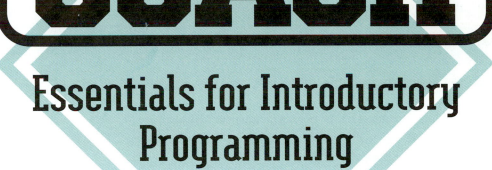

THE C++

COACH

Essentials for Introductory Programming

JEFF SALVAGE

Drexel University

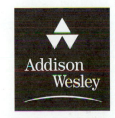
Addison Wesley

D0024256

Boston San Francisco New York
London Toronto Sydney Tokyo Singapore Madrid
Mexico City Munich Paris Cape Town Hong Kong Montreal

Sr. Acquisitions Editor: Susan Hartman Sullivan
Assistant Editor: Elinor Actipis
Cover Design: Suzanne Heiser for Night & Day Designs
Interior Design: Lisa Delgado for Delgado Design, Inc./Joyce Cosentino
Design Manager: Regina Hagen
Composition: Argosy
Copyeditor: Adrienne Rebello
Production Supervisor: Helen Reebenacker
Production Assistant: Andrea Basso
Manufacturing Buyer: Caroline Fell

Library of Congress Cataloging-in-Publication Data
Salvage, Jeff.
    C++ Coach : essentials for introductory programming / Jeff Salvage.
        p. cm.
    ISBN 0-201-70289-4 (alk. paper)
1. C++ (Computer program language) I. Title.

    QA76.73.C153 S25 2001
    005.13'3—dc21   00-044795

1 2 3 4 5 6 7 8 9 10-CRK-020100

---◆---

This book is dedicated in fond memory of Professor James B. Maginnis. He taught with an enthusiasm and a unique level of experience that started at the dawn of the modern computer era. His memory will live on in all the students he touched, challenged, and inspired throughout the years.

---◆---

TABLE OF CONTENTS

PREFACE

With all of the C++ textbooks out there, why write another one? The story goes back a couple of years, when I was on loan to a small college in Malaysia. While I was there I heard the cries of information systems students being taught C++ in too technical of a fashion. Upon my return to Drexel University, I inherited the introductory programming sequence for information systems students. I found that students were intimidated by the hard-core approach previously taken to teach C++, and realized that I had to make the class more fun and less threatening. After all, programming can be fun!

I first attempted to teach the course with the traditional text designed for computer science majors. Although I added real-world information systems examples as well as fun examples that students could comprehend easily, students complained about the difficulty in following the text. It was then that I realized we needed a textbook designed for students who weren't specifically computer science majors.

I wanted to call the book, "I Want To Pass This #*@! Computer Course," which of course, would be far too negative to be published. With a change in title and the removal of a few off-color jokes against certain football teams, *The C++ Coach: Essentials for Introductory Programming* was born.

TARGET AUDIENCE

Although some programmers are striving to become hard-core applications developers who will write the latest operating system from Microsoft, many more programmers are studying to become the information systems professionals of tomorrow. A computer science professional most likely will go on to develop operating systems and application programs like Microsoft Word or Excel. However, information systems professionals may move on to develop database applications, become network administrators, or even become database administrators.

Unfortunately, most C++ texts are written with the hard-core computer programmer in mind. Even though these introductory texts assume no knowledge of programming, they do assume that the reader has a computer programmer's aptitude and will learn quickly. The problem is aggravated when many of the examples are mathematically based and use terminology more suitable for a mathematician.

This does not mean individuals from other disciplines cannot learn how to program; it means that people without a strong mathematical background need examples that are based on information acquisition and processing as opposed to computing Pi to the millionth decimal place. Since *The C++ Coach* provides relevant, easy-to-understand examples, any student can use it, regardless of his or her major. The only prerequisite is an understanding of rudimentary mathematics, like addition, subtraction, multiplication, and division.

The C++ Coach is perfect whether you intend to program for the rest of your life, are required to take a course in school, or wish merely to gain an appreciation for programming. This text is designed to be a stand-alone volume for students learning C++, who are not majoring in computer science. It also may function as a bridge between your current level of understanding and more advanced C++ texts.

AUTHOR'S APPROACH

Because the audience for *The C++ Coach* is different from most programming texts, I have taken a unique approach by applying many techniques learned from coaching athletes to the teaching of computer programming. I have competed as an international athlete representing the United States and currently am coaching Olympic hopefuls in the sport of race walking. In many ways the teaching of race walking is similar to that of computer programming.

Race walking is a complex sport that requires combining Olympian endurance with a very complicated technique. To master it requires a great deal of practice and attention to the details of proper technique. Coaches do not start athletes by sending them into competition on the first day of practice. Instead, many coaches require athletes to repeat drills over and over again until they have mastered the techniques of the sport.

Similarly, instead of beginning with problem solving, this text teaches sound C++ syntactical fundamentals first. While learning the basic building blocks of C++, we will perform programming drills repeatedly until you understand the fundamentals and subtleties of the C++ language. This approach contrasts with many other texts trying to be complete reference manuals instead of instructional textbooks. They introduce too many constructs of the C++ language before solidifying a mastery of the basic C++ syntax.

Throughout the text we will present new features of C++, explain their syntax, and present drills that explore the subtleties of the syntax. We supplement these drills with real-world examples of programming problems and build upon the knowledge gained from these drills.

Although writing the proper programs is important, so is motivating the group and people around you to get the job done. Whether breaking up the monotony of a long race walk by joking around, or breaking up the dryness of a computer text, the idea is the same. *The C++ Coach* finds different ways to motivate and amuse you as you read through the text.

SCOPE OF COVERAGE

There are two main approaches to take in a C++ text: one, take the purest approach of teaching objects right at the get-go, or two, teach the basic constructs first and then move on to objects later.

I have tried both approaches. I have found the latter approach to be far more successful for non–computer science majors. The problem with starting with objects when no previous programming knowledge is assumed is that there are too many details to a C++ program that get in the way of attempting to produce any relevant computer programs for the information systems professional.

The text is divided into three parts.

Part I is designed to give a basic understanding of programming constructs: variables, operators, conditional statements, loops, and functions. These constructs are used to develop programs that solve relatively simple, but useful problems. Although basic problem solving is covered, this section of the text centers on mastering the basic syntax of C++.

Beginning students must grasp many concepts in the early days of programming. If too much is introduced too quickly, students will program quickly just to solve the current problem. By doing this, they miss the opportunity to understand fully the constructs that are introduced. By focusing on one construct at a time in great detail, *The C++ Coach* enables students to learn all facets of a construct and then move on to problem solving. If students are tasked with problem solving from the start, they will not venture to learn all the subtleties; instead, they will zero in on whatever will solve their problems the fastest.

In Part II, once the students have gained a firm understanding of basic C++ features, we'll concentrate on additional features of C++ such as arrays, structures, classes, pointers, and files. These features complete our arsenal of problem-solving tools, allowing us to spend more time discussing various algorithms and to focus more on true problem solving. We examine various problems and develop the simplest solution first. This solution may be easy to write, but it is usually inefficient. Then we introduce more efficient (although more complex) solutions. This allows students to appreciate that a working solution is not necessarily a good solution. In addition, in many cases we show mistakes commonly made by novice C++ programmers and then show the evolution of the problem-solving process.

Part III discusses the benefits and implementations of some simple C++ data structures. Stacks, queues, linked lists, trees, and hash tables are all covered. Although a stack's access restrictions may not make it the most applicable data structure for non-computer science majors, it is included because it is a simple way to introduce the concepts of a data structure. We introduce queues to solve the access restrictions while still maintaining a simple implementation scheme. To reinforce the concepts of pointers and to provide a more robust data structure, we implement both linked lists and trees. Finally, to show that speed does matter, we show an implementation of a simple hash table so that students can have a concrete example of the tradeoffs between speed and size of a data structure. Understanding the various data structures helps an information systems professional appreciate the issues of performance when dealing with real-world problems.

PEDAGOGY

Drills

The C++ Coach has many strengths that separate it from other C++ texts. We all know that you cannot learn to program merely by reading a textbook in a narrative format. *The C++ Coach* combats this by providing about 150 drills that provide students with immediate feedback on their understanding of what they just learned. The drills are presented as questions, and their complete solutions with detailed explanations are included at the end of each chapter.

The following is a sample of a few drills from the chapter on conditional statements. It shows how students can get immediate feedback with variations of the same problem, changed slightly, so they can master all aspects of the concept we are teaching.

What is the output of the following code?

```
//Drill 3-2

#include <stdlib.h>
#include <iostream.h>

void main()
{
    int DrillValue=1;

    if (DrillValue>2)
        cout<<"The first statement prints"<<endl;
    cout<<"The second statement prints"<<endl;
    cout<<"The third statement prints"<<endl;

}
```

Students can then flip to the end of the chapter to get the answer and explanation.

The output of the code provided for the drill is as follows:

```
The second statement prints
The third statement prints
```

The code initializes the variable **DrillValue** to the value 1. It then evaluates the expression **(DrillValue>2)**. Since **(1>2)** is false, the expression evaluates to false and the statement immediately following the **if** statement is not executed. The following two **cout** statements are not affected by the evaluation of the **if** statement, so they are executed.

What is the output of the following code?

```cpp
//Drill 3-4

#include <stdlib.h>
#include <iostream.h>

void main()
{
    int DrillValue=1;

    if (DrillValue>2)
      {
        cout<<"The first statement prints"<<endl;
        cout<<"The second statement prints"<<endl;
      }
    cout<<"The third statement prints"<<endl;
}
```

The output of the code provided for the drill is as follows:

```
The third statement prints
```

The code initializes the variable **DrillValue** to the value 1. It then evaluates the expression **(DrillValue>2)**. Since **(1>2)** is false, the expression evaluates to false. In this example, there is a curly brace, '{', following the **if** statement. This signifies to treat all the statements enclosed within it and the close curly brace '}' as a single entity. Since the expression evaluated to false, all the statements contained within the curly braces will not be executed. Therefore, the first two **cout** statements are skipped. The final **cout** statement is not affected by the evaluation of the **if** statement, so it is executed.

DIAGRAMS

The old cliché, "A picture is worth a thousand words," is very appropriate for programming textbooks. *The C++ Coach* makes extensive use of diagrams in later chapters. Three of the biggest areas of difficulty beginner programmers have are in the areas of recursion, pointers, and linked lists. This is compounded when students learn trees, which combine the concepts of the three difficult areas in one concept.

The following diagram is just one in a sequence of diagrams showing every step of an insertion algorithm for linked lists:

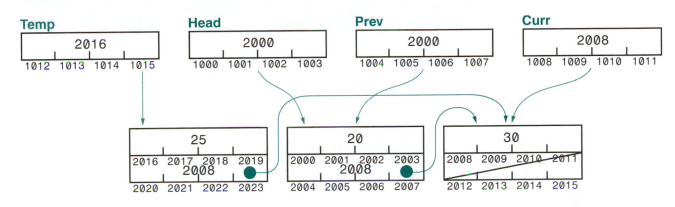

A full explanation of all aspects of what the algorithm is doing at each step is detailed for each diagram.

Recursion is difficult because students have a hard time realizing what happens from function call to function call. Therefore, when we trace through a recursive program, we show a diagram of a simplified version of the system stack on each call.

For example, here we show a diagram along with a representation of the recursive calls for the Insert method of the tree class.

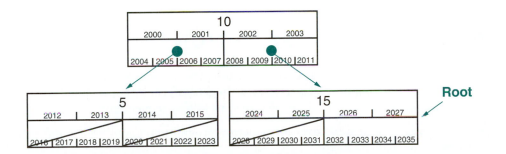

call root Called from 3 NULL Left 2 2024 Left 1 2000 Initial

When learning pointers and linked lists, students have difficulty visualizing the relationship between the pointer variables, memory locations, and variables. By providing diagrams showing the effect of each line of code in the associated algorithms, we illustrate exactly what most students are wondering about. Unlike texts that sparingly provide diagrams for these concepts, these diagrams are provided for every step of the explanation of these algorithms.

Programmer's Notebook

You'll find Programmer's Notebook text boxes throughout the chapters. These boxes highlight important programming issues. Here are just a few examples of those provided to alert students to common mistakes in programming:

PROGRAMMER'S NOTEBOOK

Be aware that a common mistake is to use a one instead of the letter l when typing **endl**.

Be aware that the **cin** operator >> is in the opposite direction of the **cout** operator <<.

Be aware that neither an equal sign nor a semicolon are required for a define statement!

End-of-Chapter Material

At the end of each chapter, all new terms introduced within the chapter are listed with condensed definitions of the terms. Additionally, any C++ keywords introduced are also listed, with explanations of their purpose.

In each chapter you will find a case study that focuses on the skills developed in the chapter in a practical real-world example. Through most of the text, our case study focuses on a business owner creating a system that will process payroll for his company. It is simple and clear to follow. We provide the problem statement, discuss its solution, and then provide the coded solution. By immediately reinforcing the skills learned in the chapter, retention will be greatly improved.

Finally, each chapter is followed with a series of short answer–style questions and programming assignments so that students can practice what they have learned in the chapter.

DIFFERENT COURSE OPTIONS

This book is designed for a one- or two-semester introductory programming sequence for non-computer science majors. In general, each chapter builds on your programming arsenal and is ideally designed to follow sequentially.

- For a course designed to cover introductory programming and basic data structures, read Chapters 2–16.

- For a course designed to cover introductory programming, but excluding basic data structures, read Chapters 2–11.

- For a course designed to cover introductory programming, but with limited time, read Chapters 2–7 and Chapter 9, and Sections 10.3–10.4 in Chapter 10.

- If you want to cover objects earlier, you could follow this sequence of chapters: Chapters 2–5, 10, 11, then Chapters 6–9 (Chapters 12–16 can be included as well).

TO THE STUDENTS

So you're taking a computer course—odds are, you'll either love it or hate it. It's the job of this text to help you through it. Regardless of why you are taking the course, you need to learn the material presented by your teacher. If you follow my advice, you will make the process a lot easier. The book is designed to be interactive. *Do not* just read the drills—try them! You will learn much more that way. Although some of the examples are dry and simply there to help with your mastery of the C++ syntax, many more are colorful statements from things I enjoy. The sports theme shows up in many examples, but I have also included many names and quotes from movies. Try to see if you can figure them out. Hopefully I am not dating myself too badly.

SUPPLEMENTS

The following supplements will be made available online for qualified instructors only: the instructors manual, complete answers to the exercises in the chapters, source code to all programs, test banks of sample exams, and lecture notes in a Power Point format.

ACKNOWLEDGMENTS

Many people's efforts go into the creation of a textbook, not just the author's. Obvious thanks go to my editors Susan Hartman Sullivan and Elinor Actipis, without whose efforts *The C++ Coach* would not have reached publication; Helen Reebenacker for her assistance in the production cycle of the text; and Michael Hirsch for making sure the world knows about this text. Additional thanks go to Robert Arnold (Drexel University); without his help in creating the exercises included in this text and his efforts with proofing the text, I would never have completed it on time. Further thanks go to Elmer G. Swartzmeyer (Georgia State University, Computer Information Systems Department), whose help with the appendixes and case studies was invaluable. Additionally, I have to thank Jim Goens and John Cunningham for providing the flexibility in my consulting that assisted greatly with my meeting publishing deadlines.

Along the way, many people helped with the many stages of the manuscript. Thanks go to Carla Matusow, Michele Sykes, Kimberly Williams, Pat Henry, and Alan Treacy for their help in the early preparation of the manuscript. Additional thanks go to my reviewers Robert G. Baird (Salt Lake Community College), Frederick H. Colclough, Julia Hassett (Oakton Community College), Edward J. Rodowicz (Brevard Community College), and Judith A. Scholl (Austin Community College).

A special thanks goes to Dr. Nira Herrmann, who makes teaching at Drexel a pleasure.

CHAPTER 1

Introduction

The C++ Coach will teach you many constructs and concepts related to programming in C++. Some of these concepts are common to all programming languages, some are common to "modern" programming languages, and still others are found only in C++ style languages. Why *are* there so many different programming languages? Where did they all come from? Are so many different languages still necessary?

1.1 WHAT IS A PROGRAMMING LANGUAGE?

Before we can compare and contrast programming languages and the concepts behind them, first we must decide what a programming language is.

A **programming language** is an agreed-upon format of symbols that allow a programmer to instruct a computer to perform certain predefined tasks.

Symbols are used to communicate a programmer's intent to a computer; how understandable these symbols are determines the level of the programming language. Some languages are written in an English-style prose, very readable by the programmer, but more difficult for the computer to understand. Others are easy for the computer to understand, but very difficult for the programmer to comprehend.

1.2 EARLIEST COMPUTER LANGUAGES

The earliest computers really didn't have much of a programming language. To instruct these computers to accomplish tasks, early computer programmers entered a series of numbers by manually flipping switches. Making the programming of these machines even more difficult was the fact that these numbers were not entered in the more common decimal form, but in an encoding scheme called binary numbers. Binary numbers are an encoding scheme where values are represented by a series of 1's and 0's. By combining 1's and 0's, different numbers can be represented. These machines were extremely difficult to program and thus were used only to solve simple problems that were repeated over and over again.

It didn't take long for computer scientists to realize that in order for computers to be more useful, they would require a programming environment that was a bit more robust than manually flipping switches.

Two major leaps forward were the creation of an **assembly language** and the introduction of **punch cards**. An assembly language utilized a series of pneumonics to represent commonly used instructions. Additionally, to increase the readability of the program, numbers could be entered in our commonly used decimal notation instead of the cryptic binary format previously used.

Another milestone was the creation of punch cards to facilitate the entry and storage of these programs. A punch card was a cardboard card in which a machine popped holes, thereby allowing the representation of an instruction and its operators. These punch cards could be assembled into a program by piling the cards in the proper order and placing them in the machine to be read in sequence.

Although punch cards and the associated assembly language were monumental leaps forward, they still provided immense problems when dealing with nontrivial programs.

One big issue was that assembly language program written for one computer system would not work on another computer system. This meant that when your company upgraded its computer system you would be forced to rewrite many of your applications. Additionally, you might have to spend time learning the new assembly language required for the new computer system.

Another issue was that although the available assembly languages were easy for the computer to understand and better than dealing with the 1's and 0's of a straight machine language, they didn't map themselves well to real-world problems.

1.3 EARLY ATTEMPTS AT NEW LANGUAGES

Two popular computer languages were developed to combat these problems: **COBOL** and **FORTRAN**. These languages were developed to meet the different needs of computer users. COBOL, which stands for Common All Purpose Business Language, was used primarily for business processing. For example, it was used to write programs to handle a company's payroll or to store a company's inventory. In contrast, FORTRAN, which stands for formula translation, was designed primarily to perform mathematical calculations extremely quickly.

Both these languages were a major improvement over the existing assembly language in terms of the time required to develop applications. These languages raised the level of the machine to the programmer. By providing built-in commands for commonly used operations, the language allowed programmers to solve their problem, by writing less, but more understandable, code.

Aside from reducing the time it would take to solve a problem, another big advantage is that standards were developed so that the language was the same from computer system to computer system. This meant that programs written for one computer system could be run on another computer system without having to be rewritten.

Although these programming languages were written so they were more understandable by humans, they required translation into a language the computer system could understand. As new computer systems were developed, they would include a translator for these standard languages that would convert the standard language into one the computer could understand.

Controversy arose over whether these languages produced programs that were slower to execute than hand-written assembly language programs. While one camp of computer system developers were trying to improve the efficiency of the machine code generated by these new languages, other camps were developing new, "better" computer languages. The quest for the Holy Grail of computer languages began.

Almost with a religious furor, languages were developed to deal with all types of situations: business applications, mathematical applications, and artificial intelligence applications; and then the quest to develop a single language that would meet all users' needs.

The quest for a single programming language cycles into popularity from time to time. One of the most ambitious attempts was PL1. It was IBM's attempt at combining the best of FORTRAN and COBOL. What they got was a language that many feel was very complex and not as useful as either FORTRAN or COBOL for their respective tasks.

1.4 NEXT GENERATION LANGUAGE

As computer technology, capacity, and speed increased, the need for better and more diverse languages developed. Even teaching languages were developed, such as Pascal, which were intended only to teach sound programming principles, and not intended for business or scientific applications.

Many of these languages addressed the needs of the programmers writing applications, but they didn't address the needs of the programmers developing the operating systems of the day. Today we are familiar with operating systems such as Windows NT and UNIX, which are written for more than one type of computer system. This way, when Microsoft wants to develop a version of Windows NT for another computer platform, they only need a program that translates the language in which they developed the operating system to the machine on which they want it to run. The most popular of these languages was C.

Because of C's popularity, it became much more than a language used for developing operating systems. Programmers quickly started to use C to write applications for many different needs. The programs produced were efficient and rivaled the performance of hand-written assembly language programs. Indeed, with today's efficient compilers and complex computer systems, C's produced machine code often runs faster than hand-developed assembly language.

As C increased in popularity and a large group of reusable programs were developed, new issues arose. How could programs be reused more effectively?

1.5 OBJECT-ORIENTED LANGUAGES

A new methodology was developed for creating reusable programs. The concept was to create objects that closely wrapped a computer program and the data on which it operated. It would allow programmers access to the data only in ways intended by the original programmer, so that programmers with less knowledge could not damage the data.

Languages like Smalltalk were developed on this approach, but more importantly, programmers wanted to be able to leverage their existing programs and therefore, the development of object-oriented extensions to languages that previously existed were created. Object-oriented Pascal and C++ were two of these extensions.

Because they were not created from scratch, the object-oriented extensions sometimes required kludgey language syntax.

Recently a new language, **Java**, has come on the scene. Java is an object-oriented-based language that is very similar to C++. It has many of the same features as C++, but without the awkwardness of some of the syntax. Additionally,

Java can be run on any computer without having to recompile your code for that machine. This is a huge advantage when dealing with Internet-based applications, but it has disadvantages as well. One big problem with JAVA is that its performance is much slower than C++. Its simpler syntax removes some of the power C++ gives the programmer. It also is inherently slower because the program must be translated into machine language by the computer executing it. This added step is acceptable in small applications that are run from the web, but for enterprise-wide application development it will present a performance issue.

C/C++ are still the programming languages of choice for the development of many performance-driven applications.

1.6 BASIC ALGORITHMS

Although we have introduced you to the concept of different programming languages, we have not introduced you to the concept behind giving instructions to a computer that will perform tasks that you wish.

Instead of jumping right into a programming example, let's practice by first trying to understand the concept of algorithms. **Algorithms** are the steps required to solve problems. Instead of thinking about algorithms in terms of a computer program, let's try to understand the algorithms behind a process with which you are already familiar. It is important to learn how to understand a process completely and then be able to explain it in simple steps before trying to write a program to accomplish a task.

DRILLS

Drill

Write down the steps required to describe how you would brush your teeth in the morning.

Drill

Write down the steps required to parallel park a car.

END-OF-CHAPTER

◆ Key Terms

Algorithm	The steps required to solve a problem.
Assembly language	An "unfriendly" programming language composed of a series of pneumoics to represent instructions that are commonly used.

COBOL	One of the early computer languages developed for business transactions.
Compiler	A program that translates a source code program into a language the machine understands.
FORTRAN	One of the early computer languages developed for mathematic calculations.
C	A computer language developed in order to develop operating systems like UNIX.
Java	A new computer language that is object-oriented and portable to run on any machine.
Programming language	An agreed-upon format of symbols that allow a programmer to instruct a computer to perform certain predefined tasks.
Punch cards	A mechanism to enter a program into a computer that stores the program on cardboard cards with holes punched out to represent the program.

◆ Answers to Drills

Drill 1-1

In giving instructions to brush one's teeth in the morning, assume that the person receiving the instructions would take nothing for granted. This is the way a computer operates: A computer does exactly what you tell it, not what you meant to tell it.

Teeth-Brushing Solution (my dentist would be so proud!)

1. To brush your teeth, first get out of bed.

2. Remove your blanket and swing your legs over the edge of the bed.

3. Stand up and walk toward the bathroom.

4. If the door is closed, open it.

5. Walk into the bathroom.

6. Turn on the light.

7. Walk toward the sink.

8. Turn on the cold water faucet.

9. Pick up a cup and fill it with water.

10. Place the cup down on the counter.

11. Pick up the toothpaste.

12. Unscrew the cap.

13. Pick up the toothbrush.

14. Place the head of the toothbrush under the running water.

15. Remove the toothbrush from the water.

16. Point the toothpaste, open end down, toward the head of the toothbrush.

17. Squeeze the tube lightly so that a little of the paste is squeezed onto the toothbrush.

18. Stop squeezing the toothpaste.

19. Put the toothpaste down.

20. Bring the toothbrush up to your mouth.

21. Move the toothbrush up and down the surface of your teeth.

22. Repeat until all teeth are well cleaned.

23. Pick up the cup of water.

24. Pour some of the water in your mouth.

25. Swoosh the water around your mouth.

26. Spit the water out.

27. Repeat if necessary until all the toothpaste is out of your mouth.

28. Rinse the toothbrush off.

29. Place the toothbrush back where you got it.

30. Place the cap on the toothpaste.

31. Place the toothpaste back where you got it.

32. Shut the water off.

33. Shut the light off.

34. Exit the bathroom.

35. Close the door behind you.

If we dissect this solution, we will see that I have not left much to chance. When programming a computer this is essential. You will also see that steps like #4 require decisions. Most computer programs will execute having to make decisions along the way as to whether or not to take additional steps. In step #22 we see another concept of programming, the concept of looping. Often it is required to repeat a step a number of times before moving to the next step.

A final issue to notice is that I did not end the algorithm with the completion of the brushing of my teeth, but with the returning of the bathroom to its initial conditions. It will be important when we program to make sure that we do not leave resources that we use unreturned to the computer when our programs finish executing.

Drill 1-2

There is no easy answer to this drill. The question was asked to stress an important point. Make sure that you get complete instructions about what you are supposed to be solving.

If you were asked to write instructions to parallel park a car, you should immediately think of other questions to ask before attempting to solve the problem; for example, does the car have automatic or manual transmission? If it has a manual transmission, where is reverse?

Only by fully specifying a problem can a programmer be sure that he or she is solving the right problem. All too often programmers develop applications that may function without error, but do not solve the problem for which they were intended.

Fundamental C++ Programming

2.1 OUR FIRST PROGRAM

Most traditional C++ texts start out with a program that prints a "hello, world" message to the screen. Because this somewhat overused example appears all too often, we decided to include a slightly more interesting example, shown in the following code.

```
//Jeff Salvage's favorite football team
#include <stdlib.h>
#include <iostream.h>
```

```
void main()
{
  cout<<"Jeff loves the Pittsburgh Steelers!";
}
```

This code is referred to as **source code**. It can be converted to an **executable program** that the computer can run. The output will look like the following:

```
Jeff loves the Pittsburgh Steelers!
```

The cout Command

The single line that appears on this screen is the one that was passed to the **cout** object. It is displayed exactly the way it was typed. No font information or style is assigned or displayed; instead, the default system font is used. If more text than can be displayed on a single line is passed to **cout**, the text wraps around on the next line.

PROGRAMMER'S NOTEBOOK

cout is one of many objects that are predefined in C++ to allow us to develop programs easily. As we proceed through the text, we will introduce more of these predefined objects.

Let's look at the program line by line and pick it apart to become familiar with everything written.

The program begins with a single statement indicating its purpose. This statement is preceded by two forward slashes, //, indicating to the compiler that the remainder of the line is a **comment** and should be ignored. Comments indicate to the programmer or to the person reading the program the intent of the program or section of code. A comment describing the program's purpose is important for every program, no matter how simple. Comments will be explained in more detail shortly.

You will use the same lines of code at the beginning of every C++ program that you write:

```
#include <stdlib.h>
#include <iostream.h>
```

These lines tell the compiler to possibly include additional information that the program needs when it is compiled. They are commonly referred to as **precompiler** directives. In our example it was necessary for the compiler to know where **cout** was defined. C++ provides these definitions in a file called **iostream.h**. Additional definitions are specified in other files that are like **iostream.h**; another fairly commonly used file is **stdlib.h**. Although not required for many programs, this standard library is used enough that it is simpler to add it than to try to remember the additional information within it.

In the code, the following line defined the main **function** of the program. A **function** is a block of code intended to accomplish a single task. The function is referred to by a name—in this case, **main**. The **main** function is a special function that is executed automatically when the program is run. We will learn much more about functions in later chapters, but for now realize that every program must have at least one function, **main**.

```
void main()
```

The opening curly brace, {, indicates the beginning of the function.

The code:

```
cout<<"Jeff loves the Pittsburgh Steelers!";
```

instructs the computer to output the expression, "Jeff loves the Pittsburgh Steelers!" to the screen. The closing curly brace, }, indicates the end of the function, and in this case, the program.

Let's review what each piece of our program looks like when we annotate each line with a description of its functionality:

```
//Jeff Salvage's favorite football team          ← Comment

#include <stdlib.h>                              ← Precompiler Directives
#include <iostream.h>

void main()                                      ← Function
{                                                ← Beginning of Function
    cout<<"Jeff loves the Pittsburgh Steelers!"; ← Instructions
}                                                ← End of Function
```

By using the **cout** object, the computer can output anything you like to the screen. **cout** can accept many different values, and then figures out how to display them to the screen. If you wish to display a character, number, or series of characters, simply place it to the right of the **<<** operator and **cout** will display it. If you wish to display multiple values, you can place them all on one line and separate each value by a **<<** operator. Therefore, if you want to display the number 123 and the number 456 right next to each other, use the following code:

```
cout<<123<<456;
```

Note the semicolon at the end of the instruction. Statements in C++ are terminated with the semicolon character. It is a way for the programmer to indicate to the compiler the location of the end of a statement.

Let's try modifying the program to output another message so that another statement appears after the one about the Steelers. To appease the varying tastes of the audience of this book, try one of the following three examples:

1. If you are a Steelers fan then have the program output "The author has great taste in Football!!!"
2. If you are the fan of another team, provide a statement to that effect.
3. If you are not a football fan, say something along those lines.

Try to write the programs and run them without looking at our answers.

Your program should look like one of the three following programs:

```
//Simple program for Pittsburgh Steeler fans
#include <stdlib.h>
#include <iostream.h>

void main()
{
  cout<<"Jeff loves the Pittsburgh Steelers!";
  cout<<"The author has great taste in Football!!!";
}
```

```
//Simple program for non-Pittsburgh Steeler fans
#include <stdlib.h>
#include <iostream.h>

void main()
{
  cout<<"Jeff loves the Pittsburgh Steelers!";
  cout<<"I love the Denver Broncos!!!";
}
```

```
//Simple program for Non-Football fans
#include <stdlib.h>
#include <iostream.h>

void main()
{
  cout<<"Jeff loves the Pittsburgh Steelers!";
  cout<<"Who cares? It's only football!!!";
}
```

Hopefully, you ran your programs and did not just read the answers. What happened? If you wrote your program similar to any of the previous three examples, I bet it didn't produce the results you expected. You probably assumed each text phrase would appear on a separate line. Felix Unger in "The Odd Couple" once said that when you assume, you make an ass out of you and me. Unfortunately, C++ assumes nothing. If you do not tell C++ to place them on separate lines, it won't. So if you used code similar to the preceding examples, your output would have been as follows.

First Program's Output

```
Jeff loves the Pittsburgh Steelers!The author has great taste in Football!!!
```

Second Program's Output

```
Jeff loves the Pittsburgh Steelers!I love the Denver Broncos!!!
```

Third Program's Output

```
Jeff loves the Pittsburgh SteelersWho cares? It's only football!!!
```

To force text to appear on separate lines, the **endl** keyword is required. Although the **endl** keyword may appear cryptic, it is an abbreviation for "end line." Simply add the **endl** keyword directly after the text phrase by adding the **<<** operator on the line containing the **cout** object. The correct code appears in the following program:

```
//Example using endl
#include <stdlib.h>
#include <iostream.h>

void main()
{
  cout<<"Jeff loves the Pittsburgh Steelers!"<<endl;
  cout<<"The author has great taste in Football!!!";
}
```

Notice that the **endl** is not in quotes. What do you think would happen if you typed quotes around the **endl** as follows?

```
//Incorrect endl example
#include <stdlib.h>
#include <iostream.h>

void main()
{
  cout<<"Jeff loves the Pittsburgh Steelers!"<<"endl";
  cout<<"The author has great taste in Football!!!";
}
```

Answer: Everything would appear on one line and the characters "endl" would appear in between the two lines as follows:

```
Jeff loves the Pittsburgh Steelers!endlThe author has great taste in Football!!!
```

PROGRAMMER'S NOTEBOOK

Be aware of the common mistake of using the number one instead of the letter l when typing endl.

To improve the ability of **cout** to format text on the output screen, C++ has provided special characters that allow the user to indicate when a carriage return or tab is displayed:

\n is the carriage return
\t is the tab

The following is a simple example showing the power of including these special characters within the text phrase that we pass to the **cout** command:

```
//Example of using \n and \t on output

#include <stdlib.h>
#include <iostream.h>

void main()
{
   cout<<"This is the 1st line\nThis is the 2nd line\n";
   cout<<"This is the 3rd line\tThis is still on the 3rd line, but tabbed over";
}
```

The output of this would be:

```
This is the 1st line
This is the 2nd line
This is the 3rd line     This is still on the 3rd line, but tabbed over
```

2.2 SIMPLE OPERATORS

So far, our programs only echo back phrases to the user that we typed directly into the program. Our society would not be so heavily dependent upon computers if this were their only power. A programmer begins to tap a computer's power by writing simple programs that perform calculations.

C++ allows the user to perform all the numerical operations with which you are familiar. A computer uses symbols called **operators** to indicate that an operation is to be performed. Addition, subtraction, multiplication, and division are all supported, using the familiar operators +, − ,* , and /, respectively. Another operator, modulus, is performed using the % operator, which returns the remainder of a division operation. However, we will concentrate on the more familiar operators first. Observe the following simple program to calculate and output the Pittsburgh Steelers' winning percentage when they have won 14 of 16 games:

```
//Example of a simple division

#include <stdlib.h>
#include <iostream.h>

void main()
{
  cout<<"The Pittsburgh Steelers won 14 games and lost only 2 games."
      <<endl;
  cout<<"Their winning percentage is "<<(14.0/16.0);
}
```

If you run the program you will get the following output:

```
The Pittsburgh Steelers won 14 games and lost only 2 games.
Their winning percentage is 0.875
```

Notice that the winning percentage did not display as "(14.0/16.0)." Instead, it displayed as 0.875. C++ automatically evaluates the value of an expression by performing the operations indicated by the operators and uses the result in the statement. Here the result of dividing 14.0 by 16.0 is 0.875. Therefore, 0.875 is used and displayed by the **cout** statement.

Expressions may contain more than just values and operators. They may also contain parentheses. Parentheses tell the computer to calculate the operations inside the parentheses before performing the rest of the calculations. The order in which the operations are performed is referred to as the precedence of the operations. So far, these operations follow the same precedence as they did in elementary school mathematics. Therefore, when reading from left to right, we perform all the operations in the parentheses first, then all multiplications and divisions, then all additions and subtractions. As we introduce more operators, the issue of precedence becomes more complicated. Therefore, we have included a chart of the precedence of all the operators introduced in this chapter at the end of the chapter.

PROGRAMMER'S NOTEBOOK

Why is it that we wrote 14.0/16.0 instead of 14/16? C++ defaults to the simplest calculation it can perform. If we wrote 14/16, both numbers would be treated as integers. Since they are both integers, it would perform whole number integer division, just like we did in grade school. The remainder or decimal portion would be discarded. Therefore the dividend of 14/16 would be 0. Clearly not the value that we wish displayed.

PROGRAMMER'S NOTEBOOK

Why is it that we added parenthesis around 14.0/16.0 when normal arithmetic would not require it? Some older compilers require parenthesis around expressions used with the cout object. We placed them there to ensure the program will compile properly regardless of what compiler you have selected.

DRILLS

The following program is designed to test your order of precedence knowledge. Try working out each example first, then type the program and execute it. Compare your results to the answers found at the end of the chapter.

Drill **2-1**

```
//Drill 2-1
//Precedence drill

#include <stdlib.h>
#include <iostream.h>

void main()
{
    cout<<(4+5*6-3/3+6)<<endl;
    cout<<((4+5)*6-(3/3+6))<<endl;
    cout<<((4+5)/(1+2))<<endl;
    cout<<(4*5*(3+3))<<endl;
    cout<<(2-2/2+2*2-3)<<endl;
}
```

PROGRAMMER'S NOTEBOOK

A word of caution: C++ performs operations in the most efficient way possible. Computers usually can compute integer arithmetic faster than floating point arithmetic. Therefore, if C++ sees two integers and an operator, it will perform an integer operation of that operator. This does not make a difference if you are adding, subtracting, or multiplying the two numbers, since an integer plus an integer, an integer minus an integer, or an integer multiplied by an integer will always equal an integer. However, if you have an integer divided by an integer, you may wish to get a floating point result. C++ will by default give you an integer result. The result would be the whole portion of the division with the remainder truncated. Therefore 4/3 would result in the value 1 and 2/3 would result in the value 0. A way to correct this problem will be shown shortly.

▌▌ 2.3 VARIABLES

With the knowledge learned so far, we could perform simple calculations, but would not be able to remember the results once calculated. To perform complex calculations, we need a mechanism to store the results. A **variable** is the way a computer stores a value in memory. C++ allocates the appropriate amount of space for a variable and assigns the variable a name and type. The **variable name** is used to reference the stored value throughout the program. The **variable type** indicates to C++ how much space to allocate and how to process and display the variable when it is used within the program.

Variables of different types exist so that we can store different types of values. One type is the integer. An integer is a whole number. Typically we represent integers as a number following the pattern: . . . , –3, –2, –1, 0, 1, 2, 3 . . .

We can see that positive numbers, negative numbers, and the number zero are all included. C++ provides the variable type **int** to allow the creation of a variable of type integer. However, selection of **int** as a variable type requires some thought. The maximum and minimum size of a variable must be taken into account. Does the program you are writing require storing a grade on an exam with a maximum value of 100 and a minimum value of 0? Does the program you are writing require storing the total number of people in the United States? That number would be upward of a couple of hundred million people.

C++ provides multiple integer types depending upon the range of values the integer variable you are declaring requires. The situation is complicated because there is no set range for the **int** variable type. Depending upon the machine on which you are executing your code, the **int** variable type can range from either –32,768 to 32,767 or –2,147,483,648 to 2,147,483,647. To be sure of which range you are going to get, you can use the variable types **short** and **long**, which will give you the ranges just listed, respectively.

Not all values we store are whole numbers. Often we must store decimal numbers. Similar to integers, C++ provides multiple options for selecting the type of variable to use when storing decimal numbers. A programmer can select from **float, double**, or **long double** when creating a decimal variable. They are listed in increasing order of capacity and precision.

Another simple variable type is a character. C++ provides the **char** type to allow the storage characters. Any of the variables discussed so far can store only one value per variable declared. Later, we will learn ways of storing more than one value in a variable easily.

Variable Names

A variable name in C++ begins with a letter or an underscore followed by any number of letters, underscores, or digits. When picking a variable name, it should be representative of the value that you are storing. Try to stay away from variable names like **x**. If the represented value is the number of students in a class, a good variable name might be **NumberStudents**. As your programs get larger, more readable variable names will make the program easier to follow.

A variable name cannot be a keyword already used by C++. Therefore, variable names like **int**, **char**, or **cout** are illegal.

Additionally, although not a rule imposed by the C++ language, it is a good practice to use a naming convention that capitalizes the first letter of each word used in the variable name. It allows the reader of the code to differentiate the words in a variable name easily. Another good convention is to be consistent with any abbreviations that you might use repeatedly through your code. For instance, Number could be abbreviated as Num or Nbr. It really doesn't matter which abbreviation you choose, as long as you use the same one throughout your code.

To use a variable in C++, we must tell the compiler that the variable exists before we actually access it. This is called declaring a variable. Declaring or allocating a variable means that we are indicating to the computer the type of variable that we wish to use as well as the name that we will use to reference it from within the program. To actually declare the variable, we need to specify the variable type followed by a space, followed by the variable name, and end the statement with a semicolon. It is always a good idea to add a comment on the same line indicating the purpose of the variable. See the following format as a template for declaring variables:

```
VariableType VariableName; //A comment goes here
```

Letters used in variable names can be either lower- or uppercase. But be aware that a variable spelled with different capitalization is considered a different variable. When a language differentiates between two variable names that are identical except for the case of the letters in their names, the language is considered **case sensitive**. Therefore, C++ is case sensitive.

Many beginning programmers may wish to use a dash in a variable name. There is a very good reason why C++ does not allow it. Can you guess what it is? Maybe the following bit of code will help illustrate the problem:

```cpp
//Example of improper use of a dash
#include <stdlib.h>
#include <iostream.h>

void main()
{
   int x; //Proper declaration of the variable x
   int y; //Proper declaration of the variable y
   int x-y; //Improper declaration of the variable x-y

   cout<<x-y; //Output statement of ???
}
```

If C++ allowed you to declare a variable called **x-y**, then it couldn't distinguish between the operation **x** minus **y** and the variable **x-y**. When writing computer programs it is important that we do not create ambiguous conditions. If there is no clear indication of what we intend the computer to accomplish, then the computer will not be able to guess what we intend.

PROGRAMMER'S NOTEBOOK

Note that type specifications are written in lowercase.

The following is an example of declaring an integer called **Wins**, another integer called **Losses**, and a character called **Team**.

```
int Wins;
int Losses;
char Team;
```

As a shortcut, you can declare variables of the same type by separating them by a comma as shown in the following code.

```
int Wins, Losses;
char Team;
```

Let's look at a complete program example that declares variables, assigns them values, performs simple calculations, and then outputs the result. Let's write a program that starts by assigning the number of wins and losses for a team. Then it calculates and outputs the total number of games played.

```
//Calculate total games played
#include <stdlib.h>
#include <iostream.h>

void main()
{
   int Wins; //Number of Wins
   int Losses; //Number of Losses
   int TotalGames; //Total Games Played

   Wins = 12;
   Losses = 4;

   TotalGames = Wins+Losses;

   cout<<"The total number of games played ="<<TotalGames;
}
```

PROGRAMMER'S NOTEBOOK

Notice we have included a new operator, =.

The equal sign is the assignment operator in C++. The equal sign assigns the value to its right to the variable immediately to its left.

The previous example shows three assignments. The first is a simple assignment of a single integer value, 12, to a variable, **Wins**. After the statement executes, the variable **Wins** evaluates to the value 12. The second assignment is also an example of the same type of assignment. The value 4 is assigned to the variable **Losses**.

The third assignment is slightly different. Unlike the previous assignments, the value on the right is not a single integer. In contrast, it is an expression of variables. To assign the proper value to the variable **TotalGames**, the computer must evaluate the value of the expression **Wins+Losses**. Since **Wins** evaluates to 12 and **Losses** evaluates to 4, **Wins+Losses** will evaluate to 16. Therefore, the variable **TotalGames** is equal to 16 after the assignment statement is executed.

Even though C++ allows you to place the declarations of your variables anywhere in the code, it is generally good practice to declare your variables at the beginning of the main section of your code. Exceptions to this rule are explained later.

PROGRAMMER'S NOTEBOOK

The rules that we just learned for declaring variables are the same rules we will apply when we learn to create other identifiers like function and class names.

DRILLS

Try to determine which of the following are valid variable names:

Drill 2-2

```
_JeremyL
H#2
floating
FreddieJoe
Xx
_1312
6_05
April_needs_to_rake_my_leaves
A$
Int
char
```

■■■ 2.4 COMMENTS

Earlier, we mentioned that it is important to add comments to your C++ code. There are several reasons for this practice:

1. To indicate to yourself the overall purpose of your code and what you are trying to accomplish in each section of code.
2. To indicate to whoever reads your code its overall purpose and what you are trying to accomplish in each section of code.
3. To put the person grading your paper in a better mood so you get a higher grade.

The first two reasons seem similar, but are very different. You may think your code is self-explanatory and does not require any additional statements for you to understand it. However, as a once guilty member of that party, I can tell you first-hand that when you look at code that you wrote a few weeks earlier, it is not as easy to read as you thought.

Therefore, when you comment, you really should comment as if you are commenting for the second reason. Assume that the person reading the code has no knowledge of the program. This assumption will lead to complete documentation and a clear, concise program.

The third reason is one of practicality. If you are writing a program that will be reviewed by someone else, whether at school or work, the person reading it will have an easier time if it is well commented. This usually is reflected directly in your grade or job evaluation. If your instructor struggles to understand your code, then he or she is not going to be as generous in evaluating your work.

To comment in C++ is extremely simple: just place two slashes, //, on a line and everything remaining on that line will be commented out. The following example of C++ code shows the use of this single-line comment by showing the commented areas of code in bold face:

```
int X; //This is a comment about the variable X
int Y; //This is another comment

//This whole line is a comment
int Z;

This would produce an error, because there is no //before the line
```

Another version of commenting in C++ is the multiline comment. It uses the following pair of symbols: /* and */. Anything typed between the /* and the */ is considered to be a comment. Again, in the following example, the commented areas of C++ code are shown in bold face.

```
int X; /*This is a comment about the variable X */
int Y; /*This is another comment */
/*This line and the next line
are both comments */
int Z;
This would produce an error, because there is no /* comment before the line*/
```

See the following example of a program with both types of comments:

```
//Different style of comments program
#include <stdlib.h>
#include <iostream.h>


/* This is a block comment that will not be included in the code because it
is contained within the comment indicators. All code contained within will
be ignored.

void main()
{
   cout<<"This will be ignored!";
}

This is the end of the block comment */


//The following is the real code

void main()
{
   cout<<"This will print!";
}
```

The following page is a template for you to use. It is often helpful to have a premade template in a file for your comments. Even before you start typing your program, it helps not only because it reminds you to add your comments, but also because it separates your code into distinct sections. Although you have not learned all the sections yet, you can just delete the ones that you aren't using. The different sections also help you to place your code in the proper order.

```
/**********************************************************/
/* Program Name:                                          */
/* Program Purpose:                                       */
/**********************************************************/

/**********************************************************/
/* Includes:                                              */
/**********************************************************/

/**********************************************************/
/* Constants & Defines:                                   */
/**********************************************************/

/**********************************************************/
/* Typedefs:                                              */
/**********************************************************/

/**********************************************************/
/* Structures:                                            */
/**********************************************************/

/**********************************************************/
/* Classes:                                               */
/**********************************************************/

/**********************************************************/
/* Class Name:                                            */
/* Purpose:                                               */
/**********************************************************/

/**********************************************************/
/* Globals:                                               */
/**********************************************************/

/**********************************************************/
/* Functions Prototypes:                                  */
/**********************************************************/

/**********************************************************/
/* Main:                                                  */
/**********************************************************/

/**********************************************************/
/* Functions:                                             */
/**********************************************************/

/**********************************************************/
/* Function Name:                                         */
/* Function Purpose:                                      */
/**********************************************************/
```

DRILLS

Indicate the errors in the following code:

Drill 2-3

```
//Drill 2-3

/ This is the first comment of the program

/* This is also a valid comment

#include <stdlib.h>
#include <iostream.h>

void main()
{
   /* This is the firs valid comment inside the main routine */ */
   int X; Here is a variable X
   X=5;
   cout<<X;

}
//End of the program
```

Here is another drill for you to try to identify the errors:

Drill 2-4

```
//Drill 2-4

#include <iostream.h>
#include <stdlib.h>

//Here is the second drill\\

/******This one is special*******/
void main()
{
   int X;
   int Y;

Code needs to be added here;

}
/End of the program */
```

2.5 SIMPLE INPUT

To create programs that are versatile enough to run more than one time, we require a method of changing the values upon which the program performs its calculations. The easiest way to accomplish this is to read values from the user.

The simplest way to read values from the user in C++ is the **cin** object.

The cin Commmand

The **cin** command works by typing **cin>>** and then placing a variable to the right of the **>>** operator. In essence, the **cin** command is taking a value from the keyboard and is funneling it to the variable through the **>>** operator. Much like **cout**, **cin** will allow multiple values to be read on a single line. Each value must be read into a separate variable and separated by a **>>** operator.

PROGRAMMER'S NOTEBOOK

Be aware that the cin operator >> is in the opposite direction of the cout operator <<.

The following program accepts information from the user and then echoes it back to the screen:

```
//Simple input example

#include <stdlib.h>
#include <iostream.h>

void main()
{
   int NumWins;
   int NumLosses;

   cout<<"Enter the number of wins for the Pittsburgh Steelers ";
   cin>>NumWins;

   cout<<"Enter the number of losses ";
   cin>>NumLosses;

   cout<<"The number of wins for Pittsburgh = "<<NumWins<<endl;
   cout<<"The number of losses for Pittsburgh = "<<NumLosses;
}
```

The next program is similar, but it accepts less input from the user and calculates the number of losses automatically. It can do this because the program realizes that the number of losses is equal to 16 minus the number of wins. (In football there are 16 games in a regular season.)

```
//2nd simple input example

#include <stdlib.h>
#include <iostream.h>

void main()
{
   int NumWins; //Stores the number of wins entered by the user
   int NumLosses; //Stores the number of losses calculated by the user

   //Get the number of wins.
   cout<<"Enter the number of wins for the Pittsburgh Steelers ";
   cin>>NumWins;

   //Calculate the number of losses assuming there are 16 games in a season.
   NumLosses=16-NumWins;

   //Output the results.
   cout<<"The number of wins for Pittsburgh = "<<NumWins<<endl;
   cout<<"The number of losses for Pittsburgh = "<<NumLosses;
}
```

2.6 CONSTANTS

Often in programming we want to represent a value that will not change during the execution of the program. These values are called **constants**. They are added to the program for two purposes.

First, by adding a name to associate with the value, your program will become more readable. In the previous example, we wrote the value 16 as the number of games in a season. A person reading the program would not immediately understand the purpose of the value 16 without reading the comment. We accomplish this by adding a constant called **TotalNumGames** and setting it to 16.

In addition, another benefit occurs if the value 16 appeared in the program many times. If the number of games in a season changed to another value, we would have to change it in many places, thus increasing our risk of adding an error to the program. With the use of constants we have to change the value only in a single place.

You may be wondering why we just do not use a variable instead of coming up with a new way to define a constant. The answer is twofold. First, a variable has the ability to change within the program, and we wouldn't want you to inadvertently change a value that shouldn't be changed. With a constant there is no way to change it. Second, a constant actually requires less space when the final program is created. Without getting overly complex, a compiler must allocate space for each variable. With a constant, the compiler does a search and replace operation, similar to one you would do with a word processor, before you compile your program. No additional memory is required when creating the final program.

To declare a constant, you type a pound sign, followed by the word **define**, followed by a space, followed by the name of the constant, followed by the value for the constant. This can be seen in the following template:

```
#define ConstantName ConstantValue
```

PROGRAMMER'S NOTEBOOK

Be aware that neither an equal sign nor a semicolon are required for a define statement!

The following is the rewritten version of the previous program, now correctly using a constant to represent the total number of games:

```cpp
//2nd simple input example with the use of a constant

#include <stdlib.h>
#include <iostream.h>

#define TotalNumGames 16

void main()
{
  int NumWins; //Stores the number of wins entered by the user
  int NumLosses; //Stores the number of losses calculated by the user

  //Get the number of wins.
  cout<<"Enter the number of wins for the Pittsburgh Steelers ";
  cin>>NumWins;

  //Calculate the number of losses assuming there are 16 games in a season.
  NumLosses=TotalNumGames-NumWins;

  //Output the results.
  cout<<"The number of wins for Pittsburgh = "<<NumWins<<endl
     <<"The number of losses for Pittsburgh = "<<NumLosses;
}
```

2.7 TYPES OF ERRORS

Much like writing a paper for English class, when we write a computer program we often do not create the perfect program the first time. In English class, a teacher indicates your mistakes in grammar and content. When we write a computer program, the compiler indicates some of your mistakes. Unfortunately, the compiler is not as "intelligent" as your English teacher.

By now you probably have experienced many types of problems with the programs you have entered in the computer. These errors can be divided into two primary groups: **syntax errors** and **run-time errors**.

Syntax errors are defined as errors within the grammar of your program and are determined at the time you compile your application. All of the errors demonstrated so far are considered syntax errors.

In contrast, run-time errors occur during the execution of the actual program. A run-time error obeys the syntax of the C++ language, but causes an error for another reason. A simple example of this is if you try to divide a number by zero. Since the result of dividing a number by zero is undefined, the computer does not know what to do and can only produce an error.

Try running the following program:

```cpp
//Run-time error example

#include <stdlib.h>
#include <iostream.h>

void main()
{
  int FirstNumber; //Stores the first number
  int SecondNumber; //Stores the second number

  cout<<"Enter the first number"<<endl;
  cin>>FirstNumber;

  cout<<"Enter the second number"<<endl;
  cin>>SecondNumber;

  //Output the results.
  cout<<"The first number / second number = ";
  cout<<(FirstNumber/SecondNumber);
}
```

If you ran the program and entered 15 for the first number and 5 for the second number, your results are as expected:

```
Enter the first number
15
Enter the second number
5
The first number / second number = 3
```

If you ran the program and entered 0 for the first number and 5 for the second number, your results are as expected:

```
Enter the first number
0
Enter the second number
5
The first number / second number = 0
```

However, if you ran the program and entered 5 for the first number and 0 for the second number, there are no valid results. The program would run properly until it attempted the calculation of 5/0. The results appear similar to the following:

```
Enter the first number
5
Enter the second number
0
The first number / second number =
Div By Zero
```

At the point of the division by zero, the program would terminate.

▐▐ DRILLS

You now know enough to make it is easy to make a mistake somewhere. Practice identifying mistakes by finding the number of errors in the following program:

Drill 2-5

```
//Drill 2-5

#include <stdlib.h>
#include <iostream.h>

void main()
(
  INT Sum;
  // COMPUTE RESILT
  Sum = 25 + 37 - 19 / display results
  cout<<"The answer is "<<Sum<<"endl";
}
```

2.8 CHARACTERS

All the examples we have seen so far involve the processing of integers. However, we could just as easily write a program with character variables. A character is a letter or number enclosed in single quotes.

'A' represents the uppercase letter A.
'1' represents the number 1.
'z' represents the lowercase letter z.

Character variables can be defined as easily as integer variables. See the following program:

```
//Simple character program
#include <stdlib.h>
#include <iostream.h>

void main()
{
    char Letter1;
    char Letter2;

    Letter1='A';
    Letter2='B';

    cout<<Letter1<<endl;
    cout<<Letter2<<endl;

}
```

The output would be:

```
A
B
```

The program is simple. The variable **Letter1** stores a single character, 'A'. The variable **Letter2** stores a single character, 'B'. Then they are both output on separate lines.

DRILLS

What is the output of the following program? (It is not as simple as you might expect.)

Drill **2-6**

```
//Drill 2-6

#include <stdlib.h>
#include <iostream.h>

void main()
{
  char C,D;
  C = 'D';
  D = C;
  cout<<"D = "<<D<<endl<<"C = "<<C<<endl
      <<"or does C ="<<'C';
}
```

2.9 TYPE CONVERSIONS

Although it is not necessary to use **type conversions** often, it is important to realize that if you are switching from one type in C++ to another, it should be done intentionally.

The following code shows an example of what happens when we divide two integers and store the result in a variable of type **float**.

```
//Type conversion example
#include <stdlib.h>
#include <iostream.h>

void main()
{
  float Result;

  int Value1 = 1;
  int Value2 = 3;

  Result = Value1/Value2;

  cout<<"The result is = "<<Result;
}
```

The output is as follows:

```
The result is 0
```

We explained earlier that integer division results in an integer answer. This is true even if we store the result in a variable of type **float**. To correct the problem it is necessary to convert the integers to floating point numbers for purposes of the division.

To convert a variable or value of one type to another, place the type to which you wish to convert the variable in parentheses in front of the variable or value you wish to convert. Converting a value from one variable type to another is commonly referred to as casting a variable. See the following template:

```
(New Type) Old Variable
```

The following is the corrected program that will execute properly:

```
//Type conversion example
#include <stdlib.h>
#include <iostream.h>


void main()
{
   float Result;

   int Value1 = 1;
   int Value2 = 3;

   Result = (float)Value1/(float)Value2;

   cout<<"The result is = "<<Result;
}
```

The addition of the **float** keyword in parentheses temporarily converts **Value1** and **Value2** to floating point numbers. Although it is good practice to convert both variables to floating point numbers, the compiler will automatically take care of this as long as one of the values in the calculation is a floating point number.

2.10 COMPLEX OPERATORS

C++ provides numerous operators that allow us to shortcut the amount of typing required in our source code, and that may allow code to execute faster. The first group is designed to shortcut when you add, subtract, multiply, or divide a variable by a number or variable and then store the result in itself. See the following code as an example of the old way that we perform operations of this type:

```
//Complex operator example - old way
#include <stdlib.h>
#include <iostream.h>

void main()
{
  //Declare three variables.
  int X;
  int Y;
  int Z;

  //Initialize three variables.
  X=5;
  Y=3;
  Z=4;

  //Perform operations on three variables.
  X=X-4;
  Y=Y+2;
  Z=Z/2;
}
```

The last three statements can be simplified as follows:

```
//Complex operator example - new way
#include <stdlib.h>
#include <iostream.h>

void main()
{
 //Declare three variables.
 int X;
 int Y;
 int Z;

 //Initialize three variables.
 X=5;
 Y=3;
 Z=4;

 //Perform operations on three variables.
 X-=4;
 Y+=2;
 Z/=2;
}
```

The +=, −=, *=, and /= operators work as follows:

X + = 3; is the same as typing X = X + 3;
X − = 3; is the same as typing X = X − 3;
X * = 3; is the same as typing X = X * 3;
X / = 3; is the same as typing X = X / 3;

These four shortcuts are easily understood and are often used to simplify code.

The next two shortcut operators, ++ and −−, are helpful, but unfortunately are tricky to master.

++ is intended to shortcut the adding of 1 to a variable, and −− is intended to short-cut the subtracting of 1 from a variable. If these shortcut operators are used on a line with just a variable, there is no confusion, as shown in the following code:

```
//Simple pre-increment example
#include <stdlib.h>
#include <iostream.h>

void main()
{
   int X;
   int Y;

   X=4;
   Y=4;

   ++X;
   --Y;

   cout<<X<<'\t'<<Y;
}
```

The previous code would yield the following results:

```
5      3
```

By using the ++ or −− operator in front of the variable, C++ outputs the expected value. However, C++ allows the ++ and −− operators to be placed before or after the variable. Depending where you place it yields different results. Observe the fol-lowing code:

```
//Complex pre- and post-increment example
#include <stdlib.h>
#include <iostream.h>

void main()
{
  int X;
  int Y;
  X=4;
  Y=4;
  cout<<++X<<'\t'<--Y<<endl;
  cout<<X<<'\t'<<Y<<endl;

  int A;
  int B;
  A=4;
  B=4;
  cout<<A++<<'\t'<<B--<<endl;
  cout<<A<<'\t'<<B<<endl;
}
```

The output would be as follows:

```
5       3
5       3
4       4
5       3
```

The first set of output gives you the expected results. **X** and **Y** both start off initially as 4. If we add 1 to **X** and subtract 1 from **Y**, then it makes sense that the output is 5 and 3. The **++** and **--** add and subtract one from **X** and **Y** before they are used in the **cout** command. These values are then stored in **X** and **Y**, respectively, and therefore are available when we display them in the second **cout** statement.

However, the next two output lines produce unexpected results. You might have expected the same result as that generated by the first set. However, this does not happen. When you use the **++** operator after the variable, the old value of the variable is used in the expression, and only after it is used is 1 added to the variable. We refer to this type of incrementing as a post-increment. When the **++** is before the variable, we refer to it as a pre-increment. For now, we suggest using **++** only before the variable name. Later, as you become more familiar with C++ and have a few more keywords to use, its usefulness will be more relevant. Similar to pre-increment and post-increment are pre-decrement and post-decrement. By using the **--** operator either before or after a variable, we can decrement the variable by 1.

■ DRILLS

Try to figure out the output of the following code:

Drill **2-7**

```
//Drill 2-7

#include <stdlib.h>
#include <iostream.h>

void main()
{
   int X;
   int Y;
   int Z;

   X=5;
   Y=10;
   Z=30;

   X += 3;
   Y -=5;
   Z *=3;

   cout<<X<<'\t'<<Y<<'\t'<<Z<<endl;
}
```

Try this drill as well. What is the output of the following code?

Drill **2-8**

```
//Drill 2-8

#include <stdlib.h>
#include <iostream.h>

void main()
{
  int X;
  int Y;

  X=5;
  Y=5;

  ++X;
  cout<<X<<endl;
```

```
   --Y;
   cout<<Y<<endl;

   cout<<++X<<endl;
   cout<<X++<<endl;
   cout<<X<<endl;
}
```

Assignment at Declaration

Another useful shortcut that C++ allows is the ability to initialize a variable at the time of its declaration. See the following example of how we initialize and declare an integer.

```
#include <stdlib.h>
#include <iostream.h>

void main()
{
   int X=5;
   cout<<X;
}
```

The output follows:

```
5
```

2.11 ORDER OF PRECEDENCE CHART

The following is a list of operators introduced in this chapter and their precedence of operation. The lower the number listed the higher the precedence of the operator. Remember, a higher precedence means that we execute the higher precedence operator before the lower precedence operator. Operators with the same precedence are executed in the order that they appear from left to right.

Precedence	Operator	Use
0	( )	Parentheses
1	++	Pre-Increment/Post-Increment
	--	Pre-Decrement/Post-Decrement
	( )	Type casting/Conversion
2	*	Multiply
	/	Divide
	%	Modulus
3	+	Addition
	-	Subtraction
4	=	Assignment
	*=	Multiplicity and Assignment
	/=	Divide and Assignment
	+=	Addition and Assignment
	-=	Subtraction and Assignment

2.12 Case Study

Problem Description

An entrepreneur runs a day labor pool. He pays each worker $5.15 per hour. Write a C++ program that calculates a worker's daily pay showing the dollar sign and the amount formatted to two decimal places. Test your program for an input of odd, even, and fractional hours.

Discussion

The program requires one input, the number of hours the worker was employed. Any attempt to input the pay rate should be discouraged, since it is the same for all workers and therefore should be placed in the program as a constant. Because the worker may work fractional hours, the input variable must be a float. A double is acceptable, but should be discouraged since it is unlikely a daily worker will earn a large sum of money. Minimum flag settings should be **showpoint**, and **precision** should be set to two (see Appendix C for more details). Also, setting the **fixed** flag should be encouraged, since it will be needed for larger numbers in later chapters.

2.12 Case Study

Solution

```c++
#include <iostream.h>
#include <iomanip.h>

#define MinWage (float)5.15

void main()
{
    float Hours, Pay;
    cout << endl <<"Enter hours worked -> ";
    cin >> Hours;
    Pay = MinWage * Hours;
    cout << setprecision(2);
    cout << setiosflags(ios :: showpoint);
    //needed only for large numbers
    cout << setiosflags(ios :: fixed);
    cout << endl << "Worker\'s pay is $" << Pay << endl;
}
```

Output, First Input

```
Enter hours worked -> 7
Worker's pay is $36.05
```

Output, Second Input

```
Enter hours worked -> 8
Worker's pay is $41.20
```

Output, Third Input

```
Enter hours worked -> 8.5
Worker's pay is $38.62
```

♦ Key Terms

Case sensitive	A language that considers variables spelled with different capitalization as separate variables.
Comment	A description of the C++ code that is included in the source code, but that is not included in the actual executable. It is merely a means of documentation.
Constant	A value that does not change during the execution of the program.
Executable program	The compiled program that is ready to be understood by the computer so that it may run it without modification.
Function	A block of code intended to accomplish a single task.
Operator	A representation of an action that will be performed upon whatever operators are placed next to it.
Run-time error	An error or inconsistent result that occurs when the program is executed.
Source code	The program created by a programmer in a language that is understood by the programmer. It is converted to an executable in order to be run by the computer.
Syntax error	An error in the grammar of the program that you have written. It is discovered during compile time.
Type conversion	The changing of a value's variable type from one type to another.
Variable	A way the computer stores a value in memory.
Variable name	The name to which a variable is referred from within the source code.
Variable type	The classification of variable so that it knows how much space to allocate and how to operate upon it.

♦ C++ Keywords Introduced

`#define`	A precompiler directive that allows the user to set constant values within the program.
`#include`	A precompiler directive that allows the user to include other information in his or her program.
`char`	A variable type that stores a single character value.
`cin`	A statement that allows entry of simple input from the user and stores the result in a variable.
`cout`	A statement that allows the displaying of values from the program to the user.
`double`	A type of variable that allows the storing of a decimal value.
`endl`	A predefined value that can be used with the **cout** statement to display a carriage return on the screen.
`float`	A type of variable that allows the storing of a decimal value.
`int`	A type of variable that allows the storing of an integer value.
`long`	A type of variable that allows the storing of a large integer value.
`main`	The first function called by the program when it starts to execute.
`short`	A type of variable that allows the storing of a small integer value.

♦ Answers to Drills

Drill 2-1

The output would be as follows:

```
39
47
3
120
2
```

An explanation of each output value follows.

The first calculation is **4+5*6-3/3+6**. Reading from left to right, the first calcula- **4+5*6-3/3+6**
tion we compute is 5*6, because there are no parentheses and it is the first multiplication or division.

By replacing the 5*6 with 30, we rewrite the expression as **4+30-3/3+6**. Since
there are no parentheses we evaluate the next multiplication or division that we see
when reading from left to right, which is 3/3.

By replacing 3/3 with 1, we rewrite the expression as **4+30-1+6**. Since no parentheses, multiplications, or divisions remain, the solution to the problem is a simple
matter of adding and subtracting the numbers from left to right until we get the
answer of 39.

The second calculation is **(4+5)*6-(3/3+6)**. Reading from left to right, the first **(4+5)*6-(3/3+6)**
calculation we compute is (4+5), because 4+5 is in the first set parentheses found.

By replacing (4+5) with 9, we rewrite the initial expression as **9*6-(3/3+6)**.
Reading from left to right, we must continue to compute the values in the remaining parentheses. Therefore, we must compute the entire expression (3/3+6) before
we evaluate 9*6-. We start by computing 3/3, since it is the first multiplication or
division inside the parentheses. Then we can rewrite the expression inside the parentheses as **(1+6)**. Adding the 1 to the 6 we get 7.

By replacing (3/3+6) with 7, we rewrite the initial expression as **9*6-7**. Since no
more parentheses exist, we continue with the evaluation by computing the first multiplication or division found when reading from left to right. Therefore, the next calculation evaluated is 9*6.

By replacing (9*6) with 54 we rewrite the expression as **54-7**. The final answer is
then calculated with a result of 47.

The third calculation is **(4+5)/(1+2)**. Reading from left to right we must compute **(4+5)/(1+2)**
the values in the parentheses first. The first expression evaluated is (4+5).

By replacing (4+5) with 9, we rewrite the expression as **9/(1+2)**. Since a set of
parentheses still exists, we must compute the expression inside the remaining parentheses, (1+2).

By replacing the (1+2) with 3, we rewrite the initial expression as **9/3**. This leaves
us with a simple division to calculate the final answer, 3.

The fourth calculation is **4*5*(3+3)**. Reading from left to right, we must compute **4*5*(3+3)**
the values in the parentheses first. We compute (3+3).

By replacing (3+3) with 6, we rewrite the initial expression as **4*5*6**. This is a simple series of multiplications that can be computed to get our answer final answer of
120.

The fifth calculation is **2-2/2+2*2-3**. Reading from left to right, since there are no **2-2/2+2*2-3**
parentheses, we compute the first multiplication or division we see—2/2.

By replacing 2/2 with 1, we rewrite the initial expression as **2-1+2*2-3**. We continue evaluating the expression by finding the next multiplication or division—2*2.

By replacing 2*2 with 4, we rewrite the initial expression as **2-1+4-3**. The remaining problem is a simple series of additions and subtractions to reach the final answer
of 2.

Drill 2-2

The following is a list of each variable name, an indication of whether it is valid or invalid, and an explanation why.

_JeremyL is a valid variable name. It starts with an underscore and is followed by characters.

H#2 is not a valid variable name. It contains a #, which is an illegal character.

floating is a valid variable name. It starts with a keyword, **float**, but is different because "ing" is added to it.

FreddieJoe is a valid variable name. It starts with a character and is followed by characters. The fact that the F and J are capitalized is not relevant to whether it is a legal identifier or not. However, wherever FreddieJoe is used it must be capitalized the same way.

Xx is a valid variable name for the same reasons as FreddieJoe.

_1312 is a valid variable name. It starts with an underscore and is followed by numbers.

6_05 is not a valid variable name. It starts with a number, which is illegal.

April_needs_to_rake_my_leaves is a valid variable name. It starts with a character and contains characters and underscores.

A$ is not a valid variable name. It contains a $, which is illegal.

Int is a valid variable name, because the I is capitalized and therefore it is considered different from **int**, which could not be used as a variable name.

char is not a valid variable name, because **char** is a reserved word used to declare variables.

Drill 2-3

1. The first error is in the following code:

```
/ This is the first comment of the program
```

In order for it to be commented correctly, the / should be //.

2. The second error is in the following code:

```
/* This is also a valid comment
```

In order for this line to be commented correctly, there should be a */ at the end of the line.

3.   The third error is in the following code:

```
/* This is the firs valid comment inside the main routine */ */
```

The first `*/` ends the comment started on the previous line. The second `*/` should be removed. Note that although "first" is misspelled, it is not an error. C++ doesn't check your spelling.

4.   The fourth and final error is in the following code:

```
int X; Here is a variable X
```

There should be a `//` before the code "Here is a variable X."

Drill 2-4

There is actually only one error in the code provided for this drill. It is in the following line:

```
Code needs to be added here;
```

This line is intended to be a comment, but no comment indicators are present.

You may think that there is an error with either of the first two lines; however, they are following the rules of commenting exactly. The first line simply has a `//` as the first two characters of the line, so everything else is ignored. The second line has a `/*` and a `*/` pair with lots of asterisks in between. Asterisks are perfectly legal characters and can be placed in between the `/*` and `*/` without any problem.

Drill 2-5

How many errors did you find in the code provided? You should have found four, all of which are syntax errors.

1.   A parenthesis is used instead of a curly brace to indicate the start of the function.

2.   **INT** is capitalized instead of being in lowercase as in:

```
int Sum;
```

3.   There is no semicolon on the line **Sum = 25 + 37 − 19**. It should read as follows:

```
Sum = 25 + 37 − 19;
```

4. The comment **/display results** is mistyped. It should read as follows:

```
//display results
```

There are two other "errors," but they are not syntax errors. The first is **// COMPUTE RESILT**, which contains a spelling mistake, but because it is contained within a comment the compiler ignores it.

The second error is in the statement **cout<<"The answer is "<<Sum<<"endl";**. The "endl" should not be in quotes. This is an error in the sense that the program does not produce the output we intended. C++ will think that you mean to display the text "endl" as opposed to the carriage return that we intended. Removing the quotes around the **endl** will fix this error.

Drill 2-6

The output of the code provided in the drill is as follows:

```
D = D
C = D
or does C = C
```

This program contains two variables named **C** and **D**. It is obvious that the variable **C** contains the character 'D'. However, determining the value of the variable **D** is not as simple as it might seem. You might think that the variable **D** contains the character 'C', but it actually contains the character 'D'. This is because the variable **D** is assigned the value of the variable **C**, not the letter 'C'. Since the variable **C** contains the letter 'D', then so will the variable **D**.

When we issue the **cout** command the first value is the string "D = " and that is output exactly as it is typed. The second value is the variable **D**. As we stated, the value of the variable **D** is the letter 'D', so it is displayed on the screen. Then the **endl** is processed and a carriage return is displayed. Therefore, when the **cout** command processes the string "C = ", it is displayed on the next line.

The next value is the variable **C**. The value of the variable **C** is 'D', so a 'D' is displayed. Another **endl** is processed and the next output appears on the next line.

Then the string "or does C =" is displayed. Therefore, 'or does C =' gets displayed. The final value is the character 'C'. 'C' is different from the variable **C** and is displayed exactly as it is typed, 'C'.

Drill 2-7

The output of the code provided in the drill would be as follows:

```
8       5       90
```

The first value is 8, because 3 is added to **X** and stored back in **X**. Since **X** started as 5, the result is 8. The second value is 5, because 5 is subtracted from **Y** and stored back in **Y**. Since **Y** started as 10, the result is 5. The third value is 90, because 3 is multiplied by **Z** and stored back in **Z**. Since **Z** started as 30, the result is 90.

Drill 2-8

The output is as follows:

```
6
4
7
7
8
```

In the program both **X** and **Y** are initialized to 5. **X** is then pre-incremented to 6. The next line outputs **X** and 6 is displayed. **Y** is then predecremented to 4 and then the next line outputs **Y**, therefore 4 is displayed.

The following line pre-increments **X** to 7 and then displays 7 on the same line. The value 7 is stored in **X**. The next line postincrements **X** to 8, which means that the old value of **X** is used in the **cout** statement, so 7 is displayed. Finally, the last **cout** statement accesses the value of **X**, which was postincremented to 8 in the previous statement, so 8 is displayed.

◆ Programming Exercises

1. Correct the following code so that it will run and compile properly. The program should request two values, add them together, and output the result.

```cpp
#include <stdlib.h>
#include <iostream>

void main()
{
    char Num1; Num2;Answer;
    //Prompts for two numbers//
    cout<<"Enter the first number: ";
    cin<<Num1;
    cout<<"Enter the second number: ";
    cin<<Num1;
    //The numbers are added together
    Answer=Num1++Num2
    cout<<The answer is<<Answer;
}
```

2. Write a program that outputs the Pledge of Allegiance.

3. Write a program that requests the amount of a person's total income and the amount of a person's total bills. The program should output the amount of money the person has remaining.

4. Write a program that calculates a student's GPA for a semester. Assume that the student takes five classes and can have a grade of 0, 1, 2, 3, or 4. Output the student's overall average. Make sure that the program remembers decimal places in its calculation.

5. Write a program that accepts four numbers. The program should compute the sum, average, and product of all the numbers. The output of the program should show all the numbers that were entered and the three answers to the computations. Show the output in a table format like the following:

```
Numbers      12      15      17      18
Sum          Average         Product

-----        -----------     ---------
62           15.5            55080
```

6. Write a program that accepts five sale prices and five retail prices for merchandise a store carries. The program should output the discount amount of each item. The costs for the merchandise should be entered in as a float.

7. Write a program that accepts a percentage sales tax and five prices of products. The program should output the cost of the tax for each item.

8. Write a program that accepts an initial value of a stock and the percentage it has increased/decreased each year for four years. The program should output the value of the stock after four years. Assume the amount of the increase/decrease was reinvested each year.

   Therefore if $1000 were invested and the returns each year were 10%, 15%, 13%, and 20%, respectively, the program should output 1715.34.

♦ Additional Exercises

1. Which of the following are valid variable names?

   a. DoYouLikeFootball
   b. This_is_a_valid_variable
   c. Go-Hawks-Basketball
   d. 1234
   e. HOW_ABOUT_ALL_CAPS
   f. What_about_one_with_a_?
   g. FLOAT

2. TRUE or FALSE

   a. 'A' is the exact same thing as "A".
   b. A variable is considered an operator.
   c. Excessive comments add time to the execution of a program.
   d. Basic operations in C++ follow a different precedence than traditional mathematics.
   e. Statements in C++ are terminated with a colon.
   f. Run-time errors can be discovered when you compile your program.

3. What is the output of the following code?

```
cout<<"Programming is not that hard.";
cout<<"In fact it can be quite easy!"<<endl;
cout<<"But you have to pay close attention";
```

4. Does the following code run properly all the time, have a syntax error, or cause a run-time error?

```
#include <iostream.h>
#include <stdlib.h>

void main()
{
 int Value;
 Value=Value+5;
 cout>>Value;
}
```

5. Does the following code run properly all the time, have a syntax error, or cause a run-time error?

```
#include <iostream.h>
#include <stdlib.h>

void main()
{
 int Value;
 cout<<"Please enter a number" <<endl;
 cin>>Value;
 cout<<(Value-1)<<"Is one less than the number you entered";
}
```

6. Rewrite the following program, but remove all of the comments.

```
// This is a simple program
/* Here is the first comment
#include <stdlib.h> */
#include <iostream.h>

void main() //The program starts here
{
   //First variable : int First;
   int Second; //second variable

   /* Third variable */
   int Third;
   cout<<"Enter a value"<<endl;
   cin>>Third;

}
//End of the program!
```

7. What is the output of the following expressions?

   a. `cout<<(1+8/2+((1*4)+(5*4))/4);`
   b. `cout<<((1+1+1+1)/2+(1+1+1)/3);`
   c. `cout<<(5*5+5/5+6);`
   d. `cout<<(((3+4)+(4*7))/5);`
   e. `cout<<((3*6*7*2)+12/2);`

8. Do the following lines of code compile, and if not, why?

   a. `cout<<(3+4);`
   b. `cout<<(3+4)*1;`
   c. `cout<<4(5+6);`

9. Do the following statements produce different output?

   a. `cout<<"I will get this right!"<<endl<<endl;`
      and
      `cout<<" I will get this right!"<<endl endl;`
   b. `cout<<((3+4)*5);`
      and
      `cout<<(((3+4)*5));`
   c. `cout<<"((3+4)*5)";`
      and
      `cout<<"(3+4)*5";`
   d. `cout<<"Will you get this right?"<<'\n'<<"Of course!";`
      and
      `cout<<"Will you get this right?"<<"\n"<<"Of course!";`
      and
      `cout<<"Will you get this right?\nOf course!";`

10. Assume X is equal to 6. What is the output of the following statements?

    a. `cout<<X<<endl<<(X+1)<<endl<<X<<endl<<(X*X)<<<<endl<<X;`
    b. `cout<<endl<<"X"<<endl<<'X'<<endl<<X;`

11. For each of the following, state whether or not the statement is valid. If it is valid, state the values for X, Y, and Z. Assume each is preceded by the following code:

```
int X, Y, Z;
X = 2;
Y = 3;
Z = 5;
```

    a. `++X;`
    b. `XYZ;`
    c. `X++;`
    d. `Y+=X;`
    e. `Y+=X*Z;`
    f. `X++Y;`
    g. `X+=2;`
       `Y=2/2;`
       `Z=X*Y;`
    h. `++Y++;`
    i. `Y = X+++Y++;`

a12. Assume that X is of type int. If the following code was executed:

```
int X;
cin>>X;
cout<<X;
```

what would be the output if the following values were entered?

a. 5
b. 2000
c. a
d. 34.5
e. −34
f. −4.2

13. Redo exercise 12, but assume that X is now of type float.

3

Conditional Statements

Chapter Objectives

- ♦ Introduce decision-making concepts
- ♦ Explain the if statement syntax
- ♦ Explain conditional expression evaluation
- ♦ Explain the else statement
- ♦ Explain nested if statements
- ♦ Introduce new operators associated with condition expressions
- ♦ Introduce the `bool` variable type

Currently, our computer consists of a glorified calculator with simple input and output operations. A useful computer requires the ability to make decisions. The key to programming the computer to make correct decisions is making sure we understand how to represent and evaluate the expression representing the decision properly. Therefore, we will inspect the evaluation of the truthfulness of an expression in great detail. Mastery of the evaluation of conditional expressions will also pay dividends when we study looping statements in future chapters, so your time will be well spent.

3.1 IF STATEMENTS

C++ offers several ways for decisions to be made, the simplest of which is the `if` statement.

A template for the statement follows:

```
if (expression)
  program statement;
```

An **if** statement consists of an expression that determines whether or not a program statement executes. An expression can be the comparison of two values. To compare values, you may use any of the following operators:

<	less than
>	greater than
<=	less than or equal to
>=	greater than or equal to
==	equal to
!=	not equal to

By placing either a variable or a constant value on both sides of the operator, an expression can be evaluated to either true or false. Here are some sample true expressions:

1 == 1
2 >= 1
2 >= 2
1 <= 2
1 < 2
1 != 2
'a' != 'c'
'A' != 'a'
'D' == 'D'

Here are some samples of false expressions:

1 == 2
2 <= 1
2 < 2
3 > 4
1 >= 2
1 != 1
'a' == 'A'
'D' != 'D'

When the condition in an **if** statement evaluates to true, the statement immediately following it is executed. If the **if** statement evaluates to false, the statement immediately after it is not executed. The following code is an example.

```
//Example of an if statement
#include <stdlib.h>
#include <iostream.h>

void main()
{
  if (1==1)
      cout<<"This will print, because 1=1\n";
      cout<<"This would print, even if 1==1 were not true, "
          <<"because it is not part of the if statement"<<endl;

   if (1==2)
      cout<<"This will not print, because 1 does not equal 2"<<endl;
      cout<<"This would print, even if 1==2 were not true, "
          <<"because it is not part of the if statement "<<endl;

}
```

The output of the code will be as follows:

```
This will print, because 1=1
This would print, even if 1=1 were not true, because it is
not part of the if statement
This would print, even if 1=2 were not true, because it is
not part of the if statement
```

The first line of output "This will print, because 1=1" is displayed because the expression in the first **if** statement evaluates to true. Since the expression is true, the next statement in the program is executed. Therefore, the **cout** statement outputs "This would print, even if 1=1 were not true, because it is not part of the **if** statement." The second **if** statement evaluates to false, because 1 does not equal 2. Therefore, the next **cout** statement is skipped. Finally, the last **cout** statement "This would print, even if 1=2 were not true, because it is not part of the **if** statement" is displayed because it is not part of the **if** statement.

▌▌ DRILLS

Drill 3-1

Indicate whether each expression is true or false.

1. (5 >= 4)
2. (-3 < -4)
3. (5 == 4)
4. (5 != 4)
5. (4 >= 4)
6. (4 <= 4)

Multiple Statements with an If

If you want more than one statement to execute when a condition evaluates to true, enclose the statements you wish to execute within a set of curly braces. By placing the character { in the code before the statements and the character } after the statements, the statements in between are treated as a group. Either all the statements are executed or all the statements are skipped.

The following example illustrates this point:

```
//If statement example with multiple statements in the body
#include <stdlib.h>
#include <iostream.h>

void main()
{
  if (1==1)
    {
      cout<<"This will print because 1 is equal to 1\n";
      cout<<"This will print because it is inside the curly braces\n";
    }

  if (2==1)
    {
      cout<<"This will never print because 1 is not equal to 2\n";
      cout<<"This will also never print, because it is contained within the curly braces\n";
    }
}
```

The output would be the following:

```
This will print because 1 is equal to 1
This will print because it is inside the curly braces
```

The first two **cout** statements are executed because the expression (**1==1**) is true. Since it is true, all of the statements contained within the set of curly braces directly after the first **if** expression are executed. Since the expression (**2==1**) is not true, all the statements contained within the set of curly braces directly after the second **if** expression are not executed.

▌ DRILLS

What is the output of the following code?

Drill 3-2

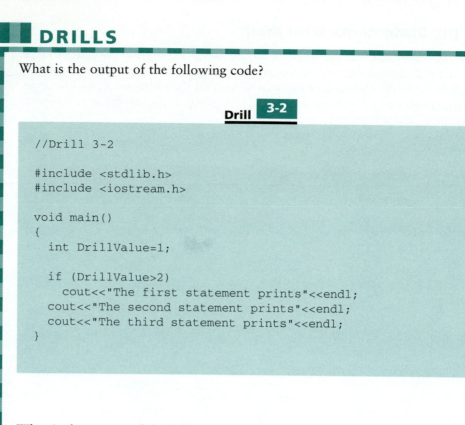

```
//Drill 3-2

#include <stdlib.h>
#include <iostream.h>

void main()
{
  int DrillValue=1;

  if (DrillValue>2)
    cout<<"The first statement prints"<<endl;
  cout<<"The second statement prints"<<endl;
  cout<<"The third statement prints"<<endl;
}
```

What is the output of the following code?

Drill 3-3

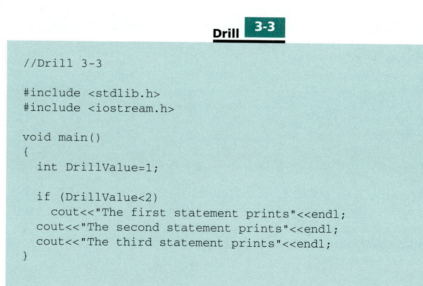

```
//Drill 3-3

#include <stdlib.h>
#include <iostream.h>

void main()
{
  int DrillValue=1;

  if (DrillValue<2)
    cout<<"The first statement prints"<<endl;
  cout<<"The second statement prints"<<endl;
  cout<<"The third statement prints"<<endl;
}
```

What is the output of the following code?

Drill 3-4

```
//Drill 3-4

#include <stdlib.h>
#include <iostream.h>

void main()
{
  int DrillValue=1;

  if (DrillValue>2)
    {
     cout<<"The first statement prints"<<endl;
     cout<<"The second statement prints"<<endl;
    }
  cout<<"The third statement prints"<<endl;
}
```

What is the output of the following code?

Drill 3-5

```
//Drill 3-5

#include <stdlib.h>
#include <iostream.h>

void main()
{
    int DrillValue=1;

    if (DrillValue<2)
      {
       cout<<"The first statement prints"<<endl;
       cout<<"The second statement prints"<<endl;
      }
    cout<<"The third statement prints"<<endl;
}
```

Decision-Making Programs

Now that we understand the basic operations of **if** statements, let's write our first program where a decision is required. The program will ask the user to enter the amount of a product a company has on hand. If the number is greater than 0, then the program outputs that the item is "in stock." Otherwise, it outputs that the item is "sold out." The code follows.

```
//The simple inventory program
#include <stdlib.h>
#include <iostream.h>

void main()
{
  //Declaration of variable
  int Number;

  //Gathering value from user
  cout<<"Enter the number of items you have ";
  cin>>Number;

  //Determine appropriate output
  if (Number <= 0)
    cout<<"Sold Out";
  if (Number > 0)
    cout<<"In Stock";
}
```

This program is broken into two parts. The first part is the declaration and initialization section, which declares a variable called **Number** (an integer). It then prompts the user for a number to enter and accepts that number in the variable **Number**.

The second part of the program compares the number to zero. If it is less than zero, then the message **Sold Out** is displayed. If the value is greater than zero, the message **In Stock** is displayed.

PROGRAMMER'S NOTEBOOK

It is important to be careful when writing expressions. A very common mistake, made even by advanced programmers, is to accidentally use the = operator instead of the == operator when performing a comparison.

C++ will allow the use of a single equal sign in the **if** statement, but your results may not be as expected. See the following example:

```
//Improper use of = operator in an if expression

#include <stdlib.h>
#include <iostream.h>

void main()
{
   int DrillValue=5;
   if (DrillValue=1)
      cout<<"The expression is true"<<endl;
   cout<< DrillValue;
}
```

You would expect the output to be as follows:

```
5
```

However, the output is as follows:

```
The expression is true
1
```

At this point you are probably thinking there is a typographical error in the book, but there is not. A single equal sign in C++ indicates an assignment, not a comparison. The statement **(DrillValue=1)**, therefore, assigns the variable **DrillValue** the value 1. C++ still needs to evaluate the expression, and since there is no comparison expression, C++ evaluates the variable. C++ **evaluates variables or numerical expressions to be true if they evaluate to anything other than zero.** If they evaluate to zero, then the expression is false. Therefore, since our variable contains a 1, it is true and the **cout** statement is executed. After the **if** statement, **DrillValue** is displayed. However, the value of **DrillValue** is now 1 not 5, so 1 is output.

DRILLS

What is the output of the following code?

Drill `3-6`

```
//Drill 3-6

#include <stdlib.h>
#include <iostream.h>

void main()
{
  int DrillValue=2;
  if (DrillValue=5)
    cout<<"The expression is true"<<endl;
  cout<<DrillValue;
}
```

What is the output of the following code?

Drill `3-7`

```
//Drill 3-7

#include <stdlib.h>
#include <iostream.h>

void main()
{
  int DrillValue=2;
  if (DrillValue=0)
    cout<<"The expression is true"<<endl;
  cout<<DrillValue;
}
```

More Examples

Let's modify our early program, which outputs the difference between the amount of your income versus the amount of your expenses. This time, let's add an output message that indicates whether or not you are spending more than you are making.

```cpp
//Improved expenses program

#include <stdlib.h>
#include <iostream.h>

void main()
{
  //Declaration of variables
  float Income;
  float Expenses;

  //Gathering input
  cout<<"Please enter the amount of your income"<<endl;
  cin>>Income;

  cout<<"Please enter the amount of your expenses"<<endl;
  cin>>Expenses;

  //Determine appropriate output
  if (Income > Expenses)
    cout<<"You did a good job, make sure you invest it wisely";

  if (Income < Expenses)
    cout<<"You need to be more frugal";

  if (Income == Expenses)
    cout<<"You have spent exactly what you earned!";
}
```

The program is straightforward. First, the variables to store a person's income and expenses are declared. Then the values are input from the user and evaluated using three conditional statements. Each is used to check a specific condition.

The first condition checks whether the income entered is a larger number than the expenses entered. If so, the first **cout** statement is executed.

Whether the first condition is true or false, the second condition is now checked. It checks to see if the income entered is a smaller number than the expenses entered. If so, the second **cout** statement is executed.

Regardless of the results of the first two **if** statements, the third condition is checked. It checks to see if the income entered is equal to the expenses entered. If so, the third **cout** statement is executed.

Another Example

With a bit more functionality in our C++ arsenal, let's improve our earlier program, which calculated the winning percentage for the Pittsburgh Steelers. Instead of just printing out the number of wins or the winning percentage, let's print out a message that will change depending upon how well the Pittsburgh Steelers are doing.

Our program is as follows:

```cpp
//Improved football example with if statements

#include <stdlib.h>
#include <iostream.h>

#define TotalNumGames 16

void main()
{
  //Declare variables.
  int NumWins;
  int NumLosses;

  //Get the number of wins.
  cout<<"Enter the number of wins for the Pittsburgh Steelers"
      <<endl;
  cin>>NumWins;

  //Compute the number of losses.
  NumLosses=TotalNumGames-NumWins;

  //Output the number of win & losses.
  cout<<"The number of wins for the Steelers = "<<NumWins<<endl
      <<"The number of losses for Steelers = "<<NumLosses<<endl;

  //Output a message depending on the number of wins.
  if (NumLosses>NumWins)
    cout<<"The Pittsburgh Steelers had a losing season,"
        <<" You must have entered the values wrong!";

  if (NumLosses<NumWins)
    cout<<"The Pittsburgh Steelers had a winning season, as we would expect!";
  if (NumLosses==NumWins)
    cout<<"The Pittsburgh Steelers finished 500.";

}
```

The program begins by declaring two variables to store the number of wins and the number of losses for the Steelers. It then asks the user for the number of wins. Because we know that there are 16 games in a season, we can compute the number of losses by subtracting the number of wins from 16. Now we have the information we need to determine the proper output message.

In all cases we display the message indicating the number of wins and the number of losses. Then we compare the number of wins and losses using a greater-than sign. If the number of losses is greater than the number of wins, then the statement "The Pittsburgh Steelers had a losing season, you must have entered the values wrong!" is displayed. What can I say, I'm a Pittsburgh Steeler fan. Then the next `if` statement is evaluated. If the number of losses is less than the number of wins, then the statement "The Pittsburgh Steelers had a winning season, as we would expect!" is displayed. Finally, if the number of losses equals the number of wins, the last statement is displayed, "The Pittsburgh Steelers finished 500."

Although this program executes correctly, from an efficiency standpoint, there are two problems with it. If the first condition is true, then there is no need to check the other conditions. Similarly, if the first two conditions are false, the third condition must be true and there is no need to waste time checking a condition at all.

3.2 ELSE AND ELSE IF STATEMENTS

C++ provides the `else if` and `else` keywords to handle these cases. When an `if` statement's expression evaluates to false, the next `else if` condition is evaluated, if is it true, then the statement(s) directly after it is executed. Otherwise, any additional `else if` statements are evaluated in the same fashion. After all the `else if` statements, if they all evaluate to false and an `else` statement is included, then the statement(s) directly following the `else` keyword will be executed.

```
if (condition)
   do something
else if (condition 2)
   do something else
else
   do something else
```

Now we can rewrite our previous program to be more efficient using **else if** and **else** keywords.

```
//Improved football example with if, else if, and else statements

#include <stdlib.h>
#include <iostream.h>

#define TotalNumGames 16

void main()
{
  //Declare Variables
  int NumWins;
  int NumLosses;

  //Get the number of wins.
  cout<<"Enter the number of wins for the Pittsburgh Steelers";
  cin>>NumWins;

  //Compute the number of losses.
  NumLosses=TotalNumGames-NumWins;

  //Output the number of win & losses.
  cout<<"The number of wins for the Steelers ="<<NumWins
      <<" The number of losses for Steelers ="<<NumLosses;

  //Output a message depending on the number of //wins.
  if (NumLosses>NumWins)
    cout<<"The Pittsburgh Steelers had a losing season,"
        <<" You must have entered the values wrong!";

  else if (NumLosses<NumWins)
    cout<<"The Pittsburgh Steelers had a winning season, as we would expect!";

  else
    cout<<"The Pittsburgh Steelers finished 500.";
}
```

The code is more efficient, because if

```
if (NumLosses>NumWins)
```

evaluates to be true, then the **cout** statement is executed and the program terminates. Otherwise, the **else if** statement is evaluated.

```
else if (NumLosses<NumWins)
```

If this is true, then the corresponding `cout` statement is executed and the program terminates. Finally, if the first two conditions are false, we know the last statement will be true, so the `else` statement forces the final `cout` statement to be executed without the need for an additional comparison.

PROGRAMMER'S NOTEBOOK

Be aware that you are not restricted in the number of `else if` statements contained within an `if` statement.

Another Example

See the following program that will display the text name of a single digit integer read from the user. It uses as many `else if`s as are required by the problem:

```cpp
//Example showing conversion from number to word

#include <stdlib.h>
#include <iostream.h>

void main()
{
    int Digit;

    cout<<"Enter a single digit"<<endl;
    cin>>Digit;

    if (Digit > 10)
        cout<<"That is too large of a number to display";
    else if (Digit<1)
        cout<<"That is too small of a number to display";
    else if (Digit==1)
        cout<<"One";
    else if (Digit==2)
        cout<<"Two";
    else if (Digit--3)
        cout<<"Three";
    else if (Digit==4)
        cout<<"Four";
    else if (Digit==5)
        cout<<"Five";
    else if (Digit==6)
        cout<<"Six";
    else if (Digit==7)
        cout<<"Seven";
    else if (Digit==8)
        cout<<"Eight";
    else if (Digit==9)
        cout<<"Nine";
    else
        cout<<"Ten";
}
```

The program starts by declaring a variable and reading a value from the user. The first comparison is accomplished with an **if** statement. All the comparisons except the last one are all implemented with **else if** statements. The last comparison is not required, because the only number that could remain at that point is the number 10.

An important feature of this program is that it checks for valid input. In this program the first **if** and **else if** statements check to ensure the number entered is between 1 and 10. A program is considered more robust if it doesn't crash or return inaccurate results when unexpected data is entered.

Another Example

Here is another example of using **if**, **else if**, and **else** keywords.

```
//Example showing letter grade for a numeric grade

#include <stdlib.h>
#include <iostream.h>

void main()
{
  int Grade;

  cout<<"Enter a numerical grade"<<endl;
  cin>>Grade;

  if (Grade>=90)
    cout<<"A";
  else if (Grade>=80)
    cout<<"B";
  else if (Grade>=70)
    cout<<"C";
  else if (Grade>=60)
    cout<<"D";
  else
    cout<<"F";
}
```

Note: *In this example, without the* **else if** *it would be difficult, given what we know so far, to construct a simple* **if** *statement program that printed the desired letter grade for a numerical grade.*

The program is simple. It starts by declaring and reading in a numerical grade. It then compares the grade entered to 90. Any grade greater than or equal to 90 outputs the letter A, and the program terminates. If the grade is not greater than or equal to 90, it must be less than 90. Therefore, when we have a grade that is in the 80s the first **else if** statement is enough to check for a B. Similarly, we check for a C and D. Finally, if the grade is not greater than or equal to a 60, we output F.

DRILLS

What is the output of the following code if DrillValue equals 5? What is the output of the following code if DrillValue equals 8? What is the output of the following code if DrillValue equals 1?

Drill **3-8**

```
// Drill 3-8

#include <stdlib.h>
#include <iostream.h>

void main()
{
   int DrillValue=5;// or DrillValue=8 or DrillValue=1

   if (DrillValue>5)
     cout<<"DrillValue is greater than five"<<endl;
   else if (DrillValue<5)
     cout<<"DrillValue is less than five"<<endl;
   else
     cout<<"DrillValue is equal to five"<<endl;
}
```

What is the output of the following code if DrillValue equals 5? What is the output of the following code if DrillValue equals 8? What is the output of the following code if DrillValue equals 1?

Drill 3-9

```
// Drill 3-9
#include <stdlib.h>
#include <iostream.h>

void main()
{
   int DrillValue=5; //or DrillValue=8 or DrillValue=1
   if (DrillValue>5)
      {
      cout<<"DrillValue is greater than five"<<endl;
      cout<<"The if expression evaluated to true"<<endl;
      }
   else if (DrillValue<5)
      {
      cout<<"DrillValue is less than five"<<endl;
      cout<<"The else if expression evaluated to true"<<endl;
      }
   else
      {
```

```
            cout<<"DrillValue is equal to five"<<endl;
            cout<<"The else statements were executed"<<endl;
        }
}
```

What is the output of the following code if DrillValue equals 5? What is the output of the following code if DrillValue equals 8? What is the output of the following code if DrillValue equals 1?

Drill **3-10**

```
//Drill 3-10

#include <stdlib.h>
#include <iostream.h>

void main()
{
   int DrillValue=5; // or DrillValue=8 or DrillValue=1
   if (DrillValue>5)
      cout<<"DrillValue is greater than five"<<endl;
      cout<<"The if expression evaluated to true"<<endl;

   else if (DrillValue<5)
      cout<<"DrillValue is less than five"<<endl;
      cout<<"The else if expression evaluated to true"<<endl;

   else
      cout<<"DrillValue is equal to five"<<endl;
      cout<<"The else statements were executed"<<endl;
}
```

What is the output of the following code if DrillValue equals 5? What is the output of the following code if DrillValue equals 8? What is the output of the following code if DrillValue equals 1?

Drill 3-11

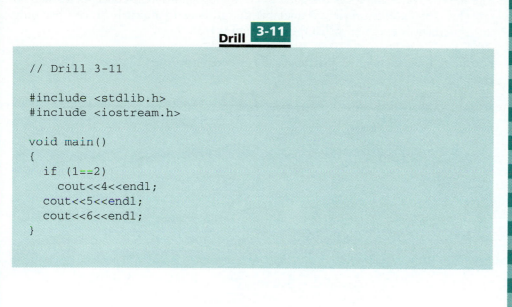

```
// Drill 3-11

#include <stdlib.h>
#include <iostream.h>

void main()
{
  if (1==2)
    cout<<4<<endl;
  cout<<5<<endl;
  cout<<6<<endl;
}
```

What is the output of the following code?

Drill 3-12

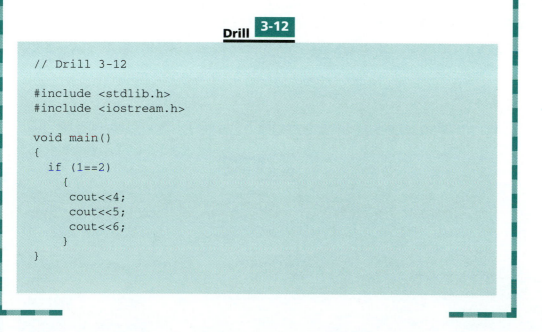

```
// Drill 3-12

#include <stdlib.h>
#include <iostream.h>

void main()
{
  if (1==2)
    {
      cout<<4;
      cout<<5;
      cout<<6;
    }
}
```

▋▋ MORE DRILLS

The next set of examples is designed to combine the different concepts learned so far. This is an excellent review. Remember that if there are no curly braces then only one statement is executed when the condition is true.

For the following code, what happens if 1 is entered for **DrillValue**; what if 2 is entered?

Drill **3-13**

```
// Drill 3-13

#include <stdlib.h>
#include <iostream.h>

void main()
{
  int DrillValue;
  cin>>DrillValue;

  if (DrillValue==1)
   {
    cout<<"The Yankees can buy the best players in baseball!"<<endl;
    cout<<"The Steelers have to get players from the draft"<<endl;
   }
    cout<<"We can only hope for the Eagles.";
}
```

For the following code, what happens if 1 is entered for **DrillValue**; what if 2 is entered?

Drill **3-14**

```
//Drill 3-14

#include <stdlib.h>
#include <iostream.h>

void main()
{
  int DrillValue;
  cin>>DrillValue;

  if (DrillValue==1)
    cout<<"The Yankees can buy the best players in baseball!"<<endl;

    cout<<"The Steelers have to get players from the draft"<<endl;

    cout<<"We can only hope for the Eagles.";
}
```

White Space Issues

It is important to note that white space (tabs, carriage returns, and spaces) does not affect the running of the code.

The following code runs properly, but certainly is not as readable as a properly formatted program.

```
#include<stdlib.h>
#include<iostream.h>
void main(){int x;cin>>x;if (x==1) cout<<"1st statement";
cout<<"Second statement"; cout<<"Third statement";}
```

3.3 COMPOUND CONDITIONAL STATEMENTS

C++ gives us additional expression operators to help us map a problem or algorithm to a program. Often we require these operators, because the condition that we wish to express cannot be represented as a simple single comparison. It is not uncommon to require **Boolean logic** operators like and, or, and not to help us represent a condition properly.

&& is used to represent the logical anding of two conditions. If you are unfamiliar with **Boolean logic** here is a simple truth table of all the possible conditions:

```
TRUE && TRUE = TRUE

TRUE && FALSE = FALSE

FALSE && TRUE = FALSE

FALSE && FALSE = FALSE
```

|| is used to represent the logical or. Here is a truth table of all of the possibilities:

```
TRUE || TRUE = TRUE

TRUE || FALSE = TRUE

FALSE || TRUE = TRUE

FALSE || FALSE = FALSE
```

In addition, C++ provides the ! operator to negate the value of an expression. Here is a truth table of all the possibilities:

```
! TRUE = FALSE

! FALSE = TRUE
```

Here is an example of a program that contains a **compound conditional statement**. It will check two conditions instead of one to display a message.

```cpp
//Compound conditional example

#include <stdlib.h>
#include <iostream.h>

#define Dallas 'D'
#define Pittsburgh 'P'
#define TotalNumGames 16

void main()
{
  int NumWins; //stores the number of wins entered by the user
  int NumLosses;//stores the number of losses calculated by the user

  char Team; //Stores a character representing the team you wish.

  //Get the number of wins.
  cout<<"Enter the Number of Wins for a Team"<<endl;
  cin>>NumWins;

  cout<<"Enter a 'P' for Pittsburgh and a 'D' for Dallas"<<endl;
  cin>>Team;

  //Calculate the number of losses assuming there are 16 games in a season.
  NumLosses=TotalNumGames-NumWins;

  //Output the results.
  if (Team == Dallas && NumWins > NumLosses)
    cout<<"Dallas had a winning season, they must have a soft schedule!";

  else if (Team == Dallas && NumWins <= NumLosses)
    cout<<"Dallas did not have a winning season";

  else if (Team == Pittsburgh && NumWins > NumLosses)
    cout<<"Pittsburgh is on the way to the Super Bowl";

  else if (Team == Pittsburgh && NumWins <= NumLosses)
    cout<<"Must be a typo, Pittsburgh always wins";

  else if (Team != Pittsburgh && Team != Dallas)
    cout<<"A typo on entering the team has occurred";

}
```

The program starts the same way as the other football program that we wrote. However, this time we also accept a character indicating the team to be displayed. The program then determines which of the output statements to execute by evaluating the **compound condition** in each **if** statement.

Since the **&&** operator is used between each conditional expression, both sub-conditions must be true in order for the entire expression to evaluate to true. Note that the last **else if** statement could have been written as an **else** statement. However, we wrote out the expression to demonstrate another example of the **&&** operator.

DRILLS

The best way to become comfortable with these operators is to try lots of examples. Look at the following code, guess the results, and then type the program and observe the results when you execute the operators.

Drill **3-15**

```
//Drill 3-15

#include <stdlib.h>
#include ,iostream.h>

void main()
{
    int DrillValue1=5;
    int DrillValue2=3;
    int DrillValue3=10;

    if ((DrillValue1==5) && (DrillValue2==3))
      cout <<"#1 prints\n";
    if ((DrillValue1==5) || (DrillValue2==3))
      cout <<"#2 prints\n";
    if ((DrillValue1==5) && (DrillValue2==4))
      cout<<"#3 prints\n";
    if ((DrillValue1==5) || (DrillValue2==4))
      cout<<"#4 prints\n";
    if ((DrillValue3==DrillValue1) || (DrillValue3==DrillValue2) ||
        (DrillValue3==DrillValue3))
      cout<<"#5 prints\n";
    if ((DrillValue3==DrillValue1) && (DrillValue3==DrillValue2) &&
        (DrillValue3==DrillValue3))
      cout<<"#6 prints\n";
    if ((DrillValue3==DrillValue1) && (DrillValue3==DrillValue2) ||
        (DrillValue3==DrillValue3))
      cout<<"#7 prints\n";
    if ((DrillValue3==DrillValue1) || (DrillValue3==DrillValue2) &&
        (DrillValue3==DrillValue3))
      cout<<"#8 prints\n";
}
```

3.4 NESTED CONDITIONAL STATEMENTS

C++ provides additional options that provide maximum flexibility in implementing conditional statements. C++ allows conditional statements to be nested within each other. This shouldn't add too much confusion—it simply requires treating the inner **if** statement like an individual **if** statement, which is evaluated as any other statement.

See how we modify our previous football program so that it takes advantage of the nesting ability of **if** statements.

```cpp
//Nested if statement example

#include <stdlib.h>
#include <iostream.h>

#define TotalNumGames 16
#define Dallas 'D'
#define Pittsburgh 'P'

void main()
{
  int NumWins; //Stores the number of wins entered by the user
  int NumLosses; //Stores the number of losses calculated by the user

  char Team; //Stores a character representing the team you wish

  //Get the number of wins.
  cout<<"Enter the Number of Wins for a Team"<<endl;
  cin>>NumWins;

  cout<<"Enter a 'P' for Pittsburgh and a 'D' for Dallas"<<endl;
  cin>>Team;

  //Calculate the number of losses assuming there are 16 games in a season.
  NumLosses=TotalNumGames-NumWins;

  //Output the results.
  if (Team==Dallas)
  {
   if (NumWins>NumLosses)
     cout<<"Dallas had a winning season, they must have had a soft schedule!";
   else
     cout<<"Dallas did not have a winning season";
  }
  else if (Team==Pittsburgh)
   {
    if (NumWins>NumLosses)
      cout<<"Pittsburgh is on the way to the Superbowl";
    else
      cout<<"Must be a typo, Pittsburgh always wins";
   }
  else

    cout<<"A typo on entering the team has occurred.";

}
```

In the previous program, we gather input from the user, calculate the number of losses and then determine what output should be displayed. The first **if** statement is a check to compare the variable **Team** to 'D'. If the **Team** variable equals 'D', then the inner **if** statement is evaluated. This statement determines whether or not Dallas had a winning season and outputs the appropriate message. If the first if statement evaluated to false, then the **else if** statement compares the Team variable to 'P'. If the **Team** variable equals 'P', then the inner if statement is executed to determine whether or not the Steelers had a winning season and outputs the appropriate message. If neither outer **if** statement evaluates to true, then the outer **else** statement executes and the message "A typo on entering the team has occurred."

By using nested **if**, **else if**, and **else** statements we can accomplish the same as we did in the compound condition, but in this case we can accomplish it with less comparisons and therefore have a more efficient program.

DRILLS

The following program is designed to test your order of precedence knowledge. Try working out each example first, then type the program and execute it. Compare your results to the answers found at the end of the chapter.

Drill 3-16

```
//Drill 3-16

#include <stdlib.h>
#include <iostream.h>

void main()
{
   int DrillValue1=5;
   int DrillValue2=3;

   if (DrillValue1==5)
     if (DrillValue2==3)
       cout<<"#1 prints";
     else
       cout<<"#2 prints";
   else
     cout<<"#3 prints";
}
```

If we change the program so that **DrillValue2=2**, the output would now change.

Drill 3-17

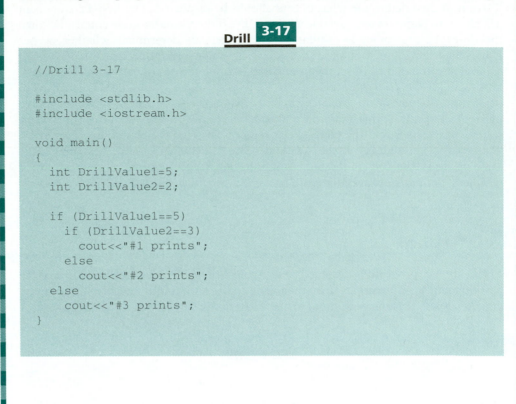

```
//Drill 3-17

#include <stdlib.h>
#include <iostream.h>

void main()
{
    int DrillValue1=5;
    int DrillValue2=2;

    if (DrillValue1==5)
      if (DrillValue2==3)
        cout<<"#1 prints";
      else
        cout<<"#2 prints";
    else
      cout<<"#3 prints";
}
```

This is because the inner **if** statement expression now evaluates to false and the second **cout** statement is selected for output.

Similarly, if we modified the program so that **DrillValue1=1**, we would see the following:

Drill **3-18**

```
//Drill 3-18

#include <stdlib.h>
#include <iostream.h>

void main()
{
  int DrillValue1=1;
  int DrillValue2=3;

  if (DrillValue1==5)
    if (DrillValue2==3)
      cout<<"#1 prints";
    else
      cout<<"#2 prints";
  else
    cout<<"#3 prints";
}
```

It is possible to rewrite the preceding code using a compound condition statement as follows:

```
#include <stdlib.h>
#include <iostream.h>

void main()
{
  int DrillValue1=1;
  int DrillValue2=3;

  if (DrillValue1==5) && (DrillValue2==3)
    cout<<"#1 prints";
  else if (DrillValue1==5) && (DrillValue2!=3)
    cout<<"#2 prints";
  else
    cout<<"#3 prints";
}
```

However, although your output would be identical, an extra evaluation occurs in the first **else if** statement. The **(DrillValue1==5)** is evaluated a second time, whereas it really wouldn't be required if we used a nested **if** statement.

In general, if an evaluation occurs multiple times in a series of **if/else if/else** statements with compound expressions, it may be more efficient to use a nested **if/else if/else** statement instead.

3.5 SUBTLE EXPRESSION EVALUATION

So far we have an excellent foundation for the evaluation of expressions, but unfortunately not all expressions are so clear cut in their evaluation. Conditional statements in C++ can be much subtler.

DRILLS

Remember, if an expression evaluates to 0 it is false, otherwise it's true. Try the following examples as well. What is the output of the following code?

Drill 3-19

```
//Drill 3-19

#include <stdlib.h>
#include <iostream.h>

void main()
{
  if (1)
    cout<<"#1 prints";
  else
    cout<<"#2 prints";
}
```

What is the output of the following code?

Drill 3-20

```
//Drill 3-20

#include <stdlib.h>
#include <iostream.h>

void main()
{
  if (0)
    cout <<"#1 prints";
  else
    cout<<"#2 prints";
}
```

What is the output of the following code?

Drill 3-21

```
//Drill 3-21

#include <stdlib.h>
#include <iostream.h>

void main()
{
  int DrillValue=5;

  if (DrillValue)
    cout<<"#1 prints";
  else
    cout<<"#2 prints";
}
```

What is the output of the following code?

Drill 3-22

```
//Drill 3-22

#include <stdlib.h>
#include <iostream.h>

void main()
{
  int DrillValue=0;

  if (DrillValue)
    cout<<"#1 prints";
  else
    cout<<"#2 prints";
}
```

What is the output of the following code?

Drill `3-23`

```
//Drill 3-23

#include <stdlib.h>
#include <iostream.h>

void main()
{
  int DrillValue=0;

  if (++DrillValue)
    cout<<"#1 prints "<<DrillValue;
  else
    cout<<"#2 prints "<<DrillValue;
}
```

What is the output of the following code?

Drill `3-24`

```
//Drill 3-24

#include <stdlib.h>
#include <iostream.h>

void main()
{
  int DrillValue=-1;

  if (++DrillValue)
    cout<<"#1 prints "<<DrillValue;
  else
    cout<<"#2 prints "<<DrillValue;
}
```

What is the output of the following code?

Drill 3-25

```
//Drill 3-25

#include <stdlib.h>
#include <iostream.h>

void main()
{
  int DrillValue=0;

  if (DrillValue++)
    cout<<"#1 prints "<<DrillValue;
  else
    cout<<"#2 prints "<<DrillValue;
}
```

What is the output of the following code?

Drill 3-26

```
//Drill 3-26

#include <stdlib.h>
#include <iostream.h>

void main()
{
  int DrillValue=-1;

  if (DrillValue++)
    cout<<"#1 prints "<<DrillValue;
  else
    cout<<"#2 prints"<<DrillValue;
}
```

3.6 SHORT CIRCUIT CONDITIONAL EVALUATION

Did you ever notice that when you are calculating whether an expression is true or not that sometimes you don't have to calculate the rest of the expression? This is because regardless of the rest of the expression, your answer will remain the same.

For example:

```
#include <stdlib.h>
#include <iostream.h>

void main()
{
  if ((1==1) || (2==3) ||(4==5) || (6==7))
    cout<<"It prints";
}
```

After the (1==1) is calculated to be true, the rest of the equation is irrelevant. Since the first part of the equation is true and everything else is or'd together, nothing else is required to be calculated. Since one of the purposes of C++ is to be as fast as possible, C++ ignores what is irrelevant. We call this a **short circuit evaluation** of a condition expression.

Why is this important to us as C++ programmers? It's more than just "the need for speed." If we ignore this feature of C++ we sometimes find that code does not function as expected.

Although the following code is a bit cryptic and should not be used in the "real world," it does illustrate the hazards that can be associated with short circuit evaluation. Try to determine the output of the following code.

```
#include <stdlib.h>
#include <iostream.h>

void main()
{
  int DrillValue=3;

  if ((1==1) || (++DrillValue==4))
    cout<<"Inside the if statement DrillValue="<<DrillValue<<endl;
  cout<<"After the if statement DrillValue="<<DrillValue<<endl;
}
```

It should be obvious that the expression evaluates to true. The **(1==1)** subcondition will evaluate to true. However, because of short circuiting, the second subcondition is never evaluated. If it is never evaluated, the **++DrillValue** is never executed. Therefore, **DrillValue** remains the same as it did before the **if** statement. So the output would be as follows:

```
Inside the if statement DrillValue=3
After the if statement DrillValue=3
```

DRILLS

What is the output of the following code?

Drill 3-27

```
//Drill 3-27

#include <stdlib.h>
#include <iostream.h>

void main()
{
   int DrillValue=3;

   if ((1==1) || (DrillValue++==4))
     cout<<"DrillValue="<<DrillValue;
}
```

What is the output of the following?

Drill 3-28

```
//Drill 3-28

#include <stdlib.h>
#include <iostream.h>

void main()
{
   int DrillValue=3;

   if ((1==1) && (DrillValue++==4))
     cout<<"DrillValue="<< DrillValue;
}
```

What is the output of the following?

Drill 3-29

```
//Drill 3-29

#include <stdlib.h>
#include <iostream.h>

void main()
{
  int DrillValue=3;

  if ((1==2) || (DrillValue++==4))
    cout<<"DrillValue="<<DrillValue;
}
```

What is the output of the following?

Drill 3-30

```
//Drill 3-30

#include <stdlib.h>
#include <iostream.h>

void main()
{
  int DrillValue=3;

  if ((1==2) && (DrillValue++==4))
    cout<<"DrillValue="<<DrillValue;
}
```

What is the output of the following?

Drill `3-31`

```
Drill 3-31

#include <stdlib.h>
#include <iostream.h>

void main()
{
   int DrillValue=3;

   if (((1==3) || (DrillValue++==4)) && (1==1))
     cout<<"DrillValue="<<DrillValue;
}
```

What is the output of the following?

Drill `3-32`

```
//Drill 3-32

#include <stdlib.h>
#include <iostream.h>

void main()
{
   int DrillValue=3;

   if (((1==1) || (DrillValue++==4)) && (1==1))
     cout<<"DrillValue="<<DrillValue;
}
```

What is the output of the following?

Drill `3-33`

```
//Drill 3-33

#include <stdlib.h>
#include <iostream.h>

void main()
{
   int DrillValue=4;

   if ((1==1) && (++DrillValue==5))
     cout<<"DrillValue="<<DrillValue;
}
```

3.7 SWITCH STATEMENTS

Using multiple **if**, **else if**, and **elses** can become burdensome as well as look quite busy on the page. C++ gives you a better way to handle multiple options— it's called the **switch** statement. If you have an expression that evaluates to a single integer or character as in:

```
if (SwitchValue == 1)
  ...
else if (SwitchValue == 2)
  ...
else if (SwitchValue == 3)
  ...
```

or

```
if (SwitchValue == 'a')
  ...
else if (SwitchValue == 'b')
  ...
else if (SwitchValue == 'c')
  ...
```

then you can use a **switch** statement. A **switch** statement follows the following template:

```
switch (Expression)
{
 case Val1:
   program statements;
   break;
 case Val2:
   program statements;
   break;
 case Val3:
   program statements;
   break;
 default:
   program statements;
}
```

PROGRAMMER'S NOTEBOOK

A switch statement cannot operate on nonscalar variables like float or double.

Here is a simple example that reads in the first character of a team and then outputs the full name of the team.

```
//Switch statement example

#include <iostream.h>
#include <stdlib.h>

#define Yankees 'Y'
#define Mets 'M'
#define Phillies 'P'

void main()
{
   cout<<"Enter your team's 1st letter"<<endl;

   char Lteam;
   cin>>Lteam;
```

```
switch (Lteam)
{
 case Yankees:
   cout<<"Yankees";
   break;
 case Mets:
   cout<<"Mets";
   break;
 case Phillies:
   cout<<"Phillies";
   break;
 default:
   cout<<"It was a strike, nobody";
}
 cout<<" won the world series!";
}
```

Therefore, if a 'Y' is entered, the following expression is output:

```
Yankees won the world series!
```

If an 'M' is entered, the following expression is output:

```
Mets won the world series!
```

If a 'P' is entered, the following expression is output:

```
Phillies won the world series!
```

If a 'X' is entered, the following expression is output:

```
It was a strike, nobody won the world series!
```

The **default** case works like the **else** in an **if, else if, else** statement. It executes only if all the other cases did not execute.

Notice the keyword **break** after each case. C++ behaves unintuitively if the keyword **break** is not placed there. Without a **break** keyword, once a case evaluates to true, all the remaining **case** statements will execute. Therefore, you usually will place a **break** keyword at the end of each case in a **switch** statement.

Observe the difference in the following code, which does not have **break** statements included:

```
//Switch statement example without breaks

#include <iostream.h>
#include <stdlib.h>

#define Yankees 'Y'
#define Mets 'M'
#define Phillies 'P'

void main()
{
  cout<<"Enter your team's 1st letter"<<endl;

  char Lteam;
  cin>>Lteam;

  switch (Lteam)
  {
   case Yankees:
     cout<<"Yankees";
   case Mets:
     cout<<"Mets";
   case Phillies:
     cout<<"Phillies";
   default:
     cout<<"It was a strike, nobody";
   }
   cout<<" wins the world series!";
}
```

When executing the preceding code and entering a 'Y' for **Lteam**, we would get the following output:

```
YankeesMetsPhilliesIt was a strike, nobody wins the world series!
```

If we enter 'M', we would get the following output.

```
MetsPhilliesIt was a strike, nobody wins the world series!
```

Clearly, this is not the desired result.

Here is an example of using a **switch** statement to evaluate a simple mathematical expression:

```cpp
//Calculator example using a switch statement
#include <stdlib.h>
#include <iostream.h>

void main()
{
  float Value1, Value2;
  char Operator;
  cout<<"Enter your expression."<<endl;
  cin>>Value1>>Operator>>Value2;

  switch(Operator)
  {
   case '+':
     cout<<Value1+Value2;
     break;
   case '-':
     cout<<Value1-Value2;
     break;
   case '*':
     cout<<Value1*Value2;
     break;
   case '/':
     if (Value2 == 0)
       cout<<"Division by Zero!"<<endl;
     else
       cout<<Value1/Value2;
     break;
   default:
     cout<<"Unknown operator"<<endl;
     break;
  }
}
```

The operation of the program is straightforward. Three values are read from the user: two numbers and a character representing the operation to be performed. The **switch** statement selects which of the operations should be performed and then executes that operation. The result is output and then the program terminates.

Look at the next portion of a program as an enhancement of the previous one. The program takes advantage of a shortcut feature in a **case** statement. When more than one case is to be associated with the statement, we can simply list one below the other. This allows multiple input values to represent a multiplication value. The following code snippet shows the middle part of the **case** statement and allows either 'X', 'x', or '*' for multiplication:

```
case '-':
  cout<<Value1-Value2;
  break;
case '*':
case 'x':
case 'X':
  cout<<Value1*Value2;
  break;
case '/':
  if (Value2 == 0)
    cout<<"Division by Zero!"<<endl;
```

DRILLS

What is the output of the following code if the letter 'A' is entered? What is the output of the following code if the letter 'C' is entered? What is the output of the following code if the letter 'Z' is entered?

 Drill **3-34**

```
//Drill 3-34

#include <stdlib.h>
#include <iostream.h>

void main()
{
  char TestChar;

  cin>>TestChar;
```

```
    switch (TestChar)
    {
        case 'a':
        case 'A':
          cout<<"The Letter A";
        case 'b':
        case 'B':
          cout<<"The Letter B";
        case 'c':
        case 'C':
          cout<<"The Letter C";
        default:
          cout<<"You do not know your ABC's!";
    }
}
```

What is the output of the following code if the letter 'A' is entered? What is the output of the following code if the letter 'C' is entered? What is the output of the following code if the letter 'Z' is entered?

Drill **3-35**

```
//Drill 3-35

#include <stdlib.h>
#include <iostream.h>

void main()
{
  char TestChar;

  cin>>TestChar;

  switch (TestChar)
  {
   case 'a':
   case 'A':
     cout<<"The Letter A";
     break;
   case 'b':
   case 'B':
     cout<<"The Letter B";
     break;
   case 'c':
   case 'C':
     cout<<"The Letter C";
     break;
   default:
     cout<<"You do not know your ABC's!";
  }
}
```

3.8 BOOL DATA TYPE

Often, we want our programs to store the results of a conditional expression or a Boolean value. In older compilers, a programmer would have to use an integer variable. Usually, if the integer equaled 0, it represented false. If the integer equaled 1, it represented true. Although this method works, it is not extremely readable.

To improve the situation, some programmers used the **#define** precompiler directive to establish constants for true and false. Although this was an improvement over using one and zero, it would not prevent variables created as integers from containing values other than the ones indicated by the **#define** precompiler directives.

Therefore, C++ introduced the **bool** data type and keyword. A **bool** can represent only true or false. This allows us to store Boolean values in a readable and safe manner.

The following example of a program asks the user three questions and then outputs a message based on whether all three questions are answered true.

PROGRAMMER'S NOTEBOOK

Notice that you cannot read a **true** value or a **false** value from the keyboard.

```
//Bool data type example

#include <stdlib.h>
#include <iostream.h>

void main()
{
  bool Answer1;
  bool Answer2;
  bool Answer3;

  char Response;


  //Get first response
  cout<<"Did you like the movie Star Wars? (Enter 'Y' for Yes, 'N' for No"<<endl;
  cin>>Response;

  if (Response == 'Y')
    Answer1 = true;
  else
    Answer1 = false;

  //Get second response
  cout<<"Did you like the movie The Empire Strikes Back?";
  cout<<" (Enter 'Y' for Yes, 'N' for No"<<endl;
  cin>>Response;
```

```
if (Response == 'Y')
  Answer2 = true;
else
  Answer2 = false;

//Get third response
cout<<"Did you like the Movie Return of the Jedi?";
cout<<" (Enter 'Y' for Yes, 'N' for No"<<endl;
cin>>Response;

if (Response == 'Y')
  Answer3 = true;
else
  Answer3 = false;

//Evaluate all three answers at once.
if ((Answer1 == true) && (Answer2 == true) && (Answer3 == true))
  cout<<"You are a Jedi Knight!";
else
  cout<<"You have much to learn young pedawon";
}
```

A final note: If you are comparing a Boolean value to true as in the final **if** statement in the preceding program, you can use a shortcut to write it. By writing the conditional statement as follows, you are still comparing to true; it's just that the **true** keyword is assumed:

```
//Evaluate all three answers at once.
  if ((Answer1) && (Answer2) && (Answer3))
    cout<<"You are a Jedi Knight!";
  else
    cout<<"You have much to learn young pedawon";
}
```

3.9 Case Study

Problem Description

An entrepreneur operating a day labor pool divides his workers into three skill levels. Unskilled workers receive $8.15 per hour, semiskilled workers $12.55 per hour, and skilled workers $18.60 per hour. Write a program that calculates a worker's daily pay showing the dollar sign and the amount formatted to two decimal places. Test your program for an input of odd, even, and fractional hours. Your program input should consist of the hours worked and a skill level indicator.

Discussion

The program requires two inputs, the skill indicator and number of hours the worker was employed. Any attempt to input the pay rates should be discouraged, since the pay scales are fixed and entry of excessive data could lead to errors. The pay rates should be placed in the program as constants. Either a **switch** statement or multiple **if** statements may be used; however, **switch** is the better choice. We will show both implementations. Because the worker may work fractional hours, the input variable must be a float. A double is acceptable, but should be discouraged since it is unlikely a daily worker will earn a large sum of money. Minimum flag settings should be **showpoint**, and **precision** should be set to two. Also, setting the fixed flag should be encouraged, since it will be needed for larger numbers in later chapters.

Solution 1, If Statements

```
#include <stdlib.h>
#include <iostream.h>
#include <iomanip.h>

#define LWage (float) 8.15
#define MWage (float) 12.55
#define HWage (float) 18.60

void main()
{

    float Hours;
    float Pay;
    float Rate;
    int SkillIndicator;

    cout << setprecision(2);
    cout << setiosflags(ios :: showpoint);
    cout << setiosflags(ios :: fixed); //Needed only for large numbers
    cout << endl << "Enter hours worked -> ";
    cin >> Hours;
    cout << "Enter skill indicator (1,2,3) -> ";
    cin >> SkillIndicator;
    if (SkillIndicator == 1)
       Rate = HWage;
    else if (SkillIndicator == 2)
       Rate = MWage;
    else if (SkillIndicator == 3)
       Rate = LWage;
```

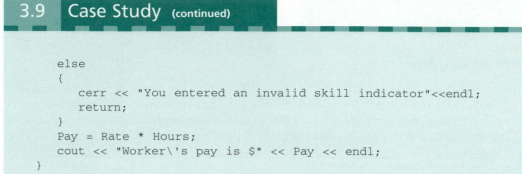

```
    else
    {
        cerr << "You entered an invalid skill indicator"<<endl;
        return;
    }
    Pay = Rate * Hours;
    cout << "Worker\'s pay is $" << Pay << endl;
}
```

Output, First Input

```
Enter hours worked -> 7
Enter skill indicator (1,2,3) -> 3
Worker's pay is $57.05
```

Output, Second Input

```
Enter hours worked -> 8
Enter skill indicator (1,2,3) -> 2
Worker's pay is $100.40
```

Output, Third Input

```
Enter hours worked -> 8.5
Enter skill indicator (1,2,3) -> 1
Worker's pay is $158.10
```

Output, Fourth Input

```
Enter hours worked -> 10.5
Enter skill indicator (1,2,3) -> 4
You entered an invalid skill indicator
```

3.9 Case Study (continued)

Solution 2, Switch Statements

```
#include <stdlib.h>
#include <iostream.h>
#include <iomanip.h>


#define LWage (float) 8.15
#define MWage (float) 12.55
#define HWage (float) 18.60

void main()
{
  float Hours;
  float Pay;
  float Rate;
  char SkillsIndicator;

  cout << setprecision(2);
  cout << setiosflags(ios :: showpoint);
  cout << setiosflags(ios :: fixed);
  //Needed only for large numbers
  cout << endl <<"Enter hours worked -> ";
  cin >> Hours;
  cout << endl<< "Enter skill indicator (A,B,C) -> ";
  cin >> SkillsIndicator;
  switch (SkillsIndicator)
  {
     case 'A':
     case 'a':
       Rate = HWage;
       break;
     case 'B':
     case 'b':
       Rate = MWage;
       break;
     case 'C':
     case 'c':
       Rate = LWage;
       break;
    default:
       cerr << endl << "You entered an invalid skill indicator";
       return;
  }

  Pay = Rate * Hours;
  cout << endl <<"Worker's pay is $" << Pay;
}
```

Output, First Input

```
Enter hours worked -> 7
Enter skill indicator (A,B,C) -> c
Worker's pay is $57.05
```

Output, Second Input

```
Enter hours worked -> 8
Enter skill indicator (A,B,C) -> B
Worker's pay is $100.40
```

Output, Third Input

```
Enter hours worked -> 8.5
Enter skill indicator (A,B,C) -> A
Worker's pay is $158.10
```

Output, Fourth Input

```
Enter hours worked -> 10.5
Enter skill indicator (A,B,C) -> s
You entered an invalid skill indicator
```

◆ Key Terms

Boolean logic	A system of mathematics dealing with values that can be either true or false, and the operations that can occur.
Compound conditional statement	An expression the involves more than one subexpression.
Nested conditional statement	Conditional statements that are written inside of other conditional statements.
Short circuit evaluation	An efficient method of evaluating conditional statements.

◆ C++ Keywords Introduced

`<`	An operator performing the less-than comparison.
`>`	An operator performing the greater-than comparison.
`<=`	An operator performing the less-than or equal-to comparison.
`>=`	An operator performing the greater-than or equal-to comparison.
`==`	An operator performing the equal-to comparison.
`!=`	An operator performing the not-equal-to comparison.
`&&`	An operator used to perform the logical anding of two conditions
`||`	An operator used to perform the logical oring of two conditions.
`!`	An operator used to negate a value.
`bool`	A variable type that allows the storage of a Boolean value.
`break`	A keyword that ends the execution of a `switch` statement and continues processing at the next instruction following the `switch` statement.
`case`	A keyword that allows specific values to be tested against in a `case` statement.
`else`	A keyword that indicates what statement(s) should be executed when an `if` statement evaluates to false.

if	A keyword that indicates what statement(s) should be executed when the expression following it evaluates to true.
switch	A statement that allows a shorthand notation for a series of

◆Answers to Drills

Drill 3-1

1. (5 >= 4) is true. When the operator >= is used, the expression is true if the value to the left is greater than the value to the right (in this case it is) or if the value to the left is equal to the value to the right (in this case it is not). Since only one of these cases must be true for the expression to be evaluated to true, the expression is evaluated to true.

2. (−3 < −4) is false. When the operator < is used, the expression is true if the value to the left is less than the value to the right. Although 3 is less than 4, the value −3 is not less than the value −4.

3. (5 == 4) is false. When the operator == is used, the expression is true if the value to the left is exactly the same as the value to the right. Since 5 is the value on the left and 4 is the value on the right, the values are not the same.

4. (5 != 4) is true. When the operator != is used, the expression is true if the value to the left of the operator is not the same as the value to the right of the operator. Since 5 is not the same as 4, the expression evaluates to true.

5. (4 >= 4) is true. When the operator >= is used, the expression is true if the value to the left is the greater than value to the right (in this case it is not) or if the value to the left is the same as the value to the right (in this case it is). Since only one of these cases must be true for the expression to be evaluated to true, the expression is evaluated to true.

6. (4 <= 4) is true. When the correct <= is used, the expression is true if the value to the left is less than the value to the right (in this case it is not) or if the value to the left is the same as the value to the right (in this case it is). Since only one of these cases must be true for the expression to be evaluated to true, the expression is evaluated to true.

Drill 3-2

The output of the code provided for the drill is as follows:

```
The second statement prints
The third statement prints
```

The code initializes the variable **DrillValue** to the value 1. It then evaluates the expression **(DrillValue>2)**. Since **(1>2)** is false, the expression evaluates to false and the statement immediately following the **if** statement is not executed. The following two **cout** statements are not effected by the evaluation of the **if** statement, so they are executed.

Drill 3-3

The output of the code provided for the drill is as follows:

```
The first statement prints
The second statement prints
The third statement prints
```

The code initializes the variable **DrillValue** to the value 1. It then evaluates the expression **(DrillValue<2)**. Since **(1<2)** is true, the expression evaluates to true and the statement immediately following the **if** statement is executed. This causes the first line of output to appear. The following two **cout** statements are not affected by the evaluation of the **if** statement, so they are executed, causing the final two lines of output to appear.

Drill 3-4

The output of the code provided for the drill is as follows:

```
The third statement prints
```

The code initializes the variable **DrillValue** to the value 1. It then evaluates the expression **(DrillValue>2)**. Since **(1>2)** is false, the expression evaluates to false. In this example, a curly brace, {, follows the **if** statement. This means that all the statements enclosed within it and the close curly brace, }, are treated as a single entity. Since the expression evaluated to false, all the statements contained within the curly braces will not be executed. Therefore, the first two **cout** statements are skipped. The final **cout** statement is not affected by the evaluation of the **if** statement, so it is executed.

Drill 3-5

The output of the code provided for the drill is as follows:

```
The first statement prints
The second statement prints
The third statement prints
```

The code initializes the variable **DrillValue** to the value 1. It then evaluates the expression **(DrillValue<2)**. Since **(1<2)** is true, the expression evaluates to true. In this example, a curly brace, {, follows the **if** statement. This means that all the statements enclosed within it and the close curly brace, }, are treated as a single entity. Since the expression evaluated to true, all the statements contained within the curly braces will not be executed. Therefore, the first two **cout** statements are executed, and the first two lines of output are generated. The final **cout** statement is not affected by the evaluation of the **if** statement, so it is executed as well.

Drill 3-6

The output of the code provided for the drill is as follows:

```
The expression is true
5
```

The variable **DrillValue** is initialized to the value 2. The expression (**DrillValue=5**) is then evaluated. Because a single equal sign is used, the value 5 is assigned to the variable **DrillValue**. Since there is no comparison expression, C++ evaluates the variable **DrillValue**. Since **DrillValue** is not equal to zero, it is evaluated to true. Therefore, the first output line appears. Now when the second **cout** statement is evaluated, it outputs the current value of **DrillValue**, 5.

Drill 3-7

The output of the code provided for the drill is as follows:

```
0
```

The variable **DrillValue** is initialized to the value 2. The expression (**DrillValue = 0**) is then evaluated. Because a single equal sign is used, the value 0 is assigned to the variable **DrillValue**. Since there is no comparison expression, C++ evaluates the variable **DrillValue**. Since the variable **DrillValue** is equal to zero, it is evaluated to false. Therefore, the first **cout** statement is ignored. Now, when the second **cout** statement is evaluated, it outputs the current value of **DrillValue**, 0.

Drill 3-8

The output of the code provided for the drill, when **DrillValue=5**, is as follows:

```
DrillValue is equal to five
```

When **DrillValue** equals five, the expression (**DrillValue>5**) evaluates to false. The **else if** expression, (**DrillValue>5**) is then evaluated and is also found to be false. Since both the **if** and the **else if** expression were false, the **else** statement is executed and the **cout** statement produces the appropriate output.

The output when **DrillValue=8** is as follows:

```
DrillValue is greater than five
```

When **DrillValue** equals eight, the expression **(DrillValue>5)** evaluates to true. Therefore, the first **cout** statement is executed and produces the appropriate output. Since the **if** statement evaluated to true, the **else if** and **else** statements are ignored.

The output when **DrillValue=1** is as follows:

```
DrillValue is less than five
```

When **DrillValue** equals one, the expression **(DrillValue>5)** evaluates to false. The **else if** expression **(DrillValue<5)** is then evaluated and is found to be true. This causes the second **cout** statement to be executed and the appropriate output produced. The **else** statement is ignored, since the **else if** statement evaluated to true.

Drill 3-9

The output of the code provided for the drill, when **DrillValue=5**, is as follows:

```
DrillValue is equal to five
The else statements were executed
```

When **DrillValue** equals five, the expression **(DrillValue>5)** evaluates to false. Since both statements following the **if** are enclosed within curly braces, they are both skipped. Then the **else if** expression **(DrillValue<5)** is evaluated and is also found to be false. Again, since both statements following the **else if** statement are enclosed in curly braces, they are both skipped. Since both the **if** and the **else if** expressions were false and the two **cout** statements following the else are enclosed in curly braces, the two **cout** statements that follow the **else** statement are executed and produce the appropriate output.

The output when **DrillValue=8** would be as follows:

```
DrillValue is greater than five
The if expression evaluated to true
```

When **DrillValue** equals eight, the expression **(DrillValue>5)** evaluates to true. Since the two **cout** statements that follow the **if** statement are enclosed within curly braces, they are both executed and produce the appropriate output. Since the **if** statement evaluated to true, the **else if** and **else** statements are ignored.

The output when **DrillValue=1** would be as follows:

```
DrillValue is less than five
The else if expression evaluated to true
```

When **DrillValue** equals one, the expression **(DrillValue>5)** evaluates to false. Since both statements following the **if** statement are enclosed within curly braces, they are both skipped. The **else if** expression **(DrillValue<5)** is then evaluated and is found to be true. Since the two **cout** statements that follow the **else if** statement are enclosed within curly braces, they are both executed and produce the appropriate output. The **else** statement is ignored, since the **else if** statement evaluated to true.

Drill 3-10

Actually, this was a trick question, because the program would not compile. If it does not compile, it cannot produce any output. The problem is that the curly braces are missing. Without them, the compiler treats the second **cout** statement of each set as a separate statement from the **if** statement. When the compiler then sees an **else if** and **else** statement, it cannot associate it with the previous **if** statement, and causes a compiler error.

Drill 3-11

The output of the code provided for the drill is as follows:

```
5
6
```

The expression (1==2) is false, so the body of the **if** statement does not execute. Because there are no curly braces, only the first statement is considered part of the **if** statement.

Drill 3-12

The output of the code provided for the drill is as follows:

The expression (1==2) is still false; however, this time all the statements are enclosed in curly braces, so none of them will execute and there is no output from the snippet. Although there is no output, this does not mean that our program has an error. Some programs can run without any output.

Drill 3-13

The output of the code provided for the drill is as follows:

If a 1 is entered for **DrillValue**, then the expression **(DrillValue==1)** is true and the following is the output:

```
The Yankees can buy the best players in baseball!
The Steelers have to get players from the draft
We can only hope for the Eagles.
```

The first two lines are printed because the **if** expression was true, but the second line would output whether the expression evaluates to true or false.

If a 2 is entered for **DrillValue**, then the expression **(DrillValue==1)** is false and the following is the output:

```
We can only hope for the Eagles.
```

The first two lines are skipped because the **if** expression was false. As before, the last statement is output regardless, since it is outside the **if** statement. Try to determine the output of the same exact code without the {}.

Drill 3-14

The output of the code provided for the drill is as follows:

If a 1 is entered for **DrillValue**, then the expression **(DrillValue==1)** is true and the following is the output:

```
The Yankees can buy the best players in baseball!
The Steelers have to get players from the draft
We can only hope for the Eagles.
```

The first line is printed because the **if** expression was true, but the second two lines would have printed anyway.

If a 2 is entered for **DrillValue**, then the expression **(DrillValue==1)** is false and the following is the output:

```
The Steelers have to get players from the draft
We can only hope for the Eagles.
```

The first line is skipped because the **if** expression was false. As before, the last two statements are output regardless, since they are outside the **if** statement.

Drill 3-15

The output of the code provided for the drill is as follows:

```
#1 prints
#2 prints
#4 prints
#5 prints
#7 prints
```

Let's look at each example and determine why or why not the corresponding output statement was executed.

```
if ((DrillValue1==5) && (DrillValue2==3))
   cout <<"#1 prints";
```

The previous **if** statement evaluates to true because **DrillValue1** is equal to 5 and **DrillValue2** is equal to 3. Since there is a logical and operator between them, both statements must be true for the entire condition to be true. Therefore **#1 prints** is output.

```
if ((DrillValue1==5) || (DrillValue2==3))
   cout <<"#2 prints";
```

The previous **if** statement evaluates to true because **DrillValue1** is equal to 5 and **DrillValue2** is equal to 3. Since there is a logical or operator between them, if either statement is true the entire condition evaluates to true. Since both subconditions are true, the requirement of the or operator is fulfilled and the expression is evaluated to true. Therefore, the statement **#2 prints** is output.

```
if ((DrillValue1==5) && (DrillValue2==4))
  cout<<"#3 prints";
```

The previous **if** statement evaluates to false because although **DrillValue1** is equal to 5, **DrillValue2** is not equal to 4. Since there is a logical and operator between them, both subconditions must be true for the entire expression to evaluate to true. Therefore, nothing is output from this **if** statement.

```
if ((DrillValue1==5) || (DrillValue2==4))
   cout<<"#4 prints";
```

The previous **if** statement evaluates to true; although **DrillValue1** is equal to 5 and **DrillValue2** is not equal to 4, the logical or operator between them indicates that only one of the subconditions must be true for the entire expression to evaluate to true. Therefore, the statement **#4 prints** is output.

```
if ((DrillValue3==DrillValue1) || (DrillValue3==DrillValue2) ||
    (DrillValue3== DrillValue3))
  cout<<"#5 prints";
```

The previous **if** statement evaluates to true. Although **DrillValue3**, which equals 10, is not equal to **DrillValue1**, which equals 5; and **DrillValue3** does not equal **DrillValue2**, which equals 3; **DrillValue3** does equal **DrillValue3**. Since the subconditions are connected with a **logical or** operator, only one of the subconditions must be true for the entire expression to evaluate to true. Therefore, the expression **#5 prints** is output.

```
if ((DrillValue3==DrillValue1) && (DrillValue3==DrillValue2) &&
    (DrillValue 3==DrillValue3))
  cout<<"#6 prints";
```

The previous **if** statement evaluates to false because **DrillValue3**, which equals 10, is not equal to **DrillValue1**, which equals 5, and **DrillValue3** does not equal **DrillValue2**, which equals 3, so **DrillValue3** does equal **DrillValue3**. Since the subconditions are connected with a logical and operator, all of the subconditions must be true for the entire expression to evaluate to true. Therefore, nothing is output from this **if** statement.

```
if ((DrillValue3==DrillValue1) && (DrillValue3==DrillValue2) ||
    (DrillValue3==DrillValue3))
  cout<<"#7 prints";
```

The previous **if** statement evaluation is a little tricky. In order for it to be true, **(DrillValue3==DrillValue1) && (DrillValue3==DrillValue2)** must be true or **(DrillValue3==DrillValue3)** must be true. Since we know that the subexpression **(DrillValue3==DrillValue3)** is true, we can ignore the subexpression **(DrillValue3==DrillValue1) && (DrillValue3== DrillValue2)**. Therefore, the expression **#7 prints** is output.

```
if ((DrillValue3==DrillValue1) || (DrillValue3==DrillValue2) &&
    (DrillValue3==DrillValue3))
  cout<<"#8 prints";
```

The final example evaluates to true if the subexpression **(DrillValue3== DrillValue1) || (DrillValue3==DrillValue2)** is true and the expression **(DrillValue3==DrillValue3)** is true. We know that **(DrillValue3==DrillValue3)** is true, so we need to determine if **(DrillValue3==DrillValue1) || (DrillValue3==DrillValue2)** is true. For it to be true, **(DrillValue3==DrillValue1)** must be true or **(DrillValue3==DrillValue2)** must be true. Since neither subexpression is true, the entire expression is false and nothing is output.

Drill 3-16

The output of the code provided for the drill is as follows:

```
#1 prints
```

The evaluation of the program is as follows: First **DrillValue1** is assigned 5 and **DrillValue2** is assigned 3. Then the first **if** statement's expression is evaluated. If **DrillValue1** is equal to 5, which it is, then the nested **if** statement is evaluated. If **DrillValue1** is not equal to 5, then the statement **#3 prints** is output. To evaluate the inner **if** statement, we compare **DrillValue2** to 3. Since they are equal, the statement **#1 prints** is output; otherwise the statement, **#2 prints** would be displayed.

Drill 3-17

The output of the code provided for the drill is as follows:

```
#2 prints
```

Drill 3-18

The output of the code provided for the drill is as follows:

```
#3 prints
```

The statement **#3 prints** is output, because now the first expression is false and the program skips down to last **else** clause.

Drill 3-19

The output of the code provided for the drill is as follows:

```
#1 prints
```

The output of the previous **if** statement would be **#1 prints**, because 1 is a non-zero number and all nonzero numbers evaluate to true.

Drill 3-20

The output of the code provided for the drill is as follows:

```
#2 prints
```

The output of the previous **if** statement would be **#2 prints**, because 0 evaluates to false.

Drill 3-21

The output of the code provided for the drill is as follows:

```
#1 prints
```

The output of the previous **if** statement would be **#1 prints**, because **DrillValue** is equal to five, five is a nonzero value, and nonzero values are true.

Drill 3-22

The output of the code provided for the drill is as follows:

```
#2 prints
```

The output of the previous **if** statement would be **#2 prints**, because **DrillValue** is equal to zero and all zero values are false. Since the **if** expression evaluates to false, the **else** statement is executed.

Drill 3-23

The output of the code provided for the drill is as follows:

```
#1 prints
```

The output of the previous **if** statement would be **#1 prints**, although **DrillValue** is initialized to 0, **DrillValue** is pre-incremented to 1 before it is evaluated in the **if** expression. Since 1 is a nonzero value and nonzero values evaluate to true, the first statement is executed.

Drill 3-24

The output of the code provided for the drill is as follows:

```
#2 prints
```

The output of the previous **if** statement would be **#2 prints**, because although **DrillValue** is initialized to −1, **DrillValue** is pre-incremented to 0 before it is evaluated in the **if** expression. Since 0 is equal to zero and zero values evaluate to false, the second statement is executed.

To help illustrate what really happens when we use the pre-increment, here is the equivalent code to the previous drill, but without the pre-increment operator:

```cpp
#include <stdlib.h>
#include <iostream.h>

void main()
{
  int DrillValue=-1;

  DrillValue=DrillValue+1;

  if (DrillValue)
    cout<<"#1 prints "<<DrillValue;
  else
    cout<<"#2 prints "<<DrillValue;
}
```

Drill 3-25

The output of the code provided for the drill is as follows:

```
#2 prints
```

The output of the previous statement is **#2 prints** because **DrillValue** is initialized to 0. You might think that **DrillValue** is incremented to 1, but the increment in this case is a postincrement. The postincrement does not occur until after the value of **DrillValue** is used in the **if** expression. Since 0 is used during the evaluation and 0 is evaluated to false, the second **cout** statement is printed.

To help illustrate what really happens when we use the postincrement, here is the equivalent code to the previous drill, but without the postincrement operator:

```cpp
#include <stdlib.h>
#include <iostream.h>

void main()
{
    int DrillValue=0;

    if (DrillValue)
    {
        DrillValue=DrillValue+1;
        cout<<"#1 prints "<<DrillValue;
    }
    else
    {
        DrillValue=DrillValue+1;
        cout<<"#2 prints "<<DrillValue;
    }
}
```

Drill 3-26

The output of the code provided for the drill is as follows:

```
#1 prints
```

The output of the previous statement is **#1 prints** because **DrillValue** is initialized to –1. You might think that **DrillValue** is incremented to 0, but the increment in this case is a postincrement. The postincrement does not occur until after the value of **DrillValue** is used in the **if** expression. Since –1 is used during the evaluation and –1 is evaluated to true, the first **cout** statement is printed.

To help illustrate what really happens when we use the postincrement, here is the equivalent code to the previous drill, but without the postincrement operator:

```
#include <stdlib.h>
#include <iostream.h>

void main()
{
   int DrillValue=-1;

   if (DrillValue)
   {
     DrillValue=DrillValue +1;
     cout<<"#1 prints "<<DrillValue;
   }
   else
   {
     DrillValue=DrillValue+1;
     cout<<"#2 prints"<<DrillValue;
     }
}
```

Drill 3-27

The output of the code provided for the drill is as follows:

```
DrillValue=3
```

Since **(1==1)** is true and the expression **((1==1) || (DrillValue++==4))** is connected with a logical or operator, there is no need to evaluate the subcondition **(DrillValue++==4)** because we know the entire expression to be true. Therefore, **DrillValue** will remain at its original value 3. The **cout** statement is executed and the output is **DrillValue=3**.

Drill 3-28

The output of the code provided for the drill is as follows:

Since the expression in the **if** statement has a logical and operator and the sub-condition **(1==1)** is true, we are required to evaluate the subcondition **(DrillValue++==4)**. The subcondition **(DrillValue++==4)** evaluates to false since the 1 is not added to **DrillValue** until after the value of **DrillValue**, 3, is used in the condition. Therefore, no output occurs from the code snippet. If, however, we added an additional **cout** statement after the **if** statement, we would find that the value of **DrillValue** would now be 4, since it was postincremented in the evaluation of the **if** statement.

Drill 3-29

The output of the code provided for the drill is as follows:

This program is very similar to the previous one we evaluated. Since the first sub-condition is false and there is a logical or operator in the main expression, we are required to evaluate the **(DrillValue++==4)** subexpression as well. This evaluates to false as it did in the previous example. Since both subconditions are false, then the entire expression is false and nothing prints. If we added an additional **cout** statement after the **if** statement like we did in the previous example, we would find that the value of **DrillValue** would now be 4, since it was postincremented in the evaluation of the **if** statement.

Drill 3-30

The output of the code provided for the drill is as follows:

This program is very similar to the previous one we evaluated. Since the only part of the code to change is the logical operator from a logical or (| |) to a logical and (&&), we really need to consider only one thing. Since the first subcondition, **(1==2)**, evaluates to false and the logical operator connecting the subcondition is an **and**, we need not evaluate the remainder of the expression. The main expression evaluates to false and nothing is output from the code snippet. However, if we added an additional **cout** statement after the **if** statement, we would find that unlike the previous examples, since the subcondition **(DrillValue++==4)** is not evaluated, the value of **DrillValue** would still be 3, since the postincrement statement is never evaluated.

Drill 3-31

The output of the code provided for the drill is as follows:

```
```

The **if** statement requires the evaluation of the **((1==3) || (DrillValue++==4))** subcondition first. Since the subsubcondition **(1==3)** is false, we are required to evaluate the other sub-subcondition, **(DrillValue++==4)**. This evaluates to false as well and there is no output from the program. So there is no need to evaluate the **(1==1)** subexpression. However, the value of **DrillValue** is changed to 4 as it was in the previous examples.

Drill 3-32

The output of the code provided for the drill is as follows:

```
DrillValue=3
```

This **if** statement requires the evaluation of the **((1==1) || (DrillValue++==4))** subcondition first. Since the subsubcondition **(1==1)** is true, we are not required to evaluate the other sub-subcondition, **(DrillValue++==4)**. Since the other subexpression, **(1==1)**, is true, the main expression evaluates to true. The output would be **DrillValue=3**, because the subexpression **(DrillValue++==4)** was never evaluated so the postincrement of **DrillValue** never occurred.

Drill 3-33

The output of the code provided for the drill is as follows:

```
DrillValue=5
```

In the previous code snippet the subexpression **(1==1)** is evaluated to true. Since the logical operator is an **and**, we must evaluate the second subexpression **(++DrillValue==5)**. Since the second subexpression contains a pre-increment, we add one to **DrillValue** before making the evaluation. This makes the value of **DrillValue** equal to 5 and the subexpression true. Therefore, the main expression evaluates to true and the output of the snippet is **DrillValue=5**.

Drill 3-34

The output of the code provided for the drill is as follows:

If the letter 'A' is entered, the output would be:

```
The Letter AThe Letter BThe Letter CYou do not know your ABC's
```

When the letter 'A' is entered for **TestChar**, it is processed through the **switch** statement. The first case, 'A', evaluates to true and therefore the first **cout** executes. However, because there is no **break** included in the **case**, all the other cases, including the default, are evaluated to true and all the **cout** statements are executed.

If the letter 'C' is entered, the output would be:

```
The Letter CYou do not know your ABC's
```

When the letter 'C' is entered for **TestChar**, it is processed through the **switch** statement. The first case, 'A', evaluates to false and therefore the first **cout** is skipped. The next case, 'B', is tried, which also evaluates to false and therefore, the second **cout** statement is skipped. Then the third case is tested, 'C', and it evaluates to true. Therefore, the third **cout** statement is executed. However, because there is no **break** included in the **case**, the remaining, default, cases are evaluated to true and the **cout** statement is executed.

If the letter 'Z' is entered, the output would be:

```
You do not know your ABC's
```

When the letter 'Z' is entered for **TestChar**, it is processed through the **switch** statement. The first three cases evaluate to false, so the first three **cout** statements are skipped. The default case is evaluated to true and the last **cout** statement executes.

Drill 3-35

The output of the code provided for the drill is as follows:

If the letter 'A' is entered, the output would be:

```
The Letter A
```

When the letter 'A' is entered for **TestChar**, it is processed through the **switch** statement. The first case, 'A', evaluates to true and therefore the first **cout** statement executes. Because there is a **break** directly following the **cout** statement, no other evaluation of the **case** statement is necessary.

If the letter 'C' is entered, the output would be:

```
The Letter C
```

When the letter 'C' is entered for **TestChar**, it is processed through the **switch** statement. The first case, 'A', evaluates to false and therefore the first **cout** statement is skipped. The next case, 'B', is tried, which also evaluates to false and therefore, the second **cout** statement is skipped. Then the third case is tested, 'C', and it evaluates to true. Therefore, the third **cout** statement is executed. Because there is a **break** directly following the **cout** statement, no other evaluation of the case statement is necessary.

If the letter 'Z' is entered, the output would be:

```
You do not know your ABC's
```

When the letter 'Z' is entered for **TestChar**, it is processed through the **switch** statement. The first three cases evaluate to false, so the first three **cout** statements are skipped. The default case is evaluated to true and the last **cout** statement executes. In this case, it didn't matter if the **break** keyword was used.

◆ Programming Exercises

1. In the last section, you had to write a program that asks for the amount of money in the bank and how much you want to deposit and withdraw. Rewrite the program, but this time add in error checks to make sure that there is enough money in the account to cover the withdrawals.

2. Modify the previous football program so that it checks to see that only valid input is accepted.

3. Write a program that accepts a list of grades. The program should output the average of the grades entered and then output the average, excluding the lowest and highest grades.

4. Write a program that will act as a simple calculator. It should ask the user for a floating point number, an operation, and another floating point number.

    The program should first check that the operator is either +, -, *, or /. If it is, then it should output the result of performing the operation on the two floating point numbers.

    If the operation is a division, it should check to make sure the divisor is not equal to zero. If it is, it should print the warning message "Divide by zero."

    If the operation entered is not a +, -, *, or / then the program should print the message "Illegal Operation."

5. Write a program to convert English units to metric units. The program should ask for a value to be entered. Then the program should prompt the user with options for each type of conversion. The program should then output the conversion.

    The program should include the following conversions:

    - 1 inch = 2.54 centimeters

    - 1 gallon = 3.785 liters

    - 1 mile = 1.609 kilometers

    - 1 pound = .4536 kilograms

    Make sure that your program will accept only valid choices for the type of conversion to perform.

6. Write another program that converts from metric to English units. The program should include the following conversions:

    - 1 cm = .394 inches

    - 1 liter = .264 gallons

    - 1 kilometer = .622 miles

    - 1 kilogram = 2.2 pounds

    Make sure that your program will accept only valid choices for the type of conversion to perform.

7. Write a program that accepts a single-digit integer from the user and outputs the word that represents that number. If a number other than a single digit is entered, the program should output "Error on Input." The program must be written with a switch statement.

8. Write a program that presents the user with a menu for an automatic teller machine. The program should ask the user for a pin number. Since currently we cannot store the amount people have in their accounts from program to program, ask the user for this as well. Then the program should display a menu that prompts the user to select an option from the following list:

(B)alance, (D)eposit, (W)ithdrawal, and (Q)uick Cash.

If Balance is selected, simply echo the balance back to the user.

If Deposit is selected, ask the user for the amount to deposit, add it to the previous balance, and output the new balance.

If Withdrawal is selected, ask the user for the amount to withdraw; check to see that it is available; if so, subtract it from the previous balance and output the new balance; and if there is not enough money to make the withdrawal, display an error message.

If Quick Cash is selected, present the user with another menu: 20, 50, 100, 300. Assuming there is enough money in the account, withdraw it. Otherwise display an error message.

You must implement both menus with **switch** statements.

◆ Additional Exercises

1. Show the output of the following code when the values are equal to these choices:

```cpp
int ExerciseValue1, ExerciseValue2;

if (ExerciseValue1<3)
  cout<<"got here" <<endl;

if (ExerciseValue2>1)
  cout<<"got here too" <<endl;

cout<<"got here also" <<endl;
```

    a.   ExerciseValue1 is equal to 1 and ExerciseValue2 is equal to 2
    b.   ExerciseValue1 and ExerciseValue2 are equal to 0
    c.   ExerciseValue1 and ExerciseValue2 are equal to 5
    d.   ExerciseValue1 is equal to 3 and ExerciseValue2 is equal to 1
    e.   ExerciseValue1 is equal to 2 and ExerciseValue2 is equal to 2000

2. Show the output of the following code when the values are equal to these choices:

```
int ExerciseValue1, ExerciseValue2, ExerciseValue3;

if (ExerciseValue1<2)
{
   cout<<"got here" <<endl;
   ExerciseValue3= ExerciseValue1++;
}

if (ExerciseValue2>2)
{
   cout<<"got here too" <<endl;
   ExerciseValue3=ExerciseValue2-;
}

if (ExerciseValue3!=2)
   cout<<"got here also"<<endl;

cout<<x<<' '<<ExerciseValue2<<' '<<z<<endl;
```

   a. ExerciseValue1=1, ExerciseValue2=2, ExerciseValue3=2
   b. ExerciseValue1=2, ExerciseValue2=3, ExerciseValue3=2
   c. ExerciseValue1=4, ExerciseValue2=1, ExerciseValue3=2
   d. ExerciseValue1=0, ExerciseValue2=4, ExerciseValue3=3

3. Show the output of the following code when the values are equal to these choices:

```
int ExerciseValue1, ExerciseValue2, ExerciseValue3;

if (ExerciseValue1<2)
{
   cout<<"got here"<<endl;
   ExerciseValue3=ExerciseValue1+5;
}

else if (ExerciseValue2>2)
{
   cout<<"got here too"<<endl;
   ExerciseValue3=ExerciseValue2-;
}

else if (ExerciseValue3<=6)
{
   cout<<"got here also"<<endl;
}

else
   cout<<"always print me";
```

    a.   ExerciseValue1=1, ExerciseValue2=2, ExerciseValue3=2
    b.   ExerciseValue1=2, ExerciseValue2=3, ExerciseValue3=4
    c.   ExerciseValue1=4, ExerciseValue2=1, ExerciseValue3=2
    d.   ExerciseValue1=0, ExerciseValue2=4, ExerciseValue3=3
    e.   ExerciseValue1=3, ExerciseValue2=2, ExerciseValue3=6

4.   What is the output of the following code:

```
#include <stdlib.h>
#include <iostream.h>
void main()
{
  int ExerciseValue1=5;

  if (ExerciseValue1=0)
    cout<<"Output 1";
  else
    cout<<"Output 2";
}

cout<<ExerciseValue1<<' '<<ExerciseValue2<<' '<<ExerciseValue3<<endl;
```

5.   True or False

    a.   An **if** statement can have only one **else if** and **else** statement associated with it.
    b.   An if statement evaluates to true if the expression evaluates to any value other than –1.
    c.   It is possible to have an **else if** statement without associating it with an **if** statement.
    d.   It is possible to have **if** and **else if** statements without having an **else** statement.

6.   Assume the variable ExerciseValue1 is equal to zero before the expression is evaluated. Indicate whether the expression evaluates to true or false:

    a.   (ExerciseValue1++==1)
    b.   (ExerciseValue1=0)
    c.   (ExerciseValue1=1)
    d.   assume ExerciseValue1=0, (ExerciseValue1==0)

7.   Do the following expressions evaluate to true or false?

    a.   (3<4) || (3>4)
    b.   (3!=3) && (4 = 4)
    c.   (15>=15) && (16==16) || (14<2)
    d.   (15>=15) && ((16==16) || (14<2))
    e.   ((15>=15) && (16==16)) || (14<2)

8. Do any of the conditional statements not get checked because of short circuiting? Assume that ExerciseValue1=2, ExerciseValue2=3, ExerciseValue3=1:

   a. (ExerciseValue2==2) &&((ExerciseValue1>=1)||(ExerciseValue3<=9))
   b. ((ExerciseValue3<3)||(ExerciseValue2<5)||
       (ExerciseValue1+ ExerciseValue3<5))&&(1)
   c. ((ExerciseValue2<3)||(ExerciseValue2<5)||
       (ExerciseValue1+ ExerciseValue3<5))&&(0)
   d. !((ExerciseValue2>3)||(ExerciseValue2>5)||
       (ExerciseValue1+ ExerciseValue3<5))&&(!0)

9. Show the output of the following code when the values are equal to these choices:

```
if (ExerciseValue1 > 10)
  if (ExerciseValue2 < 5 )
    cout<<"Output 1"<<endl;
  else
    cout<<"Output 2"<<endl;
else if (ExerciseValue1<10)
  cout<<"Output 3"<<endl;
else
  cout<<"Output 4"<<endl;
```

   a. ExerciseValue1=12, ExerciseValue2=7
   b. ExerciseValue1=3, ExerciseValue2=10
   c. ExerciseValue1=99, ExerciseValue2=1
   d. ExerciseValue1=5, ExerciseValue2=5
   e. ExerciseValue1=5, ExerciseValue2=1

10. Show the output of the following code when the values are equal to the choices:

```
if (ExerciseValue1<5)
  cout<<"Less than 5"<<endl;
else if
  cout<<"Less than 10"<<endl;
else
  cout<<"Neither case"<<endl;
```

   a. ExerciseValue1 = 12
   b. ExerciseValue1 = 10
   c. ExerciseValue1 = 7
   d. ExerciseValue1 = 5
   e. ExerciseValue1 = 1

11. Write the truth table that simulates an exclusive or (XOR). Here is the equivalent expression using || and &&: ExerciseValue1&&(! ExerciseValue2) || (!ExerciseValue1)&& ExerciseValue2.

12. Rewrite the following code to use a switch statement:

```
if (choice==1)
  cout<<"The choice was 1";
else if (choice ==2)
  cout<<"The choice was 2";
else if (choice ==3)
  cout<<"The choice was 3";
else if (choice ==4)
  cout<<"The choice was 4";
```

13. What is the output of the following code for each value of choice?

```
#include<stdlib.h>
#include<iostream.h>

main()
{
    int Choice = //value is placed here
    switch (Choice)
    {
      case 1:
        cout<<"Print first value\n";
        break;
      case 2:
        cout<<"Print second value\n";
        break;
      case 3:
        cout<<"Print third value\n";
        break;
      default:
        cout<<"The case is not specified\n";
        break;
    }
}
```

   a. Choice = 1
   b. Choice = 3
   c. Choice = 4
   d. Choice = 0

14. Redo the preceding example but remove all the breaks from the code and show what the output would be.

CHAPTER

4

Loops

Chapter Objectives

- ◆ Introduce the concept of executing code more than one time

- ◆ Introduce the concept of for loops

- ◆ Introduce the concept of while loops

- ◆ Introduce the concept of do loops

- ◆ Reinforce condition evaluation, presented in the previous chapter

- ◆ Introduce nested loops

Another important characteristic of a powerful programming language is the ability to perform a statement or series of statements over and over again. C++ accomplishes this with one of three looping constructs: **for** loops, **while** loops, and **do** loops. It is important to master the **conditional expression** evaluation discussed in the previous chapter before attempting to learn C++'s looping constructs. The evaluation of conditional expressions and looping expressions is the same. The expression evaluation section in the previous chapter provides more detail than this chapter does.

4.1 FOR LOOPS

The choice of **loop** construct is mainly one of style. In fact, any loop construct can be represented using any of the other loop constructs. However, there is usually a natural choice of looping type for your problem. We usually select a **for** loop when the problem is easily definable into the following distinct sections:

1. A starting condition(s)

2. A condition when to stop

3. A statement(s) to execute as the body of the loop

4. An increment statement

While loops are similar, but we usually use them when the initial condition(s) are defined elsewhere. Often this can occur when the initial condition is set with a **cin**

125

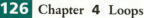

command. A **do loop** is used when the body of the loop is executed at least once. Often this is used when a menu system is being developed.

The **for** loop is very versatile with lots of options. This does not have to be confusing. If we break the loop into separate components, remember the order in which they are executed, and evaluate them carefully, the evaluation of **for** loops can be simple.

The following is a template to use for the **for** loop:

```
for(initial expression; looping condition; looping statement)
    body of loop;
```

Follow this sequence for successful evaluation of a **for** loop:

1. The initial expression is evaluated. It sets the starting value of the loop and can have more than one value if a comma is used to separate the statements.
2. The looping condition is evaluated. If false, the loop terminated. *You can review conditional evaluations and their subtleties in Chapter 3.*
3. The body of the loop executes.
4. The looping statement is evaluated. This generally changes a variable that stores the looping index or iteration.
5. Go to step 2.

Similar to a conditional statement, which can have a single statement following it or a series of statements enclosed within a set of curly braces, the looping statement can have more than one statement by enclosing the statements in a set of curly braces.

Here is an example of a simple **for** loop that outputs the numbers from 1 to 10:

```
//Simple for loop example outputing numbers 1-10

#include <stdlib.h>
#include <iostream.h>

void main()
{
    int LoopCounter; //counter to track the # from 1-10

    //Loop from 1 to 10, outputting each on a separate line
    for(LoopCounter=1; LoopCounter<=10; LoopCounter++)
      cout<<LoopCounter<<endl;
}
```

The previous program starts by declaring one variable, `LoopCounter`. It is used to keep track of the number that we are going to output on each line. The variable `LoopCounter` also keeps track of the number of times we have executed the loop. One execution of the loop is often referred to as an **iteration**. Therefore, the variable `LoopCounter` also keeps track of the number of iterations of the loop.

After the variable has been declared it is time to execute the `for` loop. The `for` loop starts by initializing the variable `LoopCounter` to 1. Then the condition is checked to see if the variable `LoopCounter` is less than or equal to 10. Since it is not, the body of the `for` loop executes and the 1 is output on a line. To complete the first iteration of the `loop`, the variable `LoopCounter` is incremented to 2.

Each iteration of the `for` loop continues in the same manner. The current value of `LoopCounter` is output and then `LoopCounter` is incremented. Therefore 1, 2, 3, 4, 5, 6, 7, 8, 9, and 10 are output on separate lines. Although the program doesn't use `LoopCounter` after the loop, it should be noted that the value of `LoopCounter` is 11 after the loop terminates.

Here is another example of a simple `for` loop that calculates the sum of the numbers from 1 to 10:

```
//Simple for loop example

#include <stdlib.h>
#include <iostream.h>

void main()
{
    int LoopCounter;   //counter to track the # from 1-10
    int Sum=0;   //Stores the sum of the # from 1-10

    //Loop from 1 to 10 adding each # to the sum
    for(LoopCounter=1; LoopCounter<=10; LoopCounter++)
      Sum=Sum+LoopCounter;

    //Output the result
    cout<<Sum;
}
```

The previous program starts by declaring two variables.

The first variable, `LoopCounter`, is used to keep track of the number that we are going to add to the sum. The variable `LoopCounter` also keeps track of the number of times we have executed the loop.

The second variable, `Sum`, will keep track of the sum as we add the numbers together. However, it is important that we do not assume a value for `Sum` before we use it. Therefore, it must be initialized to zero.

After the variables have been declared and **Sum** has been initialized, it is time to execute the **for** loop. The **for** loop starts by initializing the variable **LoopCounter** to **1**. Then the condition is checked to see if the variable **LoopCounter** is less than or equal to 10. Since it is not, the body of the **for** loop executes and the **1** is added to the variable **Sum**. To complete the first iteration of the loop, the variable **LoopCounter** is incremented to 2.

Each iteration of the **for** loop continues in the same manner. The current value of **LoopCounter** is added to the variable **Sum** and then **LoopCounter** is incremented. Therefore **1+2+3+4+5+6+7+8+9+10** is added to the variable **Sum** for a total of 55, which is then output. Although the program doesn't use **LoopCounter** after the loop, it should be noted that the value of **LoopCounter** is 11 after the loop terminates.

▌▐ DRILLS

The previous examples were written with proper style and contained a clear purpose. However, C++ code often can be a little more complicated and subtle. Therefore, we will demonstrate some subtle, not so practical examples to help clarify exactly how C++ loops function. Although this would be bad practice in the real world, these subtle loops have the **++** operator in weird places. If you can figure these out, then you understand basic looping and will be prepared to read any code that is handed to you.

What is the output of the following code?

Drill `4-1`

```
//Drill 4-1

#include <stdlib.h>
#include <iostream.h>

void main()
{
    int LoopCounter;
    for (LoopCounter=0; LoopCounter<10; LoopCounter++)
      cout<<++LoopCounter<<endl;
}
```

What is the output of the following code?

Drill `4-2`

```
//Drill 4-2

#include <stdlib.h>
#include <iostream.h>
```

```
void main()
{
    int LoopCounter;
    for (LoopCounter=0; LoopCounter<10; LoopCounter++)
      cout<<LoopCounter++<<endl;
}
```

What is the output of the following code?

Drill 4-3

```
//Drill 4-3

#include <stdlib.h>
#include <iostream.h>

void main()
{
    int LoopCounter;
    for (LoopCounter=0; LoopCounter++<10; LoopCounter++)
      cout<<LoopCounter<<endl;
}
```

What is the output of the following code?

Drill 4-4

```
//Drill 4-4

#include <stdlib.h>
#include <iostream.h>

void main()
{
    int LoopCounter;
    for (LoopCounter=0; ++LoopCounter<10; LoopCounter++)
      cout<<LoopCounter<<endl;
}
```

Be aware that a loop may not execute the body at all, or it may execute the body for an infinite amount of time if the loop expression is either initially false or always true.

Multiple Initial Values

Sometimes when writing **for** loops, they require more than one initial statement. Although the additional initialization could be written directly before the **for** loop, it makes more sense to include it within the loop. C++ provides a shortcut for this situation.

By adding a comma in between statements, multiple statements can be listed and are executed in order. See the previous code rewritten with the shortcut added:

```
//Example using comma in a for loop
#include <stdlib.h>
#include <iostream.h>

void main()
{
    int Sum;
    int LoopCounter;

    for(LoopCounter=1, Sum=0; LoopCounter <= 10; LoopCounter++)
      Sum+=LoopCounter;   //note we also added the += operator
    cout<<Sum;
}
```

The only differences are that we moved the initialization of **Sum** into the loop and used the **+=** operator in the looping statement.

Here is a slightly more robust example of the sum program. We add the numbers starting with the value stored in **LowNum** and including all numbers up to and including the value stored in **HighNum**. **LowNum** and **HighNum** are values entered by the user.

```
//Example adding all numbers between LowNum & HighNum
#include <stdlib.h>
#include <iostream.h>

void main()
{
    int LowNum,HighNum;
    int Sum;
    int LoopCounter;
```

```
    cout<<"Enter the lower number"<<endl;
    cin>>LowNum;
    cout<<"Enter the higher number"<<endl;
    cin>>HighNum;

    for(LoopCounter=LowNum, Sum=0;LoopCounter<=HighNum;LoopCounter++)
        Sum+=LoopCounter;
    cout<<Sum;
}
```

The program works in the same way as the previous one. However, instead of using hardcoded values for the lower- and uppermost values when calculating the sum, we use variables. These upper- and lowermost values are often referred to as the bounds of the loop.

Loops are excellent for calculating and displaying series of values. Here is an example of a program that will print out all the numbers between **LowNum** and **HighNum** and their squares:

```
//Example outputting all numbers between LowNum & HighNum and their squares

#include <stdlib.h>
#include <iostream.h>

void main()
{
    int LowNum,HighNum;
    int LoopCounter;

    cout<<"Enter the lower number"<<endl;
    cin>>LowNum;
    cout<<"Enter the higher number"<<endl;
    cin>>HighNum;

    for(LoopCounter=LowNum;LoopCounter<=HighNum;LoopCounter++)
        cout<<LoopCounter<<'\t'<<LoopCounter*LoopCounter<<endl;
}
```

The program starts by asking the user to provide the lower and upper bound of the loop. The lower bound is set to **LowNum** and the upper bound is set to **HighNum**. The loop initializes **LoopCounter** to **LowNum** and will continue printing the value of **LoopCounter** and its square until **LoopCounter** is greater than **HighNum**.

Poorly Formatted For Loops

It is possible to write the entire **for** loop inside one statement, although this leads to extremely unreadable code. To emphasize the point, here is the following loop written as one line (Please don't try this at home; we're professionals!):

```
#include <stdlib.h>
#include <iostream.h>

void main()
{
 for (int LoopCounter=0;++LoopCounter<10;cout<<LoopCounter<<endl,LoopCounter++);
}
```

It is also possible to have an empty loop expression. This would create an infinite loop, since no condition is specified. You should not try this with other programs running on your computer, because if you don't have a way for the program to terminate, you may get caught in a loop that you can't break out of.

```
for(;;)
```

Just as in conditional statements, statements within a set of curly braces are treated as one unit. The following example includes two statements enclosed within a set of curly braces:

```
#include <stdlib.h>
#include <iostream.h>

void main()
{
    int LoopCounter;

    for (LoopCounter=0; LoopCounter<5; LoopCounter++)
    {
        cout<<"This is the first statement when LoopCounter = "
             << LoopCounter <<endl;
        cout<<"This is the second statement when LoopCounter = "
             << LoopCounter <<endl;
    }
    cout<<"This is the statement outside the loop"<<endl;
}
```

The output would be:

```
This is the first statement when LoopCounter = 0
This is the second statement when LoopCounter = 0
This is the first statement when LoopCounter = 1
This is the second statement when LoopCounter = 1
This is the first statement when LoopCounter = 2
This is the second statement when LoopCounter = 2
This is the first statement when LoopCounter = 3
This is the second statement when LoopCounter = 3
This is the first statement when LoopCounter = 4
This is the second statement when LoopCounter = 4
This is the statement outside the loop
```

The loop executes initializing **LoopCounter** to 0. Since **LoopCounter** is less than 0, the body of the loop executes. In this case, both **cout** statements are considered the body of the loop. Therefore, both **cout** statements are executed each time the conditional expression evaluates to true. The body of the loop executes five times and then the loop terminates. Finally, the last **cout** statement executes and the program terminates.

▌▌ DRILLS

Here are some more examples. See if you can figure out what they output, then type them in and see if you were correct. Be careful, we have purposely written the examples so the indentation of the statements may not be proper.

What is the output of the following?

Drill 4-5

```cpp
//Drill 4-5

#include <iostream.h>
#include <stdlib.h>

void main()
{
    int LoopCounter;
    for(LoopCounter=1;LoopCounter<5;LoopCounter++)
      cout<<LoopCounter<<endl;
      cout<<LoopCounter+4<<endl;
      cout<<LoopCounter<<endl;
}
```

What is the output of the following?

Drill **4-6**

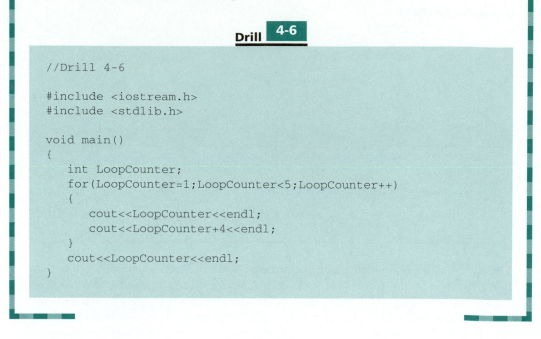

```
//Drill 4-6

#include <iostream.h>
#include <stdlib.h>

void main()
{
    int LoopCounter;
    for(LoopCounter=1;LoopCounter<5;LoopCounter++)
    {
        cout<<LoopCounter<<endl;
        cout<<LoopCounter+4<<endl;
    }
    cout<<LoopCounter<<endl;
}
```

4.2 WHILE LOOPS

Sometimes a **for** loop is burdensome if we don't need all the different sections of the **for** loop. Although we can leave them blank, often it is easier to use another type of loop. The most common is the **while** loop.

The following is a template for a **while** loop:

```
while (condition)
{
    body of loop;
}
```

The **while** loop starts by checking if the **condition** is true. If it is, then it executes the body of the loop. If it is not, it skips the body of the loop and is finished. There is no guarantee that the body of the loop will execute even once. Many beginning programmers make the mistake of executing the body of the loop before they check to see if the condition is true.

The following **while** loop sums all the numbers from 1 to 10:

```
#include <iostream.h>
#include <stdlib.h>

void main()
{
    int Num=1;
    int Sum=0;

    while (Num<=10)
    {
        Sum+=Num;
        Num++;
    }
    cout<<Sum;
}
```

The program starts by declaring and initializing a variable, **Num,** to keep track of the current number as well as a variable, **Sum,** to store the sum as we calculate it.

The loop expression compares the variable **Num** to see if it is less than or equal to 10. If it is, then we continue with the loop adding the current number to **Sum,** and incrementing the current number by 1.

When the **Num** variable equals 11, the loop terminates and the **Sum, 55,** is output. By using the **++** operator properly we can combine the statements in the body of the loop and remove the curly braces. However, now the code becomes more unreadable. This method is not recommended for beginning programmers. It is shown here because you may run across code written by a C++ whiz in this fashion.

```
#include <iostream.h>
#include <stdlib.h>

void main()
{
    int Num=1;
    int Sum=0;

    while (Num<=10)
        Sum+=Num++;
    cout<<Sum;
}
```

Here is another example of a **while** loop to display the number and its squares.

```cpp
#include <iostream.h>
#include <stdlib.h>

void main()
{
    int LoopCounter=1;
    while (LoopCounter<=10)
    {
        cout<<LoopCounter<<'\t'<<LoopCounter*LoopCounter<<endl;
        LoopCounter++;
    }
}
```

The following is the output:

```
1      1
2      4
3      9
4      16
5      25
6      36
7      49
8      64
9      81
10     100
```

The value of **LoopCounter** is initialized to 1 before the loop. Then the value of **LoopCounter** is compared to 10. Since **LoopCounter** is less than or equal to 10, the body of the loop executes and **1** and **1** are output. **LoopCounter** is then incremented to 2. Since 2 is less than or equal to 10, the body of the loop is executed. **2** and **4** are output. This continues until **10** and **100** are output. Then **LoopCounter** is incremented to 11 and the looping condition fails and the loop terminates.

DRILLS

Try to predict the output of these examples and then run them to see if you are correct.

Drill **4-7**

```
//Drill 4-7
#include <iostream.h>
#include <stdlib.h>

void main()
{
    int LoopCounter=1;

    while(LoopCounter<=10)
      cout<<LoopCounter++<<endl;
}
```

What is the output of the following code?

Drill **4-8**

```
//Drill 4-8

#include <iostream.h>
#include <stdlib.h>

void main()
{
    int LoopCounter=1;

    while(LoopCounter++<=10)
      cout<<LoopCounter++<<endl;
}
```

What is the output of the following code?

Drill 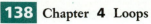 4-9

```
//Drill 4-9

#include <iostream.h>
#include <stdlib.h>

void main()
{
    int LoopCounter=1;

    while(++LoopCounter<=10)
      cout<<LoopCounter++<<endl;
}
```

What is the output of the following code?

Drill 4-10

```
//Drill 4-10

#include <iostream.h>
#include <stdlib.h>

void main()
{
    int LoopCounter=1;

    while(++LoopCounter<=10)
      cout<<++LoopCounter<<endl;
}
```

4.3 DO LOOPS

The final type of loop is a **do** loop. A **do** loop is used when you require a loop to execute at least one time. The format of a **do** loop is as follows:

```
do
{
    body of loop;
}  while (looping condition);
```

The following loop will present a message asking whether or not to continue. This process will continue as long as the user enters either a **y** or a **Y**.

```
//Do loop example

#include <stdlib.h>
#include <iostream.h>

void main()
{
    char Ans;
    do
    {
        cout<<"The Steelers Rule!!!\n";
        cout<<"Do you want another greeting?\n";
        cout<<"Enter y for yes, n for no\n";
        cout<<"and then press return: ";
        cin>>Ans;
    }  while (Ans == 'y' || Ans == 'Y');
    cout << "Good bye!\n";
}
```

The program starts by declaring a variable that will store the answer to the question of whether the user wishes to continue. Then the **do** loop is executed. Regardless of the looping condition, the **cout** statements are executed. Then the user is prompted to enter a character to indicate if he or she wishes to continue. If the character is a lowercase y or an uppercase Y, the looping condition is true and the loop executes again. This is repeated until the answer read is not equal to y or Y. Once the loop is terminated, the final **cout** message is displayed.

Examples Using All Forms of Loops

If you were required to write a program that will ask the user for ten numbers and output the maximum number, there are many ways to approach the problem.

Here are two solutions. Let's look at the thought process and code behind each. The first version sets the **Max** variable to 0. Then it loops ten times asking for a value from the user. After each value is entered, it is compared to the previous maximum value. If the value entered is greater than the previous maximum value, then the maximum value is replaced with the current value. When the **for** loop terminates, the value stored in **Max** is the greatest value entered by the user. Observe the following code:

```
//Maximum value - version 1

#include <stdlib.h>
#include <iostream.h>

#define NumValues 10

void main()
{
   int Max=0;   //The maximum value so far

   int Curr;   //The currently read value
   int LoopCounter;

   for (LoopCounter = 0; LoopCounter < NumValues; LoopCounter++)
   {
      cout<<"Enter a number:"<<endl;
      cin>>Curr;
      if (Curr > Max)
        Max = Curr;
   }
    cout<<"The maximum is "<<Max<<endl;
}
```

If the values entered were 100, 40, –4, 101, 99, 75, 197, 5, –100, 54, then the answer **197** would be output correctly. However, what would happen if we entered the following sequence of numbers: –1,–2,–3,–4,–5,–6,–7,–8,–9,–10? We would get an output of **0**. Clearly, that is not the desired result. The problem is that we made an incorrect assumption. The assumption was that the maximum value was at least 0. This is a common mistake. How do we solve this problem? We might think that if we set the **Max** variable to the largest negative number, we would solve our problem. However, what is the most negative number that we can store? That is not an easy question to answer. An easier solution is to set the **Max** variable to the first value entered and then loop through the remaining numbers. This solution that works for all input is shown in version 2 of the program.

```
//Maximum value - version 2

#include <stdlib.h>
#include <iostream.h>

#define NumValues 10

void main()
{
  int Max;  //The maximum value so far

  int Curr;  //The currently read value
  int LoopCounter;

  cout<<"Enter a number:"<<endl;
  cin>>Max;

  for (int LoopCounter = 1; LoopCounter < NumValues; LoopCounter++)
    {
      cout<<"Enter a number:"<<endl;
      cin>>Curr;
      if (Curr > Max)
         Max = Curr;
    }

  cout<<"The maximum is "<<Max<<endl;
}
```

What if the problem was changed to read numbers until the user indicates that he or she wants to quit? The user would enter numbers and then be asked if he or she wishes to continue to enter more numbers. This would continue until the user enters a Q or q for quit. To solve this problem, we are better off using a different type of loop. By using a **while** loop, we can solve this problem easily.

```
//Maximum value - version 3

#include <stdlib.h>
#include <iostream.h>




void main()
{
  int Max;  //The maximum value so far

  int Curr;  //The currently read value
  char Answer;

  cout<<"Enter a number:"<<endl;
  cin>>Max;
  cout<<"Do you wish to continue?"<<endl;
  cin>>Answer;
```

```
while (Answer != 'Q' && Answer != 'q')
   {
    cout<<"Enter a number: "<<endl;
    cin>>Curr;
    if (Curr > Max)
       Max = Curr;
    cout<<"Do you wish to continue?"<<endl;
    cin>>Answer;
   }
  cout<<"The maximum is "<<Max<<endl;
 }
```

In version 3 of the maximum value program we no longer have to indicate the total number of values to be entered. Instead, we use the variable **Answer** to indicate when we wish to stop reading values from the user. When **Answer** equals an upper- or lowercase Q, the **while** loop terminates and the maximum value is output.

Let's see how we would write a program that will ask the user a yes/no question twenty times. The program should track the number of yes results and the number of no results. This program will accept an upper- or lowercase Y for yes and an upper- or lowercase N for no. Finally, the program should output the total number of yes and no responses.

```
#include <stdlib.h>
#include <iostream.h>

#define NumValues 20

void main()
{
 int NumYes=0;   //Yes responses
 int NumNo=0; //No responses
 int LoopCounter;

 char Curr;   //The currently read value
 for (LoopCounter = 0; LoopCounter < NumValues; LoopCounter++)
    {
     cout<<"Do you think the Steelers will win the Superbowl?";
     cin>>Curr;
     if ((Curr == 'Y') || (Curr == 'y'))
        NumYes++;
     if ((Curr == 'N') || (Curr == 'n'))
        NumNo++;
    }

 cout<<"The number of yes responses = " << NumYes <<endl;
 cout<<"The number of no responses = " << NumNo <<endl;

}
```

The problem with the existing solution is that it does not account for invalid input from the user. A simple solution is shown in version 2. Here we add an additional variable to track the number of invalid responses.

```
//Survey program - version 2

#include <stdlib.h>
#include <iostream.h>

#define NumValues 20

void main()
{
  int NumYes=0;   //Yes responses
  int NumNo=0; //No responses
  int NumInvalid=0; //Invalid responses
  int LoopCounter;

  char Curr;   //The currently read value
  for (LoopCounter = 0; LoopCounter < NumValues; LoopCounter++)
    {
      cout<<"Do you think the Steelers will win the Superbowl?";
      cin>>Curr;
      if ((Curr == 'Y') || (Curr == 'y'))
        NumYes++;
      else if ((Curr == 'N') || (Curr == 'n'))
        NumNo++;
      else
        NumInvalid++;
    }

  cout<<"The number of yes responses = " << NumYes <<endl;
  cout<<"The number of no responses = " << NumNo <<endl;
  cout<<"The number of invalid responses = " << NumInvalid <<endl;

}
```

The previous program tracks the number of yes responses in the variable **NumYes** and the number of no responses in the variable **NumNo**. Each variable is initialized to 0. Then a **for** loop is executed to ask the question twenty times. Each time a Y or a y is entered, the variable **NumYes** is incremented. Each time an N or an n is entered, the variable **NumNo** is incremented. If a Y, a y, an N, or an n is not entered, the variable **NumInvalid** is incremented. After twenty questions are asked and answered, the **for** loop terminates and the number of yes, no, and invalid responses are output.

Although the previous solution solves the immediate issue, it would be better if the program would reask the question when invalid input is entered. A simple solution to this problem would be to reduce the counter by one when the user enters an invalid input. See the following solution.

```
//Survey program - version 3

#include <stdlib.h>
#include <iostream.h>

#define NumValues 20

void main()
{
 int NumYes=0;  //Yes responses
 int NumNo=0; //No responses
 int LoopCounter;

 char Curr;  //The currently read value

 for (LoopCounter = 0; LoopCounter < NumValues; LoopCounter++)
   {
     cout<<"Do you think the Steelers will win the Super Bowl?";
     cin>>Curr;
     if ((Curr == 'Y') || (Curr == 'y'))
        NumYes++;
     else if ((Curr == 'N') || (Curr == 'n'))
        NumNo++;
     else
         LoopCounter--;
   }

 cout<<"The number of yes responses = " << NumYes <<endl;
 cout<<"The number of no responses = " << NumNo <<endl;

}
```

DRILLS

At this point, any of the following programs should be relatively easy to write. Try them now. We have posed the question and then discussed how to solve each of them.

Drill 4-11

Write a program that displays the numbers from 1 to 15 on the screen.

Drill 4-12

Write a program that displays the numbers from 15 to 1 on the screen.

Drill 4-13

Write a program that asks the user for a value. It should start by displaying the value entered by the user and decreasing it by .5. Continue displaying and decreasing the value by .5 as long as the value is positive.

Drill 4-14

Write a program to read integers from the user. Display their sum. Continue to do this until the sum of the three numbers entered by the user is negative.

Drill 4-15

Write a program that displays every odd number from 1 to 100.

Drill 4-16

Write a program that asks for grades until a negative one is entered. Have the program compute and print the average of the grades to the nearest integer.

Drill 4-17

Write a program that will display all the even numbers between two values entered by the user. The list should include the values entered by the user if they are even. This one is harder because you need to test if the first number is even.

4.4 NESTED LOOPS

Just as we nested **if** statements, we may need to nest loops. Let's start with a simple unnested loop that will roll a pair of dice ten times. To simulate the roll of a die we can use the **rand()** function that is built into C++. It will return a pseudorandom number, but the range will be too large for our purposes. To ensure the random number is generated between 1 and 6, we can use the modulus operator. It returns the remainder of an integer division. Therefore, if we divide by 6 and add 1 we will be sure to get an answer between 1 and 6. The code would look as follows:

```
//Die rolling program

#include <stdlib.h>
#include <iostream.h>

void main()
{
    int Die1, Die2, Sum=0;
    int LoopCounter;
```

```
for (LoopCounter=0; LoopCounter<10; LoopCounter++)
{
    Die1=rand()%6+1;
    Die2=rand()%6+1;
    cout<<Die1<<'\t'<<Die2<<endl;
    Sum+=Die1+Die2;
}
cout<<"SUM="<<Sum<<endl;
}
```

PROGRAMMER'S NOTEBOOK

Many programmers have problems with the modulus operator. Think of placing boxes in a case. Imagine that you could fit a maximum of six boxes in a case. The modulus operator is the number of boxes left over when you have filled as many cases as possible. If the maximum number of boxes in a case is six, then you may have between zero and five boxes left over.

If we wanted to display ten individual sums of ten sets of rolls, we would require a nested loop as follows:

```
//Nested looped die rolling program

#include <stdlib.h>
#include <iostream.h>

void main()
{
    int Die1, Die2, Sum=0;
    int RollCounter, SetCounter;

    for(SetCounter=0; SetCounter<10; SetCounter++)   //Outer loop
    {
        for (int RollCounter=0; RollCounter<10; RollCounter++) //Inner loop
        {
            Die1=rand()%6+1;
            Die2=rand()%6+1;
            cout<<Die1<<'\t'<<Die2<<endl;
            Sum+=Die1+Die2;
        }
        cout<<"SUM="<<Sum<<endl;
    }
}
```

The inner loop of our new program is the same as the main loop of the program before it. However, in this implementation we have added an outer loop. The outer loop controls the number of times the inner loop is executed and then outputs the sum of the rolls of the inner loop.

DRILLS

Try to guess the output of these examples and then run the code and compare your results.

What is the output of the following code?

Drill 4-18

```
//Drill 4-18

#include <iostream.h>
#include <stdlib.h>

void main()
{
  int InnerLoopCounter, OuterLoopCounter;

  for(int OuterLoopCounter=0; OuterLoopCounter<3; OuterLoopCounter++)
    {
      for(int InnerLoopCounter=0; InnerLoopCounter<4; InnerLoopCounter++)
        {
          cout<<OuterLoopCounter<<' '<<InnerLoopCounter<<endl;
        }
    }
}
```

What is the output of the following code?

Drill 4-19

```
//Drill 4-19

#include <iostream.h>
#include <stdlib.h>

void main()
{
    int InnerLoopCounter;
    int OuterLoopCounter;

    for(int OuterLoopCounter=0 ; OuterLoopCounter<5; OuterLoopCounter++)
    {
        for(int InnerLoopCounter=OuterLoopCounter; InnerLoopCounter<5;
            InnerLoopCounter++)
        {
         cout<< OuterLoopCounter <<' '<< InnerLoopCounter <<endl;
        }
    }
}
```

What is the output of the following code?

Drill 4-20

```
//Drill 4-20

#include <iostream.h>
#include <stdlib.h>

void main()
{
    int InnerLoopCounter;
    int OuterLoopCounter;

    OuterLoopCounter=0;

    while (OuterLoopCounter<5)
    {
        cout<<OuterLoopCounter++<<'\t';
        InnerLoopCounter=0;

        while(InnerLoopCounter<3)
        {
            cout<<++InnerLoopCounter<<'\t';
        }

        cout<<endl;
    }
}
```

Drill 4-21

Write a program that draws a rectangle based on a width and height entered by the user. The rectangle should be drawn using asterisks (*). If the input is 7 and 3, then the output should look as follows:

```
* * * * * * *
* * * * * * *
* * * * * * *
```

4.5 EARLY LOOP TERMINATION— BREAK AND CONTINUE KEYWORDS

Sometimes we execute a loop and decide that it should discontinue to process for a reason other that the looping expression evaluates to false. C++ allows us to handle cases like these with the **break** statement.

PROGRAMMER'S NOTEBOOK

Caution should be taken when using the **break** statement. Using it instead of a properly written loop will lead to less readable code and cause maintenance problems as your programs get large.

The following example of a program will read values from the user and multiply them together. When a zero is entered the program should stop.

```cpp
//Example of using a break statement

#include <iostream.h>
#include <stdlib.h>

void main()
{
    //Declare variables
    int Product=1;
    int UserInput;

    //Loop until 0 is entered.
    do
    {
        cout<<"Enter an Integer, Enter 0 to quit"<<endl;
        cin>>UserInput;
        if (UserInput == 0)
            break;
        Product *= UserInput;

    } while(UserInput != 0)


    //Output the result
    cout<<"The Product is "<<Product;
}
```

In the previous program, the **break** was needed because we did not wish to perform the multiplication when a zero was entered by the user. Upon encountering a **break** statement, the execution of the loop stops and the program continues at the first statement after the loop containing the **break** statement.

Another way of controlling a loop is using the **continue** statement, which allows the user to skip the remainder of the loop and continue with normal loop processing from there.

The following program is slightly different from the previous one. Here, we wish to gather ten values from the user and multiply all nonzero values together.

```cpp
//Example of using a continue statement

#include <iostream.h>
#include <stdlib.h>

#define NumValues 10

void main()
{
    //Declare variables
    int Product=1;
    int UserInput;
    int LoopCounter;

    //Loop 10 times
    for (LoopCounter = 0; LoopCounter < NumValues; LoopCounter++)
    {
        //Gather input from user
        cout<<"Enter an Integer "<<endl;
        cin>>UserInput;

        //Ensure input is valid
        if (UserInput == 0)
            continue;

        //Multiply value by previous value, if we get here!
        Product *= UserInput;

    }

    //Output result
    cout<<"The Product is "<<Product;
}
```

PROGRAMMER'S NOTEBOOK

Caution: Using the `continue` statement instead of a properly written loop will lead to less readable code and cause maintenance problems as your programs get large.

Observe the previous program rewritten without a **continue** statement. It is often more readable if you omit the **continue** and write the loop more directly.

```
//Rewritten example of using a continue statement

#include <iostream.h>
#include <stdlib.h>

#define NumValues 10

void main()
{
   //Declare variables
   int Product=1;
   int UserInput;
   int LoopCounter;

   //Loop 10 times
   for (LoopCounter = 0; LoopCounter < NumValues; LoopCounter++)
   {
      //Gather input from user
      cout<<"Enter an Integer "<<endl;
      cin>>UserInput;

      //Ensure input is valid
      if (UserInput != 0)
         Product *= UserInput; //Multiply value by previous value
   }

   //Output result
   cout<<"The Product is "<<Product;

}
```

4.6 Case Study

Problem Description

An entrepreneur operating a day labor pool divides his workers into three skill levels. Unskilled workers receive $8.15 per hour, semiskilled workers $12.55 per hour and skilled workers $18.60 per hour. Write a program that calculates a worker's daily pay showing the dollar sign and the amount formatted to two decimal places. Test your program for an input of odd, even, and fractional hours. Your program input should consist of the hours worked and a skill level indicator. The program should run continuously until terminated by the operator, at which time the sum of all wages paid that day should be displayed.

Discussion

The program requires two inputs, the skill indicator and number of hours the worker was employed. Any attempt to input the pay rates should be strongly discouraged, since the pay scales are fixed and entry of excessive data could lead to errors. The pay rates should be placed in the program as constants. Either a **switch** statement or multiple **if** statements may be used; however, **switch** is the better choice. Because the worker may work fractional hours, the input variable must be a float. A double is acceptable, but should be discouraged since it is unlikely a daily worker will earn a large sum of money. Minimum flag settings should be **showpoint**, and **precision** should be set to two. Also setting the **fixed** flag should be encouraged, since it will be needed for larger numbers later. Since we have no knowledge of how many employees are going to be paid, the **for** loop should not be used. Either the **while** or **do while** are good choices. Both solutions will be shown. The notion of a loop means that entries for multiple employees are the norm. The student should be strongly discouraged from adding statements such as "Do you want to continue -Y/N". Entering the terminating value one time is much more economical than answering Y/N after each set of data.

Solution 1, While Loops

```
#include <stdlib.h>
#include <iostream.h>
#include <iomanip.h>

#define LWage (float) 8.15
#define MWage (float) 12.55
#define HWage (float) 18.60

void main()
{
    float Hours = 1;
    float Pay;
    float Rate;
    float Sum = 0.0;

    int SkillIndicator;

    cout << setprecision(2);
    cout << setiosflags(ios :: showpoint);
    cout << setiosflags(ios :: fixed); //Needed only for large numbers
```

```
while(Hours > 0) //Hours must have a starting value
  {
     cout << endl << endl << "Enter negative value to end or";
     cout << endl <<"Enter hours worked -> ";
     cin >> Hours;
     if (Hours >= 0)
     {
        cout << "Enter skill indicator (1,2,3) -> ";
        cin >> SkillIndicator;

        if (SkillIndicator == 1)
          Rate = HWage;
        else if (SkillIndicator == 2)
          Rate = MWage;
        else if (SkillIndicator == 3)
          Rate = LWage;
        else
        {
           cerr << "You entered an invalid skill indicator";
           continue;
        }

        Pay = Rate * Hours;
        cout << "Worker's pay is $" << Pay;
        Sum += Pay;
     }
  }
  cout << endl <<"Total workers' daily pay is $" << Sum <<endl;
}
```

Output

```
Enter negative value to end or
Enter hours worked -> 12
Enter skill indicator (1,2,3) -> 2
Worker's pay is $150.60

Enter negative value to end or
Enter hours worked -> 10
Enter skill indicator (1,2,3) -> 3
Worker's pay is $81.50

Enter negative value to end or
Enter hours worked -> -1

Total workers' daily pay is $232.10
```

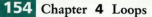

4.6   Case Study (continued)

Solution 2, Do While Loops

```cpp
#include <stdlib.h>
#include <iostream.h>
#include <iomanip.h>
#include <ctype.h>
#define LWage (float) 8.15
#define MWage (float) 12.55
#define HWage (float) 18.60
void main()
{
   float Hours = 1;
   float Pay;
   float Rate;
   float Sum = 0.0;
   char SkillIndicator;
   cout << setprecision(2);
   cout << setiosflags(ios :: showpoint);
   cout << setiosflags(ios :: fixed); //Needed only for large numbers
   do
   {
     cout << endl <<"Enter a negative value to end or";
     cout << endl <<"Enter hours worked -> ";
     cin >> Hours;
     if (Hours > 0)
     {
        cout << endl << "Enter skill indicator (A,B,C) -> ";
        cin >> SkillIndicator;
        SkillIndicator = toupper(SkillIndicator); // Toupper in ctype.h
        switch (SkillIndicator)
        {
           case 'A':
             Rate = HWage;
             break;
           case 'B':
             Rate = MWage;
             break;
           case 'C':
             Rate = LWage;
             break;
           default:
             cerr << endl << "You entered an invalid skill indicator";
             continue;
        }
      Pay = Rate * Hours;
      cout << "Worker's pay is $" << Pay << endl;
      Sum += Pay;
    }
  } while(Hours >= 0);
  cout << endl<<"Total workers' daily pay is $" << Sum;
}
```

Output

```
Enter a negative value to end or
Enter hours worked -> 12

Enter skill indicator (A,B,C) -> B
Worker's pay is $150.60

Enter a negative value to end or
Enter hours worked -> 10

Enter skill indicator (A,B,C) -> C
Worker's pay is $81.50

Enter a negative value to end or
Enter hours worked -> -1

Total workers daily pay is $232.10
```

END-OF-CHAPTER

♦ Key Terms

Conditional expression	An expression used to indicate what the proper conditions are to execute the loop.
Iteration	One repetition of a loop.
Loop	A structure whose contents are repeated over and over again.
Nested loop	A loop that has another loop defined within it.

♦ C++ Keywords Introduced

`break`	A keyword indicating that the program should exit the loop and continue processing at the first statement following the existing loop.
`continue`	A keyword indicating that the program should not execute the remainder of the body of the loop, but it should continue processing the loop as if nothing else occurred.

`do`	A looping construct that always executes the body of the loop at least once. It repeats as long as a specified condition evaluates to true.
`for`	A looping construct that allows the specification of an initial statement, a condition to evaluate to continue processing the loop, and a looping statement.
`while`	A looping construct that repeats as long as a specified condition evaluates to true.

♦ Answers to Drills

Drill 4-1

The previous program has the following output:

```
1
3
5
7
9
```

The previous program is executed as follows: `LoopCounter` is initialized to 0. Since 0 is less than 10, 1 is added to `LoopCounter` via a pre-increment before it is output, then **1** is output.

`LoopCounter` is incremented in the looping statement to 2. Then `LoopCounter` is compared to 10 and since it is still less than 10, we move on to the body of the loop where `LoopCounter` is incremented again before it is output as **3**.

Then `LoopCounter` is incremented in the looping statement to 4. `LoopCounter` is compared to 10 and since it is still less than 10, we move on to the body of the loop where `LoopCounter` is incremented again before it is output as **5**.

Again, `LoopCounter` is incremented in the looping statement to 6, and compared to 10. Since it is still less than 10, we move on to the body of the loop where `LoopCounter` is incremented again before it is output as **7**.

`LoopCounter` is incremented in the looping statement to 8. Then `LoopCounter` is compared to 10 and is still less than 10, so we move on to the body of the loop where `LoopCounter` is incremented again before it is output as **9**.

Finally, `LoopCounter` is incremented in the looping statement to 10. When `LoopCounter` is compared to 10 again, it is no longer less than 10, so the loop terminates.

Drill 4-2

The output of the code provided for the drill is as follows:

```
0
2
4
6
8
```

The previous program is executed as follows: **LoopCounter** is initialized to 0. Since 0 is less than 10, the loop moves to the body that outputs the value of **LoopCounter** before incrementing it. **0** is output and then 1 is added to **LoopCounter**, making **LoopCounter** equal to 1. Then, the looping statement is executed and **LoopCounter** is incremented to 2.

LoopCounter is compared to 10 and is still less than 10, so the body of the loop is executed. The body of the loop outputs the value of **LoopCounter** before incrementing it. **2** is output and then 1 is added to **LoopCounter** making **LoopCounter** equal to 3. The looping statement is then executed and **LoopCounter** is incremented to 4.

This process continues, with **6** and **8** being output. Once **8** is output, it is incremented to 9 with the postincrement. The looping statement then increments it to 10. The condition evaluates whether **LoopCounter** is less than 10; it fails and exits the loop.

Drill 4-3

The output of the code provided for the drill is as follows:

```
1
3
5
7
9
```

The previous program is executed as follows: **LoopCounter** is initialized to 0. Although an increment exists on the conditional statement, it is a postincrement command and therefore occurs after the evaluation is made. So 0 is compared to 10 and is less than 10, so the body of the loop executes. However, the value of **LoopCounter** is incremented to 1 after the evaluation of the condition. Therefore, **1** is output from the body of the loop.

LoopCounter is then incremented to 2 in the looping statement. Since 2 is the value of **LoopCounter** used to evaluate the condition expression, and 2 is less than 10, the body of the loop executes. Before it executes, the postincrement command increments **LoopCounter** to 3. **3** is then output from the body of the loop.

This process continues with **5**, **7**, and **9** being output. After **9** is output, the looping statement increments the value to 10. 10 is compared to 10 in the expression and found to be false, so the loop terminates.

Drill 4-4

The output of the code provided for the drill is as follows:

```
1
3
5
7
9
```

The previous program is executed as follows: **LoopCounter** is initialized to 0. The increment in the expression is a pre-increment, therefore it occurs before the evaluation is made. So 1 is compared to 10 and is less than 10, so the body of the loop executes and a **1** is output.

LoopCounter is then incremented to 2 in the looping statement. 2 is then incremented with the pre-increment statement to 3. **LoopCounter** uses the value of 3 to evaluate the condition expression, and 3 is less than 10, so the body of the loop executes and **3** is output.

This process continues with **5**, **7**, and **9** being output. After **9** is output, the looping statement increments the value to 10. 10 is then pre-incremented to 11. 11 is compared to 10 and is not less than 10, so the loop terminates.

Drill 4-5

The output of the code provided for the drill is as follows:

```
1
2
3
4
9
5
```

The loop starts with **LoopCounter** initialized to 1. Since 1 is less than 5, the body of the loop executes. Even though the indentation makes it appear that all three **cout** statements are included in the body of the loop, only the statement **cout<<LoopCounter<<endl;** is part of the body of the loop. Therefore, the number **1** is output and the looping statement is executed incrementing **LoopCounter** to 2. Separating the following two **cout** statements out of the problem, we are now left with a simple loop that compares **LoopCounter** to 5, outputs the value, and increments **LoopCounter**. This continues until **4** is output and **LoopCounter** is incremented to 5. When **LoopCounter** equals 5, the looping condition fails, and the loop terminates.

The next statement, **cout<<LoopCounter+4<<endl;**, executes and **9** is output. The calculation of **LoopCounter+4** is not stored in **LoopCounter**, so when the final statement, **cout<<LoopCounter<<endl;**, executes a **5** is also output.

Drill 4-6

The output of the code provided for the drill is as follows:

```
1
5
2
6
3
7
4
8
5
```

The loop starts with `LoopCounter` initialized to 1. Since 1 is less than 5, the body of the loop executes. In this case, the body of the loop contains two `cout` statements. **1** and **5** are output from the first and second statements, respectively. Then the looping statement is executed, incrementing `LoopCounter` to 2.

We now have a simple loop that compares `LoopCounter` to 5, outputs the two values, `LoopCounter` and `LoopCounter+4`, and then increments `LoopCounter`. This continues until **4** and **8** are output and `LoopCounter` is incremented to 5. When `LoopCounter` equals 5, the looping condition fails, and the loop terminates.

One statement exists outside the loop, so `LoopCounter` is output again; however, because of the increment in the looping statement, `LoopCounter` is output as **5**.

Drill 4-7

The output of the code provided for the drill is as follows:

```
1
2
3
4
5
6
7
8
8
10
```

`LoopCounter` is initialized to 1. `LoopCounter` is then compared to see if it is less than or equal to 10. It is, so the body of the loop executes. 1 is output and then `LoopCounter` is incremented to 2 by the postincrement in the body of the loop. 2 is less than or equal to 10, so the body of the loop is executed again. 2 is output and `LoopCounter` is postincremented to 3. This continues with 3, 4, 5, 6, 7, 8, 9, and 10 being output. `LoopCounter` is then postincremented to 11 and the looping condition fails, thus terminating the loop.

Drill 4-8

The output of the code provided for the drill is as follows:

```
2
4
6
8
10
```

LoopCounter is initialized to 1. **LoopCounter** is compared to 10 and is less than or equal to 10, so the looping condition will execute. However, because of the postincrement on **LoopCounter** in the looping condition, **LoopCounter** is incremented to 2 before the body of the loop executes. The value of **LoopCounter**, **2**, is then output and postincremented to 3. **LoopCounter** is compared to 10 and then postincremented to **4**, which is output. This continues with **6**, **8**, and **10** being output. After **10** is output, **LoopCounter** is postincremented to 11 and the looping condition fails, so the loop terminates.

Drill 4-9

The output of the code provided for the drill is as follows:

```
2
4
6
8
10
```

LoopCounter is initialized to 1. **LoopCounter** is pre-incremented to 2 before it is compared to 10. Since 2 is less than or equal to 10, the looping condition will execute. **2** is then output, since the increment is a postincrement and occurs after the **cout** statement. When the looping condition is evaluated again, **LoopCounter** already equals 3 and is pre-incremented to 4. 4 is less than or equal to 10, so we continue with **6**, **8**, and **10** being output. Once **10** is output, **LoopCounter** is postincremented to 10, then pre-incremented to 11, so when it is compared to 10, the looping condition fails and the loop terminates.

Drill 4-10

The output of the code provided for the drill is as follows:

```
3
5
7
9
11
```

LoopCounter is initialized to 1. **LoopCounter** is then pre-incremented to 2 before it is compared to 10. Since 2 is less than or equal to 10, the looping condition will execute. **LoopCounter** is then pre-incremented to 3 before the output of the **cout** statement occurs. Then **3** is output. When the looping condition is evaluated again, **LoopCounter** is pre-incremented again and equals 4. 4 is less than or equal to 10, so we continue with **5**, **7**, and **9** being output. Once **9** is output, **LoopCounter** is pre-incremented in the looping condition statement, causing **LoopCounter** to equal 10. Since 10 is less than or equal to 10, the looping statement is executed again. **LoopCounter** is incremented again by 1, and **11** is output. Now, when the looping condition is evaluated again and **LoopCounter** is incremented to 12, 12 is not less than or equal to 10 and the loop terminates.

Drill 4-11

To solve this problem, we would need some kind of loop. The most obvious choice is a **for** loop. The **for** loop is chosen because there exists a logical beginning point **(LoopCounter=1)**, a logical ending point **(LoopCounter==15)**, and a looping statement **(LoopCounter++)**. The body of the loop is a single statement that outputs the current value. The code would look as follows:

```cpp
//Displays the numbers from 1 to 15

#include <stdlib.h>
#include <iostream.h>

void main()
{
    int LoopCounter;

    for (LoopCounter=1; LoopCounter<=15; LoopCounter++)
        cout<< LoopCounter <<endl;

}
```

Drill 4-12

This problem is extremely similar to the previous problem. The same tenants hold true for it that hold true for the previous problem. Again, a **for** loop is the perfect choice. We need to change the initial statement to set **LoopCounter** to equal 15, to change the looping condition to compare to >=1, and for the looping statement to decrement **LoopCounter**, so that we reverse the order in which the number is displayed.

The code is as follows:

```
//Displays the numbers from 15 to 1

#include<stdlib.h>
#include<iostream.h>

void main()
{
    int LoopCounter;

    for (LoopCounter=15; LoopCounter>=1; LoopCounter--)
      cout<<LoopCounter<<endl;


}
```

Drill 4-13

This program requires a bit more thought. What do we require?

• A counter

• A loop

From first glance it would not seem like there is that much of a difference between the first two problems. However, the value to start the counter is not set as in the previous examples. Therefore, to gather the information from the user, we use a **cin**. Since we are using the **cin** command, there is no need for an initial looping statement, so instead of using a **for** loop we use a **while** loop. Finally, we are no longer incrementing by an integer; therefore, our looping variable must be a **float** to enable it to store decimal values.

The solution follows:

```
//Displays numbers by .5 from the 1 entered
//as long as the number is positive

#include<stdlib.h>
#include<iostream.h>

void main()
{
    float LoopCounter;
```

```
    cout<<"Enter a number"<<endl;
    cin>> LoopCounter;

    while (LoopCounter > 0)
    {
        cout<< LoopCounter <<endl;
        LoopCounter = LoopCounter -.5;
    }
}
```

Drill 4-14

To solve the problem we will require four variables. The first three are integers called **Value1**, **Value2**, and **Value3**, which will be used to store the numbers that we are reading from the user. The fourth will also need to be an integer called **Sum**. **Sum** will contain the sum of **Value1**, **Value2**, and **Value3**, and will be used both for output and in the looping condition. If we chose a **for** loop or **while** loop to solve the problem, we would need to initialize **Sum** so that it doesn't terminate the loop on the first try. The following solution is inefficient.

```
//Reads integers Value1, Value2, Value3. Prints their sum.
//Continues until the sum of Value1, Value2 and Value3 is
negative.

#include<stdlib.h>
#include<iostream.h>

void main()
{
    int Value1, Value2, Value3;
    int Sum=1;

    while (Sum >= 0)
    {
        cout<<"Enter three numbers"<<endl;
        cin>>Value1>>Value2>>Value3;
        Sum=Value1+Value2+Value3;
        cout<<"There sum is "<<Sum<<endl;
    }
}
```

A better way to solve the problem is to use a **do..while** loop, because we want the loop to execute at least once. That implementation is as follows and is obviously more logical as well as a bit faster.

```
//Reads integers Value1, Value2, Value3. Prints their sum.
//Continues until the sum of Value1, Value2, and Value3 is negative.
//Do-while solution

#include<stdlib.h>
#include<iostream.h>

void main()
{
   int Value1, Value2, Value3;
   int Sum;

   do
   {
      cout<<"Enter three numbers"<<endl;
      cin>>Value1>>Value2>>Value3;
      Sum=Value1+Value2+Value3;
      cout<<"There sum is "<<Sum<<endl;
   } while (Sum>=0);
}
```

Drill 4-15

Since there is a logical beginning and ending to the loop, we implement this program with a **for** loop. The loop needs to count only whole numbers, so the looping variable is an integer. The main difference from the earlier question is that the looping variable must increment by two instead of one. This can be accomplished with the **+=** operator. The code follows:

```
//Program to display odd numbers between 1 and 100.

#include<stdlib.h>
#include<iostream.h>

void main()
{
   int LoopCounter;

   for(LoopCounter = 1; LoopCounter < 100; LoopCounter += 2)
      cout<<count<<endl;
}
```

Drill 4-16

Since we want the program to read grades until a –1 is entered, at least one grade must be entered. Therefore, a **do..while** loop would be the best choice. We will require a variable to store a grade. If we assume that grades are whole numbers, we can make the grade variable an **int**.

The real question is, what type of variable do we need to compute the average of all the numbers read? We need to track the sum of all the grades as well as the total number of grades. Therefore we will require two more integer variables.

The final average can be a calculation of the sum of the grades divided by the number of grades. Since we are required to output it only once, there is no need to store it in a variable.

One problem that we have is that it is logical to add the grade to the sum and increment the number of grades within the loop; however, if a –1 is entered for the grade, adding it to the sum would cause a problem. Therefore, we require an **if** statement around the sum calculation and incrementing of the number of grades.

The code is as follows:

```
//Program to compute grades

#include <stdlib.h>
#include <iostream.h>

void main()
{
    int Sum=0;
    int NumGrades=0;
    int Grade;

    do
    {
        cout<<"Enter a grade:"<<endl;
        cin>>Grade;

        if (Grade != -1)
        {
            Sum+=Grade;
            NumGrades++;
        }
    }  while (Grade != -1);
    cout<<Sum/NumGrades;
}
```

Drill 4-17

The solution to the programming problem presented in the drill follows:

```
//Program to display even numbers between Value1 and Value2

#include<stdlib.h>
#include<iostream.h>

void main()
{
   int LoopCounter;
   int Value1;
   int Value2;

   cout<<"Enter the starting value\n";
   cin>>Value1;
   cout<<"Enter the ending value\n";
   cin>>Value2;

   if (Value1%1 == 1)  //check to see if it is odd
     Value1++;

   for(LoopCounter=Value1; LoopCounter <= Value2; LoopCounter +=2)
     cout<<LoopCounter<<endl;
}
```

The program works by asking the user for a value for **Value1** and **Value2**. If **Value1** is odd we need to increment it to the next integer value, which will be even. We can test to see if a number is odd by looking at the remainder of that number when it is divided by 2. If there is a remainder, it is odd. To determine the remainder, we use the modulus operator. The modulus operator, **%**, performs a division; however, instead of returning a result of the division, it returns the remainder of the division.

Once we have a new starting value of **Value1**, we can use a **for** loop to print out every value through **Value2**. We do not have to worry if **Value2** is even, because we are skipping by two throughout the loop.

Drill 4-18

The solution to the programming problem presented in the drill follows:

```
0 0
0 1
0 2
0 3
1 0
1 1
1 2
1 3
2 0
2 1
2 2
2 3
```

The program starts by entering the outer loop where the variable `OuterLoopCounter` is set to 0. The outer loop's conditional expression is checked. Since 0 is less than 3, the statements contained within the curly braces are executed. In this case those statements are the inner `for` loop. Therefore, the entire inner loop is executed to completion each time the outer `for` loop's conditional expression evaluates to true.

Then the inner loop starts with `InnerLoopCounter=0` and outputs a pair of numbers as `InnerLoopCounter` increments by 1 to 3. During this inner loop the value of `OuterLoopCounter` remains constant. It is not until the inner looping condition `(InnerLoopCounter<4)` is false and the inner loop terminates, that the outer looping statement `LoopCounter++` is executed. Then with `OuterLoopCounter` equaling 1, the inner loop continues. `InnerLoopCounter` is reinitialized to 0 and the inner loop is executed again. The final termination of the nested loops occurs when the outer looping condition `(OuterLoopCounter<3)` is false and the outer loop terminates.

Drill 4-19

The solution to the programming problem presented in the drill follows:

```
0 0
0 1
0 2
0 3
0 4
1 1
1 2
1 3
1 4
2 2
2 3
2 4
3 3
3 4
4 4
```

This set of nested loops is a bit more complicated, because the inner loop variable is not set to a constant, but to the outer loop counter. The outer loop starts by initializing `LoopCounter` to 0. Then the inner loop begins. `InnerLoopCounter` is initialized to `OuterLoopCounter`, which means that `InnerLoopCounter` will be initialized to 0. Then the inner loop is like any other, outputting pairs of numbers until the inner loop's looping condition is false. When this occurs, the outer looping statement, `OuterLoopCounter++`, is executed. With `LoopCounter` now equaling 1, the inner loop begins to execute. However, instead of starting from `InnerLoopCounter=0`, the inner loop starts from `InnerLoopCounter=1`. The process continues until the outer looping condition fails. Notice that each pass of the inner loop is shorter and shorter.

Drill 4-20

The solution to the programming problem presented in the drill follows:

```
0       1       2       3
1       1       2       3
2       1       2       3
3       1       2       3
4       1       2       3
```

The outer loop in this example is controlled by the variable `OuterLoopCounter`. It is initialized to 0 and output. After the value is output, it is postincremented to 1. Then the inner loop starts. In this example the inner loop will execute the same each time it is executed regardless of the value of `OuterLoopCounter`. It will display the values 1, 2, and 3, respectively. The last part of the outer loop outputs a carriage return. This process then repeats for the remaining values of `OuterLoopCounter`, 1, 2, and 3 respectively.

Drill 4-21

The code for the program presented in this drill is as follows:

```cpp
#include <stdlib.h>
#include <iostream.h>

void main()
{
  int Width;
  int Height;
  int HeightCounter;
  int WidthCounter;

  cout<<"Enter the width of the rectangle:"<<endl;
  cin>>Width;

  cout<<"Enter the height of the rectangle:"<<endl;
  cin>>Height;
```

```
for(int HeightCounter=0;HeightCounter<Height;HeightCounter++)
{
  for(int WidthCounter=0;WidthCounter<Width;WidthCounter++)
    cout<<"*";
  cout<<endl;
}
}
```

The previous program accepts two integers from the user. The first is the **Width** and the second is the **Height**. The **Width** represents the number of stars that will be displayed across the screen and the **Height** represents the number of stars that will be displayed down the screen.

The outer **for** loop controls the number of complete lines of stars that are displayed. This equals the height entered by the user. Therefore, the outer **for** loop counts up to the height entered by the user.

The inner **for** loop controls the number of stars across a single line that is displayed. This equals the width entered by the user. Therefore, the inner **for** loop counts up to the width entered by the user.

◆ Programming Exercises

1. Write a program that will read a series of 20 numbers and output the minimum value. *Make sure that it works if you enter numbers that are all much greater than zero!*

2. Write a program that will ask the user a question with four possible answers. The question should be asked 20 times. After all the input is gathered, the program should output the number of times each answer was selected.

3. Write a program that will ask the user to enter the number of different items a store carries in stock. The program should loop the number of times entered, and ask for a price and quantity on hand for each part. The program should output the total value of the inventory.

4. Write a program that asks the user for a width and height of a rectangle and then outputs a hollow rectangle. The rectangle would be composed of the characters '*' and ' '. Therefore, a rectangle with a width of 8 and a height of 4 would appear as follows:

```
* * * * * * * *
*             *
*             *
* * * * * * * *
```

To improve the program, make sure that it accepts only valid input—a number greater than 3.

5. Write a program that allows the user to select either a **for**, **while**, or **do** loop to produce output. Additionally, the user enters the highest number to output as well as how many numbers should be skipped each time. For example, if the user asks the program to count to 10 in steps of 3, then the output should be **0**, **3**, **6**, and **9**. Since 12 is larger, it should be skipped. Use the **switch** function described in the last section to decide on the correct loop to use.

6. Write a program that accepts a number and outputs whether the number is even or odd. Instead of using complicated mathematical techniques, the program should compute the results by continuously subtracting 2 until you are left with 0 or 1. The program should output "EVEN" if the final value is 0, and "ODD" if the final value is 1.

7. Write a program to calculate a student's GPA. The program should read letter grades one at a time. It should convert them to the corresponding number grade (A to 4, B to 3, C to 2, D to 1, F to 0). It should continue reading grades until the user enters a Q or q. There should be no limit to the amount of grades that can be entered. Once all grades have been entered, the overall average needs to be calculated and displayed.

8. Write a program that uses loops in order to display all the hours on a clock. The program should start with 12:00 AM and then 1:00 AM, 2:00 AM, and so on, until 12:00 PM, then 1:00 PM, 2:00 PM, and so on until 11:00 PM. When you write this program, you must use loops to go from hour to hour (you will need more than one). Do not hardcode the output with 24 **cout** statements.

◆ Additional Exercises

1. What is the output of the following code?

```
#include <stdlib.h>
#include <iostream.h>

void main()
{
    int LoopCounter;

    for (LoopCounter=0; LoopCounter<20;LoopCounter=LoopCounter+2)
      cout<<LoopCounter<<endl;
}
```

2.   What is the output of the following code

```
#include <stdlib.h>
#include <iostream.h>
void main()
{
   int LoopCounter;
   for(LoopCounter=10;LoopCounter>0;LoopCounter--)
     cout<<LoopCounter<<endl;
}
```

3. What is the output of the following code?

```
#include <stdlib.h>
#include <iostream.h>

void main()
{
   int LoopCounter;
   for(LoopCounter=0; LoopCounter>=0; LoopCounter++)
     cout<<LoopCounter<<endl;
}
```

4.   What is the output of the following code?

```
#include <stdlib.h>
#include <iostream.h>

void main()
{
   int LoopCounter;
   for (LoopCounter=0; LoopCounter<0; LoopCounter--)
     cout<<LoopCounter<<endl;
}
```

5. What is the output of the following code?

```
#include <stdlib.h>
#include <iostream.h>

void main()
{
    int LoopCounter;
    for(LoopCounter=0; LoopCounter<10; LoopCounter=LoopCounter+2)
      cout<<++LoopCounter<<endl;
}
```

6. Rewrite the following loop as a **while** loop.

```
#include <stdlib.h>
#include <iostream.h>

void main()
{
    int LoopCounter;
    for (LoopCounter=0; LoopCounter<10; LoopCounter=LoopCounter+2)
      cout<<LoopCounter<<endl;
}
```

7. What is the output of the following code?

```
#include <stdlib.h>
#include <iostream.h>

void main()
{
    int LoopCounter1, LoopCounter2;
    for (LoopCounter1=1,
      LoopCounter2=1;LoopCounter1<=5;LoopCounter2++)
      cout<<LoopCounter1++<<endl;
    cout<<--LoopCounter2<<endl;
}
```

8. What is the output of the following code?

```
#include <stdlib.h>
#include <iostream.h>

void main()
{

    int LoopCounter = 0;
    int Number=10;
    while (LoopCounter<=10)
    {
        Number++;
        cout<<LoopCounter++<<endl;
    }
    cout<<Number<<endl;
}
```

CHAPTER

5

Functions

Chapter Objectives

- ♦ Explain how to create your own functions
- ♦ Introduce parameters
- ♦ Introduce local variables
- ♦ Introduce global variables
- ♦ Introduce return values
- ♦ Introduce pass by value versus pass by reference

5.1 DEFINING A FUNCTION

To keep our programs organized and readable we need a way of breaking our programs into separate logical parts. **Functions** allow us to do this. You may not have realized it, but we have already used functions (e.g., **rand()**). However, a programming language would not be very powerful if it did not allow programmers to extend it by creating their own functions.

In C++ we define functions using the following template:

```
return type function name(function parameter list)
{
    body of function;
}
```

- A return type is any valid C++ variable type.
- A function name is any valid C++ identifier.
- A parameter list is a list of variable types followed by a variable name.

Multiple parameters are separated with commas.

Here is a simple function that has no parameters or **return values** and simply outputs a message.

```
//Simple function example
void Message()
{
    cout<<"We love the Pittsburgh Steelers!"<<endl;
}
```

Although not required by C compilers, C++ requires that we declare a function before we use it. We declare all the functions in a program at the beginning of a file. This declaration is called a **prototype**. Prototypes allow the compiler to know about all functions before we start defining them. This will help reduce confusion, especially when one function we define calls another function we define. You may think of prototypes as a table of contents of your functions.

The simplest way to write a prototype is to write exactly the same code as the first line of the function and then follow it by a semicolon. We usually write the function, then copy the first line to the clipboard, then paste it in the appropriate space in the file with a semicolon appended to it. Look back at the template file to see the exact location of the prototypes within the program file.

Following is an example of a program with the **Message** function. Note the placement of the prototype before the definition of the function. This is required. Also note that the function definition is listed after the **main** routine. Although not required, it is done out of style.

```
//Function example with a prototype
#include <stdlib.h>
#include <iostream.h>

//Prototypes
void Message();

//main routine
void main()
{
    Message();
}



//Functions

//Message function
void Message()
{
    cout<<"We love the Pittsburgh Steelers!"<<endl;
}
```

5.2 PARAMETERS AND RETURN VALUES

In our programs so far we have used variables that were visible to the entire program. With the addition of functions this will not always be the case. When we write a function, we may wish to pass a value to the function. If the value is passed as a **parameter**, a copy of that value is passed to the function. This form of parameter passing is known as **pass by value**. The function then refers to that value by the parameter name. Any changes made to that parameter will not change the original value of the variable passed.

In some languages there is a distinction between a function and a procedure, but in C++ there is no such distinction. While you can only return one value from a C++ function, later, we learn ways of having more than one value changed by a function. By default a function returns the type integer, but it is good practice to define what it returns. If we do not specify a **return value**, the return will default to 0, but we may receive a compiler warning. If the function is intended to return nothing, then we should declare the return type as **void**.

Here are some examples of some very simple functions. They do not change any values—they merely select a value and return it to the calling function.

```
//Compute the minimum of two values
int Min(int FirstValue, int SecondValue)
{
    if (FirstValue < SecondValue)
      return FirstValue;
    else
      return SecondValue;
}
```

Min accepts two integers as parameters, **FirstValue** and **SecondValue**. If **FirstValue** is greater than **SecondValue**, then **SecondValue** is returned. Otherwise, **FirstValue** is returned. If **FirstValue** equals **SecondValue**, it does not matter which value we return, as long as we return one of them. The **else** clause will return **SecondValue**, so **SecondValue** will be returned from the function.

```
//Compute the maximum of two values
int Max(int FirstValue, int SecondValue)
{
    if (FirstValue > SecondValue)
      return FirstValue;
    else
      return SecondValue;
}
```

Max accepts two integers as parameters, **FirstValue** and **SecondValue**. If **FirstValue** is greater than **SecondValue**, then **FirstValue** is returned; otherwise, **SecondValue** is returned. Similar to the **Min** example, if **FirstValue** equals **SecondValue**, it does not matter which value we return, as long as we return one of them. The **else** clause will return **SecondValue**, so **SecondValue** will be returned.

Let's see how a program that uses both the **Min** and the **Max** function would be assembled. This program will ask the user for two values and then will call the **Min** and **Max** functions in order to determine which value is the maximum and which value is the minimum. It is shown here:

```
//Program showing use of the Min and Max
//functions

#include <stdlib.h>
#include <iostream.h>

//Prototypes
int Min(int FirstValue, int SecondValue);
int Max(int FirstValue, int SecondValue);

//Main routine
void main()
{
    int UserEntered1;   //First value to be read from the user
    int UserEntered2;   //Second value to be read from the user

    cout<<"Enter the first value:"<<endl;
    cin>> UserEntered1;

    cout<<"Enter the second value:"<<endl;
    cin>> UserEntered2;

    cout<<"The maximum value of the values you entered is "
        <<Max(UserEntered1, UserEntered2)<<endl;

    cout<<"The minimum value of the values you entered is "
        <<Min(UserEntered1, UserEntered2)<<endl;
}

//Functions

//Compute the minimum of two values.
int Min(int FirstValue, int SecondValue)
{
  if (FirstValue < SecondValue)
    return FirstValue;
  else
    return SecondValue;

}
```

```
//Compute the maximum of two values.
int Max(int FirstValue, int SecondValue)
{
   if (FirstValue > SecondValue)
     return FirstValue;
   else
     return SecondValue;

}
```

By modifying the **Min** function and adding an additional parameter, **ThirdValue**, we can compare three numbers to see which is the minimum. The first check is the most complicated. If **FirstValue** is the minimum then we must check that **FirstValue** is less than **SecondValue** and also less than **ThirdValue**. If so, then **FirstValue** is returned. However, when we check if **SecondValue** is the minimum, we no longer require the check for **SecondValue** being less than **FirstValue** because if we reached this point in the program then **FirstValue** cannot possibly be the minimum. So if **SecondValue** is less than **ThirdValue**, we return **SecondValue** as the minimum. Finally, if we reach the final **else** clause, **ThirdValue** must be the minimum and it is returned.

Similar to the example of the minimum of two numbers, in the case where all three values are the same, **ThirdValue** would be returned. In the case that two values were the same, one of the two values would be returned.

```
//Compute the minimum of three values.
int Min3(int FirstValue, int SecondValue, int ThirdValue)
{
   if ((FirstValue < SecondValue) && (FirstValue < ThirdValue))
     return(FirstValue);
   else if (SecondValue < ThirdValue)
     return (SecondValue);
   else
     return (ThirdValue);

}
```

The **Max3** function works the same as the **Min3** function, except the operator has been switched to > instead of <.

```
//Compute the maximum of three values.
int Max3(int FirstValue, int SecondValue, int ThirdValue)
{
    if ((FirstValue > SecondValue) && (FirstValue > ThirdValue))
      return(FirstValue);
    else if (SecondValue > ThirdValue)
      return (SecondValue);
    else
      return (ThirdValue);

}
```

▌▌▌ DRILLS

Drill

Write a prototype for a function called **FirstDrill**. It should have two parameters: the first, **DrillParam1**, should be an integer and the second, **DrillParam2**, should be a floating point number. The function should return an integer.

Drill

Write a prototype for a function called **SecondDrill**. It should have one parameter, **DrillParam1**, which should be a Boolean. The function should return nothing.

Drill

Write a prototype for a function called **ThirdDrill**. It should have three parameters: the first, **DrillParam1**, should be a floating point number; the second, **DrillParam2**, should be an integer; and the third, **DrillParam3**, should be a character. The function should return a Boolean.

5.3 LOCAL VARIABLES

Variables can also be declared inside the function. They are considered local to the function. Variables declared outside the function declaration are global and can be accessed after any function declared after it.

If a variable name is the same as a global variable name, the local is used inside of the function and the global remains unchanged.

Let's look at a function that will read in a number of elements specified by the parameter **NumOfElements** and then return the minimum number from the values read. To calculate the **Minimum,** we need to store the lowest value so far in a variable. In addition, we require a variable to act as a counter as we read each individual value. These variables are declared as local variables.

```
// Minimum function definition

int Minimum(int NumOfElements)
{
    int Min, LoopCounter, UserEnteredVal;

    if (NumOfElements<0)
    {
      cout<<"An error has occurred.  The # of elements must be positive!"<<endl;
      return -1;
    }

    cin>>UserEnteredVal;
    Min=UserEnteredVal;

    for(LoopCounter=1; LoopCounter < NumOfElements; ++LoopCounter)
    {
        cin>>UserEnteredVal;
        if (UserEnteredVal < Min)
          Min = LoopCounter;
    }
  return (Min);
}
```

The **Minimum** function starts out by declaring the variables that we will require for this function. Then it does something very important. It does not assume the value being passed as a parameter is correct. If an improper value is sent, it displays an error message and returns from the function. Once the **return -1** is executed the rest of the function is ignored and the program continues to execute from wherever the function was called originally. There are more sophisticated ways of handling errors, but we will not concentrate on that here.

The next step in the program is to read in the first value. The reason this is done outside the loop is because we need to set the variable representing the minimum, **Min,** to a value. If we don't set it to the first value, to what would we set it? If we chose zero, what if we read a negative number? The only way to avoid reading the first value separately would be to calculate the lowest possible number.

Now the problem is simple. We read in the remainder of the numbers and compare them to the minimum. If the new number is lower than the minimum, then we replace the minimum with the new number. Notice that our loop is one less than the total number of items we are reading. This is because we already read the first number.

Finally, the minimum value is returned from the function.

5.4 SCOPE

One of the biggest problems students have with functions is dealing with the concept of **scope**. Scope deals with the visibility of variables to a function. Not all variables are visible to all functions. Global variables are, but they need to be defined at the beginning of your program. Global variables are OK to use in some cases, but are more often misused by beginner programmers. A global variable can easily be changed by accident when it is used by more than one function. It can also lead to wasted memory.

A **local variable** is defined inside a set of {} and is visible only within the {}. A variable is **global** when it is declared outside {} and outside the function.

Let's look at the following program:

```
//Program showing scope

#include <stdlib.h>
#include <iostream.h>

//Global variables
int Global1;
int Global2;

//Prototypes
void SampleFunction1(int ParamSampleFunction1);
void SampleFunction2(int ParamSampleFunction2);

//Main routine
void main()
{
    int MainLocal1;
    int MainLocal2;

    MainLocal1 = 5;
    MainLocal2 = 7;
    Global1 = 10;
    Global2 = 20;

    SampleFunction1(MainLocal1);
    SampleFunction2(MainLocal2);
    cout<<Global1<<endl;
    cout<<Global2<<endl;
}

//Functions

//SampleFunction1
void SampleFunction1(int ParamSampleFunction1)
{
    int SampleFunction1Local;

    SampleFunction1Local = ParamSampleFunction1;

    cout<<SampleFunction1Local<<endl;
    cout<<Global1<<endl;
    cout<<Global2<<endl;
}
```

```
//SampleFunction2
void SampleFunction2(int ParamSampleFunction2)
{
    int SampleFunction2Local;

    SampleFunction2Local = ParamSampleFunction2;

    cout<<SampleFunction2Local;
    cout<<Global1<<endl;
    cout<<Global2<<endl;
}
```

The previous program, although it doesn't accomplish much in the real world, demonstrates local variables, global variables, and parameters.

The variables **Global1** and **Global2** are declared before the functions and the **main** routine, and are therefore global to the entire program. This means that they can be used in all the functions and in the main routine.

The variable **ParamSampleFunction1** is defined as a parameter to the function **SampleFunction1**. This means that the variable is initialized when it is called from another function and is visible only within the function **SampleFunction1**. Another variable, **SampleFunctionLocal1**, is declared within the function **SampleFunction1** and therefore is considered a local variable to the function. This means that it can only be used only within the function **SampleFunction1**.

The variable **ParamSampleFunction2** is defined as a parameter to the function **SampleFunction2**. This means that the variable is initialized when it is called from another function and is visible only within the function **SampleFunction2**. Another variable, **SampleFunctionLocal2**, is declared within the function **SampleFunction2** and therefore considered a local variable to the function. This means that it can be used only within the function **SampleFunction2**.

The parameter and local variable of one function cannot be used in the other functions defined. Therefore, **ParamSampleFunction1** and **SampleFunctionLocal1** can be seen from **SampleFunction1** but not from **SampleFunction2**. Likewise, **ParamSampleFunction2** and **SampleFunctionLocal2** can be seen from **SampleFunction2** but not **SampleFunction1**.

The **main** routine can see the global variables **Global1** and **Global2** and the local variables defined within the main routine, **MainLocal1** and **MainLocal2**, but not any of the other variables. Many beginning programmers think that variables defined within **main** are global, but they are like any other local variables. Therefore, **MainLocal1** and **MainLocal2** are visible only within the **main** routine.

DRILLS

What is the output of the following program?

Drill 5-4

```
//Drill 5-4
//Drill showing scope

#include <stdlib.h>
#include <iostream.h>

//Prototypes
int Mystery(int Value1);



//Main Routine
void main()
{
    int Value1=1;
    int Value2=2;
    int Value3=3;

    cout<<Value1<<'\t'<<Value2<<'\t'<<Value3<<endl;

    Value2=Mystery(Value1);

    cout<<Value1<<'\t'<<Value2<<'\t'<<Value3<<endl;
}

//Functions
int Mystery(int Value1)
{
    int Value2=Value1*2;
    int Value3=5;

    cout<<Value2<<'\t'<<Value3<<endl;
    Value1=Value1*2;

    return Value1;
}
```

What is the output of the following program?

Drill 5-5

```
//Drill 5-5
//Second drill showing scope

#include <stdlib.h>
#include <iostream.h>

//Prototypes
void Mystery(int Value1);

int Value1;
int Value2;

//Main routine
void main()
{
    int Value3=3;

    Value1=1;
    Value2=2;

    cout<<Value1<<'\t'<<Value2<<'\t'<<Value3<<endl;

    Mystery(Value1);

    cout<<Value1<<'\t'<<Value2<<'\t'<<Value3<<endl;
}

//Functions
void Mystery(int Value1)
{

    int Value3=50;

    Value1=Value1*2;
    Value2=Value2*2;

    cout<<Value1<<'\t'<<Value2<<'\t'<<Value3<<endl;
}
```

5.5 EXTENDING THE LANGUAGE

By using functions we can extend the C++ language to include features that were not originally intended. Let's start with a mundane example and build until we have a set of useful functions that adds to the power of the C++ language.

Let's say we wanted to have a function called **Star**. **Star** would simply display the character '*', nothing more. We would have the following code.

```
void Star()
{
    cout<<"*";
}
```

Now we could use **Star()** in our **main** like any other feature of C++.

```
void main()
{
    //Print five stars and then a carriage return.
    Star();
    Star();
    Star();
    Star();
    Star();
    cout<<endl;
}
```

Although this seems redundant, the function **Star** is more readable than typing **cout<<"*"**.

By looking at how we used the function **Star**, we see that there is a pattern in the way we use **Star**. We call **Star()** as many times as we want to display **Star**. Therefore, it would make sense to have another function that accepts a parameter specifying the number of **Stars** we want to display.

Let's define **Stars()** to accept a parameter indicating the number of **Stars** to display and then to display a carriage return.

```
//Stars function
void Stars(int PNumStars)
{
    int LoopCounter;
    for(LoopCounter=0; LoopCounter < PNumStars; LoopCounter++)
      Star();
    cout<<endl;
}
```

Stars takes one parameter, but it also requires a local variable. This variable, **LoopCounter**, is defined within the function and will not be seen by any other function. The local variable **LoopCounter** will not affect any other variables named **LoopCounter**.

Now we can rewrite our **main** function to be much clearer.

```
void main()
{
    Stars(5);
}
```

Let's take our example a step further. What if instead of printing a simple line of stars, we used the asterisk character to display a letter? We could do this easily. Look at the following desired output:

```
* * * * * *
* * * * * *
* *
* * * *
* * * *
* *
* *
* *
* *
```

Here is a simple intuitive function that displays an F.

```
//Print letter F function
void PrintLetterF()
{
    Stars(8);
    Stars(8);
    Stars(2);
    Stars(4);
    Stars(4);
    Stars(2);
    Stars(2);
    Stars(2);
    Stars(2);
}
```

You can see where we are going. Imagine creating a function for every letter. Think about how you would implement that. Would it be as easy as it seems? We don't think so. Letters like F, E, T, L, C, and I would be easy to implement using our existing function. However, letters like O, P, and D would not work given only the **Stars** function.

Observe the letter O:

```
* * * * * * *
* * * * * * *
* *       * *
* *       * *
* *       * *
* *       * *
* *       * *
* * * * * * *
* * * * * * *
```

You might be tempted to start writing the program with two lines of eight stars, but then what would you do about the spaces in-between the stars? We need to create the following two functions:

```
//Space function
void Space()
{
    cout<<' ';
}


//Spaces function
void Spaces(int PNumSpaces)
{
 int LoopCounter;

 for(LoopCounter=0; LoopCounter<PNumSpaces; LoopCounter++)
    Space();
 cout<<endl;
}
```

With these functions implemented you might think we're set to write the **PrintLetterO()** function as follows:

```
//Print letter O function
void PrintLetterO()
{
    Stars(8);
    Stars(8);
    Stars(2);Spaces(4);Stars(2);
    Stars(2);Spaces(4);Stars(2);
    Stars(2);Spaces(4);Stars(2);
    Stars(2);Spaces(4);Stars(2);
    Stars(2);Spaces(4);Stars(2);
    Stars(8);
    Stars(8);
}
```

However, if you execute the previous version of **PrintLetterO** function, the output would be as follows:

```
*******
*******
**

**
**

**
**

**
**

**
**

**
*******
*******
```

It hardly looks like the letter O. What happened? We have a carriage return at the end of the functions **Stars** and **Spaces**. Therefore, the carriage return is causing the lines to split into separate lines. However, we can't simply remove the carriage return because we need it at the end of each line. The solution is to modify the **Stars** function so that it takes a parameter indicating whether or not a carriage return should be output. Observe the rewritten **Stars** function.

```
void Stars(int PNumStars, bool PCarriageReturn)
{
    int LoopCounter;

    for(LoopCounter=0; LoopCounter<PNumStars; LoopCounter++)
      Star();
    if (PCarriageReturn)
      cout<<endl;
}
```

To correct all the problems we must also fix the function **Spaces()**. However, we do not need to add a parameter to this function. Since we are going to use spaces in between **Stars**, there is no case in our programming requirements where we would require a carriage return to be printed; therefore we can take it out of the function entirely. The new function **Spaces()** would be written as follows:

```
void Spaces(int PNumSpaces)
{
    int LoopCounter;

    for(LoopCounter=0; LoopCounter<PNumSpaces; LoopCounter++)
        Space();
}
```

Now the **PrinterLetterF()** and **PrintLetterO()** functions would look like the following:

```
void PrintLetterF()
{
    Stars(5, true);
    Stars(5, true);
    Stars(2, true);
    Stars(3, true);
    Stars(3, true);
    Stars(2, true);
    Stars(2, true);
    Stars(2, true);
    Stars(2, true);
}

void PrintLetterO()
{
    Stars(8, true);
    Stars(8, true);
    Stars(2, false);Spaces(4);Stars(2, true);
    Stars(2, false);Spaces(4);Stars(2, true);
    Stars(2, false);Spaces(4);Stars(2, true);
    Stars(2, false);Spaces(4);Stars(2, true);
    Stars(2, false);Spaces(4);Stars(2, true);
    Stars(8, true);
    Stars(8, true);
}
```

Obviously, if we had known the intent of the functions from the beginning, then we would have had an easier time writing the functions. So let's ask ourselves what we really want to do with these functions.

It is easy to see how we could create a function for each letter in the alphabet. I once proposed to my class that we should write a program to create a banner. Just imagine your boss comes into your office and gives you tickets to tonight's hockey game. So you want to make a banner and you have only five minutes. With the program written properly, we could use our letter functions to print a banner with whatever we want on it.

Try writing a main routine calling the letter functions that we would create. Seems easy enough. Imagine we want to say "Go Flyers." Your main routine might look like:

```
void main()
{
    PrintLetterG();
    PrintLetterO();
    PrintLetterSpace();   //Note, haven't implemented
    PrintLetterF();       //all these functions
    PrintLetterL();
    PrintLetterY();
    PrintLetterE();
    PrintLetterR();
    PrintLetterS();
}
```

Except if you run it, instead of seeing the following:

```
* * * * * * *   * * * * * * *     * * * * * * *   * *         * *       * *   * * * * * * *   * * * * * *     * * * * * *
* * * * * * *   * * * * * * *     * * * * * * *   * *         * *       * *   * * * * * * *   * * * * * *     * * * * * * *
* *       * *   * *       * *     * *             * *         * *       * *   * *             * *     * *     * *
* *             * *       * *     * * * *         * *         * *       * *   * * * *         * *     * *     * *
* *   * * * *   * *       * *     * * * *         * *         * * * * * * * * * * * *         * * * * * * *   * * * * * * *
* *   * * * *   * *       * *     * *             * *         * * * * * * * * * *             * * * * * * *   * * * * * * *
* *       * *   * *       * *     * *             * *                   * *     * *           * *     * * *             * *
* * * * * * *   * * * * * * *     * *             * * * * * * *         * *     * * * * * * *   * *       * * *   * * * * * * *
* * * * * * *   * * * * * * *     * *             * * * * * * *         * *     * * * * * * *   * *       * * *   * * * * * * *
```

we will get the something similar to the following:

```
* * * * * * *
* * * * * * *
* *       * *
* *
* *   * * * *
* *   * * * *
* *       * *
* * * * * * *
* * * * * * *
* * * * * * *
* * * * * * *
* *       * *
* *       * *
* *       * *
* *       * *
* *       * *
* * * * * * *
* * * * * * *

etc...
```

The problem is simple, once we understand it. We said that we wanted a carriage return after every line, but we really want a carriage return only after the last letter of each line. We also want a space to print out after each letter.

PROGRAMMER'S NOTEBOOK

Once again we have problems because we started coding before we thought through the entire problem. This is one of the most common mistakes in programming. You must think the entire problem through before you even start to write the program.

Let's stop then and define the entire problem. We want to write a banner printing program that we can modify easily to change the expression printed. We will write the program so the output is displayed on the computer screen, but it could be redirected to a printer easily.

The final question that remains is how can we get each letter to print in a row without the carriage return appearing between each letter?

It's simple: Display the first line of the first letter, then the first line of the second letter, and continue with all the letters of the phrase. Then repeat the process with the second line of each letter. Finally, repeat the process with each of the remaining lines.

To accomplish this we need to modify our **PrintLetter** functions to except a parameter to indicate the line number and then create a loop from 1 to the number of lines.

```
//Main routine to print banner
void main()
{
    int LineCounter;

    for(LineCounter=1;LineCounter<=8;LineCounter++)
    {
        PrintLetterG(LineCounter, false);
        PrintLetterO(LineCounter, false);
        PrintLetterSpace(LineCounter, false);
        PrintLetterF(LineCounter, false);
        PrintLetterL(LineCounter, false);
        PrintLetterY(LineCounter, false);
        PrintLetterE(LineCounter, false);
        PrintLetterR(LineCounter, false);
        PrintLetterS(LineCounter, true);
    }
}
```

We also need to rewrite the **PrintLetter** functions. So now the **PrintLetter** function would look like:

```
//Updated print letter 0 function
void PrintLetter0(int Line, bool CarriageReturn)
{
   switch (Line)
   {
     case 1:
       Stars(8,CarriageReturn);
       break;
     case 2:
       Stars(8, CarriageReturn);
       break;
     case 3:
       Stars(2, false);
       Spaces(4);
       Stars(2, CarriageReturn);
       break;
     case 4:
       Stars(2, false);
       Spaces(4);
       Stars(2, CarriageReturn);
       break;
     case 5:
       Stars(2, false);
       Spaces(4);
       Stars(2, CarriageReturn);
       break;
     case 6:
       Stars(2, false);
       Spaces(4);
       Stars(2, CarriageReturn);
       break;
     case 7:
       Stars(8, CarriageReturn);
       break;
     case 8:
       Stars(8, CarriageReturn);
       break;
   }
}
```

Two more modifications can be made to the program to improve its versatility. One is to add a size parameter. The size parameter would indicate a scale for the letters to be displayed. This is a little more complicated than it sounds. It is easy to expand the letters horizontally. We could simply pass the size parameter to the **Stars** function and add a loop around the **Stars** to call **Star** the same number of times as the size. However, to increase the size vertically, we would need to call the **PrintLetter** function with size times for each line of the letter.

Another modification is to have the **PrintLetter** functions display the letter composed of the character of that letter instead of the '*' character. We leave these implementations as an exercise.

```
GGGGGGGG  OOOOOOOO    FFFFFFFF  LL            YY      YY  EEEEEEE  RRRRRRR      SSSSSSS
GGGGGGGG  OOOOOOOO    FFFFFFFF  LL            YY      YY  EEEEEEE  RRRRRRR      SSSSSSS
GG    GG  OO    OO    FF        LL            YY      YY  EE       RR    RR     SS
GG        OO    OO    FFFF      LL            YY      YY  EEEE     RR    RR     SS
GG  GGGG  OO    OO    FFFF      LL            YYYYYYYYY   EEEE     RRRRRRR      SSSSSSS
GG  GGGG  OO    OO    FF        LL            YYYYYYYYY   EE       RRRRRRR      SSSSSSS
GG    GG  OO    OO    FF        LL                YY      EE       RR   RRR          SS
GGGGGGGG  OOOOOOOO    FF        LLLLLLLL          YY      EEEEEEE  RR     RRR   SSSSSSS
GGGGGGGG  OOOOOOOO    FF        LLLLLLLL          YY      EEEEEEE  RR     RRR   SSSSSSS
```

Here's another example of a program we can develop that may seem simple in its definition, but requires some thought to develop an elegant solution. Create a function that will accept a purchase price and an amount paid as parameters. The function should output the change due to the person in the highest denominations of the bills and change. Assume that you can give change in denominations of $100, $50, $20, $10, $5, 1, 25 cents, 10 cents, 5 cents, and 1 cent.

So if the function **MakeChange** is given $511.13 as the price and $1000.00 as the amount paid, the output should be the denominations required to give a total of $488.87 in change. The output would be as follows:

```
4    $100 bills
1    $50 bill
1    $20 bill
1    $10 bill
1    $5 bill
3    $1 bills
3    quarters
1    dime
2    pennies
```

What strategy should we employ to solve this problem? We need to figure out how many of the largest of each denomination we can return. Look at the following code and then the explanation for a clear concise solution to our problem.

```cpp
//Make change program
#include <iostream.h>
#include <stdlib.h>

//Prototypes
void PrintBills(double & TotalChange, double Denomination);
void MakeChange(double PurchasePrice, double AmountPaid);

//Main routine
void main()
{
    MakeChange(511.13, 1000.00);
}

//Make change function
void MakeChange(double PurchasePrice, double AmountPaid)
{
    double TotalChange=AmountPaid-PurchasePrice;
    PrintBills(TotalChange, 100);
    PrintBills(TotalChange, 50);
    PrintBills(TotalChange, 20);
    PrintBills(TotalChange, 10);
    PrintBills(TotalChange, 5);
    PrintBills(TotalChange, 1);
    PrintBills(TotalChange, .25);
    PrintBills(TotalChange, .1);
    PrintBills(TotalChange, .05);
    PrintBills(TotalChange, .01);
}

//Print bills function
void PrintBills(double & TotalChange, double Denomination)
{
    int NumBills=(int)(TotalChange/Denomination);
```

```
TotalChange-=Denomination*NumBills;

if (NumBills > 0)
{
    if (Denomination >= 1)
cout<<NumBills<<" $"<<Denomination<<" bill";
    else
    {
        if (Denomination == .25)
          cout<<NumBills<<" quarter";
        else if (Denomination == 0.10)
          cout<<NumBills<<" dime";
        else if (Denomination == .05)
          cout<<NumBills<<"nickle";
        else if ((Denomination == .01) && (NumBills == 1))
          cout<<NumBills<<" penny";
        else
          cout<<NumBills<<" pennie";
    }

    if (NumBills > 1)
      cout<<'s';
    cout<<endl;
}
}
```

The previous program is broken down into two functions. The first, **MakeChange**, is the main routine. It accepts a purchase price and the amount paid, and outputs the correct change. Instead of complicating **MakeChange**, we call a support function called **PrintBills**. **PrintBills** does the real work. Once we calculate the amount of change required, **MakeChange** calls **PrintBills** with each denomination that we can give as change. **PrintBills** then outputs the amount given for that denomination and reduces the amount of change remaining to be given by said amount.

   PrintBills calculates the largest number of the current denomination by converting the result of the division to an integer. Since the calculation returns an integer value, it can be used directly as the amount of that denomination. Then the rest of the function simply selects the proper wording for that denomination.

5.6 PASS BY REFERENCE

Now that we have written some fairly complicated functions, let's try to write a simple function called **Swap**. **Swap** should expect two parameters, let's say, integers. It should switch the two parameters so that the values of the parameters are swapped.

So if we have the following code:

```
int Value1=5;

int Value2=3;

swap(Value1,Value2);

cout<<"Value 1 = "<<Value1<<" Value 2 = "<<Value2<<endl;
```

the output would be as follows:

```
Value 1 = 3 Value 2 = 5
```

How can we write this? Functions accept parameters that are copies of the original values. They can return a single value, but we need to change two values. Fortunately, C++, not C, provides a way to allow the parameters we pass to a function to retain their changes after the function call. This is called **pass by reference**.

To pass a value by reference means that if a change is made to that variable during the function, the variable that was passed as a parameter retains the change even after the function call.

This is accomplished by using an **&** operator in between the type of the parameter and the parameter name. See the following definition of the **Swap** function:

```
//Swap function
void Swap(int & Value1, int & Value2)
{
    int TempValue;

    TempValue=Value1;
    Value1=Value2;
    Value2=TempValue;
}
```

Swap works because **Value1** and **Value2** have their values swapped within the function, and because of the **&** operator in the parameter list, the changes are remembered.

PROGRAMMER'S NOTEBOOK

If you look back to the `PrintBills` function in the previous example, you will see that we snuck in an & for the `TotalChange` parameter. This allowed us to remember the side effects we programmed into the `PrintBills` function. You could write the function without this, but the implementation would not be as clean.

■ DRILLS

To see if you truly understand the concept of call by reference, observe the following example:

Drill 5-6

```
//Drill 5-6

#include <iostream.h>
#include <stdlib.h>

//Mystery function to test pass by reference
void Mystery(int Param1, int & Param2)
{
    Param1=Param1*5;
    Param2=Param2*2;
    cout<<Param1<<' '<<Param2<<endl;
}

void main()
{
    int Value1=1;
    int Value2=3;
    Mystery(Value1,Value2);
    cout<<Value1<<' '<<Value2<<endl;
}
```

What is the output of the following code?

Drill 5-7

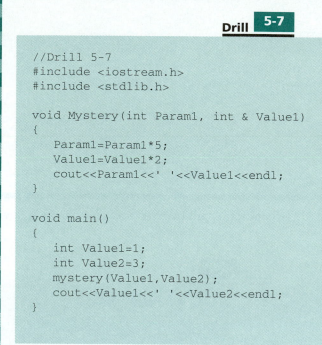

```
//Drill 5-7
#include <iostream.h>
#include <stdlib.h>

void Mystery(int Param1, int & Value1)
{
    Param1=Param1*5;
    Value1=Value1*2;
    cout<<Param1<<' '<<Value1<<endl;
}

void main()
{
    int Value1=1;
    int Value2=3;
    mystery(Value1,Value2);
    cout<<Value1<<' '<<Value2<<endl;
}
```

5.7 DECISION-MAKING FUNCTIONS

Functions are a great way of making decisions. We can either use a return value of 1 if the decision is true, or a 0 if the decision is false. If you are using a modern C++ compiler you can also return **true** or **false**. This is done by specifying the return type as **bool**. A **bool** (short for Boolean) is another variable type in C++. It can contain either the value **true** or **false**. If either of these methods are employed, then the function can be called inside an **if** statement, just like any other expression.

Let's write a function to tell whether of not a number is evenly divisible by another number (i.e., the second number can be divided into the first without a remainder).

```
//Divisible program
#include <stdlib.h>
#include <iostream.h>

//Prototypes
bool Divisible(int Value1, int Value2);

//Divisible function
bool Divisible(int Value1, int Value2)
{
    if ((Value1 % Value2) == 0)
      return true;
    else
      return false;
}



void main()
{
    if (Divisible(10,3))
      cout<<"The Numbers are divisible\n";
    else
      cout<<"The Numbers are not divisible\n";
}
```

The previous function works by making a single comparison. It computes the remainder of the two parameters using the % operator, and then compares that remainder to 0. If the remainder equals 0, then the function returns true; otherwise, it will return false. A function like this can be called inside an **if** statement, because its return value will be either true or false.

How about writing a function to tell if a number is prime? A prime number is a number that is divisible only by 1 and itself.

```
bool Prime(int Value)
{
 int LoopCounter;

for(LoopCounter=2;LoopCounter<Value;LoopCounter++)
      if (Divisible(Value, LoopCounter))
        return false;
    return true;
}
```

This function relies on the divisible function that we just wrote. By creating a simple **for** loop from two to one less than the number we are checking, to see if it is prime, we can simply call the **Divisible** function for each number. If any of the calls to **Divisible** return **true**, then the number is not prime and we return **false**. Otherwise, if we terminate the loop properly, we know the number is prime and therefore return true.

Let's write a function that returns the amount of numbers by which a number is divisible. Assume positive numbers are all that we are checking.

```
//Check for the number of values divisible by
bool NumberDivisible(int Value)
{
    int Count=0;
    int LoopCounter;
    for(LoopCounter=2; LoopCounter<Value; LoopCounter++)
        if (Divisible(Value, LoopCounter))
            Count++;

    return Count;
}
```

The previous function is not very different from the prime number function. The only change we needed to make was to declare a variable that stores the number of divisible numbers we have found so far, and to increment it each time the divisible function returns true.

If a function is declared to have a return type, then the function must have a return statement. If the function does not, you would receive a compiler error. This is why we placed a void for the return type in front of the **main** routine. Without void, the **main** function would default to returning an integer. Then, to satisfy the compiler we would have to place the statement **return** **0** at the end of the **main** function. Although this is a common practice, we chose not to do so because we thought it might add confusion in earlier chapters.

5.8 Case Study

Problem Description

An entrepreneur's business has expanded so much that employees are assigned an employee number for identification and taxes must be withheld. Overtime is now paid at 1.5 times the hourly wage for any employee working more than 40 hours per week. Write a program that calculates a worker's weekly pay formatted to show each decimal amount formatted to two decimal places. Test your program for an input of odd, even, and fractional hours. Your program input should consist of the employee's ID, the hours worked, the employee's tax rate, and each employee's hourly pay. This input should be accomplished via a single function successively called for each input. Output for each employee should show gross pay, taxes withheld, and net pay, with each of these values being tilled. The program should have a minimum of five functions and run continuously until terminated by the operator, at which time the sum of all gross wages, taxes withheld, and net pay for that week should be displayed.

Discussion

This problem specifies a minimum number of functions to encourage students to break their program into small, easily understood pieces. The constraint of forcing all inputs to be done via a single function called successively for each input is designed to provide an example of "write once, call many." Duplicate code in a program should be vehemently discouraged. The usage of separate functions for headers, lines, and footers, though not strictly necessary for this problem, is done to develop the habit for future problems. Setting the **fixed** flag is necessary for this problem since weekly pay, particularly with overtime, may exceed 999.99. Failure to set this flag would cause the large number to be displayed in exponential notation. A safety feature is built in to the **CalculateTax** function. The prompt says enter a rate—a decimal; however, if a whole number is used, it is divided by 100. The **cin.get()** function is used to keep the output window open, so results may be seen immediately. Accumulators are used for all totals for clarity, even though the accumulator for net pay is not necessary.

Solution

```
#include <stdlib.h>
#include <iostream.h>
#include <iomanip.h>

#define StdWeek 40
#define Convert (float) 100.00

//Prototypes
float GetValue(int Number);
float CalculateGross(float Gross, float TaxRate);
float CalculateTax(float Gross, float TaxRate);
void Prompt(int Index);
void DisplayHeader();
void DisplayLine( int Num, float GrossPay, float Tax, float NetPay);
void DisplayFooter(float GrossPay, float Tax, float NetPay);
```

5.8 Case Study (continued)

```cpp
void main()
{
   int EmployeeNumber;
   float Hours,TaxRate,Tax,Wage,Gross,NetPay;
   float TotalGross = 0.0, TotalTax = 0.0, TotalNet = 0.0;
   do
   {
      EmployeeNumber = int(GetValue(1));
      if (EmployeeNumber <= 0)
         break;
      Hours = GetValue(2);
      Wage = GetValue(3);
      TaxRate = GetValue(4);
      Gross = CalculateGross(Hours,Wage);
      Tax = CalculateTax(Gross,TaxRate);
      NetPay = Gross - Tax;
      DisplayHeader();
      DisplayLine(EmployeeNumber,Gross,Tax,NetPay);
      TotalGross += Gross;
      TotalTax += Tax;
      TotalNet += NetPay;
   } while(EmployeeNumber > 0);

   DisplayFooter(TotalGross, TotalTax, TotalNet);
}

float GetValue(int Number)
{
   float Value;
   Prompt(Number);
   cin >> Value;
   return Value;
}

void Prompt(int Index)
{
   switch(Index)
   {
      case 1:
         cout << "\nEnter negative to end or ";
         cout << "\nEnter employee\'s ID -> ";
         break;
      case 2:
         cout << "Enter employee\'s hours -> ";
         break;
      case 3:
         cout << "Enter employee\'s wage rate -> ";
         break;
      case 4:
         cout << "Enter employee\'s tax rate -> ";
         break;
   }
}
```

```cpp
float CalculateGross(float Hours, float Wage)
{
    float Gross, OverTime;

    if (Hours > StdWeek)
      OverTime = Hours - StdWeek;
    else
      OverTime = 0.0;

    Gross = (Wage * Hours) + (OverTime * (float).5 * Wage);
    return Gross;
}

float CalculateTax(float Gross, float TaxRate)
{
    float Tax;

    if (TaxRate > 1)
      TaxRate = TaxRate/Convert;

    Tax = Gross * TaxRate;
    return Tax;
}
void DisplayHeader()
{
    cout << endl <<"EMP NUM    GROSS PAY      TAX          NET PAY"<<endl;
    cout << setiosflags(ios::showpoint | ios :: fixed)<< setprecision(2);
}

void DisplayLine(int Num, float GrossPay, float Tax, float NetPay)
{
    cout << setw(6) << Num << setw(14) << GrossPay << setw(11)
        << Tax << setw(13) << NetPay;
    cout << endl<<endl<<"Press the Enter key to continue .... ";
    cin.get();cin.get();
}

void DisplayFooter(float GrossPay, float Tax, float NetPay)
{
  cout << endl <<"            GROSS PAY      TAX          NET PAY"<<endl;
  cout << endl <<"TOTALS" << setw(13) << GrossPay << setw(11)
        << Tax << setw(13) << NetPay;
  cout << endl<<endl<<"Press the Enter key to continue .... ";
  cin.get();cin.get();
}
```

5.8 Case Study (continued)

Output

```
Enter employee's ID -> 10101
Enter employee's hours -> 60
Enter employee's wage rate -> 18.60
Enter employee's tax rate -> .33

EMP NUM      GROSS PAY        TAX        NET PAY
 10101         1302.00      429.66       872.34

Press the Enter key to continue ....

Enter negative to end or
Enter employee's ID -> 10103
Enter employee's hours -> 40
Enter employee's wage rate -> 7.85
Enter employee's tax rate -> 20

EMP NUM      GROSS PAY        TAX        NET PAY
 10103          314.00       62.80       251.20

Press the Enter key to continue ....

Enter negative to end or
Enter employee's ID -> -9

             GROSS PAY        TAX        NET PAY

TOTALS         1616.00      492.46      1123.54

Press the Enter key to continue ....
```

◆ Key Terms

Function	A modular piece of code used to organize a program into readable maintainable parts.
Local variable	A variable that is defined within a function or set of curly braces. It is visible only within the area in which it was defined.
Global variable	A variable that is visible to the entire program. Use of a global variable should be avoided whenever possible.
Parameter	A variable that accepts a value from a function that calls it.
Pass by value	A method of passing a variable where a copy of the original value is used by the function. Any changes made to this copy do not affect the original value.
Pass by reference	A method of passing a variable where a reference to the original value is used by the function. Any changes made to this reference are reflected in the original value.
Prototype	A declaration indicating the interface of a function.
Return value	The value passed back from a function to the function that called it.
Scope	The visibility of a variable to the program.

◆ C++ Keywords Introduced

&	An operator used to indicate a parameter is passed by reference.
bool	A variable that stores either true or false.

◆ Answers to Drills

Drill 5-1

int FirstDrill(int DrillParam1, float DrillParam2);

Drill 5-2

void SecondDrill(bool DrillParam1);

Drill 5-3

bool ThirdDrill(float DrillParam1, int DrillParam2, char DrillParam3);

Drill 5-4

The results are as follows:

```
2       3       1
2       5
2       2       1
```

The main routine starts by initializing **Value1** to 1, **Value2** to 2, and **Value3** to 3. Then those values are output in the order **Value2**, **Value3**, and **Value1**. Then the function **Mystery** is called with the value 1. Once inside **Mystery**, the parameter **Value1** contains the value 1. The variables **Value2** and **Value3** are declared locally within the **Mystery** function. These variables have nothing to do with the **Value2** and **Value3** that were defined in the **main** function. **Value2** is initialized to **Value1*2** or 2. **Value3** is initialized to 5. The **cout** statement is executed and 2 and 5 are output. Then value of **Value1** is then changed to 2 and returned from the function. Remember however, that the parameter **Value1** is what is changing, not the variable defined in **main**. The **Mystery** function terminates and execution continues in the **main** with the final **cout** statement. The value of **Value2** and **Value1** are exactly what they were before the function was called. The value of **Value3** is not, because we set the variable **Value3** in the **main** function to the return value from **Mystery**.

By having the names of variables and parameters the same, we can set ourselves up for a good bit of confusion. To avoid this, a good convention is to start all global variables with a G, all local variables with an L, and all parameters with a P. This way there is little overlap.

Drill 5-5

The results are as follows:

```
1       2       3
2       4       50
1       4       3
```

The main routine starts by initializing **Value1** to 1, **Value2** to 2, and **Value3** to 3. Then those values are output in the order **Value1**, **Value2**, and **Value3**. Then the function **Mystery** is called with the value 1. Once inside **Mystery**, the parameter **Value1** contains the value 1. The variable **Value3** is declared locally within the **Mystery** function and is not related to the **Value3** declared in the **main** function. **Value2** is initialized to **Value2*2** or 4. **Value3** is initialized to 50. The **cout** statement is executed and 2, 4, and 50 are output. Nothing is returned from the function, but we leave the function and return to the **main** function. When **Value1** was changed it was the local copy that was changed. The global value did not change, but the global value of **Value2** did change, since it was not declared locally. Finally, **Value3** was declared locally, so it was changed and remained local to the function as well.

Drill 5-6

The output would be:

```
5 6
1 6
```

Let's trace through the program. 1 and 3 are passed to the **Mystery** function as **Param1** and **Param2**, respectively. **Param1** is multiplied by 5 and stored back in **Param1**. **Param2** is multiplied by 2 and stored back in **Param2**. Then **Param1** and **Param2** are output as 5 and 6 from within the function. When we leave **Mystery** the changed value of **Param2** is retained, but the changed value of **Param1** is not. So the 1 (the original main value of **Value1**) is retained, while the 6 that was the changed value of **Value2** is stored in the variable **Value2**.

Drill 5-7

The output would be as follows:

```
5 6
1 6
```

That one was a little confusing, wasn't it? The confusion is caused because a parameter and a variable in **main** are both called **Value1**. This should not matter, if you trace the program carefully.

A copy of **Value1**, 1, is passed to **Mystery** as the parameter **Param1**. A reference to **Value2** is passed to **Mystery** as the parameter **Value1**. Since the **&** is in front of the **Value1**, whatever the final value of **Value1** is in **Mystery** will also be the final value of **Value2** in the **main** function.

The first output is easy, as 1 is multiplied by 5, and 3 is multiplied by 2. When we return to the **main** function, the variable **Value1** retains its original value, whereas the variable **Value2** retains the updated value of **Value1** from the function **Mystery**.

◆ Programming Exercises

1. Write a function called **Middle** that returns the middle value of three integers that are passed as parameters.

2. Rewrite the calculator program so that each operation is performed by a function call. Each function should accept two floating point numbers as parameters and return the result as a floating point number.

3. Write a program that declares a function accepting two parameters. The first parameter is a floating pointer number and the second parameter is an integer. The program should multiply the floating point number by itself the number of times indicated by the integer. The function should return the final product back to the main function. The main routine should ask the user for the floating point number and integer. It should then call the function and store the result in a variable. Finally, the main routine should output the returned value stored in the variable.

4. Develop a complete banner system with all the letters of the alphabet implemented. Use the examples in this chapter as a start by building a function for each letter in the alphabet. Then create a function that calls the individual letter functions to spell out a phrase.

5. Modify the system that you developed so that it has additional features. The **PrintLetter?** function should take a new parameter. The parameter, PSize, should be an integer and indicate a scale for the letter. This way if you want to print really large letters, you can simply enter the number 10, and a letter ten times as large is printed. In addition, allow the user to indicate a character to be used instead of the '*'. Whatever character the user enters should be used to display the letter.

6. Write a program that accepts two integers. Create a function that tells whether the first integer is a multiple of the second. Hint: use the mod (%) operator.

◆ Additional Exercises

1. For each of the following descriptions, write a prototype:

   a. A function called **Function1** that has no parameters and returns an integer.
   b. A function called **Function2** that has no parameters and no return value.
   c. A function called **ReturnInteger** that has an integer parameter called **Value** followed by a floating point value called **Number**. The function also returns an integer.
   d. A function called **NewFunction** that accepts a floating point number called **Number** and an integer called **Number2**. The function also returns a floating point number.

2. Does the following code compile and run without error?

```
#include <stdlib.h>
#include <iostream.h>

void Function1();
void Function2();

void main()
{
   Function1()
}

void Function1()
{
   Function2()
}

void Function2()
{
   cout<<"print me";
}
```

3. Does the following code work correctly?

```
#include <stdlib.h>
#include <iostream.h>

void Function1()
{
 Function2()
}

void Function2()
{
 cout<<"print me";
}

void main()
{
 Function1()
}
```

4. Circle the variable definitions that are global in the following example.

```
#include <stdlib.h>
#include <iostream.h>

int Global1;
int Global2;

int Function2;
void Function1()
{
 int Global1;
}

int Function4;
int Function3()
{
 float Global1, Global2;
}

void main()
{
 int Global3;
 int Global4;
}
```

5. For each of the following function calls, use the following program and state whether the call to the particular function is valid, and if so, indicate the output.

```
#include <iostream.h>
#include <stdlib.h>

void Function3(int Value1, int Value2);
void Function2(int Value1);
void Function1();

int Value1 = 0;
int Value2 = 2;

void Function1()
{
 cout<<Value1<<endl<<Value2;
}


void Function2(int Value1)
{
 cout<<Value1<<endl<<Value2;
}


void Function3(int Value1, int Value2)
{
 cout<<Value1<<endl<<Value2;
}


void main()
{
 //Function call goes here
}
```

    a.   Function1();
    b.   Function2(2, 0);
    c.   Function1(2);
    d.   Function3(3,4);
    e.   Function1(3.2);
    f.   Function3(5);

6. Can an integer parameter be passed to a function that is expected to return a Boolean value?

7. Show the value of the variable **Value** at each call for the following function:

```
int Function1( int Value )
{
   if (Value>10)
   {
     cout<<Value;
     Function1(Value - 5);
   }
   else if (Value>5)
   {
     cout<<Value;
     Function1(Value - 2);
   }
   else if (Value>0)
   {
     cout<<Value;
     Function1(Value - 1);
   }
}
```

    a.   Function1(23);
    b.   Function1(17);
    c.   Function1(7);
    d.   Function1(1);
    e.   Function1(0);

8. What would be the output of the following program?

```
#include <iostream.h>
#include <stdlib.h>

int Function1(int Value1, int Value2)
int Function2(int & Value1, int Value2);
int Function3(int & Value1, int & Value2);
int Function4(int Value1, int & Value2);

int Function1(int Value1, int Value2)
{
   Value1 = 2;
   Value2 = 4;
   cout<<Value1<<endl<<Value2;
}

int Function2(int & Value1, int Value2)
{
   Value1 = 7;
   Value2 = 8;
   cout<<Value1<<endl<<Value2;
}
```

```
int Function3(int & Value1, int & Value2)
{
  Value1 = 3;
  Value2 = 3;
  cout<<Value1<<endl<<Value2;
}

int Function4(int Value1, int & Value2)
{
  Value1 = Value2;
  Value2 = Value1;
  cout<<Value1<<endl<<Value2;
}

void main ()
{
  int Value2;
  int Value1;
  Value2 = 1;
  Value1 = 0;
  cout<<Value1<<endl<< Value2;
  Function1(Value2, Value1);
  cout<<Value1<<endl<< Value2;
  Function2(Value2, Value1);
  cout<<Value1<<endl<< Value2;
  Function3(Value2, Value1);
  cout<<Value1<<endl<< Value2;
  Function4(Value2, Value1);
  cout<<Value1<<endl<< Value2;
}
```

CHAPTER

6

Simple Arrays

Chapter Objectives

- ♦ Introduce a way to store more than one value in a variable
- ♦ Introduce single dimensional arrays
- ♦ Explain how to declare arrays
- ♦ Explain how to initialize arrays
- ♦ Explain how to access arrays
- ♦ Explain how to pass arrays as parameters to functions
- ♦ Introduce multidimensional arrays

ave you noticed that so far we only have tracked one of everything in the programs we have written? What would you do if you were asked to write a program that tracked ten grades for a student? So far we have written similar programs, but the key difference was that we were not asked to track more than one grade at a time. It is simple to track a grade and the sum of grades, but how would you write a program that read ten grades from the user, summed them up, and then displayed all the grades along with the sum? The only way to accomplish this, given what we currently know, is to create a function with ten variables, one for each grade, and to write the program as follows:

```
//Example grade calculation without arrays

#include <stdlib.h>
#include <iostream.h>

void main()
{
    int Grade1, Grade2, Grade3, Grade4, Grade5;
    int Grade6, Grade7, Grade8, Grade9, Grade10;
    int Sum=0;
```

215

```
    cin>>Grade1;
    cin>>Grade2;
    cin>>Grade3;
    cin>>Grade4;
    cin>>Grade5;
    cin>>Grade6;
    cin>>Grade7;
    cin>>Grade8;
    cin>>Grade9;
    cin>>Grade10;

    Sum=Grade1 + Grade2 + Grade3 + Grade4 +
        Grade5 + Grade6 + Grade7 + Grade8 +
        Grade9 + Grade10;

    cout<<"The average of the following Grades = "
        <<Sum/10<<endl;

    cout<<Grade1<<endl;
    cout<<Grade2<<endl;
    cout<<Grade3<<endl;
    cout<<Grade4<<endl;
    cout<<Grade5<<endl;
    cout<<Grade6<<endl;
    cout<<Grade7<<endl;
    cout<<Grade8<<endl;
    cout<<Grade9<<endl;
    cout<<Grade10<<endl;
}
```

6.1 DECLARING AN ARRAY

That was a lot of typing—imagine how long the program would be if you were asked to enter 100 numbers. Clearly a better way must exist. Fortunately for us, one does. It is called an **array**. An array works similarly to any other variable. It follows the same naming convention as regular variables, except it requires an index to indicate which value in the array that you wish to access.

You can think of an array and its individual values as similar to calling a friend who has a fancy answering machine. The machine would have different mail boxes for each person in the house: 0 for Bill, 1 for Jerome, 2 for Kordell, etc. You call the house with a single phone number, just as you will reference an array with a single variable name. Then to access the individual people in the house, you use an **index**; so will you access the individual elements in an array, by using an **index**.

An array is declared as follows:

```
VariableType VariableName[Size];
```

If you want to declare (allocate) an array of 10 integers called **Grades**, you can do so as follows:

```
int Grades[10];
```

To access an individual value in an array, you place the subscript of the value you wish to access in between the brackets. Index values are from 0, the lower bound to the size of the array −1. This is one of the most confusing aspects of arrays.

Observe how the array **Grades** would appear graphically:

Array Grades

Index	0	1	2	3	4	5	6	7	8	9
Values	?	?	?	?	?	?	?	?	?	?

Initially, there are no values in the array **Grades**. Arrays in C++ are uninitialized unless the user specifies values to initialize them.

One way to set individual values in an array is as follows:

```
Grades[0]=100;
Grades[1]=99;
Grades[2]=97;
Grades[3]=99;
Grades[4]=100;
Grades[5]=98;
Grades[6]=97;
Grades[7]=95
Grades[8]=97;
Grades[9]=99;
```

Individual elements in an array can be set by specifying the index with brackets and then assigning the value you wish to place in the array in the same manner as setting any other variable.

Accessing values is equally easy. To display the first value, you would use the following code:

```
cout<<Grades[0];
```

To display the second value, you would use the following code:

```
cout<<Grades[1];
```

The last value in the array is the tenth value; you would use the following code:

```
cout<<Grades[9];
```

What would C++ do if you tried to print the eleventh value?

C++ assumes that you are smart, so it doesn't check that your operations are correct. C++ can operate quicker this way, but it can cause unpredictable results. When **Grades[10]** is accessed, you are accessing a value that is not part of the array. Therefore, whatever is stored in the memory location directly after the array will be accessed.

If you type **cout<<Grades[10]**, in most cases the worst that will happen is that you will print an erroneous value. However, if you type **Grades[10]=0**, you will store a zero directly after the array **Grades**. The potential problem with accessing memory incorrectly is that if another variable is stored there, it will be overwritten with a zero. This is obviously bad.

Well, enough about what not to do. Let's rewrite the program to read in 10 grades, but to show the power of arrays let's write it so that it reads in 100 grades.

```cpp
//Example grade calculation without arrays

#include <stdlib.h>
#include <iostream.h>

void main()
{
    int Grades[100];
    int Sum=0;
    int LoopCounter;

    for(LoopCounter=0;LoopCounter<100;LoopCounter++)
    {
        cin>>Grades[LoopCounter];
        Sum=Sum+Grades[LoopCounter];
    }

    cout<<"The grades you just entered are:"<<endl;
    for(LoopCounter=0;LoopCounter<100;LoopCounter++)
        cout<<Grades[LoopCounter]<<'\t';

    cout<<"Average = "<<Sum/100;
}
```

Although this program is not significantly smaller than the previous one, this version of the program handles 100 grades. If we rewrote the first version of the program to handle 100 grades, it would have grown immensely. If we wish to change this version of the program to 1000 grades, it would not require the source code to grow in size. All that would be required is to change the 100 to 1000 throughout the code.

However, as code grows, making sure that we replace all the 100s with 1000s can be burdensome and often leads to errors. Therefore, when dealing with arrays it is often useful to use the **define** statement to indicate the maximum size of the array. If you rewrite the previous program with a **define** for the array size, then subsequent changes to the array size need only occur in one location.

```cpp
//Example grade calculation without arrays
//but with a define

#include <stdlib.h>
#include <iostream.h>

#define MaxSize 10

void main()
{
    int Grades[MaxSize];
    int Sum=0;
    int LoopCounter;
    for(LoopCounter=0;LoopCounter<MaxSize;LoopCounter++)
    {
        cin>>Grades[LoopCounter];
        Sum=Sum+Grades[LoopCounter];
    }

   cout<<"The Grades you just entered are:"<<endl;
   for(LoopCounter=0;LoopCounter<MaxSize;LoopCounter++)
      cout<<Grades[LoopCounter]<<'\t';

   cout<<"Average = "<<Sum/MaxSize;
}
```

To help in understanding the relationship between the index and the position it holds in the array, type and run the following program. It stores the numbers 1 through 5 in an array of five integers.

```
//Example showing index locations clearly

#include <stdlib.h>
#include <iostream.h>

#define MaxSize 5

void main()
{
    int LoopCounter;
    int Values[MaxSize];
    values[0]=1;
    values[1]=2;
    values[2]=3;
    values[3]=4;
    values[4]=5;
    for(LoopCounter=0;LoopCounter<MaxSize;LoopCounter++)
      cout<<"The value at index = "<<LoopCounter<<" is "
        <<values[LoopCounter]<<endl;

}
```

The following is a graphical representation of how the array would appear after it has been initialized.

Array Values

Index	0	1	2	3	4
Values	1	2	3	4	5

As we stated earlier, array indexes start at 0, but our first number starts at 1, so the output would look like the following:

```
The value at index = 0 is 1
The value at index = 1 is 2
The value at index = 2 is 3
The value at index = 3 is 4
The value at index = 4 is 5
```

When there is no relationship between the index and the real world then there is no problem. However, what if we wanted to write a survey program that would count the number of responses. Each response is a number between 1 and 10.

If we create an array of ten values, then the first value would be stored in the zero index of the array, the second value would be stored in the one index of the array, and so on.

The program would look like the following:

```cpp
//Example of a rating program

#include <stdlib.h>
#include <iostream.h>

#define NumRatings 10
#define NumResponses 20

void main()
{
    int Rating[NumRatings]={0};//Initialize the entire array to zeros,
                            // a shortcut to be explained later.
    int LoopCounter;
    int Response;

    //Loop through 20 responses.
    for (LoopCounter=1; LoopCounter<=20;LoopCounter++)
    {
        cout<<"Enter your response"<<endl;
        cin>>Response;

        // Note without check it may work, but you can write over memory
        if (response < 1 || response > NumRatings)
          cout<<"Bad response: "<<response<<endl;
        else
          ++Rating[Response-1];
    }

    cout<<endl<<endl<<"Rating Number of responses"<<endl;
    cout<<"-------- --------------------"<<endl;

    for (LoopCounter = 0; LoopCounter<10;LoopCounter++)
      cout<<LoopCounter<<'\t'<<rating[LoopCounter-1]<<endl;
}
```

The program as written works perfectly fine; however, it is not as efficient as possible and is a little bit confusing.

First, notice that in order for the indexes of the array to line up, we must subtract 1 from each response. This slows the execution of the program down and seems nonintuitive. There is a simple solution to this problem. If we allocate the array to 11 values instead of 10, then we can store a response of 1 in index 1, a response of 2 in index 2, etc. See the following rewritten code as an improvement in both speed and clarity.

```
//Example of a more efficient rating program

#include <stdlib.h>
#include <iostream.h>

#define NumRatings 10
#define NumResponses 20

void main()
{
  //Initialize the entire array to zeros, now 11 items.
  int Rating[11]={0};
  int LoopCounter;
  int Response;

  //Loop through 20 responses.
  for (LoopCounter=1; LoopCounter<=NumResponses;LoopCounter++)
  {
    cout<<"Enter your response"<<endl;
    cin>>Response;

    // Note without check it may work, but you can write over memory
    if (Response < 1 || Response > 10)
      cout<<"Bad response: "<<Response<<endl;
    else
      ++Rating[Response];//No longer require subtraction!
  }
  cout<<endl<<endl<<"Rating Number of responses"<<endl;
  cout<<"------- --------------------"<<endl;

  //No longer require subtraction!
  for (LoopCounter = 1; LoopCounter<=10;LoopCounter++)
    cout<<LoopCounter<<'\t'<<Rating[LoopCounter]<<endl;
}
```

Although we have added an integer to the array, we have removed two subtraction commands and therefore have not increased the size of the program at all! This allows us to index the way we want to and efficiently reference the values.

Let's look at another example where we individually set array values. It is not only an excellent example of initializing, adding, and subtracting array values, but it is also an excellent example of what might happen if you do not initialize all the values of an array. Before you type the program, try to guess the output values.

```
//Example of incomplete initialization of an array

#include <stdlib.h>
#include <iostream.h>

#define MaxSize 10

void main()
{
    int Value[MaxSize];
    int LoopCounter;

    Value[0] = 197;
    Value[2] = -100;
    Value[5] = 350;
    Value[3] = Value[0]+Value[5];
    Value[9] = Value[5]/10;
    --Value[2];

    for(LoopCounter=0;LoopCounter<10;LoopCounter++)
        cout<<Value[LoopCounter]<<endl;
}
```

What is the output? There is no single correct answer because not every value in the array has been initialized. Only the 0, 2, 3, 5, and 9 values have been set. C++ assumes again that you know what you are doing and doesn't check. So whatever value was stored in memory the last time your computer used it will still be there. Often this value is 0, but you cannot count on it!

Here's what the output values would be. A '?' indicates that you cannot be sure of the result.

```
197
?
-1
547
?
350
?
?
?
35
```

6.2 ARRAY SHORTCUTS

So what can we do to initialize an array quickly? We could write a loop as follows, although it could waste a lot of execution time.

```
#define MaxSize 10

int LoopCounter;

for(LoopCounter=0;LoopCounter<MaxSize;LoopCounter++)
   Values[LoopCounter]=0;
```

A better way is to use a shorthand that C++ provides. See the following example as a way to initialize an array to 197, 0, –1, 547, 0, 350, 0, 0, 0, 35.

```
int Values[MaxSize]={197, 0, -1, 547, 0, 350, 0, 0, 0, 35};
```

However, this really doesn't seem to help if you had an array of 1000 items. If you need to specify all 1000 items, then you must list each value. After all, the computer cannot read your mind. Most of the time however, you may be initializing most of the values to 0. If this is the case, you can take advantage of a C++ feature that allows you to initialize the values that you want and then assume the rest are zero. The greatest aspect of this feature is that you do not have to do anything more than what was already mentioned. If you allocate an array larger than the number of values you initialize within the set of curly braces, then C++ assumes that since you have already initialized some values that you must want the rest of the values initialized as well. Therefore, C++ initializes the uninitialized values to 0.

Another shortcut that C++ provides allows the allocation of an array without specifying an exact size. This is handy if you are initializing many items and you do not wish to count up the number of items in between the curly braces.

The following example allocates an array of seven items from 1 through 7.

```
int Values[] = {1,2,3,4,5,6,7};
//This will allocate the array as if 7 had been placed in the [].
```

DRILLS

What is the output of the following code?

Drill 6-1

```
//Drill 6-1

#include <stdlib.h>
#include <iostream.h>

#define NumValues 10

void main()
{
    int Values[NumValues] = {5,-2,0,1};
    int LoopCounter;

    for(LoopCounter=0; LoopCounter<NumValues; LoopCounter++)
      cout<<Values[LoopCounter]<<endl;
}
```

What is the output of the following code?

Drill 6-2

```
//Drill 6-2

#include <stdlib.h>
#include <iostream.h>

#define NumValues 10

void main()
{
    int Values[] = {5,-2,0,1};
    int LoopCounter;

    for(int LoopCounter=0; LoopCounter<NumValues; LoopCounter++)
      cout<<Values[LoopCounter]<<endl;
}
```

A programmer must be careful to access only values within the bounds of an array. The lowest index accessible in an array is 0. This is considered the array's **lower bound**. The highest index accessible in an array is one less than the size of the array. This is considered the array's **upper bound**.

PROGRAMMER'S NOTEBOOK

It is important to note that you cannot copy the contents of one array to the other by using an = operator.

If you attempt to do this it will appear to work; however, a true copy is not made. Essentially the two arrays will point to the same values. If you displayed the values of both arrays you see the same values. To illustrate the problem with using an equal sign, simply change a value in the original array and redisplay both arrays. Though you would expect two different results, you will see one set of numbers repeated twice. Try executing the following code:

```cpp
//Example of improper copying of an array

#include <stdlib.h>
#include <iostream.h>

#define ArraySize 5

void main()
{
    int Source[ArraySize]={1,2,3,4,5};
    int Destination[ArraySize];
    int LoopCounter;

    //This does not copy the array Source to the array Destination.
    Destination=Source;

    //Output both arrays; both have the same values.
    for(LoopCounter=0;LoopCounter<5;LoopCounter++)
      cout<<"Source["<<LoopCounter<<"]="<<Source[LoopCounter]
        <<"\t Destination["<<LoopCounter<<"]="<<
        Destination[LoopCounter]<<endl;

    //Change the values of the Source array so that the two arrays no longer
    //are the same.
    Source[0]=10; Source[1]=11;
    Source[2]=12;
    Source[3]=13;
    Source[4]=14;

    //Output the arrays again; both contain the new values.

    for(LoopCounter=0;LoopCounter<5;LoopCounter++)
      cout<<"Source["<<LoopCounter<<"]="<<Source[LoopCounter]
        <<"\t Destination["<<LoopCounter<<"]="<<
        Destination[LoopCounter]<<endl;
}
```

Modern compilers would not even allow this to occur. In older compilers, the output would be as follows:

```
1       2       3       4       5
1       2       3       4       5
10      11      12      13      14
10      11      12      13      14
```

Later, we will discuss why arrays function this way, but for now just accept that you can't use an = operator to copy an array.

If you want to copy one array to another, use this code:

```cpp
//Example of copying an array properly

#include <stdlib.h>
#include <iostream.h>

#define ArraySize 5

void main()
{
    int Source[ArraySize]={1,2,3,4,5};
    int Destination[ArraySize];
    int LoopCounter;
    for(LoopCounter=0;LoopCounter<ArraySize;LoopCounter++)
      Destination[LoopCounter]=Source[LoopCounter];
}
```

The preceding code copies each individual element at a time, and works properly.

Let's write a function that will copy the contents of one array to another. How many parameters do you think we need? You might guess two, but you need three. Obviously, you need the source and destination arrays, but you also need an integer indicating the number of elements in the array. Remember, we have no way of knowing the number of elements in the array by looking at it. Also note that we are assuming that there is enough room in the destination array to store all the elements in the source array.

```cpp
void Copy(int Destination[], int Source[], int NumElem)
{
    int LoopCounter;

    for(LoopCounter=0;LoopCounter<NumElem;LoopCounter++)
      Destination[LoopCounter]=Source[LoopCounter];
}
```

> **PROGRAMMER'S NOTEBOOK**
>
> Notice that the Destination array is listed as the first parameter. This is done on purpose, as we will see with all array copying functions. This is to simulate the order we are already familiar with when copying. Normally we use an equal sign as in `Destination=Source`, so little has changed.

Notice the syntax that we used in declaring a function's parameters as arrays. For each parameter that is declared as an array, we use the following format:

```
VariableType ArrayName[]
```

First, the variable type of the array is indicated, then the name of the array is listed. Next to the array name is an open and close bracket. This indicates to the compiler that you are passing an array as opposed to a normal variable. With no number between the brackets, C++ assumes that your function knows how many values the array contains. This allows for a function to be written once for arrays of any size. A number can be inserted inside the brackets, but isn't necessary or recommended for general-purpose functions.

Let's look at a complete program to see how it all works together.

```cpp
#include <stdlib.h>
#include <iostream.h>

#define NumValues1 5
#define NumValues2 10

//Prototypes
void Copy(int Destination[], int Source[], int NumValues);
void InitializeArray(int Array[], int NumValues);
void OutputArray(int Array[], int NumValues);

//Main routine
void main()
{
    int Array1[NumValues1];
    int Array2[NumValues1];

    int Array3[NumValues2];
    int Array4[NumValues2];

    //Show the example with the first set of arrays.

    //Get values from users.
    InitializeArray(Array1, NumValues1);

    //Copy the values from Array1 to Array2.
    Copy(Array2,Array1,NumValues1);
```

```
      //Output the array.
      OutputArray(Array2, NumValues1);

//Functions
void Copy(int Destination[], int Source[], int NumValues)
{
    int LoopCounter;

    for(LoopCounter=0;LoopCounter<NumValues;LoopCounter++)
      Destination[LoopCounter]=Source[LoopCounter];
}

void InitializeArray(int Array[], int NumValues)
{
    int LoopCounter;

    //Loop through the arrays reading values from
    // the user.
    for(LoopCounter=0; LoopCounter<NumValues;LoopCounter++)
    {
      cout<<"Please enter a value:";
      cin>>Array[LoopCounter];
    }
}

void OutputArray(int Array[], int NumValues)
{
    int LoopCounter;

    for(LoopCounter=0; LoopCounter< NumValues; LoopCounter++)
    {
      cout<<Array[LoopCounter]<<endl;
    }
}
```

This program demonstrates how we can allocate four arrays in the **main** function. Then we call three functions for each set of arrays. We initialize one of the arrays, then copy the values of the array we initialized to the uninitialized array, and finally output the array to which we copied the values.

The four arrays are allocated as we did in the past. However, be aware that we allocated the first two to one size and the other two to another. Because we wrote the functions with a parameter indicating the number of values in the array, we are able to use the same functions to handle both arrays.

Notice how we pass an array to a function. We do not place the brackets to the right of the array name as we normally do. To pass an array to a function, we just type the array name.

You also may have noticed that although we did not use an **&** when declaring the parameters, the array's values were changed within the function and remembered in the main function. Previously we had said that all variables in C++ were passed by value (a copy), not by reference. Arrays are the exception to that rule.

When passing arrays as parameters, any changes made to the arrays from within the function are remembered outside the function.

Arrays function in this manner because of their implementation by the compiler. To shed some light into this, let's look how arrays are implemented.

Before we think about how an array is implemented, we must think about how a traditional variable is implemented. When we think about a variable, what do we think about? It has a name and a type. The name is how we reference the value of a given type that is stored in memory, and allows us an easy way to reference a specific place in memory. The type of the variable tells the computer how much memory to reserve for the variable.

An array is simply a label for the memory location of the first element of an array. To find **Array[Index]** we would calculate the memory location of **Array** and add **Index*sizeof**(element type of the array). If the memory location started at 1 we would have to calculate **Array[Index]** by:

Array[Index] = the address of Array + (Index-1)*sizeof(element type)

This slows things down and gives us only a nominal aid in understanding. Therefore, we start our indexes at 0 and gain the efficiency advantage.

Also important to note, is that if we pass an entire array to a function, instead of a reference, it would be highly inefficient due to the size of the array that would be required to be copied. Since a reference is passed, any changes made to the array will be remembered.

DRILLS

What is the output of the following code?

Drill **6-3**

```
//Drill 6-3

#include <stdlib.h>
#include <iostream.h>

#define ArraySize 5

//Prototypes
void Change(int Values[]);
void OutputArray(int Array[], int NumValues);

//Functions
void Change(int Values[], int NumValues)
{
    Values[2]=10;
    Values[4]=20;
    OutputArray(Values, NumValues);
}
```

```
void OutputArray(int Array[], int NumValues)
{
    int LoopCounter;

    for(LoopCounter=0; LoopCounter< NumValues; LoopCounter++)
    {
        cout<<Array[LoopCounter]<<endl;
    }
}

void main()
{
    int Array1[ArraySize]={1,2,3,4,5};

    //Output the array.
    OutputArray(Array1, ArraySize);

    //Call function to change values.
    Change(Array1, ArraySize);

    //Output the array.
    OutputArray(Array1, ArraySize);
}
```

6.3 CHARACTER ARRAYS

So far we have just discussed arrays of numbers, but equally important are arrays of characters. Arrays of characters allow you to store names, words, and expressions.

In the following single dimensional array of characters, notice how we use empty brackets so that we do not have to count the number of characters in the array.

```
//Example of character arrays

#include <stdlib.h>
#include <iostream.h>

void main()
{
    char Word[] = {'H','e','l','l','o','\n'};
    int LoopCounter=0;

    while(Word[LoopCounter]!='\n')
      cout<<Word[LoopCounter++];
    cout<<endl;
}
```

The previous program has a '\n' character added to the array. We used this to indicate the end of the array of characters. In reality there is a better way to accomplish this, called a string.

Although we have already seen strings, we have not really drawn attention to them. Remember the following example?

```
cout<<"We Love the Pittsburgh Steelers";
```

The double quotes are used to contain a string. This is different from the single quotes, which contain a single character.

A string is a series of characters enclosed in " ". When a string is declared, characters are declared with a '\0' character appended to the end of the array. The '\0' is a null character that indicates the end of a string to C++. This replaces the '/n' that we used in our original example.

By using the null character, we do not have to set a maximum size to the string. The only limit to the size of a string is the size of accessible memory. Although this is an advantage over other languages that require you to specify the size of a string, it is also a disadvantage. Now, if we need to know the size of a string, we must calculate it.

See how using string functionality makes allocating a string simple:

```
char Word[]="hello!";
```

Notice no special characters were needed. We could create the equivalent by allocating an array of characters and making sure that the last character in the array is a '\0';.

```
char Word[7];
Word[0] = 'h';
Word[1] = 'e';
Word[2] = 'l';
Word[3] = 'l';
Word[4] = 'o';
Word[5] = '!';
Word[6] = '\0';
```

PROGRAMMER'S NOTEBOOK

To review, an 'A' and an "A" are NOT the same thing. An 'A' is a single character, but an "A" is really two characters—an 'A' and a '\0'.

Another advantage of strings is that they can be input and output easily with `cout` and `cin` like any other variables. See the simplicity of outputting a string as follows:

```
cout<<Word;
```

No longer must we write code that loops through the array to output the values. Similarly, we can input values into strings with `cin`. The key is to have enough space in the array to accept all the characters from the user. Otherwise, the extra characters will be stored directly after the array in memory and may cause problems with your program.

```
char Buffer[256];
cout<<"Enter a name"<<endl;
cin>>Buffer;
```

Remember that the null character is stored in the string, so when you allocate an array make sure that the array size is at least equal to the number of characters to be stored plus one additional space for the null character. For example, if you wish to store the string "Hello", you need to allocate an array of six characters.

Although the ability to allocate, print out, and read in strings is important, we require additional abilities if we are going to make strings useful.

6.4 MULTIDIMENSIONAL ARRAYS

Sometimes a problem does not map itself to an array of only one dimension. Think about trying to write a program that would store a chessboard. A chessboard contains rows and columns. We would need multiple arrays to store each row of the board if we tried to implement it with the arrays that we have learned so far. Fortunately, C++ provides the ability to create multidimensional arrays, although this is only by appearance. In reality, a **multidimensional array** is really one continuous block of memory.

To declare a two-dimensional array, we use the following template:

```
VariableType ArrayName[#rows][#columns];
```

An example of declaring an array of integers called **Values** with four rows and five columns is as follows:

```
int Values[4][5];
```

The same rules exist for two-dimensional arrays as for one-dimensional arrays for indexing, accessing, and initializing. The only difference is that we need to account for the added dimension.

Remember, we start accessing by the index 0. So the first element is at row 0, column 0. To initialize the value at row 0, column 0 to 1, we use the following code:

```
Values[0][0]=1;
```

If we represented the array values graphically, with each cell containing its row and column indexes respectively, it would look as follows:

Columns

	0	1	2	3	4
0	0,0	0,1	0,2	0,3	0,4
1	1,0	1,1	1,2	1,3	1,4
2	2,0	2,1	2,2	2,3	2,4
3	3,0	3,1	3,2	3,3	3,4

(Rows)

If we wanted to initialize all the values in the array to 1, we could write a simple nested loop as follows:

```
#include <iostream.h>
#include <stdlib.h>

#define NumRows 4
#define NumCols 5

void main()
{
    int Values[NumRows][NumCols];
    int Rows;
    int Cols;

    for (Rows=0;Rows<4;Rows++)
      for(Cols=0;Cols<5;Cols++)
        Values[Rows][Cols]=1;
}
```

Let's look at a practical example. Let's write a program that reads in the prices of five items. Each item has a retail price and a discounted price. We will create an array of floating point numbers with two columns and five rows. The first column will store the retail price and the second column will store the discounted price.

Often real world problems map better to a multidimensional array. One case is when we have a pair or list of items to track. Although we can store them in two or more separate arrays, it is easier and makes more sense to store them in a multidimensional array.

Notice the use of the **define** statements to reduce the confusion of which column the retail and discounted prices are contained.

```cpp
//New way to write the code
#include <stdlib.h>
#include <iostream.h>

#define Retail 0
#define Discount 1

#define NumPrices 5
#define NumCols 2

void main()
{
    float Prices[NumPrices][NumCols];
    int LoopCounter;

    for(LoopCounter=0;LoopCounter<NumPrices;LoopCounter++)
    {
    cout<<"Enter the retail price: "<<endl;
    cin>>Prices[LoopCounter][Retail];

    cout<<"Enter the discounted price:"<<endl;
    cin>>Prices[LoopCounter][Discount];
    }
}
```

```cpp
//Old way to write the code
#include <stdlib.h>
#include <iostream.h>

#define NumPrices 5

void main()
{
    float Retail[NumPrices];
    float Discount[NumPrices];
    int LoopCounter;

    for(int LoopCounter=0;LoopCounter<NumPrices;LoopCounter++)
    {
      cout<<"Enter the retail price: "<<endl;
      cin>>Retail[LoopCounter];

      cout<<"Enter the discounted price:"<<endl;
      cin>>Discount[LoopCounter];
    }
}
```

Although the previous code may not look much different, by combining arrays we make the data more simple to handle. Think what would happen if we had to pass the array to a function. If we used the old method we would have to pass numerous arrays. With multidimensional arrays we would need to pass only 1.

Array Initialization Shortcuts

Just as we had a shortcut to initializing a single dimensional array, we can also shortcut the initialization of multiple dimensional arrays. We initialize an array of two rows and five columns of integers as follows.

```
int Values[2][5] = {{1, 2, 3, 4, 5},
                    {6, 7, 8, 9, 10}};
```

Note the commas between the rows. Also note that the extra set of curly braces are optional, but advised. The array also can be initialized as follows, but it is not nearly as readable.

```
int Values[2][5] = {1, 2, 3, 4, 5, 6, 7, 8, 9, 10};
```

It is also possible to partially initialize a multidimensional array like we did for a single-dimensional array. See the following example:

```
int Values[2][5] = {{1,2,3,4,5},
                    {6}};
```

This code initializes only the first row of the array **Values** and then the first value of the second row of the array **Values**. Since some of the array was initialized at the time of declaration, the rest of the array is initialized to 0. Therefore, a graphical representation of the array would look as follows:

Columns

Rows		0	1	2	3	4
	0	1	2	3	4	5
	1	6	0	0	0	0

DRILLS

What is the output of the following code?

Drill 6-4

```
//Drill 6-4
//Sample two-dimensional array drill

#include <stdlib.h>
#include <iostream.h>

#define NumRows 3
#define NumCols 3

void main()
{

    int SampleArray[NumRows][NumCols] = {{1,2,3},
                                         {4,5,6},
                                         {7,8,9}};


    cout<<SampleArray[1][1]<<endl;
    cout<<SampleArray[2][1]<<endl;
    cout<<SampleArray[3][3]<<endl;
}
```

What is the output of the following code?

Drill 6-5

```
//Drill 6-5
//Sample two-dimensional array drill

#include <stdlib.h>
#include <iostream.h>

#define NumRows 3
#define NumCols 3

void main()
{
    int SampleArray[NumRows][NumCols] = {{1,2,3},
                                         {4,5,6},
                                         {7,8,9}};
    int Row;
    int Col;

    for (Row=0; Row<NumRows; Row++)
      for (Col=0; Col<NumCols; Col++)
        cout<<SampleArray[Col][Row]<<endl;
}
```

6.5 MULTIDIMENSIONAL ARRAYS OF CHARACTERS

Let's create a program that stores a chessboard configuration. A chessboard consists of 64 squares arranged in eight rows and eight columns. It can contain up to eight pawns (P), two castles (C), two knights (N), two rooks (R), a queen (Q), and a king (K) for each player (white versus black). To store the pieces we need a two-dimensional array of characters. We also need to represent an unoccupied space, for which we will use the space character. Additionally, we will use a lowercase letter for one player and an uppercase letter for the other.

The representation we will store will be the beginning position of the game. See the following pictorial:

c	n	r	q	k	r	n	c
p	p	p	p	p	p	p	p
P	P	P	P	P	P	P	P
C	N	R	Q	K	R	N	C

We will use an array of characters to store the board. The only value we need to store is the character that represents the piece located in each square. If the square doesn't contain a piece, we will store a space. Otherwise, we will store the character that represents the piece that is in the square.

The array will be a two-dimensional array of characters with eight rows and eight columns. We will count the columns from left to right starting at zero and ending at seven, and the rows from top to bottom, starting at zero and ending at seven.

If we were to draw the board showing the row and column for each square, it would look as follows:

0,0	0,1	0,2	0,3	0,4	0,5	0,6	0,7
1,0	1,1	1,2	1,3	1,4	1,5	1,6	1,7
2,0	2,1	2,2	2,3	2,4	2,5	2,6	2,7
3,0	3,1	3,2	3,3	3,4	3,5	3,6	3,7
4,0	4,1	4,2	4,3	4,4	4,5	4,6	4,7
5,0	5,1	5,2	5,3	5,4	5,5	5,6	5,7
6,0	6.1	6,2	6,3	6,4	6,5	6,6	6,7
7,0	7,1	7,2	7,3	7,4	7,5	7,6	7,7

Therefore, to write the program to store the initial chessboard placement, we need to map the characters to their appropriate places in the array. This is shown in the following program:

```
//Chessboard implementation
#include <stdlib.h>
#include <iostream.h>

#define NumRows 8
#define NumCols 8

void main()
{
    char Board[NumRows][NumCols];
    int Row;
    int Col;

    //Initialize the first row.
    Board[0][0]='c';
    Board[0][1]='n';
    Board[0][2]='r';
    Board[0][3]='q';
    Board[0][4]='k';
    Board[0][5]='r';
    Board[0][6]='n';
    Board[0][7]='c';

    //Initialize the second row.
    Board[1][0]='p';
    Board[1][1]='p';
    Board[1][2]='p';
    Board[1][3]='p';
    Board[1][4]='p';
    Board[1][5]='p';
    Board[1][6]='p';
```

```
    Board[1][7]='p';

    //Initialize the third through sixth rows.
    for (Row=3; Row<6; Row++)
      for (Col=0;Col<8; Col++)
        Board[Row][Col]=' ';

    //Initialize the seventh row.
    Board[0][0]='p';
    Board[0][1]='p';
    Board[0][2]='p';
    Board[0][3]='p';
    Board[0][4]='p';
    Board[0][5]='p';
    Board[0][6]='p';
    Board[0][7]='p';

    //Initialize the eighth row
    Board[7][0]='c';
    Board[7][1]='n';
    Board[7][2]='r';
    Board[7][3]='k';
    Board[7][4]='q';
    Board[7][5]='r';
    Board[7][6]='n';
    Board[7][7]='c';
}
```

The program starts by initializing the first two rows of pieces by initializing each value one at a time. The program loops through the next four rows and sets each element to a blank space. Finally, the program initializes the last two rows by initializing each value one at a time.

This program could have been written using the shortcut for initialization of arrays, as follows:

```
//Chessboard implementation with shortcut
#include <stdlib.h>
#include <iostream.h>

#define NumRows 8
#define NumCols 8

void main()
{
    char Board[NumRows][NumCols]={
      {'c', 'n', 'r', 'q', 'k', 'r', 'n', 'c'},
      {'p', 'p', 'p', 'p', 'p', 'p', 'p', 'p'},
      {' ', ' ', ' ', ' ', ' ', ' ', ' ', ' '},
      {' ', ' ', ' ', ' ', ' ', ' ', ' ', ' '},
      {' ', ' ', ' ', ' ', ' ', ' ', ' ', ' '},
      {' ', ' ', ' ', ' ', ' ', ' ', ' ', ' '},
      {'P', 'P', 'P', 'P', 'P', 'P', 'P', 'P'},
      {'C', 'N', 'R', 'Q', 'K', 'R', 'N', 'C'}
      };
}
```

Both versions of the program merely initialize the board; it is left as an exercise to write additional functionality into the program.

Two-dimensional arrays are an excellent way to store multiple strings together as one unit. Imagine if you wanted to store a list of client names. Currently, without two-dimensional arrays, we would need to store each name as a separate variable. This would be extremely cumbersome. Let's look at a program that can store ten names, get the names from the user, and output them to the screen.

```cpp
//Chessboard implementation
//Program to demonstrate an array of strings
#include <stdlib.h>
#include <iostream.h>

//Defines
#define NumNames 10
#define MaxSize 50

//Prototypes
void InitializeNames(char Names[NumNames][MaxSize]);
void DisplayNames(char Names[NumNames][MaxSize]);


//Main routine
void main()
{
   char Names[NumNames][MaxSize];

   InitializeNames(Names);
   DisplayNames(Names);
}


//Functions
void InitializeNames(char Names[NumNames][MaxSize])
{
   int LoopCounter;
   for (LoopCounter=0;LoopCounter<NumNames;LoopCounter++)
   {
     cout<<"Enter a Name"<<endl;
     cin.getline(Names[LoopCounter], MaxSize);
   }
}

void DisplayNames(char Names[NumNames][MaxSize])
{
   int LoopCounter;

   for (int LoopCounter=0;LoopCounter<NumNames;LoopCounter++)
     cout<<Names[LoopCounter]<<endl;
}
```

Let's start analyzing the preceding program by starting with the **main** routine. In **main** we allocate **Names**, a two-dimensional array of characters. **Names** can store 10 names, each with a maximum of 50 characters. We then pass the **Names** to the **InitializeNames** function which asks the user for 10 names and stores each name in the array **Names**. Since **Names** is an array, it is passed by reference and all of the information gathered in the **InitializeNames** function is remembered when we return to the **main** routine. Then, **Names** is passed to the **DisplayNames** function where it outputs each of the names entered. Just as in single-dimensional arrays, when we pass an array to a function just the array name is passed.

6.6 Case Study

Problem Description

Instead of paying in cash, the entrepreneur now pays his employees by check. A check stub should be prepared, which shows the employee's ID, hours worked, pay rate, gross pay, tax, and net pay. Overtime at 1.5 times the hourly wage is paid for any employee working more than 40 hours per week. Write a program that prints a worker's paycheck showing the dollar sign and the amount formatted to two decimal places. Your program input should consist of the employees ID, name, the hours worked, tax rate, and hourly wage. The numeric input should be accomplished via a single function called successively for each input. The program should use functions to the maximum extent, store all inputs in arrays, and run continuously until terminated by the operator, at which time the checks for all employees should be displayed.

Discussion

This problem requires maximum use of functions to encourage students to break their program into small, easily understood pieces. The constraint of forcing all numeric inputs to be done via a single function called successively for each input is designed to provide an example of "write once, call many." Duplicate code in a program should be vehemently discouraged. Setting the **fixed** flag is necessary for this problem since a weekly pay, particularly with overtime, may exceed 999.99. Failure to set this flag would cause the large number to be displayed in exponential notation. By encapsulating all the prompts in function prompt, it is easy to add another one for the name. Function **getline()** is used to read the entire name into one row of the name array. By storing the input values in arrays, the process of input and output is clearly differentiated. The program uses a double dimension array to hold the names; however, both the prototype and actual function **DisplayCheck** show a single-dimension character array. When a double-dimension (DD) array of characters is used as a single-dimension array, the effect is to use only one row of the DD array. Variable **Count** is used to determine how many employees were entered. The escape sequence **\t** is used to **tab** to uniform positions on the output line.

Solution

```
#include <stdlib.h>
#include <iostream.h>
#include <iomanip.h>

#define NumRows 100
#define NumColumns 30
```

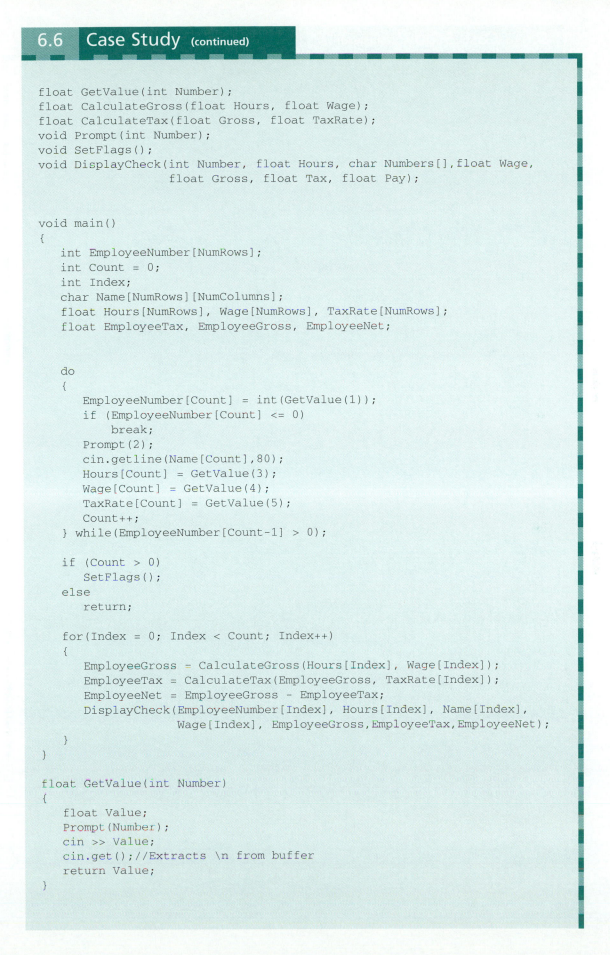

```
float GetValue(int Number);
float CalculateGross(float Hours, float Wage);
float CalculateTax(float Gross, float TaxRate);
void Prompt(int Number);
void SetFlags();
void DisplayCheck(int Number, float Hours, char Numbers[],float Wage,
                  float Gross, float Tax, float Pay);


void main()
{
   int EmployeeNumber[NumRows];
   int Count = 0;
   int Index;
   char Name[NumRows][NumColumns];
   float Hours[NumRows], Wage[NumRows], TaxRate[NumRows];
   float EmployeeTax, EmployeeGross, EmployeeNet;


   do
   {
      EmployeeNumber[Count] = int(GetValue(1));
      if (EmployeeNumber[Count] <= 0)
         break;
      Prompt(2);
      cin.getline(Name[Count],80);
      Hours[Count] = GetValue(3);
      Wage[Count] = GetValue(4);
      TaxRate[Count] = GetValue(5);
      Count++;
   } while(EmployeeNumber[Count-1] > 0);

   if (Count > 0)
      SetFlags();
   else
      return;

   for(Index = 0; Index < Count; Index++)
   {
      EmployeeGross = CalculateGross(Hours[Index], Wage[Index]);
      EmployeeTax = CalculateTax(EmployeeGross, TaxRate[Index]);
      EmployeeNet = EmployeeGross - EmployeeTax;
      DisplayCheck(EmployeeNumber[Index], Hours[Index], Name[Index],
                   Wage[Index], EmployeeGross,EmployeeTax,EmployeeNet);
   }
}


float GetValue(int Number)
{
   float Value;
   Prompt(Number);
   cin >> Value;
   cin.get();//Extracts \n from buffer
   return Value;
}
```

6.6 Case Study (continued)

```cpp
void Prompt(int Number)
{
   switch(Number)
   {
     case 1:
          cout << "\nEnter negative to end or ";
          cout << "\nEnter employee\'s ID -> "; break;
     case 2:
          cout << "Enter employee\'s name -> "; break;
     case 3:
          cout << "Enter employee\'s hours -> "; break;
     case 4:
          cout << "Enter employee\'s wage rate -> "; break;
     case 5:
          cout << "Enter employee\'s tax rate -> "; break;
   }
}


float CalculateGross(float Hours, float Wage)
{
   const int STDWEEK = 40;
   float Gross, OverTime;
   if (Hours > STDWEEK)
        OverTime = Hours - STDWEEK;
   else
        OverTime = 0.0;
   Gross = (Wage * Hours) + (OverTime * (float).5 * Wage);
   return Gross;
}


float CalculateTax(float Gross, float TaxRate)
{
   const float CONVERT = 100.00;
   float Tax;
   if (TaxRate > 1)
        TaxRate = TaxRate/CONVERT;
   Tax = Gross * TaxRate;
   return Tax;
}


void SetFlags()
{
   cout << setiosflags(ios::showpoint | ios :: fixed)<< setprecision(2);
}
```

```
void DisplayCheck(int Number, float Hours, char Numbers[],float Wage,
                  float Gross, float Tax, float Pay)
{
  int Index;
  cout << "\n\t\t|";
  cout << "\n   PAY STUB\t|";
  cout << "\n\t\t|";
  cout << "\nEmp Num\t" << Number << "\t|";
    cout << "\nHours\t" << Hours << "\t|";
    cout << "\nWage\t" << Wage << "\t|            Pay to the order of "
         << Number;
    cout << "\nGross\t" << Gross << "\t|\t\t\t\t   This Amount $"
         << Pay ;
    cout << "\nTax\t" << Tax << "\t|";
    cout << "\n          _____\t|";
    cout << "\nPay\t" << Pay << "\t|";
    for(Index = 0; Index < 3; Index++)
        cout << "\n\t\t|";
  }
```

Output

```
Enter negative to end or
Enter employee's ID -> 10101
Enter employee's name -> John Doe
Enter employee's hours -> 60
Enter employee's wage rate -> 18.60
Enter employee's tax rate -> .33

Enter negative to end or
Enter employee's ID -> 10102
Enter employee's name -> Paul L. Small
Enter employee's hours -> 40
Enter employee's wage rate -> 7.85
Enter employee's tax rate -> 20

Enter negative to end or
Enter employee's ID -> -9
```

```
    PAY STUB              |
                         |
Emp Num    10101         |
Hours         60         |
Wage       18.60         |              Pay to the order of John Doe
Gross    1302.00         |                   This Amount  $872.34
Tax       429.66         |
                         |
         _____        |
Pay       872.34         |
                         |
                         |
                         |
                         |
    PAY STUB             |
                         |
Emp Num    10102         |
Hours         40         |
Wage        7.85         |              Pay to the order of Paul L. Small
Gross     314.00         |                   This Amount $251.20
Tax        62.80         |
                         |
         _____        |
Pay       251.20         |
                         |
                         |
```

♦ Key Terms

Array	A variable that allows more than one value to be stored under the same variable name. Each value must be of the same type.
Index	An integer value used to reference individual elements of the array.
Lower Bound	The index of the lowest accessible element of the array (equal to zero).
Multidimensional Array	An array containing rows and columns of the same type of variable.
Upper Bound	The index of the highest accessible element of the array (equal to the size of the array, –1).

♦ Answers to Drills

Drill 6-1

Given the previous code, the array would allocate 10 integers with an index from 0 to 9. The values in the array would look as follows:

0	1	2	3	4	5	6	7	8	9
5	-2	0	1	0	0	0	0	0	0

The program initializes the first four values in the array **Values** to 5, –2, 0, and 1, respectively. Since some of the values of the array are initialized, any unspecified values are initialized to zero.

Then the program simply loops for 0 to 9 and outputs each value in the array along the way. Therefore, the output would be as follows:

```
5
-2
0
1
0
0
0
0
0
0
```

Drill 6-2

This program is very similar to the previous one, with one difference. The array **Values** does not have an explicit number indicating the number of integers to allocate for the array. Instead the compiler determines the number of values by counting the values to which array **Values** is initialized. In this case, there are four values, so only four values are allocated. The placement of these values can be seen as follows:

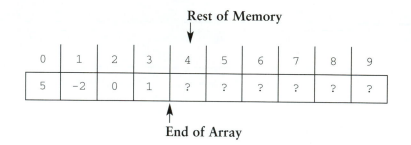

When the program begins to execute, the first four lines of output would be as follows:

```
5
-2
0
1
```

However, after the first four values are output, the program will behave unpredictably. Since only four values are allocated for the array, when we reference values beyond the upper bound of the array, we are accessing memory that is allocated to other variables and/or programs. This may cause values that belong to other variables to display, or it may cause your program to crash. This is called a run-time error. The compiler cannot detect it, but when you execute your program you do not get proper predictable results.

Drill 6-3

The output of the drill is as follows:

```
1       2       3       4       5
1       2       10      4       20
1       2       10      4       20
```

The first line of output should be obvious. The five elements of the array are initialized to 1, 2, 3, 4, and 5, respectively. When we call the **OuputArray** function, the contents of the array are sent to the screen. Then we call the **Change** function. This passes the array **Array1** to the function by reference. This means that any changes to **Array1** made within the function **Change** will be remembered when we return to the **main** routine.

Two elements of the array are changed within the function **Change**. The third and fifth elements of the array are changed to 10 and 20, respectively. Therefore, when we output the array within the function we get 1, 2, 10, 4, and 20, respectively. When we leave the function the changed values are remembered and therefore the last line of output is the same as the previous one.

Drill 6-4

The program starts by initializing a two-dimensional array. The array has three rows and three columns. Remember, the indexes start at zero, not one! Let's look at how the array would be drawn graphically:

Columns

	0	1	2
0	1	2	3
1	4	5	6
2	7	8	9

Rows

Now figuring out what values are stored in the proper location is easy. Simply cross-reference each row and column with the grid we just drew. Remember the first index is the row and the second index is the column. Therefore, the output would be:

```
5
8
???
```

The first two results are obvious, but why question marks for the third value? The third value has both a row and column of three. This is out of bounds of the array for both the row and the column. Remember when an array is defined as a size of 3, the valid indexes are from 0 to 2.

Drill 6-5

A graphic representation of the array **SampleArray** would be as follows:

Columns

	0	1	2
0	1	2	3
1	4	5	6
2	7	8	9

Rows

The output would be as follows:

```
1
4
7
2
5
8
3
6
9
```

You may be wondering why the output wasn't as follows:

```
1
2
3
4
5
6
7
8
9
```

Notice the output line of code:

```
cout<<SampleArray[Col][Row]<<endl;
```

The row and column indexes have been switched. Since there are an equal number of rows and columns in the array, this will not cause an error. It will, however, display the contents of the array in a manner you may not have expected. Instead of displaying each value of a row and then skipping to the next row, the program displays each value in a column and then switches to the next column. Therefore the elements of the array are displayed in the following order. Each element is listed by its indexes row and then column, respectively.

Row = 0, Column = 0

Row = 1, Column = 0

Row = 2, Column = 0

Row = 0, Column = 1

Row = 1, Column = 1

Row = 2, Column = 1

Row = 0, Column = 2

Row = 1, Column = 2

Row = 2, Column = 2

♦ Programming Exercises

1. Write a program that initializes an array of size 10 to random numbers. Output the values from within the array.

2. Write a program that declares an array in the main function and initializes the entire array to 0. Write a function that, when called, will ask the user to enter values into the array. Make sure that the changes to the array are remembered. Write a second function called Display that will output the results to the screen. The Display function does not have to remember changes. Use a define statement so that by changing one line of code, the rest of the program would work properly for any size array.

3. Write a function, CountIt, that accepts an array of characters and a character to search for. The function should return an integer indicating the number of times the value appears in the array passed.

4. Expand the chess program by writing a function that would accept a two-dimensional array of characters that represents the board and displays the contents of the board in text.

5. Expand the chess program by writing a function that would ask the user for a starting and ending position for a player's move and would actually execute the move. This function does not have to check to see if the player's move is actually a valid chess move; it can assume that it is.

6. Modify the chess program that you wrote so that it checks to see if the move is valid. It does not have to check if the king is in check.

7. Modify the chess program that you wrote to see if the king is in check when you make a move.

8. Write a program that will play tic-tac-toe. It should initialize the board to be empty. It should ask for a player's move and check to see that the move is valid. A valid move is one that selects an unoccupied place on the board.

The program should also check to see if a player has won after each move. The program should also check to see whether a tie has occurred.

9. Write a program that creates a 5 by 5 integer array and uses it like a spreadsheet. The program needs a function that displays the contents in the spreadsheet, a function that enters values into the sheet, and a function that will calculate values from the sheet, and place them into the proper cell. The calculations should only be addition, subtraction, multiplication, and division.

◆ Additional Exercises

1. If an array is declared as

   int Numbers[65];

   are the following lines of code valid?

   a.   Numbers[0];
   b.   Numbers[55];
   c.   Numbers[65];
   d.   [34]Numbers;
   e.   Numbers[x++]; //Assume that x is equal to 4
   f.   Numbers[65]++;

2. Referring to example #1,

   a.   How many elements are contained within the array?
   b.   Write the code to assign the number 3 to the 20th element.
   c.   Write the code to assign the number 4 to the element with the index of 20.
   d.   Using a loop, write the code that adds the element on the left to the element on the right and saves the result to the element on the right. The final value in the array should be the sum of all the values in the array.

3. Initialize an integer array of size 5 so that all the elements are equal to zero. Do this using only one line of code. How many ways can this be accomplished? Show as many ways as you can.

4. Assuming the following code is in a program, which of the following are not valid statements?

```
int Numbers[7];
int Values[10];
int Temp = 0;
```

   a.   Numbers[0] = Values[0];
   b.   Numbers[7] = Values[7];
   c.   Numbers[3] = Temp;
   d.   Numbers[temp] = Temp;
   e.   Numbers[temp] = Values[Temp];

5. Are the following statements correct? If the code produces an error, correct the problem.

    a. int Temp = 10;
        int Arr[Temp] = {0};
    b. The following is a function call:
        int StartUp(int Arr[]; int Values)

6. True or False: An array needs to have the '&' placed before it when changes to the array need to be remembered.

7. Calculate the memory location of Arr[3]. Assume that the memory starts at 1000 for the array, and the size of an integer is 4.

8. True or False: Multidimensional arrays are more efficient in that they execute faster than regular arrays.

9. True or False: Multidimensional arrays can be created for the exact same variable types as single-dimensional arrays.

10. Write a prototype for a function that returns no values and accepts a multidimensional integer array of 10 by 3, and a character array of 10 elements.

11. What is the output of the following code?

```
#include <stdlib.h>
#include <iostream.h>
void main()
{
  int Row;
  int Col;
  int SampleArray[3][3] = {{0,1,2}, {1,2,3}};

  for(Row=0; Row<3;Row++)
    for(Col=0; Col<3; Col++)
      cout<<SampleArray[i][j]<<endl;
}
```

12. Write the code required declaring an array that contains five rows of three columns of integers. Also initialize the array to contain all fives.

CHAPTER

7

Simple Arrays Applications

Chapter Objectives

♦ Obtain a stronger understanding of arrays

♦ Introduce basic string functions

♦ Introduce basic searching functions

♦ Introduce basic sorting functions

♦ Introduce basic file operations

This chapter will develop various functions dealing with arrays. Strings, searching, and sorting are all excellent examples of applications for arrays that we will implement to reinforce the concepts of the previous chapters.

7.1 STRING FUNCTIONS

Although C++ has a built-in string class, it is often helpful to take a step back in time to understand how strings used to be implemented. This helps to give us a solid understanding of creating and manipulating arrays. Later in the text, after we introduce classes, we will discuss the class implementation of strings, which is far superior to the implementation shown here.

In the olden days (before MTV) by including **string.h** we had access to many functions that operate on strings, such as: **strlen**, **strcpy**, and **strcat**. Notice that their function names are implemented in all lowercase letters. This is how C++ defines them; however, to stick to our standard, we will implement them by capitalizing the first letter of each word. We will now show you how they are implemented.

StrLen

The **StrLen** function accepts a string, defined as an array of characters, and returns the number of characters in the string excluding the null character. The prototype of the **StrLen** function is as follows:

```
int StrLen(char String[]);
```

To get a better understanding of the **StrLen** function and to get some practice with arrays, we are going to implement **StrLen**.

```
//Array implementation of StrLen
int StrLen(char String[])
{
    int Len=0;
    while(String[Len] != '\0')
      Len++;
    return Len;
}
```

The code is fairly straightforward. We initialize the **Len** variable to 0 and then step through the array until we reach the '\0'. Each character except the '\0' is counted, and finally the **Len** variable is returned from the **StrLen** function.

PROGRAMMER'S NOTEBOOK

What do you think would happen if an array of characters, not properly terminated with a '\0', were passed to StrLen? Look at the code. The only termination condition for the while loop is when the current array character equals '\0', so if a '\0' is not found, the loop will continue indefinitely. In reality, as the loop continues eventually it will randomly find a '\0' and terminate.

Let's look at an example of code using the **StrLen** function:

```cpp
//Example of the use of StrLen in a program

#include <stdlib.h>
#include <iostream.h>

#define StringSize 256

//Assume the StrLen definition is here.
void main()
{
    char Buffer[StringSize];
    char Buffer2[]={"This is another expression"};

    cout<<"Enter an expression"<<endl;
    cin>>Buffer;

    cout<<"The length of the string you just entered is "
        <<StrLen(Buffer)<<endl;
    cout<<"The length of the string with spaces is "
        <<StrLen(Buffer2)<<endl;
}
```

The output is as follows:

```
Enter an expression
hello
The length of the string you just entered is 5
The length of the string with spaces is 26
```

PROGRAMMER'S NOTEBOOK

Notice when you run the previous program that 256 is not the answer: it is the size of the allocated array, not the size of the string. Also notice that if you include a space (' ') in your string, it is counted just like any other character.

DRILLS

What is the output of the following program?

Drill **7-1**

```
//Drill 7-1

#define StringSize 100

void main()
{
   char Buffer1[StringSize]="1st String";
   char Buffer2[StringSize]="Another String";
   char Buffer3[StringSize]="";

   cout<<"The length of the 1st string is "<<StrLen(Buffer1)<<endl;
   cout<<"The length of the 2nd string is "<<StrLen(Buffer2)<<endl;
   cout<<"The length of the 3rd string is "<<StrLen(Buffer3)<<endl;
}
```

StrCpy

Recall from our discussion of arrays that you cannot copy the contents of one array to another using an **=** operator as shown here:

```
int Source[10]={1,2,3,4,5,6,7,8,9,10};
int Destination[10];
//This does not copy the array Source to the array Destination.
Destination=Source;
```

To copy strings, we need a function similar to the one that we wrote to copy arrays, but we can improve it. The previously implemented function required a third parameter that indicated the size of the array. We could use the function we wrote and calculate the string length with the **StrLen** function we just wrote; however, we can implement the string copy function (**StrCpy**) without wasting time calculating unnecessary values, as shown:

```
//Array implementation of StrCpy
void StrCpy(char Destination[], char Source[])
{
   int StringIndex=0;
   while(Source[StringIndex]!='\0')
   {
       Destination[StringIndex]=Source[StringIndex];
       StringIndex++;
   }
   Destination[StringIndex]='\0';
}
```

We use a **while** loop and continually copy the characters from the **Source** array to the **Destination** array in the string one at a time. This continues until the '\0' character is reached, and we drop out of the loop. We drop out of the loop before the '\0' is copied to the **Destination** string, so we must manually place a '\0' before leaving the function.

DRILLS

What is the output of the following code?

Drill 7-2

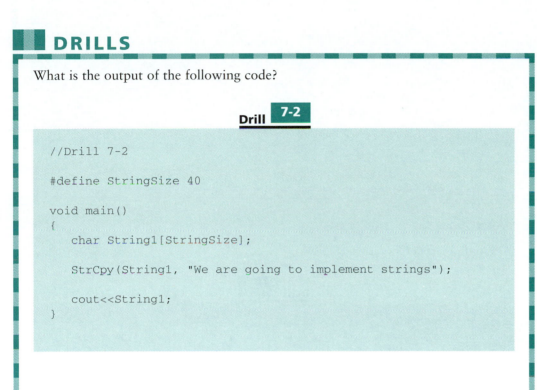

```
//Drill 7-2

#define StringSize 40

void main()
{
    char String1[StringSize];

    StrCpy(String1, "We are going to implement strings");

    cout<<String1;
}
```

What is the output of the following code?

Drill 7-3

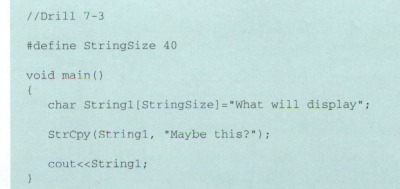

```
//Drill 7-3

#define StringSize 40

void main()
{
    char String1[StringSize]="What will display";

    StrCpy(String1, "Maybe this?");

    cout<<String1;
}
```

What is the output of the following code?

Drill 7-4

```
//Drill 7-4

#define StringSize 40

void main()
{
    char String1[StringSize]="What will display";

    StrCpy(String1, "What will output if I type all of this here instead!");

    cout<<String1;
}
```

What is the output of the following code?

Drill 7-5

```
//Drill 7-5

#define StringSize 40

void main()
{
    char String1[StringSize]= "What will output if I type all of this here instead!";

    StrCpy(String1, "What will display");

    cout<<String1;
}
```

StrCmp

Another useful function is the string compare function (**StrCmp**). We cannot compare two strings with an **==** operator as we can with other variables. Instead we need a function to compare two strings. **StrCmp** will return a 0 if the two strings are equal and a nonzero value if the two strings are not equal. The function **StrCmp** is defined as follows:

```
//Implementation of StrCmp
int StrCmp(char String1[], char String2[])
{
    int StringIndex=0;
    while((String1[StringIndex]==String2[StringIndex]) &&
        (String1[StringIndex]!='\0'))
      StringIndex++;
    return(String1[StringIndex]-String2[StringIndex]);
}
```

The implementation of this function requires some explaining. We use a simple **while** loop with a compound condition statement. The first half of the condition checks to see if the individual characters in the array are the same. If the two arrays contain different characters then this condition will fail. Otherwise, if they are the same we need the second half of the condition to terminate the loop when we have compared the last characters in the array.

If the **while** loop was terminated because the array values were different, then subtracting one character from the other will give us a nonzero value. If the two strings were identical, then the array values are both '\0', and subtracting one from the other will result in 0.

Let's look at how **StrCmp** is used in a program:

```
//Example of StrCmp in a program

#include <stdlib.h>
#include <iostream.h>

#define StringSize 256

//Assume the StrLen definition is here.
void main()
{
    char Buffer1[]={"This is a string"};
    char Buffer2[]={"This is a string"};
    char Buffer3[]={"This string is different"};

    if (StrCmp(Buffer1, Buffer2) != 0)
      cout<<"The string in Buffer 1 is different than the string in Buffer 2"
          <<endl;
    else
      cout<<"The string in Buffer 1 is the same as the string in Buffer 2"
          <<endl;
```

```
   if (StrCmp(Buffer1, Buffer3) != 0)
     cout<<"The string in Buffer 1 is different than the string in Buffer 3"
         <<endl;
   else
     cout<<"The string in Buffer 1 is the same as the string in Buffer 3"
         <<endl;
}
```

The output of the program is what we would expect:

```
The string in Buffer 1 is the same as the string in Buffer 2
The string in Buffer 1 is different than the string in Buffer 3
```

This is because the contents of **Buffer1** are exactly the same as the contents of **Buffer2**. When the contents up to a '\0' are the same in two arrays compared with the **StrCmp** function, the return value is 0. Therefore the condition expression evaluates to false and the **cout** statement associated with the **else** is executed.

In the second example, when the contents of **Buffer1** are compared to the contents of **Buffer3**, they are found to be different. Therefore, a nonzero value is returned. This makes the second conditional expression evaluate to true, thereby executing the first **cout** statement.

▌▌ DRILLS

What is the output of the following code?

Drill 7-6

```
//Drill 7-6

void main()
{
    char String1[]="What will display";
    char String2[]="WHAT WILL DISPLAY";

    if (StrCmp(String1,String2) != 0)
      cout<<"The strings are different";
    else
      cout<<"The strings are the same";
}
```

What is the output of the following code?

Drill 7-7

```
//Drill 7-7

void main()
{
    char String1[]="What will display";
    char String2[]="What will display";

    if (StrCmp(String1,String2) != 0)
      cout<<"The strings are different";
    else
      cout<<"The strings are the same";
}
```

What is the output of the following code?

Drill 7-8

```
//Drill 7-8

void main()
{
    char String1[100]="What will display";
    char String2[18]="What will display";

    if (StrCmp(String1,String2) != 0)
      cout<<"The strings are different";
    else
      cout<<"The strings are the same";
}
```

What is the output of the following code?

Drill 7-9

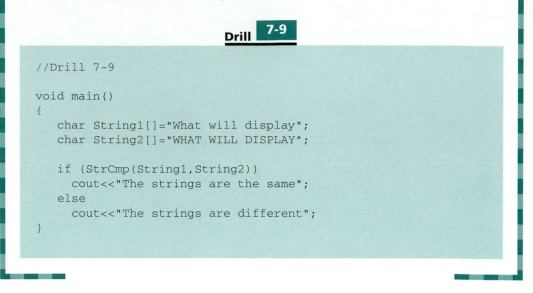

```
//Drill 7-9

void main()
{
    char String1[]="What will display";
    char String2[]="WHAT WILL DISPLAY";

    if (StrCmp(String1,String2))
      cout<<"The strings are the same";
    else
      cout<<"The strings are different";
}
```

StrCat

The string concatenation function (**StrCat**) will append the **Source** string to the end of the **Destination** string. It assumes that there is enough room in the **Destination** string to store the original string and the **Source** string appended onto it. It also assumes that both strings are null-terminated properly.

Here is an example of the **StrCat** function:

```
char Buffer[256];
StrCpy(Buffer, "The Pittsburgh Steelers are the best");
StrCat(Buffer, ", because they just won the Super Bowl!");
cout<<Buffer;
```

The output of the previous program will be as follows:

```
The Pittsburgh Steelers are the best, because they just won
the Super Bowl!
```

Now let's look at the implementation:

```cpp
//Array implementation of StrCat
void StrCat(char Destination[],char Source[])
{
    int Len=0;
    int StringIndex=0;

    //calculates the end of the destination string
    while(Destination[Len]!='\0')
      Len++;

    while(Source[StringIndex]!='\0')
    {
        Destination[Len+StringIndex]=Source[StringIndex];
        StringIndex++;
    }
    Destination[Len+StringIndex]='\0';
}
```

The first step in the **StrCat** implementation is to move to the point in the **Destination** array that is the end of the **Destination** string. This is the location of the '\0'. The code that accomplishes this should look familiar—it is basically the **StrLen** code.

The next step is to copy each element of the **Source** array to its proper place in the **Destination** array. This is accomplished by adding the length of the original string to the index into the **Source** string.

■ DRILLS

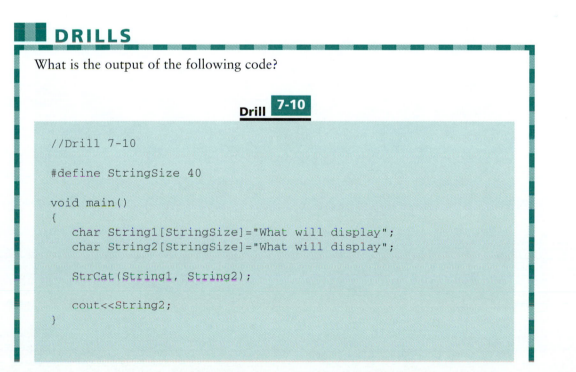

What is the output of the following code?

Drill 7-10

```cpp
//Drill 7-10

#define StringSize 40

void main()
{
    char String1[StringSize]="What will display";
    char String2[StringSize]="What will display";

    StrCat(String1, String2);

    cout<<String2;
}
```

What is the output of the following code?

Drill **7-11**

```
//Drill 7-11

#define StringSize 40

void main()
{
    char String1[StringSize]="What will display";
    char String2[StringSize]="What will display";

    StrCat(String1, String2);

    cout<<String1;
}
```

What is the output of the following code?

Drill **7-12**

```
//Drill 7-12

#define StringSize 40

void main()
{
    char String1[StringSize]="What will display if this is ";
    char String2[StringSize]="appeneded to the first string";

    StrCat(String1, String2);

    cout<<String1;
}
```

What is the output of the following code?

Drill 7-13

```
//Drill 7-13

#define StringSize 40

void main()
{
    char String1[StringSize];
    char String2[StringSize]="What will display";

    StrCat(String1, String2);

    cout<<String1;
}
```

What is the output of the following code?

Drill 7-14

```
//Drill 7-14

#define StringSize 40

void main()
{
    char String1[StringSize]="";
    char String2[StringSize]="What will display";

    StrCat(String1, String2);

    cout<<String1;
}
```

A useful exercise to see if you truly understand these string function implementations is to write the following additional string functions. They are also included in string.h (but spelled with all lowercase letters), but are worth rewriting to develop a better understanding of strings.

StrNCpy

The first is called **StrNCpy**. It is identical to **StrCpy** except instead of copying all the contents of the source string to the destination string, it copies the first *n* characters of the source to the destination string. See the following example of how it works.

```
char String1[]="Pittsburgh is great!";
char Buffer[11];
StrNCpy(Buffer,String1,10);
cout<<Buffer;
```

The output would be:

```
Pittsburgh
```

Notice that the buffer is defined to be 11 characters. Is this necessary even if we are copying only 10 characters? The answer is yes, because we must allocate space for the '\0' character.

The actual implementation of this function is left as an exercise.

StrNCat

StrNCat works similarly to **StrCat**, but instead of appending the entire source string to the end of the destination string, it only appends the first *n* characters of the source string to the destination string.

To further illustrate how the **StrNCat** function works, observe the following code:

```
char Buffer[256];
StrCpy(Buffer, "The Pittsburgh Steelers are the best");
StrNCat(Buffer, ", because they just won the Super Bowl!", 23);
cout<<Buffer;
```

The output would be:

```
The Pittsburgh Steelers are the best,  because they just won
```

Notice that "the Super Bowl!" was not appended.

The actual implementation of this function is left as an exercise.

StrNCmp

The **StrNCmp** function is similar to the **StrCmp** function, but will return a 0 if *n* characters are the same between the two strings. Otherwise it will return a nonzero number.

See the following code as an example of how the **StrNCmp** function works.

```
//Example of the StrNCmp function

char Buffer1[]="Pittsburgh won the Super Bowl";
char Buffer2[]="Pittsburgh won the playoff game";

if (StrCmp(Buffer1,Buffer2)==0)
  cout<<"The strings are the same\n";
else
  cout<<"The strings are different\n";

if (StrNCmp(Buffer1, Buffer2,10)==0)
  cout<<"The 1st 10 characters are the same\n";
else
  cout<<"The 1st 10 characters are different\n";

if (StrNCmp(Buffer1, Buffer2,25)==0)
  cout<<"The 1st 25 characters are the same\n";
else
  cout<<"The 1st 25 characters are different\n";
```

The output would be:

```
The strings are different
The 1st 10 characters are the same.
The 1st 25 characters are different.
```

The actual implementation of this function is left as an exercise.

Let's write a function that accepts two parameters, an array of characters, and a character to search for in the array of characters. If the character is contained within the array of characters, then the function will return true, otherwise it will return false.

```
//Array implementation of FindIt
bool FindIt(char Array[], char SearchValue)
{
 int Counter=0;
 bool Found=false;

 while(Array[Counter] != '\0')
 {
   if (Array[Counter] == SearchValue)
     Found=true;
   Counter++;
 }
 return Found;
}
```

FindIt starts by initializing the loop counter to 0 and the **found** flag to **false**. The **while** loop compares each value of the array to the value searched for. If it finds the value, it sets the flag **found** to true. When the **while** loop progresses to the '\0' the loop terminates. The current value of the **found** flag is returned from the function. If the search value is found more than once, the **found** flag gets assigned true multiple times, but this does not change the outcome of the function.

DRILLS

What is the output of the following code?

Drill 7-15

```
//Drill 7-15

#include <stdlib.h>
#include <iostream.h>
#include <string.h>

//Assume the string defintions are here!

void main()
{
    char String1[]="This is the first string";
    char String2[]="Yet another string";
    char String3[100];
```

```
    cout<<StrLen(String1)<<endl;
    cout<<StrLen(String2)<<endl;
    cout<<StrLen(String3)<<endl;

    StrCpy(String3,String1);
    cout<<String3<<endl;

    StrCat(String3,String2);
    cout<<String3<<endl;

    cout<<StrCmp(String2,String2)<<endl;

    if (StrCmp(String1,String2))
      cout<<"The strings are equal"<<endl;
    else
      cout<<"The strings are not equal"<<endl;

    cout<<StrLen(String3)<<endl;
}
```

Reading Strings with Spaces

All of the examples that we have tried so far were picked because they did not have a space in the middle of the string when we obtained them from the user. Try running the following code and enter the string "The Pittsburgh Steelers will be great next year!"

```
//Incorrect cin example

#include <stdlib.h>
#include <iostream.h>

#define MaxStringSize 100

void main()
{
 char Buffer[MaxStringSize];

 cout<<"Please enter a string containing a space"<<endl;
 cin>>Buffer;
 cout<<Buffer;
}
```

You would expect the output to be:

```
The Pittsburgh Steelers will be great next year!
```

Instead you would find the output to be:

```
The
```

The problem is that **cin** reads input from the user until a whitespace character is entered. Whitespace characters include the carriage return, space, and tab. Therefore, in the previous example when "The Pittsburtgh Steelers will be great next year!" is typed, only the text "The" is actually stored in the string **Buffer**.

C++ provides options to the **cin** function so that it will operate the way we want. See the following code that corrects the problem.

```cpp
//Correct cin example

#include <stdlib.h>
#include <iostream.h>

#define MaxStringSize 100

void main()
{
 char Buffer[MaxStringSize];

 cout<<"Please enter a string containing a space"<<endl;
 cin.getline(Buffer,MaxStringSize);
 cout<<Buffer;
}
```

By adding the **.getline** to the **cin** command, you are able to pass **cin** two parameters. The first is the array of characters to store the value entered from the user. The second is the maximum number of characters the user can enter into the array. This is usually set to the size of the array.

Searching

Another important operation we often wish to perform on a list of values stored in an array is to search for a specific value. Depending upon assumptions we may make on the array and the complexity of the implementation, we experience varied levels of efficiency.

We'll start with the easiest way of searching a list to see if a particular item is contained within the list. It makes no assumptions. It simply starts at the beginning of the list and searches through all the items in the list. If the item is found, we will set a flag indicating it has been found. This is known as a **linear search**.

7.2 LINEAR SEARCH

See the following code for the implementation of this simple search algorithm:

```cpp
//Linear search no assumptions

#include <stdlib.h>
#include <iostream.h>

#define ArraySize 100

int Array[ArraySize];   //Global Array to be searched

void main()
{
    int LoopCounter;
    int SearchItem;
    bool FoundFlag=false;

    //Initialize the array somehow

    //Get the value to search for
    cout<<"Enter the item to search for"<<endl;
    cin>>SearchItem;

    //Search for the value
       for (LoopCounter-0; LoopCounter<ArraySize;LoopCounter++)
          if (Array[LoopCounter]==SearchItem)
             FoundFlag=true;

    //Check if the value was found
       if (FoundFlag)
          cout<<"Item was found";
}
```

This will work; however, once the item is found we no longer need to continue to search the list. When the value is not found, we have to look through every value, but why not stop once we have found the desired value? The implementation of such an algorithm is as follows:

```
//Improved linear search no assumptions

#include <stdlib.h>
#include <iostream.h>

#define ArraySize 100

int Array[ArraySize]; //Global array to be searched

void main()
{
    int LoopCounter;
    int SearchItem;
    bool FoundFlag=false;

    //Initialize the array somehow

    //Get the value to search for
    cout<<"Enter the item to search for"<<endl;
    cin>>SearchItem;

    //Search for the value
    for (LoopCounter=0; ((LoopCounter<ArraySize) &&
                         (FoundFlag==false)); LoopCounter++)
      if (Array[ArraySize]==SearchItem)
        FoundFlag=true;

    //Check if the value was found
      if (FoundFlag)
        cout<<"Item was found";
}
```

Notice the compound condition in the loop that not only checks for the end of the array, but also checks whether the flag for finding the item has been found as well.

However, in the real world if you had to search a large number of items, would you want to do it this way? Of course not. We would at least want the list to be sorted. If we assume a sorted list, then we modify the search so that if the value being searched for is not found, we can stop once we have searched all the values less than the searched value. This implementation is shown as follows:

```
//Further improved linear search
//Assumes array is in order

#include <stdlib.h>
#include <iostream.h>

#define ArraySize 100

int Array[ArraySize]; //Global array to be searched

void main()
{
    int LoopCounter;
    int SearchItem;
    bool FoundFlag=false;

    //Initialize the array somehow and ensure that they are sorted!
    for (LoopCounter=0;LoopCounter<100;LoopCounter++)
      Array[LoopCounter]=LoopCounter;

    //Get the value to search for
    cout<<"Enter the item to search for"<<endl;
    cin>>SearchItem;

    //Search for the value
    for (LoopCounter=0; ((LoopCounter<ArraySize) && (FoundFlag==false)
                        (Array[LoopCounter]<=SearchItem));LoopCounter++)
      if (Array[LoopCounter]==SearchItem)
          FoundFlag=true;

    //Check if the value was found
    if (FoundFlag==true)
      cout<<"Item was found";
}
```

Notice we have added another condition to the loop. Why is the condition
`&& (Array[LoopCounter]<=SearchItem)` as opposed to
`(Array[LoopCounter]<SearchItem)`, since we are checking for when they
are less than the search item in order to drop out of the loop?

If we don't allow the condition where `(Array[LoopCounter] ==
SearchItem)` then the `FoundFlag` will never be set to 1.

Sorting

Now that we have a basic understanding of arrays, let's start to use them for practical purposes. Once we have the ability to track a large group of values, some of the first operations we want to perform on the values is to sort and search the values in an array.

What do we mean by sorting? We mean that we are going to rearrange the values of the array so that they go from the highest value to the lowest value or from the lowest value to the highest value.

There are many ways of sorting an array. These methods vary in efficiency, complexity, and the amount of space required to complete the sort. We will implement two basic sorts in this chapter and a more complex sort in the next chapter. Each sort has its own characteristics. For instance, some sorts are of values we wish to sort are small; however, it becomes incredibly inefficient when the number of items we are sorting becomes large. The issues involved in deciding which sorting method is better are the same issues an information systems professional must deal with when determining what the best method is for storing and retrieving information in a database.

■■■ 7.3 BUBBLE SORT

The first of these sorts is called the **bubble sort**. The reason it is called the bubble sort is that we pass over the values in the array, comparing adjacent elements, and if the value to the left is greater than the value to the right, we swap them. By the end of a pass over the data, the greatest value in the array "bubbles" to the top of the array. As we continually pass over the array, we continually place one more value in the proper place after each pass. If we make the same number of passes over the array as the number of items in the array, then all the elements in the array will be sorted from lowest to highest.

Before we look at the code to implement the bubble sort, let's make sure we understand what we wish to accomplish.

Let's start with the following list in a array of six integers:

0	1	2	3	4	5
53	13	1	90	120	5

We start by comparing the value in Array[0] to Array[1], or 53 to 13. Since 53 is greater than 13, we swap them. So the array now looks as follows:

0	1	2	3	4	5
13	53	1	90	120	5

But our work is not done yet, even for the first pass. Now we compare the value in Array[1] to the value in Array[2], or 53 to 1. Since 53 is greater than 1, we swap them and the array looks as follows:

0	1	2	3	4	5
13	1	53	90	120	5

We continue the process and compare Array[2] to Array[3], or 53 to 90. Since 53 is not greater than 90 there is no reason to swap them and the array remains the same as before.

0	1	2	3	4	5
13	1	53	90	120	5

The final check of the first pass is Array[3] to Array[4], or 120 to 5. Since 120 is greater than 5, we swap the two values and the array looks as follows:

0	1	2	3	4	5
13	1	53	90	5	120

Guaranteed Sorted ⟶

Notice that 120 is in its final position within the array. Depending upon the elements in the array, more than one value might be in the proper place, but only one value, the largest, is guaranteed to be in the proper place.

Also notice that in order to compare all the values in the array, we need only $n-1$ comparisons where n is equal to the number of elements in the array.

Now we need to repeat the process until all the values in the array are in the proper order. The following is what the array looks like after each pass of the bubble sort algorithm:

After 1 Pass

0	1	2	3	4	5
13	1	53	90	5	120

Guaranteed Sorted ⟶

After 2 Passes

0	1	2	3	4	5
1	13	53	5	90	120

Guaranteed Sorted ⟶

After 3 Passes

0	1	2	3	4	5
1	13	5	53	90	120

Guaranteed Sorted ⟶

After 4 Passes

0	1	2	3	4	5
1	5	13	53	90	120

Guaranteed Sorted ⟶

Notice that although there are six elements in the array, we only required four passes to completely sort the array. In the worst case we require one less pass than the number of elements. This is because, if on each pass we place at least one value in its proper place then after *n*-1 passes, where *n* is the number of values in the array, we have *n*-1 items in place. By default if only one item is left, then it must be in its proper place. Also, if we are writing the most efficient code possible we would want the **BubbleSort** function to stop once we have the entire array sorted.

To improve understanding of the code, we are going to review three implementations of the **BubbleSort** function. All will work, but each one will be more efficient than the previous one.

```
//First version
void BubbleSort (int Array[], int NumItems)
{
    int NumPasses;
    int InnerLoopCounter;
    int Temp;

    //Outer loop controlling # of passes
    for (NumPasses=0; NumPasses<NumItems-1; NumPasses++)

      // Inner loop controlling # of comparisons per pass
      for (InnerLoopCounter=0; InnerLoopCounter<NumItems-1; InnerLoopCounter++)

        // Compare adjacent array values
        if (Array[InnerLoopCounter] > Array[InnerLoopCounter+1])
        {
          Temp = Array[InnerLoopCounter]; // Perform swap of two adjacent values
          Array[InnerLoopCounter]=Array[InnerLoopCounter+1];
          Array[InnerLoopCounter+1]=Temp;
        }
}
```

With the preceding comments, the code is fairly self-explanatory, so why do we need two other versions? If you stepped through the code step by step, you would observe unnecessary comparisons occurring.

The inner loop sets the index from 0 to **NumItems-2**. Although it is obvious to start at 0, it is not so obvious to end at **NumItems-2**. We would normally loop from 0 to **NumItems-1** to cover all the values in an array of **NumItems** elements. However, since we need to compare two adjacent values we have no need to go to the last value in the array, but the one before the last, which has the index of **NumItems-2**.

Looping from 0 to **NumItems-2** will work, but is inefficient. On the first pass we need to loop from 0 to **NumItems-2**; however, after the first pass is it still necessary to make all those comparisons? In a word, no.

We stated that each pass places an item in the proper place, so why should we compare it to anything? We know that no swap will occur. Therefore, we can modify the inner loop by reducing the upper bound of the index by the number of items guaranteed to be in the proper place. In our program, the number of values guaranteed to be in the proper place is indicated by the variable **NumPasses**. So to accomplish a more efficient algorithm we need to subtract **NumPasses** from the inner loop index **InnerLoopCounter**. The modified code is as follows:

```
//Second version with fewer comparisons
void BubbleSort (int Array[], int NumItems)
{
    int NumPasses;
    int InnerLoopCounter;
    int Temp;

    //Outer loop controlling # of passes
    for (NumPasses=0; NumPasses<NumItems-1; NumPasses++)

        // Inner loop controlling # of comparisons per pass
        for (InnerLoopCounter=0; InnerLoopCounter<NumItems-1-NumPasses;
            InnerLoopCounter++)

        // Compare adjacent array values
        if (Array[InnerLoopCounter] > Array[InnerLoopCounter+1])
        {
            Temp = Array[InnerLoopCounter]; // Perform swap of two adjacent values
            Array[InnerLoopCounter]=Array[InnerLoopCounter+1];
            Array[InnerLoopCounter+1]=Temp;
        }
}
```

Although the second version is an improvement, we can easily improve it further. Image if you had the following array to sort:

0	1	2	3	4	5
1	2	3	4	5	6

The items in this list are already in order; however, the first and second versions of the algorithm require the same number of comparisons as if they weren't in order. Wouldn't it be better to check if the array were sorted and if it were to stop the routine? How can we do this without significantly slowing the routine when the values of the array are not in order? The easiest way is to set a flag so that when a swap occurs we remember it. If no swap occurs the flag will not be set and it is the signal to terminate the routine.

```
0//Third version with flag to stop when sorted
void BubbleSort (int Array[], int NumItems)
{
    int NumPasses;
    int InnerLoopCounter;
    int Temp;
    bool SwapOccurred = true;

    //Outer loop controlling # of passes
    for (NumPasses=0; ((NumPasses<NumItems-1) && (SwapOccurred==true));
        NumPasses++)
    {
      SwapOccurred=false;
      // Inner loop controlling # of comparisons per pass
      for (InnerLoopCounter=0; InnerLoopCounter<NumItems-1;
          InnerLoopCounter++)
      // Compare adjacent array values
      if (Array[InnerLoopCounter] > Array[InnerLoopCounter+1])
      {
        SwapOccurred=true;
        // Perform swap of two adjacent values
        Temp = Array[InnerLoopCounter];
        Array[InnerLoopCounter]=Array[InnerLoopCounter+1];
        Array[InnerLoopCounter+1]=Temp;
      }
    }
}
```

DRILLS

Drill 7-16

Trace though the **BubbleSort** function and determine what the following arrays would look like after one pass through the outer loop of the **BubbleSort** function, two passes through the outer loop of the **BubbleSort** code, and three passes through the outer loop of the **BubbleSort** code.

A pass is equivalent to the execution of the inner for loop for a single value of **NumPasses**. So the first pass is when **NumPasses**=0, the second pass is when **NumPasses**=1, and the third pass is when **NumPasses**=2.

Drill 7-17

Trace through the **BubbleSort** function and determine what the following arrays would look like after each pass through the outer loop of the bubble sort code.

0	1	2	3	4	5
3	120	100	33	142	1

7.4 INSERTION SORT

A slightly more efficient sort than the bubble sort is the **insertion sort**. It works under the premise that it is easier to insert items into a previously sorted list one at a time than to bubble them up as in the previous routine.

Let's start with the same list we used in our **BubbleSort** example:

0	1	2	3	4	5
53	13	1	90	120	5

⟵ Guaranteed Sorted

Imagine you had a list of 1 item, 53. Now you want to add a second item to that list, say 13. You would move any items in the sublist greater than 13 to the right, so you move the 53 to the right and insert the 13. So your list looks as follows:

0	1	2	3	4	5
13	53	1	90	120	5

⟵ Guaranteed Sorted

This list has two values, 13 and 53, sorted in a sublist.

Now we wish to insert the 1. We need to move any values in the sublist greater than 1 to the right. Therefore, we move 53 and 13 to the right and then insert the 1. So our list now looks as follows:

0	1	2	3	4	5
1	13	53	90	120	5

← Guaranteed Sorted

This list has three values, 1, 13, and 53, sorted in a sublist.

Now we wish to insert the 90. We need to move any values greater than 90 in the sublist to the right. Since no values are greater than 90, we don't have to move any values to the right, so the list remains the same, and looks as follows:

0	1	2	3	4	5
1	13	53	90	120	5

← Guaranteed Sorted

Although nothing has changed, we now consider the 90 in the sublist that has been sorted.

Now we wish to insert 120. We need to move any values in the sublist greater than 120 to the right. Again, we don't have to move any values to the right, so as before the list remains unchanged and looks as follows:

0	1	2	3	4	5
1	13	53	90	120	5

← Guaranteed Sorted

Finally, we wish to insert the 5. We need to move any values greater than 5 to the right. Therefore, we move 120, 90, 53, and 13 to the right and then insert the 5. So our list now looks as follows:

0	1	2	3	4	5
1	5	13	53	90	120

All Values Are Guaranteed Sorted

Now we have a completely sorted list and need to write a program that mimics the actions we just demonstrated in sorting the list.

As with **BubbleSort**, we need an outer and an inner loop. The outer loop controls the value we are going to insert into the previously sorted list, and the inner loop moves from the insert value to the left until finding the proper insertion point. While the inner loop moves left, we need to copy the values greater than the insertion value to the right. The first move of a value greater than the insertion value will cause the insertion value in the array to be overwritten, so at the beginning of each inner loop, we need to copy the insertion value to a temporary variable.

The code is as follows:

```
void InsertSort(int Array[], int NumItems)
{
    int InsertItem;
    int InnerLoopCounter;
    int Temp;

    for (InsertItem=1; InsertItem<NumItems; InsertItem++)//controls values to insert
    {
      Temp=Array[InsertItem]; //Store insert value in a temporary variable
                            //Inner loop
      for (InnerLoopCounter=InsertItem-1; InnerLoopCounter>=0 &&
          Temp < Array[InnerLoopCounter]; InnerLoopCounter--)
        Array[InnerLoopCounter+1] = Array[InnerLoopCounter]; //Move values to right
      Array[InnerLoopCounter+1] = Temp; //Place insert value in proper place.
    }
}
```

▌ DRILLS

Drill 7-18

An excellent drill to demonstrate the workings of the insertion sort is to use the same example that we did with the bubble sort. Show what the array looks like after one pass of the outer loop, two passes of the outer loop, and three passes of the outer loop.

0	1	2	3	4	5
6	5	4	3	2	1

Drill 7-19

Here is another example, which demonstrates different patterns with a more randomized initial array. Show what the array looks like after each pass of the outer loop.

0	1	2	3	4	5
3	120	100	3	142	1

As a final review of both the bubble and insertion sort, let's compare the two sorts side by side on the same set of data.

Initial Values

Bubble Sort   **Insertion Sort**

0	1	2	3	4	5
6	5	4	3	2	1

0	1	2	3	4	5
6	5	4	3	2	1

The first pass of the bubble sort compares the 6 to the 5 and swaps them. Then it compares the 6 to the 4 and swaps them. This continues all the way thru the array until the 6 is in the moved all way to the right. In doing so, all the other values have moved one position to the left.

The first pass of the insertion sort compares the 5 to the 6 and the 6 is moved to the right. The pass ends with the 5 being placed in the left-most position of the sublist.

After One Pass

Bubble Sort   **Insertion Sort**

0	1	2	3	4	5
5	4	3	2	1	6

0	1	2	3	4	5
5	6	4	3	2	1

The second pass of the bubble sort compares the 5 to the 4 and swaps them. Then it compares the 5 to the 3 and swaps them. This continues all the way through the array until the 5 is in the moved to the left of the 6. In doing so, all the other values have moved one position to the left.

The second pass of the insertion sort compares the 4 to the 6 and moves the 6 to the right one position. Then it compares the 4 to the 5 and moves the 5 to the right one position. The pass ends with the 4 being placed in the left-most position.

After Two Passes

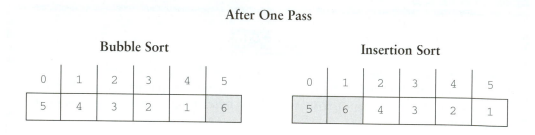

Bubble Sort   **Insertion Sort**

0	1	2	3	4	5
4	3	2	1	5	6

0	1	2	3	4	5
4	5	6	3	2	1

It now should be clear that the bubble sort works by placing the sorted values in their proper places on the right-most side of the array, whereas the insertion sort works by sorting the values with relation to one another on the left side of the array.

The remainder of the passes are shown.

After Three Passes

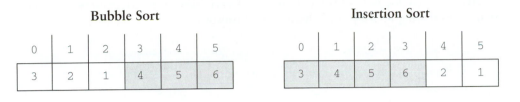

Bubble Sort

0	1	2	3	4	5
3	2	1	4	5	6

Insertion Sort

0	1	2	3	4	5
3	4	5	6	2	1

After Four Passes

Bubble Sort

0	1	2	3	4	5
2	1	3	4	5	6

Insertion Sort

0	1	2	3	4	5
2	3	4	5	6	1

After Five Passes

Bubble Sort

0	1	2	3	4	5
1	2	3	4	5	6

Insertion Sort

0	1	2	3	4	5
1	2	3	4	5	6

7.5 FILES

So far we have written programs that rely on either input from the user or the information being coded directly into the program itself. Obviously, there will be times when we either need to save information permanently or get input from a permanent source. Files are an excellent way to accomplish both of these objectives.

Writing to Files

Think about a program that sorts 100 numbers. Instead of outputting the values to the screen, we can output the results to a file and observe the results later. To accomplish this we need new routines that handle input and output to a file. C++ provides these routines in another header file. Therefore, you must include the following header file to indicate to the compiler that we will be using files.

```
#include <fstream.h>
```

C++ provides handles to files so that we can access them by name. In essence, we need a handle to a file, just like we need a handle on a briefcase. In C++, if we wish to create a filename we will write to, we use a variable of type **ofstream**. The template for creating an output file handle is as follows:

```
ofstream FileHandle;
```

To declare a variable called **NewFile** that will be a handle to an output file use the following code:

```
ofstream NewFile;
```

Although the previous statement declares a variable, we still have not created a file. Remember the variable is only a handle to the file. To open a file, we need to issue an open command to the file handle that we created. This is shown in the following template:

```
fileHandle.open("Filename.FileExtention");
```

The following is an example of declaring a file handle and opening a file called "Students.txt":

```
ofstream NewFile;
newfile.open("Students.txt");
```

This will create a file on the disk called **Students.txt**. However, C++ does not actually create the file, the operating system does. C++ makes a call to the operating system. Be careful; if a file already exists called **Students.txt**, it will be erased.

By default, C++ will open the file in the directory in which the executable is located. However, you can also create a file with a specific path as in:

```
newfile.open("a:Students.txt");
```

However, what would happen if you tried the following code?

```
newfile.open("a:\Directory\Students.txt");
```

The character \ would be interpreted incorrectly. Instead you are required to use the following when dealing with \ characters within file paths.

```
newfile.open("a:\\Directory\\Students.txt");
```

Hopefully, the file opened properly. If we just hope, we may get in trouble, so C++ provides a way to check. By using the following statement we can check if the file we attempted to open actually opened:

```
if (newfile.fail())
    cout<<"Error opening output file"<<endl;
else
   //Rest of the program
```

Now that you have the file open, it is ready to receive information. Output is accomplished in the same manner as with the **cout** command. Type the variable containing the handle to the file and the **<<** operator. Now type anything you wish to be placed in the file to the right of the **<<** operator. See the following template:

```
FileHandle<<InformationToBeWritten;
```

This is shown in the following code:

```
//Example of a string being written to a file
NewFile <<"This is written to the disk file" <<endl;

//Example of a string being displayed on the screen
cout <<"While this is written to the screen" <<endl;
```

When we are finished outputting all the desired information to a file, we must remember to close the file. This is accomplished by issuing the following command:

```
NewFile.close();
```

The following complete program demonstrates all of these concepts. It takes the contents of a two-dimensional array of characters and outputs each row as a string on a separate line of a file.

```cpp
#include <stdlib.h>
#include <iostream.h>
#include <fstream.h>

#define NumNames 5
#define NameSize 50

void main()
{
    char Names[NumNames][NameSize]={
            "King Arthur",
            "Sir Galahad",
            "Sir Lancelot",
            "Sir Bedevere",
            "Sir Robin"};

    int NameCounter;

    ofstream KnightsFile;

    KnightsFile.open("HolyGrail.dat");

    if (KnightsFile.fail())
    {
        cout<<"Error opening output file"<<endl;
        return;
    }

    for(NameCounter = 0; NameCounter < NumNames; NameCounter++)
        KnightsFile<<Names[NameCounter]<<endl;

    KnightsFile.close();
}
```

The output file would appear as follows:

```
King Arthur
Sir Galahad
Sir Lancelot
Sir Bedevere
Sir Robin
```

DRILLS

Will the following code snippet open a file called "DrillOutput.dat" in the directory "Drills" on the C drive? If not, explain why.

Drill 7-20

```
ofstream DrillOutput;

DrillOutput.open("C:\Drills\DrillOutput.dat");
```

Will the following code snippet open a file called "OutputFile.dat" or "FileOut.dat"? Explain your answer.

Drill 7-21

```
ofstream OutputFile;

OutputFile.open("FileOut.dat");
```

Does the following code snippet output the expression "DrillOutput.dat" to the file "DrillOutput.dat"? If not, explain why.

Drill 7-22

```
ofstream DrillOutput.dat;

DrillOutput.open("DrillOutput.dat");

DrillOutput<<"DrillOutput.dat";

DrillOutput.close();
```

Reading From Files

What about reading information from a file? We follow the same basic format as when we create an output file, but we use a different variable type for the file handle. Instead of using an **ofstream** variable type, we use an **ifstream** variable type. To declare a file handle called **InFile** so that we can open a file to read its contents, use the following code:

```
ifstream InFile;
```

Although the type of variable is different, the way we open it is the same.

```
InFile.open("a:students.txt");
```

To read from the file into a variable, we use the same operator as we do with the **cin** command, **>>**. The **>>** operator will direct the first value from the input file to the variable to the right of the **>>** operator. To read more than one value at a time, simply separate each value with a **>>** operator as you would do in the **cin** command. See the following code as an example of reading two integers from the previously opened **InFile** file:

```
int Value1;
int Value2;

InFile>>Value1>>Value2;
```

Now let's look at the complete program as an example:

```
//Example of computing grades from files

#include <stdlib.h>
#include <iostream.h>
#include <fstream.h>
```

```
void main()
{
    int StudentId;
    int HighId;
    float Grade;
    int NumStudent;
    float Highest =-1; //Assumes grades will be >=0

    ifstream Infile;
    InFile.open("Students.dat");

    for (NumStudent=0; NumStudent<3; NumStudent++)
    {
      Infile >> StudentId >> Grade;
      if (Grade>Highest)
      {
          Highest=Grade;
          HighId=StudentId;
      }
    }
    cout <<HighId
         <<" is the student with the highest GPA of "
         <<Highest<<endl;
    InFile.close();
}
```

The program starts by declaring the necessary variables and opening the "Students.dat" file. Then the program loops through the file, reading three records. Each record consists of a student id and a grade. If the grade is higher than the previous highest grade, it is recorded along with the associated student id as the new highest. When the loop terminates, the highest record is displayed.

If the input file "Students.dat" contained the following:

```
123 3.5
234 3.2
923 1.7
```

Then the output of the program would look like the following:

```
123 is the student with the highest GPA of 3.5
```

Let's modify the program a little bit. Try to set it up so that user enters a student id and then the program reads the student records in the input file until that particular student is found or all the student records have been examined. Then, as before, the program will display the GPA associated with the student.

```cpp
//Example of searching a file of grades

#include <stdlib.h>
#include <iostream.h>
#include <fstream.h>

void main()
{
   int StudentId;
   int SearchValue;
   float GPA;
   ifstream InFile;
   int NumStudent;
   bool Done=false;

   InFile.open("Students.dat");

   cout << "Enter student number:"<<endl;
   cin >> SearchValue;

   for (NumStudent=0; NumStudent<3 && !Done; NumStudent++)
   {
     InFile >> StudentId >> GPA;
     if (StudentId == SearchValue)
     {
        cout << "GPA is: " << GPA;
        Done = true;
     }
   }
   InFile.close();
}
```

The program is similar to the previous one; however, now we add an additional condition to the looping condition. This breaks the loop when the student id searched for is found.

In all of the previous examples, we have assumed that we know the number of items in the file, but in most cases this is unknown. However, C++ provides a simple method to test to see if the values supposedly read were read correctly and that we did not reach the end of the input file.

In the following example, we replace the **for** loop with a **while** loop. Part of the condition in the **while** loop is the check to see if the file handle, **infile**, is true. It will become false when invalid values are read or when the end of the file is reached.

```
while(InFile && !Done)
  {
    InFile >> StudentId >> GPA;
    if (StudentId == SearchValue)
      {
        cout << "GPA is: " << GPA;
        Done = true;
      }
  }
```

As long as everything is read properly **InFile** will return true. If the file is at the end or the wrong type of values are read, a false condition is returned and the loop is terminated.

Let's write a slightly more advanced program. This program should ask the user for a bank account number. The program should then read input from a file called "AccountInfo.dat." "AccountInfo.dat" contains records consisting of an account number (integer), transaction (character, D for deposit, W for withdrawal), and an amount (floating point number). The program should calculate a balance and output it:

```
//Bank account program that accesses files

#include <stdlib.h>
#include <iostream.h>
#include <fstream.h>

void main()
{
    int Account, SearchAccount;
    float Transaction, Balance=0;
    char TransType;
    ifstream InFile;

    InFile.open("AccountInfo.dat");
    cout << "Enter account number:"<<endl;
    cin >> SearchValue;
```

```
    while(InFile)
    {
      InFile >>Account>>TransType>>Transaction;
      if (InFile)
      {
          if (Account == SearchAccount)
          {
              if (TransType=='D')
                Balance+=Transaction;
              else if (TransType=='W')
                Balance-=Transaction;
              else
                cout<<"Error in input file"<<endl;
          }
      }
    }
    cout<<endl<<"The account balance is "<<Balance;
    InFile.close();
}
```

Imagine if the file "AccountInfo.dat" contains the following:

```
675 D 1000.0
512 D 500.0
275 D 100.0
675 D 500.0
675 W 250.0
675 D 75.0
275 W 50.0
675 W 100.0
```

Therefore, if the program was run and **675** was entered as the account number, then the balance would be calculated by performing all the operations with an account number of **675** associated with it. Therefore, the deposits 1000.0, 500.0, and 75 are added together, with the withdrawals of 250.0, 50.0, and 100.0 subtracted to get a total of 1175.0

The program starts by opening the **AccountInfo.dat** file and asking the user for the account number to tally. The program then loops through the file reading a record at a time. After each record is read, we check to make sure that the **infile** file handle still contains a valid value. If so, we process the values; otherwise we terminate the loop and output the total for the account.

DRILLS

What is wrong with the following program, which should read in four integers from a file and output the values read to the screen?

Drill 7-23

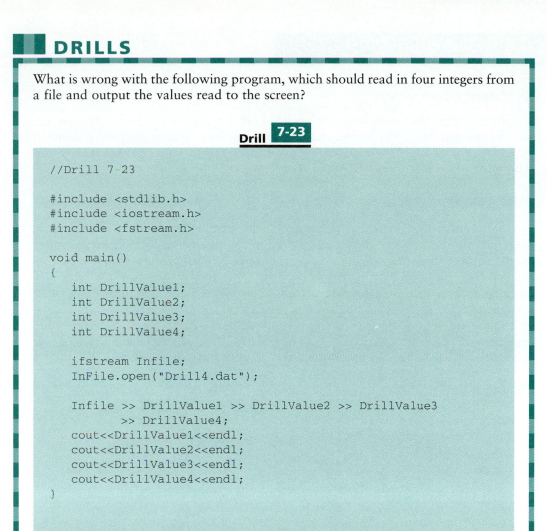

```
//Drill 7-23

#include <stdlib.h>
#include <iostream.h>
#include <fstream.h>

void main()
{
    int DrillValue1;
    int DrillValue2;
    int DrillValue3;
    int DrillValue4;

    ifstream Infile;
    InFile.open("Drill4.dat");

    Infile >> DrillValue1 >> DrillValue2 >> DrillValue3
           >> DrillValue4;
    cout<<DrillValue1<<endl;
    cout<<DrillValue2<<endl;
    cout<<DrillValue3<<endl;
    cout<<DrillValue4<<endl;
}
```

7.6   Case Study

Problem Description

Continuing from the example that we started in the case study of Chapter 6, input all employees' numbers, full names, wage rates, and tax rates in employee number sequence. Store each of these values in separate arrays. Produce a report that shows as output name, number, wage rate, and tax rate, ordered by name.

Discussion

As the specified values are read in, another array, **ptr**, will be given a row number. Then a bubble sort will be used to rearrange these row numbers by alphabetical value of the names. The string compare function **strcmp** is used in the sort. The **strcmp** function has the form **int strcmp(string1, string2)**. The function returns a negative value if string1 is less than **string2**, a positive value if **string1** is greater than **string2**, and a zero if **string1 = string2**. Using an extra array of integers is a more economical approach to this sorting problem than trying to rearrange multiple arrays. The header <string.h> must be included. Note that since the first and last names are in one string, the names are arranged in first-name sequence.

Solution

```
#include <iostream.h>
#include <iomanip.h>
#include <string.h>

//Constants
#define Rows 100
#define Cols 30

//Functions
float GetValue(int Number);
void Prompt(int Value);
void Sort(int Size, int Ptr[], char Name[][Cols]);
void DisplayHeader();
void DisplayLine(int Ptr, int Num[], char Name[], float Wage[],
                float TaxRate[]);
```

```cpp
void main()
{
    int EmployeeNumber[Rows], Ptr[Rows], Index = 0;
    char Name[Rows][Cols];
    float Wage[Rows],TaxRate[Rows];

    do
    {
        EmployeeNumber[Index] = int(GetValue(1));
        if (EmployeeNumber[Index] <= 0)
          break;
        Prompt(2);
        cin.getline(Name[Index],80);
        Wage[Index] = GetValue(4);
        TaxRate[Index] = GetValue(5);
        Ptr[Index] = Index;
        Index++;
     } while(EmployeeNumber[Index-1] > 0 && Index < Rows);

    if (Index > 0)
      Sort(Index, Ptr, Name);
    else
      return;

    DisplayHeader();

    for (int i = 0; i < Index; i++)
    {
        DisplayLine(Ptr[i],EmployeeNumber,Name[Ptr[i]],Wage,
                TaxRate);
    }
}
float GetValue(int Number)
{
    float Value;
    Prompt(Number);
    cin >> Value;
    cin.get();//Extracts \n from buffer
    return Value;
}
```

```
void Prompt(int Value)
{
  switch(Value)
  {
    case 1:
      cout << "\nEnter negative to end or ";
      cout << "\nEnter employee\'s ID -> "; break;
    case 2:
      cout << "Enter employee\'s name -> "; break;
    case 3:
      cout << "Enter employee\'s hours -> "; break;
    case 4:
      cout << "Enter employee\'s wage rate -> "; break;
    case 5:
      cout << "Enter employee\'s tax rate -> "; break;
  }
}


void Sort(int Size, int Ptr[], char Name[][Cols])
{
  int Outer, Inner, Temp;
  bool Sorted = false;
  for(Outer = 0;(Outer < Size-1 && !Sorted);Outer++)
  {
    Sorted = true;
    for(Inner =0; Inner < Size-1-Outer; Inner++)
    {
      if(strcmp(Name[Ptr[Inner]], Name[Ptr[Inner+1]]) > 0)
      {
        Temp = Ptr[Inner+1];
        Ptr[Inner+1] = Ptr[Inner];
        Ptr[Inner] = Temp;
        Sorted = false;
      }
    }
  }
}


void DisplayHeader()
{
  cout << "\nEMP NAME                   EMP NUM    WAGE    TAX RATE\n";
  cout << setiosflags(ios::showpoint | ios :: fixed)<< setprecision(2);
}

void DisplayLine(int Ptr, int Num[], char Name[], float Wage[],
                 float TaxRate[])
{
  cout << endl << setw(25) << setiosflags(ios :: left) << Name;
  cout << setiosflags(ios :: right) << Num[Ptr];
  cout << setw(10) << Wage[Ptr] << setw(10) << TaxRate[Ptr];
}
```

7.6 Case Study (continued)

Output

```
Enter negative to end or
Enter employee's ID -> 10101
Enter employee's name -> Zeta Alphonse
Enter employee's wage rate -> 18.60
Enter employee's tax rate -> .33

Enter negative to end or
Enter employee's ID -> 10102
Enter employee's name -> Bill Markham
Enter employee's wage rate -> 7.85
Enter employee's tax rate -> .20

Enter negative to end or
Enter employee's ID -> 10103
Enter employee's name -> Al Alphonse
Enter employee's wage rate -> 10.50
Enter employee's tax rate -> .26

Enter negative to end or
Enter employee's ID -> -9

EMP NAME                EMP NUM    WAGE    TAX RATE

Al Alphonse             10103      10.50     0.26
Bill Markham            10102       7.85     0.20
Zeta Alphonse           10101      18.60     0.33
```

END-OF-CHAPTER

◆ Key Terms

Bubble Sort	A simple sorting method that will order an array of values by making repeated passes over the array.
Insertion Sort	A simple sorting method that will order an array of values by making repeated passes over the array.
Linear Search	A simple searching method that determines whether a value is contained within an array by progressing through the array from the first index to the last.

◆Key Terms

StrCat	A function to append the contents of one string to the end of another.
StrCmp	A function that compares two strings to see if they contain the same values.
StrCpy	A function to copy the contents of one string to another.

◆C++ Keywords Introduced

`fstream.h`	Include file required for using files in C++.
`ifstream`	Variable type for creating input files.
`ofstream`	Variable type for creating output files.

◆Answers to Drills

Drill 7-1

The output to the drill is as follows:

```
The length of the 1st string is 10
The length of the 2nd string is 14
The length of the 3rd string is 0
```

Remember the length of a string as defined by **StrLen** is the number of characters in the string excluding the '\0' character. Remember, **StrLen** has nothing to do with the size of the array itself.

Therefore, the drill is simple. We must count the number of characters in each of the strings and output them. The first two are simple, they are 10 and 14. The last one may be tricky. There are no characters other than the '\0' placed there by the double quotes. Therefore the length of the last string is 0.

Drill 7-2

The drill allocates an array called **String1**, which contains 40 characters. We call the **StrCpy** function to copy the string **"We are going to implement strings"** into the newly allocated array. There is enough room in the array for the entire string, so it copies without a problem. Then we output the string and the output is as follows:

```
We are going to implement strings
```

Drill 7-3

The drill allocates an array called **String1**, which contains 40 characters. It is initialized to the string **"What will display"**. We call the **StrCpy** function to copy the string **"Maybe this?"** into the newly allocated array. It writes over the previous string leaving the array with the contents of the string **"Maybe this?"** in its place. There is enough room in the array for the entire string, so it copies without a problem. Then we output the string and the output is as follows:

```
Maybe this?
```

Drill 7-4

The drill starts like the others, but there is a big problem. When the string **"What will output if I type all of this here instead!"** is copied, there is not enough room in the array **String1** to store it. Since there is not enough room, we cannot predict the results; therefore, we get a run-time error.

Drill 7-5

The drill starts out by attempting to initialize the array **String1** to **"What will output if I type all of this here instead!"**; however, there is not enough room allocated in **String1** to initialize it. Because the string is attempting to be initialized to a string greater than its size, the compiler will produce a syntax error and no output will occur.

Drill 7-6

The output to the drill would be:

```
The strings are different
```

Although the characters in both strings spell out the same thing, the characters in the second string are capitalized. Remember, C++ is case sensitive, therefore the strings are considered different, and a nonzero value is returned from **StrCmp**. Since a nonzero value is returned, the conditional expression evaluates to true and the first **cout** statement executes.

Drill 7-7

The output to the drill would be:

```
The strings are the same
```

This time the characters in both strings spell out the same thing and the capitalization of the strings is the same. A value of zero is therefore returned from **StrCmp**. Since a zero value is returned, the conditional expression evaluates to false and the second **cout** statement executes.

Drill 7-8

The output to the drill would be:

```
The strings are the same
```

This is very similar to the previous drill; however, the size of the arrays is different. **StrCmp** does not look at the size of the array in its comparision. It only looks at the characters that make up the string contained within the array. Since both arrays contain the same strings and both arrays have enough space to store each string, the program executes identically to Drill 7-6.

Drill 7-9

You might think that the output would be as follows:

```
The strings are different
```

However, you would be wrong. The output is as follows:

```
The strings are the same
```

As in previous examples, **StrCmp** returns a nonzero value, since the two strings are different. However, unlike the previous examples, the conditional expression does not compare the return value of **StrCmp** using a not-equal operator. Instead, no operator is indicated. Therefore, if we remember back to our conditional expression evaluation, we will remember that any nonzero value is evaluated to true. Therefore, the first **cout** statement is executed.

Drill 7-10

The output of the drill is as follows:

```
What will this display
```

This was actually a trick question. You may have thought the output should have been "What will this displayWhat will this display". That would be correct if we choose to output the value of **String1**. However, we choose to output **String2**, which is not affected by the **StrCat** function.

Drill 7-11

The output of the drill is as follows:

```
What will this displayWhat will this display
```

This is the result of what you might have expected from Drill 7-10. The string in the array **String2** is appended to the end of the string in array **String1**. Then the newly formed string in the array **String1** is output.

Drill 7-12

There would be no predictable output from this drill. When the **StrCat** function attempts to append the string contained in the array **String2** to the string contained in array **String1**, the amount of space allocated for the array **String1** is exceeded. Therefore, a run-time error occurs.

Drill 7-13

There would be no predictable output from this drill. When the **StrCat** function attempts to append the string contained in the array **String2** to the string contained in the array **String1**, we find that there is no valid string contained in array **String1**. Without a valid string, there is no way for **StrCat** to determine the proper place to append the string contained in the array **String2**. Therefore, a run-time error occurs.

Drill 7-14

The output of the drill would be as follows:

```
What will this display
```

The array **String1** contains a string with no characters other than the '\0' and an empty string is a valid string as long as it has the '\0' contained within it. Therefore, the **StrCat** function merely copies the string contained in the array **String2** to the array **String1**. Then **String1** is output as shown.

Drill 7-15

The output of the drill would be as follows:

```
24
18
error
This is the first string
This is the first stringYet another string
0
These strings are equal
42
```

The first output is the number of characters in **String1** excluding the '\0'. The second output is the number of characters in **String2** excluding the '\0'. The third output would produce an error. This is because **String3** is not a valid string at all—it is an array of characters that was not initialized. It can contain anything. It will probably produce a run-time error, but we cannot be certain. The word "error" is showed in the output, but the word "error" would not really appear.

The next output is the string contained in **String3**. This is the same value as the string contained in **String1**, since **String1** was copied to **String3** in the previous statement.

We then concatenate the string contained in **String2** to the end of **String3**. This causes the combination of **String1** and **String2** to be displayed.

We then compare the string contained in **String2** to the string contained in **String2**. Since **String2** is passed as both parameters, they are obviously the same string. **StrCmp** returns 0 when the strings passed are the same, so a 0 is output.

When **StrCmp** compares **String1** with **String2** it determines they are not the same string. **StrCmp** returns a nonzero value. Nonzero values are true, so the if statement evaluates to true. Therefore, the statement "These strings are equal" is output.

Finally, the length of **String3** is output. As before, the length is calculated as the number of characters excluding the '\0'.

Drill 7-16

The answer to the drill is as follows:

0	1	2	3	4	5
6	5	4	3	2	1

This is an excellent example to start with, because it clearly shows the progression of the array elements when each pass of the **BubbleSort** is executed.

The beginning of the first pass starts by comparing the array element in index 0, 6, to the array element in index 1, 5. Since 6 is greater than 5, the values are swapped. Then the array element in index 1, now 6, is compared to the array element in index 2, 4. Since 6 is greater than 4, the values are swapped. Since 6 is greater than all the elements in the array, as we work down the loop, 6 is swapped with the value to its right. At the end of one pass of the outer **for** loop, the array now looks as follows:

0	1	2	3	4	5
5	4	3	2	1	6

Guaranteed Sorted ⟶

When the second pass begins, we start by comparing the value in index 0 of the array, 5, with the value in index 1 of the array, 4. Since 5 is greater than 4, the values are swapped.

Much like the 6 in the previous example, the 5 is greater than all the values from index 1 to index 4. Since **NumPasses** is now equal to 1 in the loop, we will not compare the value in index 5. Therefore, the array will look as follows:

0	1	2	3	4	5
4	3	2	1	5	6

Guaranteed Sorted ⟶

When the third pass begins, we start by comparing the value in index 0 of the array, 4, with the value in index 1 of the array, 3. Since 4 is greater than 3, the values are swapped.

Much like the 6 and 5 in the previous passes, the 4 is greater than all the values from index 1 to index 3. Since **NumPasses** is now equal to 2 in the loop, we will not compare the values in indexes 4 and 5. Therefore the array will look as follows:

0	1	2	3	4	5
3	2	1	4	5	6

Guaranteed Sorted ⟶

Drill 7-17

The beginning of the first pass starts by comparing the array element in index 0, 3, to the array element in index 1, 120. Since 3 is not greater than 120, the values are not swapped. Then the array element in index 1, 120, is compared to the array element in index 2, 100. Since 120 is greater than 100, the values are swapped. Then the array element in index 2, now 120, is compared to the array element in index 3, 33. Since 120 is greater than 33, the values are swapped. Then the array element in index 3, now 120, is compared to the array element in index 4, 142. Since 120 is not greater than 142, the values are not swapped. Finally, the array element in index 4, 142, is compared to the array element in index 5, 1. Since 142 is greater than 1, the values are swapped. At the end of one pass of the outer **for** loop, the array now looks as follows:

0	1	2	3	4	5
3	100	33	120	1	142

Guaranteed Sorted →

The second pass starts with the comparision of the array element at index 0, 3, and the array element at index 1, 100. Since 3 is not greater than 100, elements are not swapped. Then the array element at index 1, 100, is compared to the array element at index 2, 33. Since 100 is greater than 33, the values are swapped. Then the array element at index 2, now 100, is compared to the array element at index 3, 120. Since 100 is not greater than 120, the values are not swapped. Then the array element at index 3, 120, is compared to the array element at index 4, 1. Since 120 is greater than 1, the values are swapped. The inner loop now terminates, because the remainder of the items in the array are already sorted. So, at the end of two passes of the outer **for** loop, the array now looks as follows:

0	1	2	3	4	5
3	33	100	1	120	142

Guaranteed Sorted →

The third pass starts with the comparision of the array element at index 0, 3, with the array element at index 1, 33. Since 3 is not greater than 33, the elements are not swapped. Then the array element at index 1, 33, is compared with the array element at index 2, 100. Since 33 is not greater than 100, the values are not swapped. Then the array value at index 2, 100, is compared with the array value at index 3, 1. Since 100 is greater than 1, the values are swapped. The inner loop now terminates, because the remainder of the items in the array are already sorted. So, at the end of three passes of the outer **for** loop, the array now looks as follows:

0	1	2	3	4	5
3	33	1	100	120	142

Guaranteed Sorted →

The fourth pass starts with the comparision of the array element at index 0, 3, with the array element at index 1, 33. Since 3 is not greater than 33, the elements are not swapped. Then the array element at index 1, 33, is compared with the array element at index 2, 1. Since 33 is greater than 1, the values are swapped. The inner loop now terminates, because the remainder of the items in the array are already sorted. So, at the end of four passes of the outer **for** loop, the array now looks as follows:

0	1	2	3	4	5
3	1	33	100	120	142

Guaranteed Sorted →

The fifth and final pass starts with the comparision of the array element at index 0, 3, with the array element at index 1, 1. Since 3 is greater than 1, the elements are swapped. The inner loop now terminates, because the remainder of the items in the array are already sorted. So, at the end of five passes of the outer **for** loop, the array is now sorted:

0	1	2	3	4	5
1	3	33	100	120	142

All Are Guaranteed Sorted

Drill 7-18

As with the bubble sort, this is an excellent example to start with, because it also clearly shows the progression of the array elements when each pass of the insertion sort is executed.

We start with the assumption that the first element, 6, is sorted in a list by itself. Then we wish to add the element at index 1, 5, to the list. We accomplish this by comparing the value 5 to the value in the index to the left, 6. Since 6 is greater than 5, we move the value 6 one index over to the right. Therefore, the value 6 is now stored in index 1. For a brief moment, the value 6 is stored in two places in the array. Then when the inner loop terminates, we place the original value we were inserting, 5, into the array at index 0.

0	1	2	3	4	5
5	6	4	3	2	1

← **Guaranteed Sorted**

After one pass of the outer loop, the array looks as depicted. The 5 and 6 are sorted within respect to each other, but unlike the bubble sort they are not in their final positions within the array.

The second pass starts, wanting to place the value at index 2, 4, in its proper place. The 4 is compared to the value to the left, 6. Since 6 is greater than 4, the 6 is copied to the right one space. Then the value at index 0, 5, is compared to 4. Since 5 is greater than 4, it is moved to the right one. Since there are no more values remaining to the left, the 4 is placed in its proper place at index 0. The array then looks as follows:

0	1	2	3	4	5
4	5	6	3	2	1

◄— Guaranteed Sorted

The third pass follows the same pattern. The 3 is compared to all the values to the left. Since all the values are greater than 3, they all move to the right one space. The 3 is then placed in the index 0 element. The array then looks as follows:

0	1	2	3	4	5
3	4	5	6	2	1

◄— Guaranteed Sorted

Only because this example had the values from greatest value to lowest value, the exact opposite of what we want, did the pattern of replacements follow exactly the same order each iteration of the loop.

Drill 7-19

0	1	2	3	4	5
3	120	100	3	142	1

We start with the assumption that the first element, 3, is sorted in a list by itself. Then we wish to add the element at index 1, 120, to the list. We accomplish this by comparing the value 120 to the value in the index to the left, 3. Since 3 is not greater than 120 we assume that 120 is in the proper place with relation to the previously sorted sublist. Although nothing has changed, the values 3 and 120 are now considered in the sublist.

0	1	2	3	4	5
3	120	10	33	142	1

◄— Guaranteed Sorted

We now wish to add the element at index 2, 100, to the list. We accomplish this by comparing the value 100 to the value in the index to the left, 120. Since 120 is greater than 100, we move the value 120 one index over to the right. So the value 120 is now stored in index 2. For a brief moment, the value 120 is stored in two places in the array. Then the value at index 0, 3, is compared to 100. Since 3 is not greater than 100, we are finished searching for the place to insert the value 100 Then when the inner loop terminates, we place the original value we were inserting, 100, into the array at index 1. The array now has the values 3, 100, and 120 sorted in a sublist. The array looks as follows:

0	1	2	3	4	5
3	100	120	33	142	1

◄— Guaranteed Sorted

We now wish to add the element at index 3, 33, to the sublist. We accomplish this by comparing the value 33 to the value in the index to the left, 120. Since 120 is greater than 33, we move the value 120 one index over to the right. So the value 120 is now stored in index 3. Then the value at index 1, 100, is compared to 33. Since 100 is greater than 33, we move the value 100 one index over to the right. So the value 100 is now stored in index 2. Finally, the value at index 0, 3, is compared to 33. Since 3 is not greater than 33, we do not move the value 33 to the right. Then the inner loop terminates and we place the original value we were inserting, 33, into the array at index 1. The array now has the values 3, 33, 100, and 120 sorted in a sublist. The array looks as follows:

0	1	2	3	4	5
3	33	100	120	142	1

← Guaranteed Sorted

Now we wish to add the element at index 4, 142, to the sublist. We accomplish this by comparing the value 142 to the value in the index to the left, 120. Since 120 is not greater than 142 we assume that 142 is in the proper place with relation to the sublist that we have previously sorted. Although nothing has changed, the values 3, 33, 100, 120, and 142 are now considered in the sublist.

0	1	2	3	4	5
3	33	100	120	142	1

← Guaranteed Sorted

The final pass places the value at index 5, 1, in the proper place. One is compared to the values to the left and in each case the values to the left are greater than 1. Therefore, all the values in the sublist are moved to the right one. Finally, 1 is placed in its proper place at index 0. The final array looks as follows:

0	1	2	3	4	5
1	3	100	120	33	142

All Values Are Guaranteed Sorted

Drill 7-20

The code in this drill will not open the file called "DrillOutput.dat" in the directory "Drills" on the C drive, because the statement
`DrillOutput.open("C:\Drills\DrillOutput.dat");` contains a \ character in the directory path. In order for a directory to be specified, we need to use the special escape sequence \\ to indicate a \ in the directory path.

Drill 7-21

The code in this drill will open a file called "FileOut.dat". The name of the `ofstream` variable is not related to the name of the file opened on the computer.

Drill 7-22

The code in this drill will not output the expression "DrillOutput.dat" to the file "DrillOutput.dat", because the name of the variable in its declaration of the ofstream variable is illegal. If the declaration was `ofstream DrillOutput` then it would have been output correctly.

Drill 7-23

The code for this drill does everything properly to read in four integers from a file and then output them to the screen; however, it does not close the file when we are through with it. This will eventually lead to problems and should be avoided.

◆ Programming Exercises

1. Write a function, `StrNCpy`, that accepts two arrays of characters and an integer. The first array should be the destination array, and the second array should be the source array. `StrNCpy` should copy the number of characters indicated by the third parameter from the source array to the destination array.

2. Write a function, `StrNCmp`, that accepts two arrays of characters and an integer. `StrNCmp` should return a 0 if the first n (the third parameter) characters of each array are identical, otherwise it should return a nonzero value.

3. Write a function, `StrNCat`, that accepts two arrays of characters and an integer. The first array should be the destination array, and the second array should be the source array. `StrNCat` should copy the number of characters indicated by the third parameter from the source array to the end of the destination array.

4. Write a function called `Duplicates` that accepts an array of integers and an integer indicating the number of elements in the array. The function returns `true` if a duplicate exists in an array. If a duplicate does not exist then it should return `false`.

5. Rewrite the bubble sort routine so that it sorts the array in descending order.

6. Rewrite the insertion sort routine so that it sorts the array in descending order.

7. Write a program that performs a bubble sort of arrays of characters instead of integers.

8. Write a program that performs an insertion sort for arrays of characters instead of integers.

9. Write a program that opens a file and outputs the number of integers that are contained within the file.

10. Write a program that opens a file and counts how many characters are contained within the file.

11. Write a program that accepts a string from the user and searches a file to see if the string appears in the file. The program should indicate whether or not the string appears in the file. If it does, the program should display the entire line on which the string appears.

12. Write a program that asks a user for answers to a questionnaire. The program should ask the user for a name and then ask the user all of the questions. The program should store the results in a file.

13. Write a program that can decode the file that was created in exercise 2, and print out a detailed description of all the questions and answers that were asked.

◆ Additional Exercises

1. True of False: In a character array, the items are not accessed individually at each index, because the whole string must be accessed at once to perform any changes.

2. What is the output of the following code?

```
char Buffer[256];

char String1[]="The Yankees are the team of the century!";
char String2[]="I am tired of Jeff's sports examples";
char String3[]="   ";

cout<<strlen(String1)<<endl;
cout<<strlen(String2)<<endl;
cout<<strlen(String3)<<endl;

cout<<strlen(Buffer)<<endl;

strcpy(Buffer,String1);
cout<<Buffer<<endl;

strcpy(String2, Buffer);
cout<<Buffer>>endl;
cout<<String2<<endl;

strncpy(Buffer, String1, 11);
strncat(Buffer, String3, 1);
strcat(Buffer, "rule!");

cout<<Buffer<<endl;
```

3. What is the output of the following code?

```
if (strcmp("AAA", "aaa"))
   cout<<"Answer 1"<<endl;
else
   cout<<"Answer 2"<<endl;
```

4. What is the output of the following code?

```
if (strcmp("String 1", "String 2"))
  cout<<"Answer 1"<<endl;
else
  cout<<"Answer 2"<<endl;
```

5. What is the output of the following code?

```
if (strncmp("String 1", "String 2", 3))
  cout<<"Answer 1"<<endl;
else
  cout<<"Answer 2"<<endl;
```

6. Show the entire calling sequence using bubble sort for the following list of numbers.

   23 45 65 12 32 76 87 13 78 55

7. Show the entire calling sequence using bubble sort for the following list of numbers.

   17 23 1 65 22 6 55 20 5 78 99

8. Show the entire calling sequence using insertion sort for the following list of numbers.

   23 45 65 12 32 76 87 13 78 55

9. Show the entire calling sequence using insertion sort for the following list of numbers.

   17 23 1 65 22 6 55 20 5 78 99

10. Show two ways to create an empty file.

11. True or False: A file can be read only if it was created by the program that is attempting to read.

12. Assume that you have a file that contains only integers. When will the following statement be false?
    `while(infile>>value1>>value2);`

13. List at least three reasons why you couldn't open a file for input.

14. List at least two reasons why you couldn't open a file for output.

8

Advanced Application of Arrays

Chapter Objectives

- ◆ Develop more complex applications with arrays

- ◆ Learn how to recursively call a function so that we may use it to develop more complex applications

- ◆ Learn the concept behind a more efficient searching method

- ◆ Implement the more efficient searching method (Binary Search)

- ◆ Learn the concept behind a more efficient sorting method

- ◆ Implement the more efficient sorting method (Quick Sort)

8.1 RECURSIVE FUNCTIONS

It is often desirable to allow a function to call itself; this is called **recursion**. I was told that the original definition for recurism in *Merriam Webster's Collegiate Dictionary* was: "See the definition of recursion." Although I am not old enough to verify if this is true, it is a very fitting definition.

The basis for using recursion is that it is often useful to divide a problem into smaller parts, solve the smaller parts, and then place them back together to get the solution.

A simple real-world use of recursion is a phone tree. The phone tree problem is that a phone call must be made to every person on a list. A "normal" or **iterative solution** would be for a single person to call everyone in the list. If the list is long, that could take a very long time.

Instead, a **recursive solution** would be to divide the list in half and have two people call everyone on the list. The recursion is the dividing of the problem into a similar, but slightly easier problem to solve. To make this solution even more effective, we might have the people who split the list in two, split the list again. This splitting can occur as many times as necessary until the number of people each person has to call is manageable. Then each person calls the remainder of the people on their list and the problem is solved easily.

For a simple application of recursion to C++, let's look at the factorial function. The factorial of a number is that number, multiplied by 1 less than that number, multiplied by 2 less than that number, until you get to 1.

We could simply write a loop from 1 to n and multiply the numbers together, or we can take a recursive approach that calculates the factorial of a number by multiplying the number by the factorial of the number one less than itself. This definition holds true for all positive numbers. However, we need one more rule to stop the recursion: the factorial of 0 equals 1.

So we can define the factorial as:

```
Factorial (Num) = Num * factorial (Num-1)
Factorial (0) = 1
```

The C++ function is defined as follows:

```
int Factorial(int Num)
{
 if (Num > 0)
    return(Factorial(Num-1)*Num);
 return(1);
}
```

The factorial is computed by multiplying the value by the result of the factorial of one less than that value. This process continues until the if condition is false. Then a value of 1 is returned. This value is multiplied by the previous value, 1, and returned. This value is multiplied by the previous value, 2, and returned. This value is multiplied by the previous value, 3, and returned. This continues until we return to the first call of the **Factorial** function.

In order for the computer to solve a problem recursively, it must keep track of each call to a function. We will not go into detail here, but will illustrate what you must understand in order to write and trace recursive functions correctly.

If we wish to compute the factorial of 4, what does the computer do?

`//`**`Step 1`**` - first call to Factorial`
`Fact(4)`
`{`
`  if (4 > 1)`
`    return(4*Factorial(3));`
	`//`**`Step 5`**` - return from `**`Fact(2)`**
	`return(2*1);`
	
	`  // The value `**`2`**` is returned`

`// `**`Step 2`**` - second call to Factorial`
`Fact(3)`
`{`
`  if (3 > 1)`
`    return(3*Factorial(2));`
	`//`**`Step 6`**` - return from `**`Fact(3)`**
	`return (3*2);`
	
	`// The value `**`6`**` is returned`

`// `**`Step 3`**` - third call to Factorial`
`Fact(2)`
`{`
`  if (2>1)`
`     return(2*Factorial(1));`
	`//`**`Step 7`**` - return from `**`Fact(4)`**
	`return(4*6);`
	
	`//The value `**`24`**` is returned`

`//`**`Step 4`**` - fourth call to Factorial`
`Fact(1)`
`{`
`  if (1 > 1)`
`    //This is false, so the other`
`    //return statement is selected`
`return(1);`
 	
`// The value `**`1`**` is returned`
	`Done!`

When we trace through a recursive function it is important to write out the function as we process it. When we make another call to the same function, it is as if we have created an additional copy of that function. Process the copy and then return to just after the point where the copy of the function was originally called.

In the previous example, each time we called **Factorial**, we made a copy of the function, traced though the execution of that function, then returned to just after the function call.

If we further analyze the **Factorial** code we can see the two main parts of a recursive function. Every recursive function must have both of these parts. The first is the **recursive step**, in which the function calls itself. It is possible to have more than one recursive step; however, as a general rule, each recursive step should reduce the problem into a smaller problem closer to the solution of the original problem. The second part, the **stopping case**, causes the function to return without calling the recursive function again.

In the factorial code the following is the recursive step:

```
return(Num*Factorial(Num-1));
```

In the factorial code the following is the stopping case:

```
return (1);
```

IntToWords is another example of a recursive function. Imagine what your solution would be if you were asked to write a function that output the digits of an integer value in words. Therefore, if you executed the following code:

```
IntToWords(3241);
```

the output would be as follows:

```
THREE TWO FOUR ONE
```

How would you solve the problem? It is not as simple as it seems. If you had only one digit, the problem is easy. See the following **Words** function. It handles the case of outputting the text equivalent for a digit by using the digit as an index into an array of strings. Our problem, however, is to handle an integer that may be many digits. Though it is easy to calculate the last digit, it is not so easy to single out the individual digits from an integer.

We can access a single digit by using the modulus operator, %, to compute the remainder when dividing by 10. See the following examples:

```
123 % 10 = 3
4321 % 10 = 1
999 % 10 = 9
5 % 10 = 5
```

We can also remove the right-most digit by dividing the number by 10. However, if we follow this pattern in writing our function, we will output the numbers backwards.

The solution is to use recursion to reverse the order of the numbers, as shown in following code:

```cpp
void IntToWords(unsigned int Num)
{
 if (Num/10 > 0)
  IntToWords(Num/10);
 Words(Num%10);
 return;
}

void Words(int Digit)
{
 switch (Digit)
 {
  case 0:
    cout<<"ZERO ";
    break;
  case 1:
    cout<<"ONE ";
    break;
  case 2:
    cout<<"TWO ";
    break;
  case 3:
    cout<<"THREE ";
    break;
  case 4:
    cout<<"FOUR ";
    break;
  case 5:
    cout<<"FIVE ";
    break;
  case 6:
    cout<<"SIX ";
    break;
  case 7:
    cout<<"SEVEN ";
    break;
  case 8:
    cout<<"EIGHT ";
    break;
  case 9:
    cout<<"NINE ";
    break;
 }
}
```

Observe what happens when we call **IntToWords** with 3241:

``//Step 1 - call
to IntToWords(3241)
if (324 > 0)
  IntToWords(324);``` | ```//Step 5 - we return to the call to
IntToWords(32) in Step 3
Words(2)

Outputs TWO``` |
| ```//Step 2 - call to
IntToWords(324)
if (32 > 0)
  IntToWords(32);``` | ```//Step 6 - we return to the call to
IntToWords(324) in Step 2
Words(4)

Outputs FOUR``` |
| ```//Step 3 - call to
IntToWords(32)
if (3 > 0)
  IntToWords(3);``` | ```//Step 7 - we return to the call to
IntToWords(3241) in Step 1
Words(1)

Outputs ONE``` |
| ```//Step 4 - call to
IntToWords(3)
if (0 > 0)
  //Evaluates to false
Words(3)

Outputs THREE``` | Done! |

We will see more practical examples of recursion when we learn sorting and searching, but until then let's practice the mechanics of recursion.

▐▐ DRILLS

Let's try some examples. What is the output of the following statement?

Drill **8-1**

```
cout<<Mystery(4);
```

when **Mystery** is defined as:

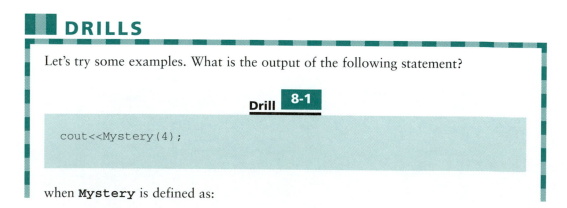

```
int Mystery(int Num)
{
if (Num<=0)
    return 1;
else
    return(Mystery(Num-2)*2);
}
```

How about the output of the following statement, using the same definition of **Mystery** as Drill 8-1?

Drill **8-2**

```
cout<<Mystery(5);
```

What happens if we change the function to the following and try the same two examples?

Drill **8-3**

```
int Mystery(int Num)
{
  if (Num==0)
    return 1;
else
    return(Mystery(Num-2)*2);
}
```

```
cout<<Mystery(4);
```

In that example not much has changed; try this example:

Drill **8-4**

```
cout<<Mystery(5);
```

Here is an interesting example of a recursive function. I was given the assignment in a graduate class to rewrite this recursive function without using recursion. My teacher was quite evil, because there is no nonrecursive solution to this problem. However, if you truly wish to test your knowledge of the mechanics of recursion, try tracing small values of *m* and *n* on paper and then type the program and see if you get the same results. Do not try large values of **Val1** and **Val2**, because they most likely will crash your computer.

```
int Recursive_Ackerman (int Val1, int Val2)
{
if (!Val1)
  return(++Val2);
else if (!Val2)
  return(Recursive_Ackerman(--Val1,1));
return(Recursive_Ackerman(Val1-1, Recursive_Ackerman(Val1,--Val2)));
}
```

PROGRAMMER'S NOTEBOOK

Be very careful when writing recursive functions. If a stopping case does not exist, they will loop until your system crashes.

8.2 BINARY SEARCH

An excellent practical use of recursion is to develop an improved solution to the linear search presented earlier. All of the searches so far are called linear searches. Although each search presented improves upon the previous search presented, as the number of items in the list grows, the search time grows linearly. So on average if it took 1 second to search 100 items, then it would take 10 seconds to search 1000 items, and 100 seconds to search 10,000 items, and 1000 seconds to search 100,000 items, etc. This is too slow.

Although the search we are about to develop can be developed without recursion, the recursive solution is elegant and simple. So we need a better way. If we start with a sorted list, the goal is to divide the problem into a smaller problem that is easier to solve. If we have a list that is sorted and we pick the middle of the list, then the value we are searching for is in one of three cases: the left of the middle, the right of the middle, or the middle value that we picked.

If it is the middle value our choice is easy. If not, we need to determine whether to search to the left or to the right side of the array. This is easy, because if the value that we are searching for is less than the middle value, we search to the left side of the array; otherwise we search to the right side of the array.

With a few simple checks, we have cut the number of items to search for in the list in half. By halving the number of values on each check we reduce the number of checks dramatically and have a much faster search. The code follows:

```
//Binary search algorithm
int Search(int Array[], int First, int Last, int Target)
{
  int Middle;

  // This is the stopping case for the recursion.
  if (Last-First<0)
    return -1;  // -1 indicates that the search was unsuccessful
  else
    {
      //Compute the middle index between first and last;
      //note that truncation occurs.
      Middle=(First+Last)/2;

      //A second stopping case for the recursion
      if (Target==Array[Middle])
        return Middle;  // Returns the location of the value as
                        //an indication search was successful

      //Check if target may be located to the left
      else if (Target<Array[Middle])
            //Search the list to the left of the middle
        return(Search(Array, First, Middle-1, Target));
    else
        //Search the list to the right of the middle
        return(Search(Array, Middle+1, Last, Target));
    }
}
```

Note that for clarity of implementation we first check the **Target** against **Array[Middle]** to see if we have found the value we are looking for. In most cases we would be failing this test, so a more efficient solution would be to check to see if the value we are searching for is to the left, then to the right, then at the middle. This would reduce the overall number of checks and speed up the search process.

Let's go through a few examples of the code searching an array for a value. We will use a graphical representation of a stack in order to keep track of the recursive calls.

With the following array, determine if the value 7 is stored.

0	1	2	3	4	5	6	7	8	9
1	4	7	9	10	17	19	20	25	100

The first call to **Search** looks like it is made with the lower bound equal to 0 and the upper bound equal to 9. This will cover the entire span of the array. It looks as follows:

```
Search(Array,0,9,7);
```

Therefore, the system stack would look as follows:

Call	First	Last	Target
1	0	9	7

During the execution of this call to **Search, Middle=4**, because $0+9=9$ and $9/2=4.5$, but it is truncated in C++ down to 4. Since **Array[Middle]==Target** evaluates to false, because **Array[4] = 10** and our target is 7, we compare **Target** to **Array[4]** with the following statement:

```
if (Target<Array[Middle])
```

Since target is less than **Array[4]**, we call **Search** again with the following parameters:

```
Search(Array,0,3,7)
```

Therefore, the stack now looks as follows:

Call	First	Last	Target
2	0	3	7
1	0	9	7

Notice that we are searching to the left. Since we know that **Middle** doesn't contain the value, we reduce the **Last** index to **Middle-1** or 3. The **First** value remains the same.

During the execution of this call to `Search`, `Middle=1`, because $0+3=3$ and $3/2=1.5$, but it is truncated in C++ down to 1. Since `Array[Middle]==Target` evaluates to false, because `Array[1] = 4` and our `Target` is 7, we compare `Target` to `Array[1]` with the following statement:

```
if (Target<Array[Middle])
```

However, unlike the previous case, our `Target` is greater than the `Middle` value. Therefore, the `else` clause is taken and the function is called with the following parameters:

```
Search(Array,2,3,7)
```

Therefore, the stack now looks as follows:

Call	First	Last	Target
3	2	3	7
2	0	3	7
1	0	9	7

Notice that we are searching to the right. Since we know that `Middle` doesn't contain the value, we increase the `First` index to the `Middle + 1` or 2. The `Last` value remains the same.

During the execution of this call to `Search`, `Middle=2`, because $2+3=5$ and $5/2=2.5$, but it is truncated in C++ down to 2. Now, `Array[Middle]==Target` evaluates to true, because `Array[2] = 7`, which is our `Target`.

So the value 2 is returned from the `Search(Array,2,3,7)` call. It returns to the `Search(Array,0,3,7)` call, which in turn returns it to the `Search(Array,0,9,7)`, which simply returns the 2 to whoever called `Search` in the first place.

Let's try one more example all the way through; this time we will search for a value that is not in the list. Let's look for the value 2 in the following array:

0	1	2	3	4	5	6	7	8	9
1	4	7	9	10	17	19	20	25	100

```
Search(Array,0,9,2);
```

Therefore, the system stack would look as follows:

Call	First	Last	Target
1	0	9	2

During the execution of this call to **Search**, **Middle=4**, because $0+9=9$ and $9/2=4.5$, but it is truncated in C++ down to 4. Since **Array[Middle]==Target** evaluates to false, because **Array[4] = 10** and our target is 2, we compare **Target** to **Array[4]** with the following statement:

```
if (Target<Array[Middle])
```

Since **Target** is less than **Array[4]**, we call **Search** again with the following parameters:

```
Search(Array,0,3,2)
```

Therefore, the system stack would look as follows:

Call	First	Last	Target
2	0	3	2
1	0	9	2

Notice that we are searching to the left. Since we know that **Middle** doesn't contain the value we reduce the last index to **Middle-1** or 3. The **First** value remains the same.

During the execution of this call to **Search**, **Middle=1**, because $0+3=3$ and $3/2=1.5$, but it is truncated in C++ down to 1. Since **Array[Middle]==Target** evaluates to false, because **Array[1] = 4** and our **Target** is 2, we compare **Target** to **Array[1]** with the following statement:

```
if (Target<Array[Middle])
```

Since **Target** is less than **Array[4]**, we call **Search** again with the following parameters:

```
Search(Array,0,0,2)
```

Therefore, the system stack would look as follows:

Call	First	Last	Target
3	0	0	2
2	0	3	2
1	0	9	2

Since **Target** is not less than **Array[Middle]** we continue our search to the right. Since we know that **Middle** doesn't contain the value, we increase the **First** index to **Middle+1** or 1. The **Last** value remains the same.

We call **Search** again with the following parameters:

```
Search(Array,1,0,2)
```

Therefore, the system stack would look as follows:

Call	First	Last	Target
4	1	0	2
3	0	0	2
2	0	3	2
1	0	9	2

Now when we enter **Search**, **Last-First** is less than 0 and therefore we return −1. −1 is passed back through all the function calls and finally returned to the original caller of **Search**.

The **binary search** may seem really fast, but that is only because we are comparing it to linear searches that are not very efficient. Being a speed monger, I want my searches to be even faster. Clearly the need exists. Search engines like Yahoo! require incredible speeds to return your search criteria as quickly as they do with thousands of simultaneous requests being made. However, we will save these examples for later.

8.3 QUICK SORT

We learned the bubble sort and the insertion sort, because their implementations are relatively simple. However, if you were given a large number of items, we would not try to sort using these methods.

When in life have you been required to sort a large group of values? I remember sorting baseball cards as a kid. There were about 800 cards in a set, each with a number on the back. If you wanted to determine if you had all the cards, you sorted them and then scanned the cards to see if any were missing. However, I didn't sort my cards by placing one item in place at a time. It would take too long. As a child, without even thinking about it, I came up with a better way. I broke all the cards into piles of 100. All the cards for 0–99 went in one pile, 100–199 in another, 200–299 in another, etc. Then one pile at a time, I broke the pile into ten smaller piles, placing 0–9 in one pile, 10–19 in another, etc. Finally, I picked up the piles of ten and sorted them in a manner similar to the insertion sort.

Without knowing it, I had developed a recursive algorithm. Remember a recursive algorithm is one that breaks a large problem into smaller problems that are similar. To improve our sorting algorithm, we are going to divide our problem into smaller problems and then sort them.

To solve our new sorting problem we will need to break the problem into two parts. The first part is what we will call **Partition**. **Partition** is responsible for splitting the values we need to sort into two smaller sublists of values that also need to be sorted. Then, we need the recursive solution that will call the **QuickSort** routine, which continues to call **Parition** until our sublists are no larger than one item.

Our new algorithm will work if each time we divide the list we place one item in its proper place. The algorithm is more efficient because it is quicker to sort smaller sublists than it is to try to sort one large list all at once.

We will write a function called **Partition**. **Partition** will pick a pivot value. Then it will divide the list of values so that all values less than the pivot value are to the left and all values greater than the pivot value are to the right. This means that when we are finished with the **Partition** function, the pivot value will be in the proper place. The items to the left and right of the pivot value are not necessarily sorted. They will be sorted by subsequent calls to the **QuickSort** function.

To implement the division of an array, realize that we do not physically divide the array. By using indexes into an array as the upper and lower bounds, we can establish a range of the array. So to implement **QuickSort**, we will pass three values: the entire array, and the lower and upper bounds of the portion of the array that we wish to sort.

With this approach, the **QuickSort** function is actually a simple implementation (if you are comfortable with recursion).

To start **QuickSort**, we call **QuickSort** with the array we wish to sort, 0, as the lower bound, and *n-1* as the upper bound, where *n* is the number of values in the array. If **QuickSort** is passed a lower bound that is not less than the upper bound, then **QuickSort** stops. When the upper bound is less than the lower bound, it means that they have crossed paths on the array and we are finished. The **QuickSort** code is as follows:

```
//The main QuickSort algorithm
void QuickSort(int Array[], int LB, int UB)
{
  int Part;
  if (LB<UB) //stopping case for recursion
  {
    Part=Partition(Array, LB, UB);//call to partition, divides list
    QuickSort(Array, LB, Part-1);//Call quicksort with left values
    QuickSort(Array, Part+1, UB);//Call quicksort with right values
  }
}
```

QuickSort is a three-step process. First **QuickSort** divides the list by calling the **Partition** function. Once the list is divided into two sublists, **QuickSort** calls itself twice, once for each sublist.

Once you get a feel for the recursive element of **QuickSort**, there is not much to it. The real work in **QuickSort** is not in the **QuickSort** routine at all. The real work is done in **Partition**, because although the idea of partition is simple, implementing it without using a lot of extra space is not.

For starters we needed to pick a pivot value. Without a lot of computation, there is no way to pick a pivot value that is any better than any other, so we will simply pick as the pivot the value in the lower bound of the portion of the array we wish to sort.

Let's look at the following array with the lower bound = 0 and the upper bound = 7:

0	1	2	3	4	5	6	7
50	12	19	90	11	99	15	110

The **Pivot** value would therefore be 50. We need two variables to track our current position as we move up and down the array. We want to move the **Down** index up as long as the values are less than the **Pivot** value. Then we move the **Up** index down the array while the values in the array are greater than the **Pivot** value. As long as the **Down** and **Up** indexes haven't crossed each other, we swap the value at the **Down** and **Up** indexes in the array. This process is repeated until **Down** is greater than **Up**. At that point we copy the value at the **Up** index to the original position of **Pivot** and **Pivot** to the position of the **Up** index.

Observe one complete call to **Partition**:

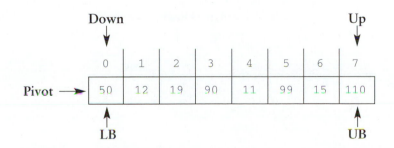

We enter `while` loop "A" and `Array[0]`, `Array[1]`, and `Array[2]` are all less than or equal to the pivot value, so `Down` increments to 3. Since `Array[3]` is greater than `Pivot`, we drop out of the `while` loop "A" with the value of `Down` equal to 3.

We start `while` loop "B" loop. `Array[7]` is greater than `Pivot` so we decrement the `Up` index to 6. We stop at `Up=6`, because the value at `Array[6]` is less than the pivot value. Since the `Down` and `Up` indexes have not crossed each other (`Down<Up`), we swap the value at `Array[down]` and the value at `Array[Up]`. After this the array looks as follows:

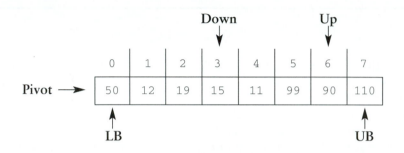

Since the `Down` index is still less than the `Up` index, the outer loop condition evaluates to true and we repeat the previous process. The values at `Array[3]` and `Array[4]` are less than `Pivot`, so the `Down` index is incremented to 5. `Array[5]` is greater than `Pivot`, so we drop out of the `while` loop "A" with the value of the `Down` index equaling 5. A graphical representation of this state is as follows:

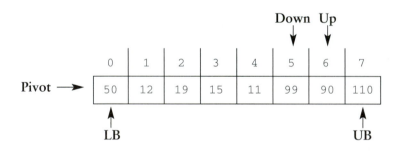

We enter `while` loop "B" with `Array[6]` greater than `Pivot`, so the `Up` index is decremented to 5. `Array[5]` is also greater than `Pivot`, so `Up` is decremented again to 4. Finally, `Array[4]` is not greater than `Pivot`, so the `while` loop "B" terminates with the `Up` index equaling 4. A graphical representation of this state is as follows:

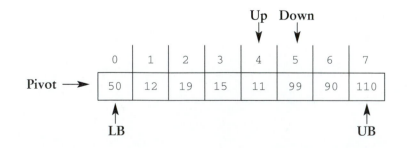

Since the **Up** index is no longer greater than the **Down** index, we complete the **Partition** by copying **Array[Up]** to **Array[LB]** and then copy **Pivot** to **Array[Up]**. So the array looks like the following:

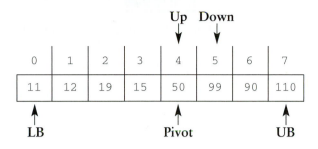

Notice all the values that are less than 50 are located to the left and all the values that are greater than 50 are to the right. Notice that those values are not necessarily in order. The code is as follows:

```
//Parition function for Quicksort routine
int Partition(int Array[], int LB, int UB)
{
  // Split the list so all items < on one side
  int Up, Down;
  int Pivot, Temp;

  Pivot = Array[LB]; // Pick the pivot item, use the lower bound.
  Up = UB;
  Down = LB;
  while (Down < Up)  //Loop until Down & Up cross paths
  {
  //Move Up array while values are < Pivot
    while ((Array[Down] <= Pivot) && (Down < UB)) //Loop A
      Down++;

    //Move Down array while values are > Pivot //Loop B
    while (Array[Up] > Pivot)
      Up--;

  if (Down < Up) //Swap values
    {
      Temp = Array[Up];
      Array[Up] = Array[Down];
      Array[Down] = Temp;
    }
  }

  //Replace LB value with a value that is less than Pivot
  Array[LB] = Array[Up];

  // Place the pivot value in the proper place
  Array[Up] = Pivot;

  return(Up); //Return the index of the pivot
}
```

DRILLS

To help you understand the workings of the **Partition** function, try computing what the following array will look like after a call to partition:

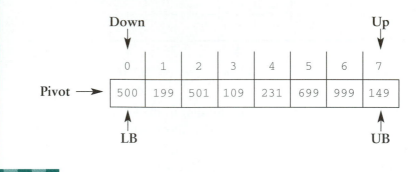

QuickSort Calling Sequence

So far, our study of the **QuickSort** has focused on the operations of the **Partition** call. Let's now assume that you understand how the **Partition** function works and investigate the operations of the main **QuickSort** function. It may help you to use a debugger to trace through the program on the computer as we trace through it on paper.

The confusing part of tracing through the **QuickSort** program is keeping track of where you are in the recursive calling sequence. We will use a graphical representation how the computer actually keeps track of each call to **QuickSort**. In actuality, a computer uses an area of memory called the system stack. Therefore, we will refer to our graphical representation as a stack as well. As additional calls to **QuickSort** are made, they will be added to the top of the stack. As calls are completed, they will be removed from the top of the stack. When the stack is empty, the **QuickSort** routine is complete and the array is sorted.

Let's try calling **QuickSort** on the same array we just tried in the drill:

0	1	2	3	4	5	6	7
500	199	501	109	231	699	999	149

The first call to **QuickSort** starts with the lower bound at 0 and the upper bound at 7. We do not know what the value of the variable **Part** is, but we know that we will call **Partition** since **LB** < **UB**. Before the call to **Partition**, the stack would look as follows:

Call	LB	UB	Part	Where
1	0	7	?	Before Part

After the call to **Partition**, the array and system stack would look as follows:

0	1	2	3	4	5	6	7
231	199	109	149	500	699	999	501

Call	LB	UB	Part	Where
1	0	7	4	Before Quick 1

QuickSort is called again with different parameters from within the first call to **QuickSort**. **QuickSort** is called with the following sequence:

```
QuickSort(Array, LB, Part-1);
```

or in this case,

```
QuickSort(Array, 0, 3)
```

Therefore, the system stack will look like:

Call	LB	UB	Part	Where
2	0	3	?	Before Partition
1	0	7	4	Before Quick 2

Now we must call the **Partition** function again, but this time we process only the first four values of the array. Upon entering the call to **Partition**, we see the following setup:

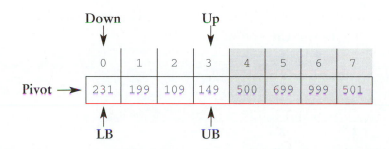

Partition picks the lower bound value, 231, as the **Pivot**. The **Down** index is incremented while stepping through **while** loop "A" to 3, because all the values in the array up to and including index 3 are less than or equal to the pivot value. Since the **Up** index is equal to 3, we no longer advance the **Down** index. Since Array[Up] is not greater than the pivot value, we drop out of **while** loop "B". Since the **Up** index is not less than the **Down** index, we swap the pivot value with the value at the **Up** index. The results are shown in the following array:

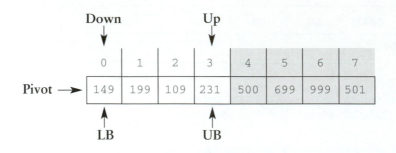

Now both the 231 and the 500 are in their final proper locations. We continue by calling **QuickSort** for a third time as follows:

```
QuickSort(Array,0,2)
```

The system stack now looks as follows:

Call	LB	UB	Part	Where
3	0	2	???	Before Partition
2	0	3	3	Before Quick 2
1	0	7	4	Before Quick 2

Partition now picks the pivot value of 149. **While** loop "A" executes until the **Down** index equals 1, since 199 is greater than the pivot value, the **Down** index stops at 1. **While** loop "B" executes until the **Up** index equals 2, since 109 is less than the pivot value. The values at the **Up** and **Down** indexes swap and the array looks as follows:

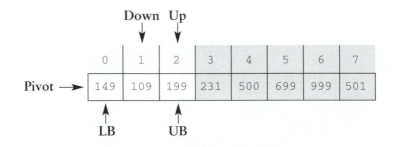

Since the **Down** index is less than the **Up** index, we enter **while** loop "A" again. The **Down** index is then incremented to 2, where **Array[Down]** is greater than **Pivot**. Then **while** loop "B" is entered and the **Up** index decrements to 1, where **Array[Up]** is less than **Pivot**. Since the **Down** index is greater than the **Up** index, we swap the pivot value with **Array[Up]** and we exit **while** loop "B". Our array now looks as follows:

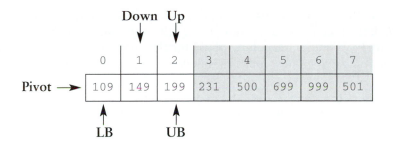

When we call **QuickSort** with the same lower and upper bounds, the function simply returns without changing the values in the array. Since the **if** statement evaluates to false and there is nothing left in the function other than the **if** statement, we return from the call to **QuickSort** and continue to process from where we called **QuickSort**. Now the system stack looks as follows and is ready to call the **QuickSort** for the second time from call #3 of **QuickSort**.

Call	LB	UB	Part	Where
4	0	0	???	Before if statement
3	0	2	2	Before Quick 2
2	0	3	3	Before Quick 2
1	0	7	4	Before Quick 2

The second call to **QuickSort** uses the following calling sequence:

```
QuickSort(Arr, Part+1, UB);
```

Therefore, our call to **QuickSort** would be:

```
Quicksort(Arr, 3, 2);
```

Once again, since the call to **QuickSort** is called with a lower bound not less than the upper bound, the function returns without changing the values in the array. This time however, we have finished handling call #3 for the quick sort, so it is removed from the system stack, which now looks as follows:

Call	LB	UB	Part	Where
2	0	3	3	Before Quick 2
1	0	7	4	Before Quick 2

When we resume call #2 of the **QuickSort** routine, we use the following call sequence:

```
QuickSort(Arr,4,3);
```

Again, we have a case where the lower bound is not less than the upper bound, so we return without modification to the array.

When we return to call #1 of **QuickSort**, we have successfully sorted the first five values in the array. All that remains is to sort the values in the array indexes 5, 6, and 7.

This would occur in the same manner, as previously demonstrated, starting with the calling sequence:

```
QuickSort(Arr, 5, 7);
```

When this call is returned from, the **QuickSort** routine is finished and the entire array is sorted.

8.4 Case Study

Problem Description

The case study for Chapter 8 is similar to the ones in previous chapters. Load arrays for employee's number, name, wage rate, and tax rate, having at least five entries in each array. Write an inquiry program that will accept an employee number from the keyboard and use a recursive binary search to search the employee number array for the input value. If the input employee number is in the array, then that employee's name, wage rate, and tax rate should be displayed. If the employee number is not in the array, a message to that effect should be displayed. Using a binary search is much quicker when the number of items to be searched is large. To save space we will only show a solution with ten names. Remember that these names must be listed in alphabetical order or the binary search will not operate correctly.

Discussion

This problem illustrates the notion of parallel arrays. If the employee number is found, information in the other arrays at the same row level is displayed; otherwise a message is displayed. Arrays have been preloaded with values, since the object here is searching and information extraction. A recursive binary search is used to determine if the employee number entered is loaded.

Solution 1

```
#include <stdlib.h>
#include <iostream.h>
#include <iomanip.h>

#define Rows 10
#define Cols 30

void DisplayHeader();
void DisplayLine(int Index,char Names[],float Wages[],
                 float TaxRates[]);
int BinarySearch(int Array[], int First, int Last, int Target);
```

8.4   Case Study (continued)

```cpp
void main()
{
 int EmployeeNumbers[Rows] = {10100, 10101, 10102, 10103,10104,
                             10105, 10106, 10107, 10108, 10109};

int Number, Location, First = 0, Last = 9;

char Names[Rows][Cols] = {
      "Alphonse, Al",
      "Alphonse, Zeta",
      "Davis, Nancy",
      "Heppner, Al",
      "Markham, Bill",
      "Matusow, David",
      "Nunn, John",
      "Paxton, Elizabeth",
      "Pinto, Marc",
      "Smith, Richard"};

float Wages[Rows] = {18.60, 7.85, 2.50, 5.15, 12.50, 13.55, 21.40,
                    40.10, 15.50, 4.75};
float TaxRates[Rows] = {.33, .20, .26, .20, .28, .33, .20, .39,
                        .26, .20};

do
{
   cout << endl << "Enter negative to end or ";
   cout << endl << "Enter employee\'s ID -> ";
   cin >> Number;

   if (Number <= 0)
     break;

   Location = BinarySearch(EmployeeNumbers, First, Last, Number);

   if(Location < 0)
      cout << endl <<"Employee number " << Number <<
            " not loaded"<<endl;
   else
   {
     DisplayHeader();
     DisplayLine(Location, Names[Location], Wages, TaxRates);
   }
} while(Number > 0);
```

```cpp
}

void DisplayHeader()
{
   cout << endl << "EMP NAME                     WAGE    TAX RATE"<<endl;
   cout << setiosflags(ios::showpoint | ios :: fixed)<< setprecision(2);
}

void DisplayLine(int Index,char Name[],float Wages[],float TaxRates[])
{
   cout << endl << setw(25) << setiosflags(ios :: left) << Name;
   cout << setiosflags(ios :: right);
   cout << setw(5) << Wages[Index] << setw(10) <<
           TaxRates[Index]<< endl;
}

int BinarySearch(int Array[], int First, int Last, int Target)
{
 int Middle;

 // This is the stopping case for the recursion.
 if (Last-First<0)
   return -1;  // -1 indicates that the search was unsuccessful
 else
  {
    //Compute the middle index between first & last,
    //note that truncation occurs.
    Middle=(First+Last)/2;

    //A second stopping case for the recursion
    if (Target==Array[Middle])
      return Middle;  // Returns the location of the value as
                      //an indication search was successful

    //Check if target may be located to the left
    else if (Target<Array[Middle])
          //Search the list to the left of the middle
      return(BinarySearch(Array, First, Middle-1, Target));
    else
      //Search the list to the right of the middle
      return(BinarySearch(Array, Middle+1, Last, Target));
  }
}
```

8.4 Case Study (continued)

Output

```
Enter negative to end or
Enter employee's ID -> 10101

EMP NAME                    WAGE      TAX RATE

Alphonse, Zeta              7.85      0.20

Enter negative to end or
Enter employee's ID -> 10103

EMP NAME                    WAGE      TAX RATE

Heppner, Al                 5.15      0.20

Enter negative to end or
Enter employee's ID -> 10105

EMP NAME                    WAGE      TAX RATE

Matusow, David             13.55      0.33

Enter negative to end or
Enter employee's ID -> 12345

Employee number 12345 not loaded

Enter negative to end or
Enter employee's ID -> -9
```

◆ Key Terms

Binary search	An advanced searching scheme that requires a sorted list of items to make the search more efficient.
Iterative solution	A solution that does not call itself as part of the process.
Quick sort	A recursive solution to sorting that divides the array to be sorted into smaller, easier to solve parts.
Recursion	A solution that is implemented with a function that calls itself.
Recursive step	The actual call to the recursive function from within the recursive function.
Stopping case	The condition that causes a recursive function to return to the function that called it.

◆ Answers to Drills

Drill 8-1

The output of the drill is as follows:

```
4
```

The following is a trace of the execution of the drill:

```
//Step 1 - call to Mystery(4)
if (4 <= 0)
   //Evaluates to false
else
   return(Mystery(2)*2);
```
```
//Step 4 - we return to the
call to Mystery(2) in Step 2

return (1*2);
// The value 2 is returned
```

```
// Step 2 - call to Mystery(2)
if (2 <= 0)
   //Evaluates to false
else
   return(Mystery(0)*2)
```
```
//Step 5 - we return to the
call to Mystery(4) in Step 1

return (2*2);
// The value 4 is returned
```

```
// Step 3 - call to Mystery(0)
if (0 <= 0)
   //Evaluates to true,
   //stopping case fires.
   return (1);
```
```
Done!
```

Drill 8-2

The output of the drill is as follows:

```
8
```

The following is a trace of the execution of the drill:

`//`**`Step 1`**` - call to `**`Mystery(5)`**
`if (5 <= 0)`
`  //Evaluates to false`
`else`
`   return(Mystery(3)*2);`
	`//`**`Step 5`**` - we return to the`
	`call to `**`Mystery(1)`**` in `**`Step 3`**
	
	`return (1*2);`
	`// The value `**`2`**` is returned`

`// `**`Step 2`**` - call to `**`Mystery(3)`**
`if (3 <= 0)`
`  //Evaluates to false`
`else`
`   return(Mystery(1)*2)`
	`//`**`Step 6`**` - we return to the`
	`call to `**`Mystery(3)`**` in `**`Step 2`**
	
	`return (2*2);`
	`// The value `**`4`**` is returned`

`// `**`Step 3`**` - call to `**`Mystery(1)`**
`if (1 <= 0)`
`  //Evaluates to false,`
`else`
`   return(Mystery(-1)*2)`
	`//`**`Step 7`**` - we return to the`
	`call to `**`Mystery(5)`**` in `**`Step 1`**
	
	`return (4*2);`
	`// The value `**`8`**` is returned`

`//`**`Step 4`**` - call to `**`Mystery(-1)`**
`if (-1 <= 0)`
`  //Evaluates to true`
`  //stopping case fires`
`   return (1)`
`//The value `**`1`**` is returned`
	`Done!`

Drill 8-3

The output of the drill is as follows:

```
4
```

The following is a trace of the execution of the drill:

`//Step 1 - call to Mystery(4)`
`if (4 == 0)`
`    //Evaluates to false`
`else`
`    return(mystery(2)*2);`
	`//Step 4 - we return to the`
	`call to mystery(2) in Step 2`
	
	`return (1*2);`
	`// The value 2 is returned`

`// Step 2 - call to Mystery(2)`
`if (2 == 0)`
`    //Evaluates to false`
`else`
`    return(mystery(0)*2)`
	`//Step 5 - we return to the`
	`call to mystery(3) in Step 2`
	
	`return (2*2);`
	`// The value 4 is returned`

`// Step 3 - call to Mystery(0)`
`if (0 == 0)`
`    //Evaluates to true,`
`//stopping case fires`
`    return (1)`
`//The value 1 is returned`
	`Done!`

Drill 8-4

The following is a trace of the execution of the drill:

`//Step 1 - call to Mystery(5)`
`if (5 == 0)`
`    //Evaluates to false`
`else`
`    return(Mystery(3)*2);`
	`Call to Mystery(-1)`
	`if (1 == 0)`
	`    //Evaluates to false`
	`else`
	`    return(Mystery(-3)*2)`

`// Step 2 - call to Mystery(3)`
`if (3 == 0)`
`    //Evaluates to false`
`else`
`    return(Mystery(1)*2)`
	`See Below...`

`// Step 3 - call to Mystery(1)`
`if (1 == 0)`
`    //Evaluates to false`
`else`
`    return(Mystery(-1)*2)`	

This process continues and the program will never end until the computer crashes. This is because we wrote a stopping case that may not be reached given certain inputs. We must be careful when writing recursive functions to ensure that they cannot get caught in infinite loops.

Drill 8-5

The trace of the drill follows:

Initially, the pivot value would be 500.

We enter the `while` loop "A" loop and `Array[0]` and `Array[1]` are all less than or equal to the pivot value, so the `Down` increments to 2. We drop out of the `while` loop "A" with the value of the `Down` index equal to 2.

We start the `while` loop "B". `Array[7]` is not greater than the pivot value, so we immediately drop out of `while` loop "B" with the value of the `Up` index equal to 7. Now the value at `Array[Down]` and the value at `Array[Up]` are swapped and the array looks as follows:

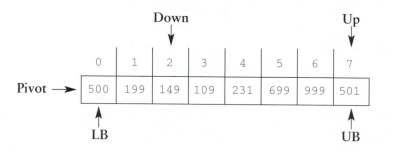

Since the `Down` index is still less than the `Up` index, we enter the `Down while` loop and `Array[2]`, `Array[3]`, and `Array[4]` are all less than or equal to the pivot value, so the `Down` index increments to 5. Since `Array[5]` is greater than the pivot value, we drop out of `while` loop "A" with the value of the `Down` index equal to 5.

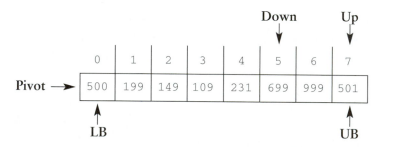

We start `while` loop "B" where `Array[7]`, `Array[6]`, and `Array[5]` are all greater than the pivot value, so we drop out of `while` loop "B" loop with the value of the `Up` index equal to 4.

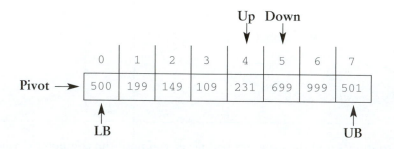
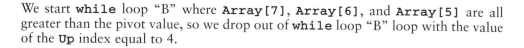

Since the **Up** index is no longer greater than the **Down** index, we complete the partition by copying **Array[Up]** to **Array[LB]** and then copy the pivot value to **Array[Up]** so the array looks like the following:

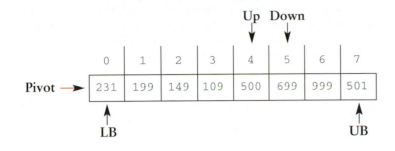

◆Programming Exercises

1. Rewrite the linear search algorithm so that it will work with an array of strings.

2. Rewrite the binary search algorithm so that is will work with an array of strings.

3. Rewrite the quick sort routine so that it sorts the array in descending order.

4. Write a program that performs a quick sort for arrays of characters instead of integers.

5. Write a program that modifies the exisiting integer quick sort so that it calls a modified version of the existing bubble sort function so that when the quick sort has an upper and lower bound less than or equal to 10 it calls the modified bubble sort. This is done because of the overhead associated with the quick sort routine. With small numbers of values to sort, bubble sort is faster.

6. Rewrite the quick sort algorithm to randomly pick a value for the pivot from the list that it is trying to sort. Write this as a program to test your results. Should this improve the speed of quick sort or decrease it, or does it remain the same?

7. Write a program that contains a function that recursively adds numbers as they are entered to a total. The function should stop accepting numbers when the user enters a 0 for the number. The function should accept only one number per call. The total should be returned to **main** where the first call was first made.

◆Additional Exercises

1. Is recursion more efficient then using a loop to do the same task?

2. Will the following function execute properly and return the correct value back to the original call? The function should show every number from the start number to the end number, inclusive, and return the number of values that have been displayed to the screen. Correct the code if necessary.

```
int Count(int Start, int End)
{
  if (Start > End)
    return (End - Start)
  else
    {
      cout<<Start;
      count(Start++);
    }
}
```

3. True or False: When searching an unordered list, the position in the list to begin the search does not matter.

4. How many checks does it take for the linear search to find 48 in the following list?

   22   34   48   51   55   62

5. How many calls to search does it take for the binary search to find 48 in the following list?

   12   17   22   34   48   51   55   62

6. List at least three real-world situations when using a linear search is better than using a binary search. List at least three real-world situations that you would use a binary search instead of a linear search. In both cases, demonstrate why you think that one will outperform the other.

7. Does the pivot always have to be the first element in the list? What is the significance, if any, of choosing this element as the pivot?

8. Describe in your own words the difference between insertion, bubble, and quick sort?

9. Is the quick sort function a recursive function? Is the partition function a recursive function? How can one function be called recursive if the other one is not?

10. Show the entire calling sequence using **QuickSort** for the following list of numbers.

    23   45   65   12   32   76   87   13   78   55

11. Show the entire calling sequence using **QuickSort** for the following list of numbers.

    17   23   1   65   22   6   55   20   5   78   99

12. In exercises 4, 6, and 8, in your opinion, which sort function did the least amount of work? Which do you think takes the least amount of time?

13. Explain the significance of using **SwapOccurred** in bubble sort.

CHAPTER
9

Pointers

Chapter Objectives

- ♦ **Introduce the concept of pointers**

- ♦ **Explain the syntax of pointers**

- ♦ **Explain how to use pointers for passing values by reference**

- ♦ **Explain how to use pointers to access arrays more efficiently**

- ♦ **Explain how to use pointers to allocate memory dynamically**

- ♦ **Practice pointer notation by rewriting string functions**

9.1 POINTERS—WHY DO WE NEED THEM?

`Pointers` are one of the most confusing concepts in C++ programming. The irony is that although a pointer in C++ is extremely powerful, it is merely a variable that stores a number. Although unknown to you, in many cases we have already used them.

Before we begin a discussion about the computer implementation of pointers, we will begin with a real-world analogy that will help us grasp the concept of pointers.

In life it is often inconvenient to carry around a great deal of personal information. Sometimes it is easier to handle a reference to that information. Most people carry with them some form of an automatic-teller card. Do you think your entire bank account information, including all your transactions, is stored on that card? Not likely, at least for the immediate future. What is stored is an account number that refers or points to your bank account information. Changes that are made to this account are remembered even when you remove your card. In fact, the card can be destroyed, but your bank is going to remember that you withdrew $200 to get the latest concert tickets. OK, it won't know that you bought concert tickets, but you get the idea.

Now ask yourself if you went into the bank without the card, would you know what your account number is for your checking or savings account? Probably not. You simply refer to the account as either your checking or savings account.

Variables and pointers in C++ work in a similar fashion to the automated-teller card example we just mentioned. A **pointer** is a method of referencing the memory location of variables.

Let's think for a moment what happens when you declare a variable as follows:

```
int Value;
```

The integer, **Value**, is declared and therefore allocated. That sounds nice, but what do we really mean by these fancy terms? By issuing the preceding statement, we are telling the program to carve out a space of memory for an integer. An integer on most modern computers takes up 4 bytes. This amount of memory is allocated and assigned a name. The name is called **Value** and that is how we have referenced it until now. However, the computer has another name for it. Its name is not so easily remembered. It is a number that represents the variable's location in memory.

Just as in our example where we had a label of either checking or savings for our numeric account number, C++ uses a variable name to represent the memory address of a variable. In C++ both the name of a variable and its memory address are useful and needed.

Before we discuss the reasons why it is important to use pointers, let's first learn their mechanics.

When declaring an integer like **Value1** or **Value2**, as shown next, a space in the computer's memory is allocated and called **Value1** or **Value2**. Let's say that the starting **memory address** of **Value1** is 1000. In reality, memory addresses are much larger and represented in another number system, but for our examples using reasonably small rounded numbers works better.

```
int Value1;
int Value2;
```

Let's make the assumption that **Value1** and **Value2** are in adjacent memory locations. This is not guaranteed, but is often the case. Therefore, if we assume that **Value1** is at memory location 1000 and an integer takes up 4 bytes, then **Value2** would start at memory location 1004.

So, the value we assign to **Value1** is stored between memory locations 1000 and 1003 and the value we assign to **Value2** is stored between memory locations 1004 and 1007. This is depicted in Figure 9.1.

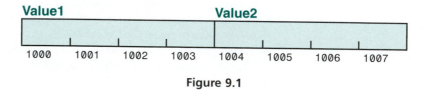

Value1   Value2

| 1000 | 1001 | 1002 | 1003 | 1004 | 1005 | 1006 | 1007 |

Figure 9.1

9.2 DECLARING POINTERS

We declare a pointer using the following template:

```
VariableType * PointerName;
```

When declaring a pointer, we first indicate the type of variable the pointer will point to, then we type an asterisk, followed by the pointer's name, and terminate with a semicolon. There must be a space between the variable type and the asterisk as well as a space between the asterisk and the pointer name.

We can declare a variable **Pointer** as a pointer to an integer as follows:

```
int * Pointer;
```

We no longer store an integer value in the variable **Pointer**, but a pointer to an integer. The ***** in between the declaration of the variable **Pointer** and the integer indicates that the variable **Pointer** will store a memory address. It also indicates that the variable stored at the memory address stored in **Pointer** is an integer.

PROGRAMMER'S NOTEBOOK

This notation can be very confusing to programmers just getting familiar with pointers. Instead, try using a typedef statement as shown next to remove some of the confusion.

A **typedef** statement in C++ will allow users to create their own types. Although not often used with the advent of classes, when dealing with pointers it is often a way of simplifying the complex syntax required.

Therefore, for each variable type for which you want to create a pointer, use the following **typedef** statement template at the beginning of your program:

```
typedef VariableType * PointerTypeName;
```

So if your program was going to use a pointer to integers, characters, and floating point numbers, you would add the following lines to the beginning of your program:

```
typedef int * intPointer;
typedef char * charPointer;
typedef float * floatPointer;
```

Now you can use these definitions to declare variables that are pointers to the specific type defined in the previous statement.

More Pointer Syntax

To store the address of the variable **Value1** in the variable **Pointer1**, we require a method to access the address of **Value1**. By using the **&** operator in front of a variable, the address of that variable is returned. This can be seen in the following code:

```
Pointer1 = &Value1;
```

The **&** operator, placed in front of a variable **Value1**, returns the address of the variable **Value1**.

  Pointer1 must be stored in memory. If we follow the same allocation scheme as we did with **Value1** and **Value2**, then **Pointer1** would be stored in the next available memory locations 1008–1011. However, instead of storing an integer variable it stores the address of **Value1**, which, in our example, is 1000 (in a real computer, the address would look more like ACD3 20FF). Figure 9.2 shows the updated memory mapping for our program.

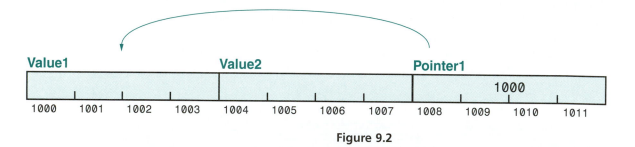

Figure 9.2

What if we want to know what value is at the address contained in the variable **Pointer**? We require an operator to indicate to the pointer to return the value it points to instead of the actual address. By using an ***** before a pointer anywhere but where we declare it, the value we desire is returned. See the following code as an example:

```
//Normal variable declaration & initialization
#include <stdlib.h>
#include <iostream.h>

typedef int * intPointer;

void main()
{
    int Value1=10;
    int Value2=20;

    //Declaration of a pointer
    intPointer Pointer1;

    // Set the pointer Pointer1 to point to Value1.
    Pointer1=&Value1;

    //Will output 10 20 10
    cout<<Value1<<' '<<Value2<<' '<<*Pointer1<<endl;

    //Reassign the pointer Pointer1 to point to Value2.
    Pointer1=&Value2;

    //Will output 10 20 20
    cout<<Value1<<' '<<Value2<<' '<<*Pointer1<<endl;
}
```

The output will look as follows:

```
10 20 10
10 20 20
```

Initially, two variables are declared, **Value1** and **Value2**, initialized to 10 and 20, respectively. For purposes of this example, let's say that they are stored in memory addresses 1000–1003 and 1004–1007, respectively. Then a pointer, **Pointer1**, is declared. It is stored in memory locations 1008–1011. **Pointer1** is initialized to the address of the variable **Value1** or 1000. This can be seen in Figure 9.3.

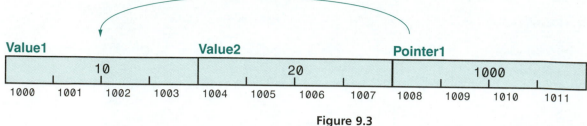

Figure 9.3

When the first **cout** statement is executed, the values 10 and 20 are displayed. When ***Pointer** is evaluated, the computer uses the value stored in **Pointer**(1000) as the location of the value to be displayed. Since 10 is located in the memory location 1000, 10 is displayed.

The program then reassigns the value of **Pointer** to the address of the variable **Value2**(1004). This is depicted in Figure 9.4.

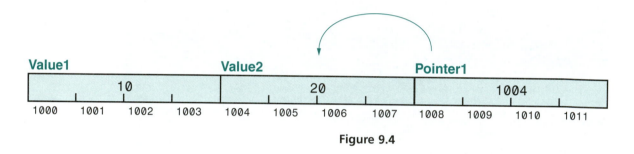

Figure 9.4

The final **cout** statement is executed and the values of **Value1** and **Value2** are displayed as before. However, now when ***Pointer1** is evaluated, the computer uses 1004 as the location of the value to be displayed. Since 20 is located at memory location 1004, 20 is displayed.

If we wish to change the value of **Value1**, we can do so in two ways. The way we are familiar with is to simply assign **Value1** to another value with the following statement:

```
Value1=NewValue;
```

However, we can also use a pointer to **Value1** to change the value of **Value1**. See the following code:

```
//Changing a value with a pointer
#include <stdlib.h>
#include <iostream.h>

typedef int * intPointer;
```

```
void main()
{
    int Value1=10;
    intPointer Pointer1;
    Pointer1=&Value1;

    cout<<Value1<<' '<<*Pointer1<<endl;

    Value1=20;
    cout<<Value1<<' '<<*Pointer1<<endl;

    *Pointer1=30;
    cout<<Value1<<' '<<*Pointer1<<endl;
}
```

The output is as follows:

```
10 10
20 20
30 30
```

Initially, the variable **Value1** is declared and initialized to 10. For the purposes of this example, let's say that **Value1** is stored at memory locations 1000–1003. Then a pointer, **Pointer1**, is declared. It is stored in memory locations 1004–1007. **Pointer1** is initialized to the address of **Value1**(1000). The **cout** statement is then executed and 10 is output for the value **Value1**.

To determine what value is output for ***Pointer1**, we must output the value at the memory location 1000, or 10.

This is depicted in Figure 9.5.

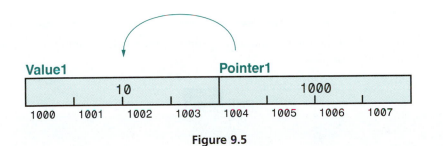

Figure 9.5

When **Value1** is changed to 20, the **cout** statement produces "20 20". This is because when **Value1** is changed, the value at memory location 1000 is changed to 20. This relationship is depicted in Figure 9.6.

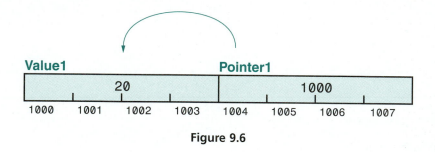

Figure 9.6

When an ***** operator is placed on the left side of a pointer and that pointer is on the left side of an equal sign, the statement causes the value to the right of the equal sign to be stored in the memory location stored in the pointer.

Therefore, when we execute the statement ***Pointer=30**, 30 is stored at the memory address stored in **Pointer**. That means the value of 30 is stored in the variable **Value1**. Therefore, the output from the final **cout** statement would be "30 30". This relationship is depicted in Figure 9.7.

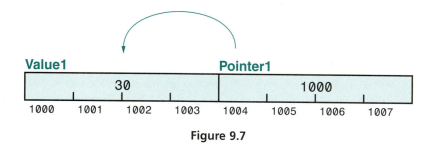

Figure 9.7

DRILLS

To see if you understand the mechanics of pointers, try to decide what the output is of the following examples:

Drill 9-1

```
//Drill 9-1
#include <stdlib.h>
#include <iostream.h>

typedef int * intPointer;

void main()
{
    //Declare variables
    int Value1;
    int Value2;
```

```
//Declare pointers
intPointer Pointer1;
intPointer Pointer2;

//Initialize variables
Value1=5;
Value2=10;

//Initialize pointers
Pointer1=&Value1;
Pointer2=&Value2;

//Output values
cout<<Value1<<' '<<Value2<<' '<<*Pointer1
    <<' '<<*Pointer2<<endl;

Value2=30;

cout<<Value1<<' '<<Value2<<' '<<*Pointer1
    <<' '<<*Pointer2<<endl;

*Pointer1=20;

 cout<<Value1<<' '<<Value2<<' '<<*Pointer1
     <<' '<<*Pointer2<<endl;

Pointer1=&Value2;

 cout<<Value1<<' '<<Value2<<' '<<*Pointer1
     <<' '<<*Pointer2<<endl;
}
```

Although this may seem like merely a nifty notation, it is quite powerful, giving us powers that we didn't have before.

Originally, one of the important uses of pointers was to allow functions to pass parameters by reference. In C, the & operator was not available in a parameter list. The only way for C to pass a value by reference was to pass the memory address. By passing a memory address, the function was able to access the original value instead of a copy. When the function made a change to the value pointed to by the pointer, it was remembered after the function call.

C++ uses the & operator to operate in a similar way. However, it hides the complexity of what is being executed from you. When you indicate to a function to pass by reference, it passes a copy of the address of the variable you wish to change to the function. Then when a change needs to be made to a variable, the program makes the change to wherever in memory the pointer is pointing, which just happens to be the original value.

Let's look in detail at the three ways of passing parameters. The first is the pass by value method that we used when we first learned to use functions. It has no side effects to the parameters and can return at most a single answer from the function.

```
//Pass by value example
#include <stdlib.h>
#include <iostream.h>

int DoubleIt(int DoubleValue)
{
    return(DoubleValue*2);
}

void main()
{
    int Value=2;
    Value = DoubleIt(Value);
    cout<<Value;
}
```

Then we learned that we can use **&** in the parameter list to cause the variables to be called by reference and thus automatically retain the changes made to it within the function.

```
//Pass by reference example in C++
#include <stdlib.h>
#include <iostream.h>

void DoubleIt(int & RefValue)
{
    RefValue=RefValue*2;
}

void main()
{
    int Value=2;
    DoubleIt(Value);
    cout<<Value;
}
```

However, there is a third way to pass values. By using pointers we can pass variables to functions and retain the changes made to them. We accomplish this by passing the variables as pointers to the variables we wish to change. We use the ***** operator to access the actual value the pointer is pointing at. Although the notation is confusing, in straight C it was the only way to accomplish a call by reference.

```
//Pointer pass by reference example

#include <stdlib.h>
#include <iostream.h>
```

```
typedef int * intPointer;

void DoubleIt(intPointer ValuePointer)
{
    *ValuePointer *= 2;
}

void main()
{
    int Value=2;
    DoubleIt(&Value);
    cout<<Value;
}
```

When the function **DoubleIt** is called, the parameter **ValuePointer** is set to a copy of the address of the variable **Value**. Let's say in this example that the address is 1000. Then, the parameter **ValuePointer** would point to the variable **Value** from within the function. Therefore, when the ***ValuePointer = *ValuePointer * 2;** is executed, the value at the memory address stored in **ValuePointer** is multiplied by 2 and stored back at the memory address stored in **ValuePointer**. This is depicted in Figure 9.8.

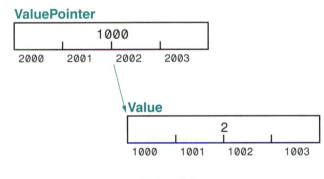

Figure 9.8

▌▌ DRILLS

What is the output of the following code?

Drill 9.2

```
//Drill 9-2

#include <stdlib.h>
#include <iostream.h>

typedef int * intPointer;
typedef char * charPointer;

void DrillFunction(intPointer Param1, charPointer Param2, float Param3);
```

```
void DrillFunction(intPointer Param1, charPointer Param2, float Param3)
{
    *Param1 = 1;
    *Param2 = 'A';
    *Param3 = 123.5;
}

void main()
{
    int Variable=100;
    char Variable2 = 'W';
    float Variable3 = 5.5;
    DrillFunction(&Variable1, &Variable2, Variable3);
    cout<<Value;
}
```

What is the output of the following code?

Drill **9.3**

```
//Drill 9-3

#include <stdlib.h>
#include <iostream.h>

typedef int * intPointer;
typedef char * charPointer;

void DrillFunction(intPointer Param1, charPointer Param2, float Param3);

void DrillFunction(intPointer Param1, charPointer Param2, float Param3)
{
    *Param1 = 1;
    *Param2 = 'A';
    Param3 = 123.5;
}

void main()
{
    int Variable=100;
    char Variable2 = 'W';
    float Variable3 = 5.5;
    DrillFunction(&Variable1, &Variable2, Variable3);
    cout<<Value;
}
```

9.3 ARRAYS AS POINTERS

If the only reason to learn pointers was to learn an archaic syntax held over from C programming, we would have left it out of the text. However, there are more reasons that we use pointers other than when we are passing parameters. We already use this method, but you are not aware of it. Do you think it would be efficient to pass really large variables to a function by copying the contents of the entire variable every time we made a function call? Probably not. Can you think of any really large variables that we have used so far? How about arrays?

Remember when we wrote the string functions? How come when we changed the destination string within the function, the string outside the function retained the change? It is because an array is passed to a function as a pointer and the actual values that were changed within the function were the original values.

Observe the following code:

```
char Array[10];
charPointer Pointer;
Pointer=Array;
```

Array is declared as an array of characters, but **Array** can also be thought of as the memory address of the beginning of an array. **Pointer** is a pointer to a character and can be assigned the starting location of the array **Array**. See Figure 9.9.

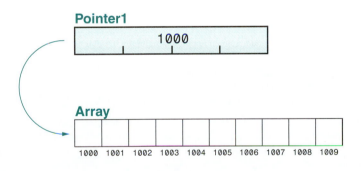

Figure 9.9

By assigning the starting address of the **Array** to **Pointer**, we can reference the same array as **Array**, but from the **Pointer** variable.

Imagine if we wanted to convert a string to uppercase. We could write the program in two ways:

```
//First method of converting a string to uppercase

#include <stdlib.h>
#include <iostream.h>

void main()
{
    char ConvertArray[]="hello";
    int Index;
    for (Index=0;ConvertArray[Index]!='\0';Index++)
      if (ConvertArray[Index] <= 'z' && ConvertArray[Index]>= 'a')
        ConvertArray[Index] += 'A' - 'a';

    cout<<ConvertArray<<endl;
}
```

In the previous program we looped through all the characters in the array **ConvertArray** until we reached the end of the string. As we passed over each character, we checked to see if it was a lowercase letter. If it was, then we converted it to an uppercase letter.

PROGRAMMER'S NOTEBOOK

The lower- to uppercase conversion is accomplished with a trick. Characters in C++ are really small integer values from 0 to 255. The difference between the lowercase letter 'a' and the lowercase letter 'b' is 1. The difference between the lowercase letter 'a' and the lower case letter 'c' is 2. All the other lowercase letters follow in a similar manner.

Likewise, the difference between the lowercase letter 'a' and the uppercase letter 'A' is 32. The difference between the lowercase letter 'b' and the uppercase letter 'B' is 32. All the upper- and lowercase letters have the same 32 difference in their numerical value. Therefore, if we know that a letter is lowercase, we can convert it to uppercase by subtracting the uppercase value from the lowercase value.

The problem with this implementation is that it forces us to calculate the position in the array many times. If you remember back to the implementation of arrays, this calculation involves an addition and multiplication, which over time can slow down the computer's operation.

Therefore, we will rewrite the program using pointers to improve the performance of our conversion. See the following example:

```
//Second method of converting a string to uppercase

#include <stdlib.h>
#include <iostream.h>

typedef char * charPointer;

void main()
{
    char ConvertArray[] = "hello";
    charPointer Pointer=ConvertArray;

    while (*Pointer != '\0')
    {
     if (*Pointer <= 'z' && *Pointer >= 'a')
       *Pointer += 'A' - 'a';
     Pointer++;
    }
    cout<<ConvertArray<<endl;
}
```

By taking advantage of pointers, we no longer are required to have the compiler calculate the array position on each reference. We simply store the starting address of the array **ConvertArray** in the pointer variable **Pointer**. We can reference each individual character in the array by dereferencing the pointer using the * operator. To pass over the entire array, we simply increment **Pointer** to the next memory address.

PROGRAMMER'S NOTEBOOK

The reason we use **Pointer** as a temporary pointer is that we need to be able to reference the beginning of the array, **ConvertArray**, when we are done. However, incrementing a pointer may cause side effects.

In this case, the array is of type **char** and requires only one byte for each value in the array. However, what would happen if the array is of a type like integer where each element is either two or four bytes long? You might think that we would have to increment **Pointer** by 2 or 4; however, this would be a burden. If C++ did things this way, we would always need to know the size of variables that would present problems. This problem would be especially bad if we decided to switch machines. Although C++ has a **sizeof** function that will return the size in bytes of a type, C++ actually takes care of the problem for us.

By declaring a pointer as a pointer to a specific type, like integer, the compiler knows how many bytes to increment a pointer when the pointer is incremented. So **Pointer++** will add one to itself if it is a pointer to a character, but add two or four to itself if it is an integer.

PROGRAMMER'S NOTEBOOK

Regardless of the type of pointer, a pointer variable of any type will require the same amount of memory.

DRILLS

What is the output of the following code?

Drill 9-4

```
//Drill 9-4
#include <stdlib.h>
#include <iostream.h>

typedef int * intPointer;

void main()
{
    int Array[10]={0,1,2,3,4,5,6,7,8,9};
    intPointer Pointer;

    Pointer=Array;
    Pointer=Pointer+3;

    cout<<*Pointer<<endl;
}
```

9.4 STRING FUNCTIONS REWRITTEN AS POINTERS

Previously, we implemented a series of string functions using arrays. Now that we understand the efficiency of pointers, let's rewrite them using pointers.

StrCpy

StrCpy can be reimplemented using pointers. Instead of arrays being listed as the parameters, we pass pointers that represent the memory addresses of the beginning of the strings. To compare the characters in the **Source** string to the '\0' character, we access each character one at a time by dereferencing the **Source** pointer. If the character at the memory location stored in the **Source** is equal to '\0', then the loop terminates. To copy from the **Source** to the **Destination** string, our implementation has taken a shortcut. We store the value that **Source** points to the memory location stored in the **Destination** pointer. In the same statement we use the postincrement function to advance both **Source** and **Destination** pointers to the next character. Finally, when the loop terminates, we add the '\0' character to the memory location stored in the **Destination** pointer.

```
//Pointer Implementation of StrCpy
void StrCpy(charPointer Destination, charPointer Source)
{
   while(*Source!='\0')
     *Destination++=*Source++;
   *Destination='\0';
}
```

The following example uses **StrCpy** implemented with pointers to copy the string "copy" from the variable **String1** to the variable **String2**. **String1** and **String2** are variables defined in **main**. **String1** is initialized to the string "copy", and **String2** is uninitialized and declared to store 10 characters. **StrCpy** is called to copy the contents of **String1** to **String2**. Then the contents of **String2** are output.

The following is the actual code for our example:

```
//Program using StrCpy (pointer implementation)

#include <stdlib.h>
#include <iostream.h>

typedef char * charPointer;

//Prototype
void StrCpy(charPointer Destination, charPointer Source);
```

```
//Pointer implementation of StrCpy
void StrCpy(charPointer * Destination, charPointer * Source)
{
    while(*Source!='\0')
        *Destination++=*Source++;
    *Destination='\0';
}

void main()
{
    char String1[]="copy";
    char String2[10];

    StrCpy(String2,String1);

    cout<<String2<<endl;
}
```

When **String1** is declared and allocated, it must allocate five characters, one for each letter and one for the '\0' in the string "copy". Let's assume these characters are allocated from memory address 1000 to memory address 1004.

When **String2** is declared and allocated, it allocates 10 characters as is indicated in the brackets. Let's assume these characters are allocated from memory address 1005 to memory address 1014.

Figure 9.10 shows the memory allocated and what is contained within it.

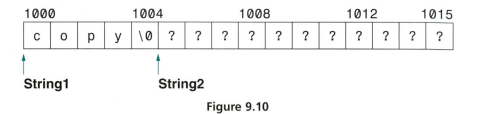

Figure 9.10

When **StrCpy** is called, the starting memory location of **String2** is passed as the pointer called **Destination**, and the starting memory location of **String1** is passed as the pointer called **Source**. Both **Source** and **Destination** are pointer variables storing copies of the memory addresses passed to **StrCpy**. This representation is shown in Figure 9.11.

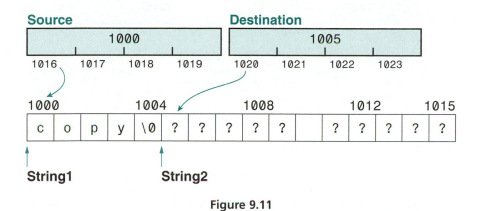

Figure 9.11

We enter the **while** loop and compare the contents at the **Source** pointer, 'c'. Since 'c' is not equal to '\0', we execute the body of the loop. The body of the loop copies the current character pointed to by the pointer **Source**, 'c', to the memory location pointed to by the pointer **Destination**, 1005. This is shown in Figure 9.12.

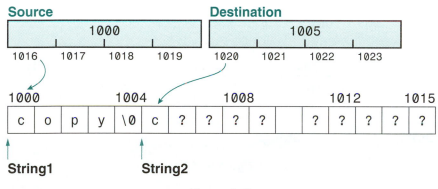

Figure 9.12

After the character is copied, both pointers **Source** and **Destination** are postincremented. Therefore, the pointer **Source** equals 1001 and the pointer **Destination** equals 1006, as shown in Figure 9.13.

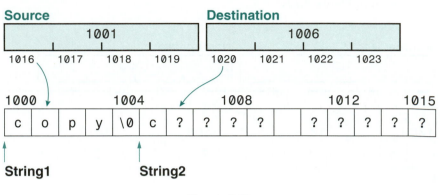

Figure 9.13

The value at the memory location pointed to by **Source** is now equal to 'o'. We reevaluate whether 'o' is equal to '\0', but it is not. Therefore, we execute the body of the loop again.

The body of the loop copies the current character pointed to by the pointer **Source**, 'o', to the memory location pointed to by the pointer **Destination**, 1006, as shown in Figure 9.14.

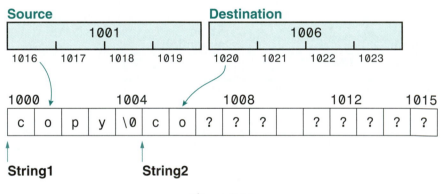

Figure 9.14

After the character is copied, both pointers **Source** and **Destination** are post incremented. Therefore, the pointer **Source** equals 1002 and the pointer **Destination** equals 1007, as shown in Figure 9.15.

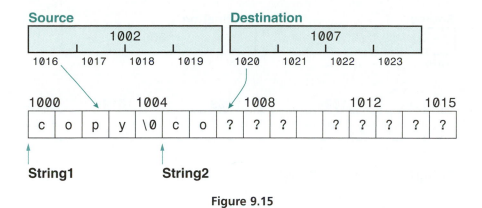

Figure 9.15

The value at the memory location pointed to by **Source** is now equal to 'p'. We reevaluate whether 'p' is equal to '\0' and it is not. Therefore, we execute the body of the loop again.

The body of the loop copies the current character pointed to by the pointer **Source**, 'p', to the memory location pointed to by the pointer **Destination**, 1007, as shown in Figure 9.16.

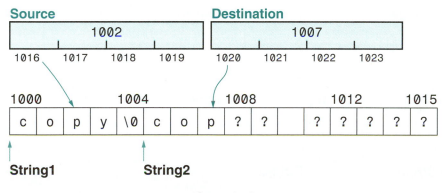

Figure 9.16

After the character is copied, both pointers **Source** and **Destination** are postin-cremented. Therefore, the pointer **Source** equals 1003 and the pointer **Destination** equals 1008, as shown in Figure 9.17.

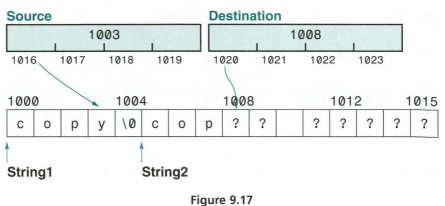

Figure 9.17

The value at the memory location pointed to by **Source** is now equal to 'y'. We reevaluate whether 'y' is equal to '\0' and it is not. Therefore, we execute the body of the loop again.

The body of the loop copies the current character pointed to by the pointer **Source**, 'y', to the memory location pointed to by the pointer **Destination**, 1008. This is shown in Figure 9.18.

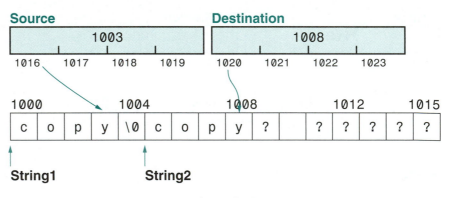

Figure 9.18

After the character is copied, both pointers **Source** and **Destination** are postincremented. Therefore, the pointer **Source** equals 1004 and the pointer **Destination** equals 1009. This is shown in Figure 9.19

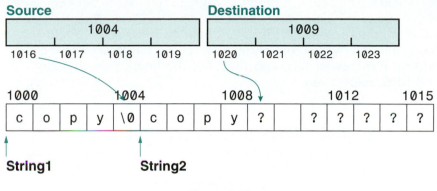

Figure 9.19

The value at the memory location pointed to by **Source** is now equal to '\0'. We reevaluate whether '\0' is equal to '\0' and this time it is. Therefore, we no longer execute the body of the loop.

The final step is to copy the '\0' to the memory location pointed to by **Destination**. Since **Destination** is equal to 1009, '\0' copied as is shown in Figure 9.20.

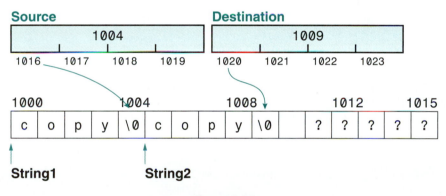

Figure 9.20

In the following implementations of **StrLen** we can check to see if the current character is '\0' without the need to compute the array position again and again. The code is almost identical to the array implementation, except we increment the **StringPointer** pointer to get to the next character instead of using an index into the array.

```
//New pointer implemantation
int StrLen(charPointer StringPointer)
{
    int Len=0;

    while(*StringPointer++ !='\0')
      Len++;
    return Len;
}
```

```
//Old array implemantation
int StrLen(char String[])
{
    int Len=0;

    while(String[Len] != '\0')
      Len++;
    return Len;
}
```

Let's step through an example of calling the new **StrLen** function with the string **String1** that contains **"Len"**. **String1** is declared in **main** and initialized to the string **"Len"**. The program is shown in the following code:

```
//Program using StrLen (pointer implementation)

#include <stdlib.h>
#include <iostream.h>

typedef char * charPointer;

//Prototype
int StrLen(charPointer StringPointer);
```

```
//Strlen function
int StrLen(char * StringPointer)
{
    int Len=0;

    while(*StringPointer++ !='\0')
        Len++;
    return Len;
}

void main()
{
    char String1[]="Len";

    cout<<StrLen(String1)<<endl;
}
```

When **String1** is declared and allocated, it must allocate four characters, one for each letter and one for the '\0' in the string **"Len"**. Let's assume these characters are allocated from memory address 1000 to memory address 1003.

PROGRAMMER'S NOTEBOOK

Remember that **StrLen** returns the number of characters in the string excluding the '\0' character.

Figure 9.21 shows the memory allocated and what is contained within it.

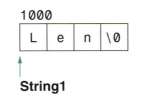

String1

Figure 9.21

When **StrLen** is called, the starting memory location of **String1** is passed as the pointer called **StringPointer**. **StringPointer** is a pointer variable storing a copy of the memory addresses passed to **StrLen**. Additionally, the integer variable **Len** is initialized to 0. This representation is shown in Figure 9.22.

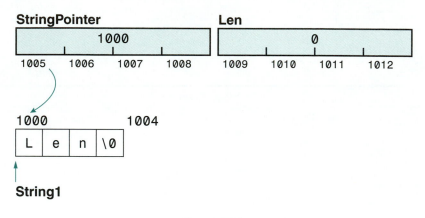

Figure 9.22

We enter the **while** loop and compare the contents at the **StringPointer** pointer, 'L'. Since 'L' is not equal to a '\0', we execute the body of the loop. However, before we execute the body of the loop, we must complete the postincrement of the **StringPointer** pointer. Therefore, **StringPointer** now contains the value 1001. The memory scheme now looks like Figure 9.23.

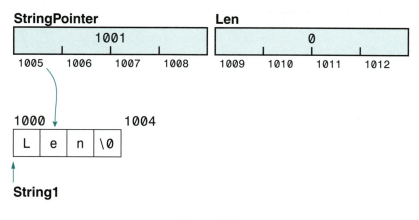

Figure 9.23

The body of the loop increments **Len** by 1 to 1, as shown in Figure 9.24.

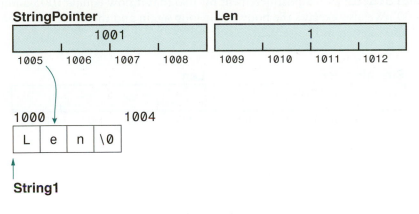

Figure 9.24

The value at the memory location pointed to by **StringPointer** is now equal to 'e'. We reevaluate whether 'e' is equal to '\0' and it is not. Therefore, we increment **StringPointer** with a postincrement by 1 so that it now equals 1002 and points to the 'n'. We also execute the body of the loop again and therefore increment **Len** to 2. This is shown in Figure 9.25.

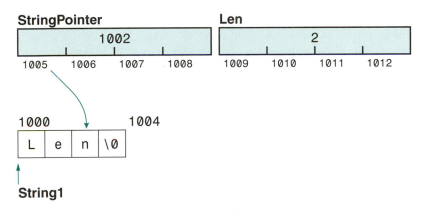

Figure 9.25

The value at the memory location pointed to by **StringPointer** is now equal to 'n'. We reevaluate whether 'n' is equal to '\0' and it is not. Therefore, we increment **StringPointer** with a postincrement by 1 so that it now equals 1003 and points to the '\0'. We also execute the body of the loop again and therefore increment **Len** to 3. This is shown in Figure 9.26.

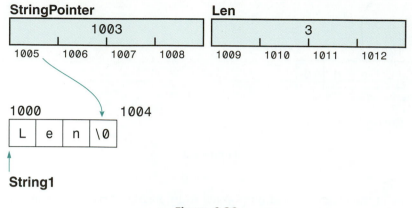

Figure 9.26

The value at the memory location pointed to by **StringPointer** is now equal to '\0'. We reevaluate whether '\0' is equal to '\0' and this time it is. Therefore, we no longer execute the body of the loop. Although **StringPointer** is postincremented one more time, it is no longer used in the function, and is irrelevant.

The final step is to return the current value of **Len**, 3, from the function.

Another example of implementing **StrLen** not only illustrates a good point, it reduces the number of increments required in the **while** loop. See the following code:

```
//Second pointer implementation of strlen
int StrLen(char * StringPointer)
{
   char * Start=StringPointer;

   while(*StringPointer !='\0')
     StringPointer++;

   return StringPointer-Start;
}
```

This version of **StrLen** stores the starting location of the string and then determines the ending location of the string. By using pointer arithmetic and subtracting the starting location from the ending location, we can determine the length of the string. Figure 9.27 contains a diagram for the string "Do or do not there is no try!"

Figure 9.27

The starting location of the string is at memory address 1000. The address of the '\0' character in the string is 1029. By subtracting 1000 from 1029 we get the proper length of the string, excluding the '\0' character.

DRILLS

Drill 9-5

Knowing how to implement **StrLen** and **StrCpy** should make it easy for you to implement **StrCat** using pointers. Try to do so.

StrCmp

The final string function we will implement with pointers is the **StrCmp** function. As with the other string functions, the parameters are passed as pointers to characters.

We compare the values at the memory location stored in the pointers as well as the current character pointed to by **String1** to the '\0' character. This condition is true, so we increment both pointers. Finally, we return the difference between the values stored at the memory locations contained in **StringPointer1** and **StringPointer2**. If these values are the same, 0 is returned. Otherwise, a nonzero value is returned.

```
//Pointer implementation of StrCmp
int StrCmp(charPointer * StringPointer1, charPointer StringPointer2)
{
    while((*StringPointer1==*StringPointer2) && (*StringPointer1!='\0'))
    {
        StringPointer1++;
        StringPointer2++;
    }
    return(*StringPointer1-*StringPointer2);
}
```

We leave as an exercise the implementation of **StrNCmp**, **StrNCpy**, and **StrnCat** with pointers instead of arrays.

9.5 DYNAMIC MEMORY AND POINTERS

Pointers give us one more very powerful feature. Until now, if we wanted to declare an array we needed to know the size of the array at the time we wrote the program. This can lead to an incredible amount of wasted memory. It is far more efficient to determine the amount of memory needed at run time and then allocate the proper size of the array.

To accomplish this, we need to declare an array as a pointer instead of a traditional array. To declare a pointer to an integer that will be used as an array, we use the same syntax as with any other pointer declaration:

```
intPointer Array;
```

To allocate an array, we could prompt the user to ask how many items he or she wants to store in the array as follows:

```
int TotalItems;

cout<<"Please enter the amount of values you wish to store in the array"
    <<endl;
cin>>TotalItems;
```

To allocate **TotalItems** worth of integers to the integer pointer **array**, use the **new** command. The **new** command uses the following template:

```
new VariableType[ArraySize];
```

The variable type listed in the **new** command can be any valid C++ variable type. The variable **ArraySize** must contain a positive integer value.

So to complete the allocation of our array in the example, we would simply write the following:

```
Array = new int[TotalItems];
```

Now, we can use the variable **Array** just as if it were declared in the traditional manner. The following code reads in **TotalItems** from the user and stores them in the array **Array**. There is absolutely no difference than if we had declared the variable **Array** in the traditional manner.

```
int Index;

for (Index=0; Index<TotalItems; Index++)
{
    cout<<"Enter a value"<<endl;
    cin>>Array[Index];
}
```

Another example of a good use of **dynamic memory** is in dealing with strings. Imagine if we wanted to store 100 names. Without dynamic memory we would be required to allocate 100 times the maximum size of any of the strings. If we decide the maximum will be 50 characters, then we would be required to declare the array as follows:

```
char Names[100][50];
```

To write the program to read in the 100 names would be fairly simple.

```
//Program to read in 100 names

#include <stdlib.h>
#include <iostream.h>

#define MaxItems 100
#define MaxSize 50

void main()
{
    char Names[MaxItems][MaxSize];
    int Name;

    for (Name=0; Name < MaxItems; Name++)
        cin.getline(Names[Name],MaxSize);
}
```

Imagine what the memory would look like if we read in names link "Fletch", "Chevy", "Geena", etc. Below is a figure depicting what the memory would look like. As you can see there is a great deal of wasted space. The first four rows of the array **Names** as well as the last four rows are shown in Figure 9.28.

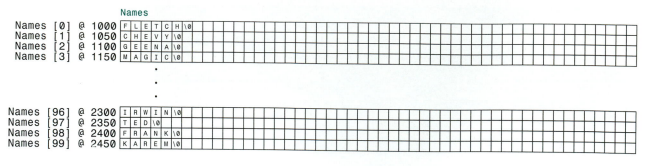

Figure 9.28

Instead of wasting so much space, we can declare an array of 100 pointers to characters. Then as we determine how much memory we require, we simply allocate it.
You might write the code as follows:

```
//Improved, but incorrect code to read in 100 names
#include <stdlib.h>
#include <iostream.h>

//Include string functions here

#define MaxSize 50
#define MaxItems 100

typedef char * charPointer;

void main()
{
    charPointer Names[MaxItems];
    char Buffer[MaxSize];

    for (int Name = 0; Name <100; Name++)
    {
      cin.getline(Buffer,MaxSize);
      Names[Name] = new char[StrLen(Buffer)];
      StrCpy(Names[Name], Buffer);
    }
}
```

The code declares an array of pointers as well as a buffer to temporarily hold the string. The buffer must be as large as the maximum string. Then it is a simple matter of calculating the size of the string, allocating the memory, setting the pointer to the allocated memory, and finally copying the string into the newly allocated memory.

The problem with this code is that **StrLen** returns the number of characters not including the '\0' character. Therefore, if we allocate only the amount returned by the **StrLen** function, we would allocate one character too few. This might not seem like a problem, but eventually your program will not function correctly. This is a very common mistake and not easily detected.

See the correct code as follows and read on to see the illustration of the more efficient memory allocation scheme:

```
//Improved and corrected code to read in 100 names

#include <stdlib.h>
#include <iostream.h>

//Include string functions here

#define MaxItems 100
#define MaxSize 50

typedef char * charPointer;

void main()
{
    charPointer Names[MaxItems];
    char Buffer[MaxSize];

    for (int Name = 0; Name <MaxItems; Name++)
      {
        cin>>Buffer;
        Names[Name] = new char[StrLen(Buffer)+1];
        strcpy(Names[Name], Buffer);
      }
}
```

Figure 9.29 is a diagram of the memory allocation for the new implementation. The array **Names** is an array of 50 pointers. Each pointer stores the **memory address** of the string associated with it. Each string occupies only as much space as is required to store the characters for each specific string and the '\0' character. The memory locations of each string may be adjacent to each other, but this is not necessarily the case.

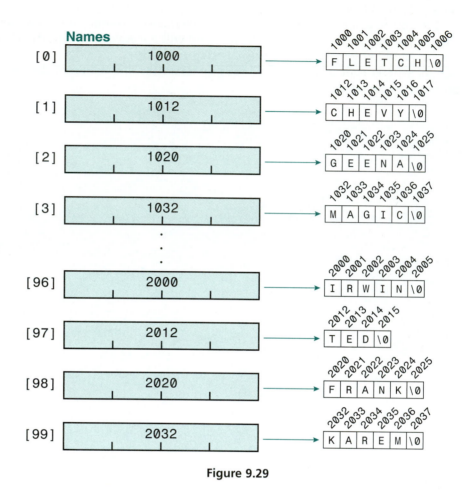

Figure 9.29

You may not have realized the problem with the first version of the dynamic string example, so in order for you to see the problem of inadequate memory, run the following example. Depending upon your compiler, you may not get exactly the same results:

```
//Example of an error using strcpy

#include <stdlib.h>
#include <iostream.h>

//Include string functions here

void main()
{
    char First[8];
    char Second[8];
    char Third[8];

    strcpy(First,"0123456789");
    strcpy(Second,"abcdefghij");
    strcpy(Third,"klmnopqrst")

    cout<<"First = "<<First<<endl;
    cout<<"Second = "<<Second<<endl;
    cout<<"Third = "<<Third<<endl;
}
```

Depending upon your compiler, your output may look like the following:

```
First = 01234567abcdefghklmnopqrst
Second = abcdefghklmnopqrst
Third = klmnopqrst
```

Why does this happen? Let's assume that strings **First**, **Second**, and **Third** are located in adjacent memory locations and then we'll look at what happens to memory after each call to **StrCpy**.

When the **StrCpy(First, "0123456789")** function is executed, the characters 0–9 are copied one character at a time to **First**, starting at the beginning location of **First**(1000). However, there is only enough room for eight characters including the '\0'. If you recall from our implementation of **StrCpy**, the copy function does not check to see that there is enough room for the string. Instead, it simply writes over whatever is directly after the string **First**. In this case, the characters '8', '9', and '\0' are written into the space that is allocated to the **Second** string. See Figure 9.30.

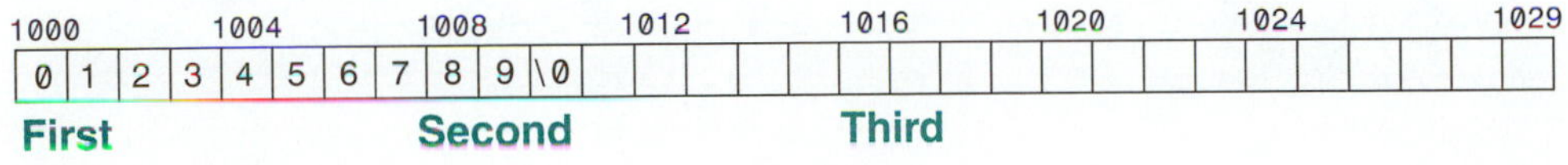

Figure 9.30

Once the second **StrCpy** function is executed, the string "abcdefghij" is copied one character at a time to **Second**, starting at the beginning location of **Second**(1008). However, the characters, '8', '9', and '\0' are already there. **StrCpy** will simply write over them. Additionally, we have the same problem as before with the string "abcdefghij" being too large to fit in the space allocated for string **Second**. As they did before, the extra characters will spill over into string **Thirds**'s space. See Figure 9.31.

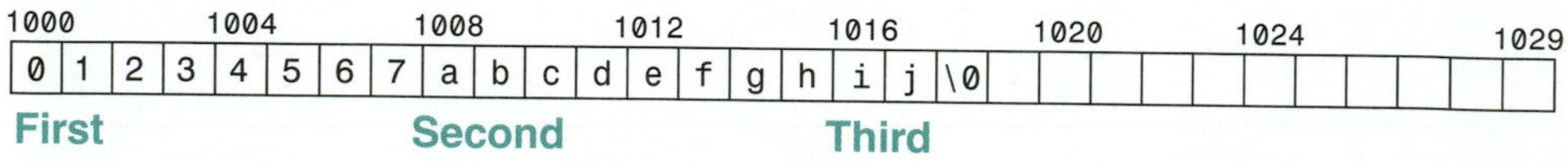

Figure 9.31

After the final **StrCpy** statement is executed, the string "klmnopqrst" is copied one character at a time to **Third** starting at the beginning location of **Third**(1016). However, the characters 'i', 'j', '\0' are already there. As before, they are simply written over. Additionally, we have the problem that the string "klmnopqrst" is larger than the space allocated for by the string **Third**, so whatever comes after the string **Third** in memory will be written over. See Figure 9.32.

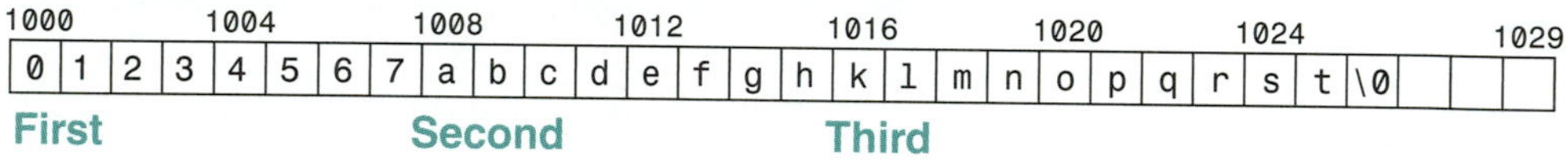

Figure 9.32

The reason the output of string **First** is "01234567abcdefghklmnopqrst" is that when we instruct the computer to display a string it will display every character until it reaches a '\0' character. Since the '\0' of strings **First** and **Second** were overwritten, all the characters until the '\0' of the **Third** string are displayed. Similarly, when we request string **Second** to be displayed, extra characters are displayed.

We have to be cautious about another subtlety. What if we wanted to write a function that allocated the array for us? It would seem like a simple task. Observe the following code:

```
//Example of an error in memory allocation

#include <iostream.h>
#include <stdlib.h>

typedef int * intPointer;

void AllocateArray(intPointer Array, int TotalSize);
```

```
void AllocateArray(intPointer Array, int TotalSize)
{
    Array = new int[TotalSize];
}

void main()
{
    intPointer Values;
    AllocateArray(Values, 10);
}
```

You would think this code works properly, and although you would not get a compile error, it does not function the way we wish. When we declare the pointer values, we are unsure of its contents. When we pass the parameter **Values** to **AllocateArray**, a copy of that unsure value is passed to the function.

Once in the function, that copy is reassigned the starting location of the memory address of the new array. However, since the array address is stored in a copy of the original value of the **Values** pointer, it is not retained when we return to the **main** routine.

To correct this we must pass the pointer by reference, using the **&** operator to retain the change. See the following corrected code:

```
//Corrected example of memory allocation

#include <iostream.h>
#include <stdlib.h>

typedef int * intPointer;

void AllocateArray(intPointer & Array, int TotalSize);

void AllocateArray(intPointer & Array, int TotalSize)
{
    Array = new int[TotalSize];
}

void main()
{
    intPointer Values;
    AllocateArray(Values, 10);
}
```

DRILLS

Drill

Write the code required to declare a pointer and allocate an array of 40 integers.

Drill

Write the code required to declare a pointer and allocate an array of 50 characters. Initialize this array to the string "Pointers can be confusing".

9.6 DELETING MEMORY

Another important issue with using dynamic memory is giving the memory we use back to the operating system when we are done with it. Until now, we have assumed that as we are finished using memory, the computer frees up the memory automatically. However, when we allocate memory with the **new** command we must manually give the memory back to the computer when we no longer require it. Fortunately, this is extremely easy to accomplish. We simply state the keyword **delete**, followed by a set of brackets, followed by the pointer from which we wish to delete memory. This can be seen in the following template:

```
delete [] PointerName;
```

Here is an example of declaring a pointer called **Memory**, allocating 100 characters and assigning the memory address of the beginning of the array to **Memory**. Finally, we deallocate the memory using a **delete** command:

```
charPointer Memory;
Memory = new char [100];
delete [] Memory;
```

We will see many more examples of the use of **delete** when we discuss the various data structures later in this book.

DRILLS

Will the following code compile and run without error? If not, explain why.

Drill 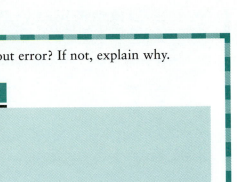 **9-8**

```
//Drill 9-8
#include <stdlib.h>
#include <iostream.h>

typedef int * intPointer;
typedef char * charPointer;

void main()
{
    charPointer Pointer;
    int Size;

    cout<<"Please enter a size of the array";
    cin>>Size;

    Pointer = new char[Size];

    //Other code

    delete [] Pointer;

}
```

Will the following code compile and run without error? If not, explain why.

Drill **9-9**

```
//Drill 9-9
#include <stdlib.h>
#include <iostream.h>

typedef int * intPointer;
typedef char * charPointer;

void main()
{
    charPointer Pointer;
    int Size;

    cout<<"Please enter a size of the array";
    cin>>Size;
```

```
    if (Size > 0)
    {
        Pointer = new char[Size];

        //Other code

        delete [] Pointer;
        delete [] Size;
    }
}
```

9.7   Case Study

Problem Description

Data for a program may come from many sources other than the program that is using it. Often, data may come from archaic systems like COBOL. When this happens, strings contain a series of spaces after them so that the strings contains the same number of characters as the maximum number of that field. We are going to simulate this by loading arrays for employee's last name, first name, and middle initial. All last names should be padded with blanks so they occupy 30 spaces. All first names should be padded with blanks so they occupy 15 spaces. Some employees have middle initials, some don't. We will write a program that will assemble the employee's full name in the form: first name space middle initial period space last name, for employees having a middle initial; and first name space last name, for employees who do not have a middle initial. Subscripts are permitted only for the initial declarations of the arrays. All subsequent array manipulation must be done with pointers.

Discussion

This problem illustrates the use of pointers to improve performance. Although the syntax is a little confusing, the solution is faster than using arrays throughout the program. It is not uncommon to have to process millions of records at a time. Therefore, this timesaving effort is well worth it.

One trick was employed so that we could use common code for the adding of the first and last names to the string. The WholeNames array is initialized to NULL characters so that we can call StrNCat instead of StrNCpy when we place the first name into the array.

Solution

```
//Includes
#include <iostream.h>
#include <iomanip.h>
#include <string.h>
#include <ctype.h>
```

```
//Typedefs
typedef char * charPointer;

//Constants
#define Cols 31
#define Rows 10
#define FirstNameSize 16
#define LastNameSize 31

//Prototypes
int AddName(charPointer NamePtr, charPointer WholeNamesPtr, int
Size);
void AddMiddleInitial(charPointer Name, char MiddleInitial);
void BuildWhole(charPointer WholeNamesPtr, charPointer LastNamesPtr,
                charPointer FirstNamesPtr, charPointer
MiddleInitialsPtr,
                int NumNames);
void StrNCat(charPointer Destination, charPointer Source, int Len);

//Main Procedure
void main()
{
  //Total number of initial names
  int  NumNames = 5;

  //Array for Full Names, note the max size is the total size for the
  //Largest First Name + the Largest Last Name + Middle Initial
  //+ the space required for spaces and periods.
  char WholeNames[Rows][FirstNameSize+LastNameSize+5]={0};
  char LastNames[Rows][Cols] = {
                                  "Montoya                       ",
                                  "Max                           ",
                                  "Buttercup                     ",
                                  "Savage                        ",
                                  "Faulk                         "};


  char FirstNames[Rows][FirstNameSize]=
      {"Inigo          ",
       "Miracle        ",
       "Princess       ",
       "Fred           ",
       "Peter          "};

  char MiddleInitials[Rows+1] =" BCDE     "";

 //We must convert the two-dimensional array to a pointer.
  BuildWhole((charPointer)WholeNames, (charPointer)LastNames,
            (charPointer)FirstNames, MiddleInitials, NumNames);
}


void AddMiddleInitial(charPointer Name, char MiddleInitial)
```

9.7 **Case Study** (continued)

```
{

    //To add a middle initial, we must place a space before and
    //a period after.
    if(MiddleInitial != ' ')
    {
        *Name++ = ' ';
        *Name++ = MiddleInitial;
        *Name++ = '.';
    }

    //Whether there is a middle initial or not, we need a space before
    //the last name.
    *Name++ = ' ';
    *Name = '\0';
}

int AddName(charPointer NamePtr, charPointer WholeNamesPtr, int Size)
{
    charPointer PtrEnd;
    int StringSize;

    //Place pointer on first non-null character in string
    PtrEnd = NamePtr + Size - 2;

    while(*PtrEnd == ' ')
      PtrEnd--;  //finds first non-blank
    StringSize = PtrEnd-NamePtr+1;

    StrNCat(WholeNamesPtr, NamePtr, StringSize);
    return StringSize;
}

void BuildWhole(charPointer WholeNamesPtr, charPointer LastNamesPtr,
                charPointer FirstNamesPtr, charPointer
MiddleInitialsPtr,
                int NumNames)
{
  int CurrentRow;
  int StringSize;

  for(CurrentRow = 0; CurrentRow < NumNames; CurrentRow++)
  {
    StringSize = AddName(FirstNamesPtr, WholeNamesPtr, FirstNameSize);
    AddMiddleInitial(WholeNamesPtr+StringSize,
                     *(MiddleInitialsPtr+CurrentRow));
    AddName(LastNamesPtr, WholeNamesPtr, LastNameSize);
```

```
      cout<<WholeNamesPtr<<endl;

      //Offsets pointer for each row by the size of the row
      FirstNamesPtr += FirstNameSize;
      WholeNamesPtr += FirstNameSize+LastNameSize+5;
      LastNamesPtr += LastNameSize;
   }
}


void StrNCat(charPointer Destination, charPointer Source, int Len)
{
   int Counter=0;
   //Calculates the end of the destination string
   while(*Destination != '\0')
      Destination++;

   while((*Source != '\0') && (Counter++ < Len))
      *Destination++=*Source++;
   *Destination = '\0';
}
```

END-OF-CHAPTER

◆ Key Terms

Pointer	A variable that stores a memory location of a variable.
Dynamic Memory	Memory that is allocated during the execution of a program.
Memory Address	The internal reference.

◆ C++ Keywords Introduced

`delete`	Returns dynamically allocated memory to the operating system.
`new`	Allocates memory dynamically.
`typedef`	Alows the user to create new data types.

◆ Answers to Drills

Drill 9-1

The output would be as follows:

```
5 10 5 10
5 30 5 30
20 30 20 30
20 30 30 30
```

Initially, the variables **Value1** and **Value2** are declared. For the purposes of this example, let's say that **Value1** is stored at memory locations 1000–1003 and **Value2** is stored at memory locations 1004–1007.

Then the pointers **Pointer1** and **Pointer2** are declared and stored in memory locations 1008–1011 and 1012–1015, respectively.

Value1 and **Value2** are initialized to 5 and 10, respectively. **Pointer1** is initialized to the address of variable **Value1**, so 1000 is stored in **Pointer1**. **Pointer2** is initialized to the address of variable **Value2**, so 1004 is stored in **Pointer2**.

Therefore when we reach Output 1, the memory is depicted in Figure 9.33.

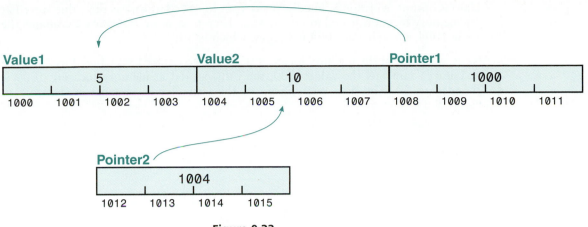

Figure 9.33

The output for the values **Value1** and **Value2** are 5 and 10, respectively. The output for ***Pointer1** is the value stored at the memory location stored in **Pointer1**. Therefore, since **Pointer1** contains the value 1000, the value at memory location 1000 is output, which is 5. Finally, the output for ***Pointer2** is the value stored at the memory location stored in **Pointer2**. Therefore, since **Pointer2** contains the value 1004, the value at memory location 1004 is output, which is 10.

Then the value at **Value2** is changed to 30. Now the relationship of the variables in memory is depicted in Figure 9.34.

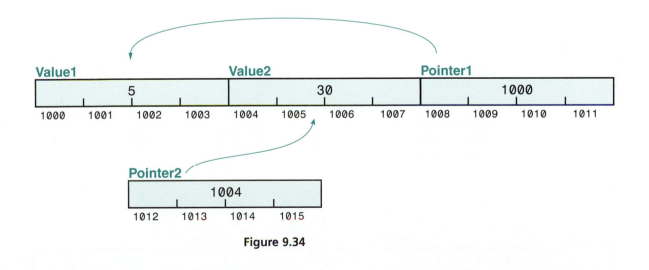

Figure 9.34

The output for the values **Value1** and **Value2** are 5 and 30, respectively. The output for ***Pointer1** is the value stored at the memory location stored in **Pointer1**. Therefore, since **Pointer1** contains the value 1000, the value at memory location 1000 is output, which is 5. Finally, the output for ***Pointer2** is the value stored at the memory location stored in **Pointer2**. Therefore, since **Pointer2** contains the value 1004, the value at 1004 is output, which is 30.

Next, the value at the memory location stored in **Pointer1** is changed to 20. Since **Pointer1** contains the value 1000, the value stored at memory location 1000 is changed to 20. The new relationship of the variables in memory is depicted in Figure 9.35.

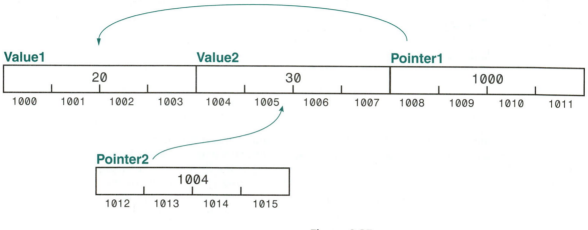

Figure 9.35

The output for the values **Value1** and **Value2** are 20 and 30, respectively. The output for ***Pointer1** is the value stored at the memory location stored in **Pointer1**. Therefore, since **Pointer1** contains the value 1000, the value at memory location 1000 is output, which is 20. Finally, the output for ***Pointer2**, is the value stored at the memory location stored in **Pointer2**. Therefore, since **Pointer2** contains the value 1004, the value at memory location 1004 is output, which is 30.

Finally, the value stored in the variable **Pointer1** is changed to the address of the variable **Value2**. Since the address of **Value1** is 1004, 1004 is stored in **Pointer1**. Now both pointer variables point to the same memory location. This relationship is depicted in Figure 9.36:

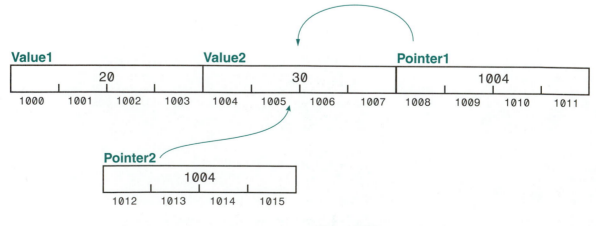

Figure 9.36

The output of **Value1** and **Value2** are 20 and 30, as before. The output for ***Pointer1** is the value stored at the memory location stored in **Pointer1**. Therefore, since **Pointer1** contains the value 1004, the value at memory location 1004 is output, which is 30. Finally, the output for ***Pointer2** is the value stored at the memory location stored in **Pointer2**. Therefore, since **Pointer2** contains the value 1004, the value at memory location 1004 is output, which is 30.

Drill 9-2

The code for this drill contains a syntax error, so it would not compile. The following line would cause an error, because the variable **Param3** is not defined as a pointer:

```
*Param3 = 123.5;
```

Drill 9-3

The output from the code of the drill would be as follows:

```
123 is the student with the highest GPA of 3.5
```

Since **Variable1** and **Variable2** are passed by reference, any changes to these values will be remembered after we return from the function **DrillFunction**. However, **Variable3** is passed by **value**, so a copy of its value is sent to **DrillFunction**. Therefore, any changes to its value are not remembered upon returning to the **main** function.

Drill 9-4

The output of the code for this drill is as follows:

```
3
```

Assume that the array **Array** starts at memory address 1000. Since the variable **Pointer** stores the address of the beginning of the array **Array**, **Pointer** would contain 1000. By adding 3 to a pointer, we are really adding enough to change the pointer to point to three values down the array. Since an integer requires four bytes of memory, we are required to add 12 to **Pointer**. Now when **Pointer** is dereferenced using the * operator, the value at memory location 1012 is returned. That value is 3.

Drill 9-5

We can take two approaches to solving the **StrCat** problem. The first is to mimic the implementation of **StrCat** from arrays and change the notation over from **Array** access to **Pointer** access. This is shown here:

```
//First pointer implementation of StrCat
void StrCat(charPointer Destination, charPointer Source)
{
   //Calculates the end of the destination string
   while(*Destination != '\0')
     Destination++;

   while(*Source != '\0')
       *Destination++=*Source++;
   *Destination = '\0';
}
```

However, if we are thinking about how pointers operate, we might realize that the **StrCat** function is merely the application of **StrCpy** to a memory address that can be calculated by adding the return value from **StrLen** to the memory address of the destination string. This implementation follows:

```
//Slicker pointer implementation of StrCat
void StrCat(charPointer Destination, charPointer Source)
{
  StrCpy(Destination+StrLen(Destination), Source);
}
```

Drill 9-6

The code required for the drill is as follows:

```
#include <iostream.h>
#include <stdlib.h>

typedef int * intPointer;

#define ArraySize 40

void main()
{
   intPointer Answer;
   Answer = new int[ArraySize];
}
```

Drill 9-7

The code required for the drill is as follows:

```
#include <iostream.h>
#include <stdlib.h>

typedef char * charPointer;

#define StringSize 50

//Assume String Function Definitions

void main()
{
    charPointer Answer;
    Answer = new char[StringSize];
    StrCpy(Answer, "Pointers can be confusing");
}
```

Drill 9-8

The code for this drill will compile without a problem. There is the potential for a run-time issue. We should either declare the **Size** variable as an unsigned integer or check to see that a negative number has not been entered for **Size**. A negative size has no meaning when allocating memory.

Drill 9-9

Even though this version of the drill has corrected the possible error of a negative size in calling **new**, we have introduced a new error. We attempt to return the memory allocated for the variable **Size** using **delete**. However, **delete** can be used only to return memory that was allocated dynamically using **new**.

◆ Programming Excercises

1. Write a function, **StrNCpy**, that accepts two pointers to characters and an integer. The first pointer should point to the destination string, and the second pointer should point to the source string. **StrNCpy** should copy the number of characters indicated by the third parameter from the source pointer to the destination pointer.

2. Write a function, **StrNCmp**, that accepts two pointers to characters and an integer. **StrNCmp** should return a 0 if the first n (the third parameter) characters of each string are identical, otherwise it should return a nonzero value.

3. Write a function, **StrNCat**, that accepts two pointers to characters and an integer. The first pointer should point to the destination string, and the second pointer should point to the source string. **StrNCat** should copy the number of characters indicated by the third parameter from the source string to the end of the destination string.

4. Write a function called **GetMaxSize** that allocates a buffer of 256 characters. It then reads ten strings from the user. The strings read should include any whitespace characters entered until a carriage return is keyed. The function should return the maximum size needed to store the largest string.

◆Additional Exercises

1. Show the output that results from the following statements. Assume that the code below precedes each:

```
intPointer Pointer1;
intPointer Pointer2;
intPointer Pointer3;
int Var1;
int Var2;
int Var3;

void main()
{
  Var1 = 10;
  Var2 = 20;
  Var3 = 30;
  }
```

a. cout<<Var1<<endl<<Var2<<endl<<Var3<<endl;

b. Pointer1 = &Var1;
    Pointer2 = &Var2;
    Pointer3 = &Var3;

    cout<<Var1<<endl<<Var2<<endl<<Var3<<endl;
    cout<<*Pointer1<<endl<<*Pointer2<<endl<<*Pointer3<<endl;

c. Var1 = 40;
    Var2 = 50;
    Var3 = 60;

    cout<<Var1<<endl<<Var2<<endl<<Var3<<endl;
    cout<<*Pointer1<<endl<<*Pointer2<<endl<<*Pointer3<<endl;

d. *Pointer1 = 60;
    *Pointer2 = 50;
    *Pointer3 = 40;

    cout<<Var1<<endl<<Var2<<endl<<Var3<<endl;
    cout<<*Pointer1<<endl<<*Pointer2<<endl<<*Pointer3<<endl;

e. Pointer1 = & Var1;
    Pointer2 = & Var3;
    Pointer3 = & Var3;

    cout<<Var1<<endl<<Var2<<endl<<Var3<<endl;
    cout<<*Pointer1<<endl<<*Pointer2<<endl<<*Pointer3<<endl;

f. Pointer1 = Pointer2;
    Pointer2 = Pointer3;
    Pointer3 = Pointer1;

    cout<<Var1<<endl<<Var2<<endl<<Var3<<endl;
    cout<<*Pointer1<<endl<<*Pointer2<<endl<<*Pointer3<<endl;

2. Using the following code, indicate each instance where a pointer is used. Also, indicate the output of the program.

```cpp
#include <stdlib.h>
#include <iostream.h>

typedef int * intPointer;

Function1(intPointer Pointer);

Function1(intPointer Pointer)
{
    int Temp;
    Temp = *Pointer++;
    cout<<Temp;
}

void main()
{
    int * LocalPointer;
    int Array[10] = {1,2,3,4,5,6,7,8,9,10};

    Function1(Array);
}
```

3. Are there syntax errors in the following code? If syntax errors exist, indicate how to fix them.

   a. ```cpp
       intPointer Pointer;
       new Pointer = int;
       ```

   b.  ```cpp
       intPointer Pointer;
       Pointer = new float;
       ```

   c. ```cpp
       intPointer Pointer;
       int Temp;
       Pointer = Temp;
       ```

   d.  ```cpp
       intPointer Pointer1;
       intPointer Pointer2;
       int Value = 1;
       Pointer2 = &Value;
       Pointer1 = Pointer2;
       ```

   e. ```cpp
       intPointer Pointer;
       Pointer = New int;
       ```

4. True or False: The same variable name can be used twice in a function if the first time it is declared as a pointer and the second time it is declared as a variable.
       ```

5. Using dynamic memory, allocate an array for three values for each of the following pointers:

    a.   `intPointer Value1;`

    b.   `floatPointer Value2;`

    c.   `charPointer Value3;`

6. Write the code to dynamically create enough memory to store the values and assign the address to each of the following:

    a.   `intPointer Value;`
         `Store the value 10`

    b.   `floatPointer Value;`
         `Store the value 22.3`

    c.   `charPointer Array;`
         `Store the string "Hello"`

    d.   `charPointer Array;`
         `Store the string "I will make this code work"`

    e.   `intPointer Array;`
         `Store the array containing 1, 3, 5, 7, and 9`

7. The following code attempts to allocate and initialize an array of integers to random values. Explain what is wrong with the following code. Show a better way to accomplish the same task.

```
intPointer Value;
for (int Index = 0; Index<10; Index++)
{
   Value = new int;
   *Value = rand();
   Sum += *Value;
}
```

10

Structures and Basic Classes

Chapter Objectives

♦ Demonstrate how to combine values of different variable types in one variable

♦ Introduce how to define a structure

♦ Explain how to use structures

♦ Explain how to use arrays of structures

♦ Introduce the concept of encapsulation

♦ Introduce C++ classes

♦ Introduce new terms associated with classes

Arrays are very powerful devices that allow us to group large amounts of data together under a single variable name; however, the examples that we used were picked specifically so that they would work with our limited knowledge of C++. How would you write a program if, instead of being asked for a simple list of either integers or characters, you were asked to combine integers, floating point numbers, and strings with one variable name? You couldn't do it, at least until now.

It is actually quite often that we want to group logically connected data that are of different types together. Just think about writing a program to store your student record. You would need strings for your name, integers to store the your ID number, and a floating point number to store your grades.

In C++ we can do this with a **structure**. A structure is a template for organizing information of various data types under a single name. It defines what types of information can be stored within it and the names by which this information will be referred. When a structure is defined, it is in essence adding a new data type to the C++ language. Once the structure is defined, it allows users to create variables of that structure as they would with any other predefined variable type.

10.1 DEFINING A STRUCTURE

The following template is used for creating a structure in C++:

```
struct StructureName
{
 VariableType1 VariableName1;
 VariableType2 VariableName2;
 VariableType3 VariableName3;
};
```

The keyword **struct** must start each structure definition. The **StructureName** is the name by which you will refer to the structure within your program.

Let's look at an example of how we would define a structure for a program. Let's create the structure for a student record. It will contain a **Name** stored as an array of twenty characters, an **ID** stored as an integer, and a **GPA** stored as a floating point number. These variables contained within a structure can be referred to as **attributes**. The following code is required:

```
struct StudentRecord
{
 char Name[20];
 int ID;
 float GPA;
};
```

A graphical representation of the structure we just created would look like Figure 10.1.

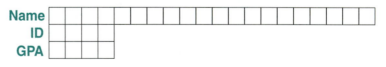

Figure 10.1

However, this is not how a structure really appears in the computer. In a computer, the information would be stored in a single dimension. This is shown in Figure 10.2.

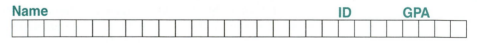

Figure 10.2

▊▊ DRILLS

Drill

Declare a structure called **DrillStructure1** that contains two integers called **Integer1** and **Integer2** as well as two floating point numbers called **Float1** and **Float2**.

Drill

Declare a structure called **DrillStructure2** that contains an array of ten integers called **Integers**, an array of ten floating point numbers called **Floats**, and an array of ten characters called **Characters**.

Declaring Variables from Structures

C++ allows us not to have to worry about the internal structure. To create a structure, we simple type the structure name, a space, and the variable name by which we want to refer to the structure within the program. This is shown in the following template:

```
StructureName VariableName;
```

Therefore, to create a variable called **GradesJohnC** of a structure called **StudentRecord**, we would use the following code:

```
StudentRecord GradesJohnC;
```

We stated earlier that it is not necessary to know the internal organization of a structure to access its fields. If we wish to access a field within a variable that is defined as a structure, we type the variable name, followed by a '.', followed by the field name. The following template shows a field being accessed from a structure with the result being sent to a **cout** statement:

```
cout<<VariableName.AttributeName;
```

If we wanted to access a single field from the previously defined **GradesJohnC** variable, we could do so with the following code in which **GradesJohnC** has its **GPA** field set to 4.0:

```
GradesJohnC.GPA=4.0;
```

We now know enough to be able to use structures within a program. So let's try. What if we wished to create a catalog of DVDs that we own? Each DVD would have a title (stored as a string), a year of release (stored as an integer), a running time (stored as an integer), and the number of stars it gets as a review (float point number). We could implement this as four individual variables, but that would be inconvenient. We can't implement it as an array because there are different types of variables representing the information we need to store. Therefore, a structure is our only option.

The following will define our **Movie** structure:

```
struct Movie
{
  char Name[100];
  int Year;
  int Time;
  float Stars;
};
```

If we wish to declare a variable of type **Movie**, we simply use the newly defined type just like any other predefined type like **int**, **float**, or **char**. See the following code in which we define a variable called **DVD1** of type **Movie**.

```
Movie DVD1;
```

Next we will want to assign values to this structure. We assign values to structures in a similar fashion as we do with regular variables. We type the variable name, place a '.' next to it with no spaces, and then type the name of the part of the structure we wish to assign. The rest of the assignment is the same as with a normal variable: simply type a single equal sign and the value or variable you wish to assign. See the following code that will assign the variable **DVD1** the year 1975, the running time 91 minutes, and the number of stars 5.

```
DVD1.Year = 1974;
DVD1.Yime = 91;
DVD1.Stars = 5;
```

To initialize the **Title**, we cannot use an equal sign. This is not because we are using structures, but simply because a **Title** is an array of characters or string and a string cannot be assigned using an equal sign. Instead, we will call the **StrCpy** function as shown:

```
StrCpy(DVD1.Title, "Monty Python and the Holy Grail");
```

Just as with arrays, if we wish to initialize the values of a structure at the time of declaration, we can do it by enclosing the values to be assigned in curly braces and separate the individual values by commas. The following code demonstrates assigning **DVD1** the same values, but at the time of declaration:

```
Movie DVD1 = {"Monty Python and the Holy Grail", 1974, 91, 5};
```

PROGRAMMER'S NOTEBOOK

It is very important to make sure that the order the values are placed in the curly braces follows the order the variables were declared in the structure. If the order is not followed, the values in the structure will be initialized incorrectly.

Now that we have declared a structure and assigned it a value, let's use it as we would any other variable. If we wanted to print the movie information contained in the structure, we would use the following code:

```
cout<<"The Movie "<<DVD1.Name<<" was made in "<<DVD1.Year
    <<" ,runs "<<DVD1.Time
    <<" minutes in length and received "<<DVD1.Stars<<" stars"<<endl;
```

The output will be:

```
The Movie Monty Python and the Holy Grail was made in 1975,
runs 91 minutes in length and received 5 stars
```

Just as we assign values using different operators with regular variables, we can do so with structures. See the following code that shows three ways of adding one to the year in the structure **DVD1**:

```
DVD1.Year = DVD1.Year + 1;
DVD1.Year += 1;
DVD1.Year++;
```

Now we can put it all together as a complete example of structures. This example will also show you how to pass structures to functions. Our example will continue to use the **Movie** structure, but will add functions that initialize a **Movie** structure and display a **Movie** structure, and a function to set the number of stars of a movie.

```
//Movie example

//Include Files
#include <stdlib.h>
#include <iostream.h>

#define MaxStringSize 100

//Structure Definitions
struct Movie
{
  char name[MaxStringSize];
  int Year;
  int Time;
  float Stars;
};

//Prototypes
void Initialize(Movie & DVD);
void Display(Movie DVD);
void CompareMovies(Movie DVD1, Movie DVD2);


//Main routine
void main()
{
 Movie DVD1, DVD2;
 Initialize(DVD1);
 Initialize(DVD2);
 CompareMovies(DVD1, DVD2);
}


//Functions
//Initialize movie function
void Initialize(Movie & DVD1)
{
  cout<<endl<<"Enter the title of the movie"<<endl;
  cin>>DVD1.Name;
  cout<<endl<<"Enter the year the movie was made"<<endl;
  cin>>DVD1.Year;
```

```
   cout<<endl<<"Enter the running time of the movie"<<endl;
   cin>>DVD1.Time;
   cout<<endl<<"Enter the number of stars of the movie"<<endl;
   cin>>DVD1.Stars;
}


//Display movie function
void Display(Movie DVD1)
{
   cout<<"The Movie "<<DVD1.Name
       <<" was made in "<<DVD1.Year<<" ,runs "<<DVD1.Time
       <<" minutes in length and received "<<DVD1.Stars
       <<" stars"<<endl;
}


//Compare movie function
void CompareMovies(Movie DVD1, Movie DVD2)
{
 if (DVD1.Stars > DVD2.Stars)
   {
    Display(DVD1);
    cout<<" and is the better Movie" <<endl;
   }
 else if (DVD2.Stars > DVD1.Stars)
    {
     Display(DVD2);
     cout<<" and is the better Movie" <<endl;
    }
   else
    {
     Display(DVD1);
     Display(DVD2);
     cout<< "are both rated the same"<<endl;
    }
}
```

▌ DRILLS

Drill 10-3

Write the code required to create a variable called **StructureVariable** of the structure declared in Drill 10-1.

Drill 10-4

Write the code required to set the attribute **Integer1** to 100 for the variable created in Drill 10-3.

Drill 10-5

Write the code required to create a variable called **StructureVariable** of the structure declared in Drill 10-2.

Drill 10-6

Write the code required to initialize the first five integers of the attribute `Integers` in the variable declared in Drill 10-5 to 1, 2, 3, 4, and 5, respectively.

10.2 ARRAYS OF STRUCTURES

At the beginning of this chapter we stated that arrays could not contain more than one type of variable; however, with arrays of structures we can accomplish this. The following code demonstrates how easy it is to declare arrays of structures.

```
Movie Collection[10]; //Declares an array of ten movies
//Will assign the first title in the collection array to Fletch

strcpy(Collection[0].Name, "Fletch");
```

You can initialize the array of structures at the time of declaration similarly to the way you did with a single structure or simple array. See the following example that initializes a collection of movies:

```
Movie Collection[]={
{"Monty Python and the Holy Grail", 1975, 91, 5},
{"Fletch", 1985, 98, 5},
{"Trading Places", 1983, 118,5}};
```

These inner braces are optional, but recommended for readability, because they provide a convenient way to separate the different structures within the array.

DRILLS

Drill 10-7

Declare an array called **ArrayOfStructures** consisting of five **DrillStructure1**'s that we defined in Drill 10-1.

Drill 10-8

Write the code required to initialize the first array element of the array declared in Drill 10-7 to 1, 2, 3.5, and 4.5, respectively.

Drill 10-9

Declare an array called `ArrayOfStructures` consisting of five `DrillStrucutre2`'s that we defined in Drill 10-2.

Drill 10-10

Write the code required to initialize the first five integers of the first array element of the array declared in Drill 10-9 to 1, 2, 3, 4, and 5, respectively.

10.3 CONCEPT OF A CLASS

The introduction of **classes** is the beginning of what many people call the core of C++. By using classes we can improve upon the concepts of structures, making them more versatile. With classes, we can control the way that a variable of a class is initialized. We can also ensure that the data stored in a variable is "correct." Imagine if we had an integer variable that was supposed to represent the minute portion of a time. We would not want the value to be beyond the range of 0–59. An integer could be between the range –32,768 to 32,767. By providing control over these issues, classes provide a user-interface over our data.

Unfortunately, learning classes opens a programmer up to countless options that lead to a great deal of confusion. For our purposes, we will learn a subset of the options classes offered and focus on the concept that teaches us how to encapsulate a structure and the operations that are performed on it under one construct. In addition, we will learn the basic concepts of reusing code via inheritance.

Encapsulation enables the programmer designing the class to dictate what types of operations are permissible upon a class without permitting other programmers access to the inner workings of the class. In essence, the class designer allows other programmers to have the complexity of a class hidden and ensures that other programmers can use the class only in ways intended by the programmer designing the class.

10.4 DEFINING A CLASS

A class definition is much like combining a structure definition with the prototypes of the functions that would operate on that structure. A structure defines what attributes a variable of that structure will have without actually allocating any storage for a variable. Allocation occurs when a variable is declared based on a structure. Similarly, a class does not allocate any space until a variable of that class is declared for it. However, variables declared from classes are no longer called variables, but they are called **objects**.

A basic **class** definition follows the following template:

```
class ClassName
{
   public:
     //Public methods and attributes
    private:
       // Private methods and attributes
};
```

All class definitions start with the keyword **class**. They are followed by a class name that can be any valid C++ identifier. Then, enclosed within a set of curly braces, is a **public** and **private** section. Another section, **protected**, exists, but we will not discuss that until later.

Anything defined in the **public** section is visible outside the class definition. Anything defined in the **private** section is visible only to methods declared inside the class definition. Adding a semicolon after the closing curly brace completes the class definition.

A **method** is a function that is defined inside a class. A **method** is defined as follows:

```
ReturnType ClassName :: MethodName(Parameter List)
{
   Body of method;
}
```

Methods are similar to functions in that they can have return types and process a list of parameters; however, they differ in that methods also have access to all the public and private methods and attributes of a class.

If an object is created of a specific class, its method can be called by stating the object name, followed by a dot operator, then the method name, and then a parameter list enclosed within a set of parentheses. The parameter list may be empty; however, the set of parentheses is still required.

```
ClassName ObjectName;
ObjectName.MethodName(Parameter List);
```

An **attribute** is a variable that is defined inside a class.

The easiest way to learn classes is to define a class. Let's define a class that is a simple counter. A counter can be initialized to a value, incremented, decremented, or reset. No other modifications to the counter may be made. Once a counter is initialized it can be reset only to the value to which it is initialially set. If no value is given as a default to initialize a counter, zero is selected. Additionally, a counter can be displayed and its value returned.

Here is the class definition for `Counter`:

```
class Counter
{
    public:
        Counter();
        Counter(int IValue);
        void Increment();
        void Decrement();
        void Display();
        int Value();
        void Reset();
    private:
        int Count;
        int InitialValue;
};
```

The first two methods of the class **Counter** are special. They have the same name as the class. Methods with the same name as a class are called constructors. A **constructor** is a method that indicates to an object how to create itself. In this example, the first constructor has no parameters. We will use that as the default constructor. It will initialize the object to 0. The second constructor takes a parameter for the initial value. It sets the **Count** and **InitialValue** attributes to the value passed. The code is as follows:

```
Counter :: Counter()
{
    Count = 0;
    InitialValue = 0;
}


Counter :: Counter(int IValue)
{
    Count = IValue;
    InitialValue = IValue;
}
```

The next method is **Increment**. It simply increments the attribute **Count** by 1 and returns nothing.

```
void Counter :: Increment()
{
    Count++;
}
```

The **Decrement** method is similar to the **Increment** method. The only difference is that instead of adding one, we subtract one from **Count**.

```
void Counter :: Decrement()
{
    Count--;
}
```

The **Display** method takes the private attribute **Count** and displays it:

```
void Counter :: Display()
{
    cout<<Count<<endl;
}
```

The **Reset** methods takes the orginial value the **Counter** was set to and resets it to that value:

```
void Counter :: Reset()
{
    Count = InitialValue;
}
```

The final method **Value** returns the private attribute **Count** to the caller of the method:

```
int Counter :: Value()
{
    return Count;
}
```

The following is an example of a program using our **Counter** class. It initializes a **Counter** to 10 and then decrements it until it reaches 0. The code follows:

```
void main()
{
    Counter Count(10);

    do
    {
        Count.Decrement();
        Count.Display();
    } while(Count.Value()>0);
}
```

DRILLS

Drill 10-11

Define a class called **Radio**. Specify attributes to indicate what station it is on, what band is selected (i.e., AM/FM), whether it is on or off, and the volume setting. Specify what methods will be defined, such as **TurnOn**, **TurnOff**, **IncreaseVolume**, **DecreaseVolume**, **SetStation**, and **SwitchBand**. For each method you must indicate the parameters required (if any). Does a radio require a constructor? If so make sure you include it in the definition.

Drill 10-12

Write the definition of the methods that you specified in Drill 10-11.

10.5 Case Study

Problem Description

For this case study, let's create another class that would simulate an alarm clock. The alarm clock class should:

- Store a time in hours, minutes, and seconds
- Keep track if we are in the AM or PM
- Initialize a clock to a specific time
- Increment the clock to the next second
- Set the alarm
- Display the current time

Solution

```
class AlarmClock
{
   public:
     AlarmClock();
     AlarmClock(int H, int M, int S, char A_P);
     void Display();
     void SetAlarmTime(int H, int M, int S,
                        char A_P);
     void Increment();

   private:
//Time attributes
     int Hours;
     int Minutes;
     int Seconds;
     char AM_PM;

//Alarm attributes
     int Ahours;
     int Amintues;
     int Aseconds;
     char A_AM_PM;
     bool On;

    //Private methods
       CheckAlarm();
};
```

The first two methods of the class **AlarmClock** are the constructors. In this example, the first constructor has no parameters. We will use that as the default constructor. It will initialize the object to 12:00:00 AM. The second constructor takes a parameter for hours, minutes, seconds, and AM/PM. It will map each of these parameters to the private attributes accordingly. Additionally, both constructors must set the **On** attribute to false so the alarm clock does not go off unless specified.

```
AlarmClock :: AlarmClock()
{
  Hours=12;
  Minutes=0;
  Seconds=0;
  AM_PM = 'A';
  On=false;
}
```

```
AlarmClock :: AlarmClock(int H, int M, int S, int A_P)
{
  Hours=H;
  Minutes=M;
  Seconds=S;
  AM_PM = A_P;
  On=false;
}
```

The next method is **Display**, which will display the private time attributes using a **cout** command.

```
void AlarmClock :: Display()
{
  cout<<Hours<<":"<<Minutes<<":"<<Seconds<<" ";
  if (AM_PM=='A')
    cout<<"AM"<<endl;
  else
    cout<<"PM"<<endl;
}
```

10.5 Case Study (continued)

The next method is **SetAlarm**. **SetAlarm** will map the parameters for hours, minutes, seconds, and AM/PM to the proper private attributes. It will also set the flag **On** to **true**.

```
void AlarmClock :: SetAlarmTime(int H, int M, int S, char A_P)
{
 Ahours=H;
 Aminutes=M;
 Aseconds=S;
 A_AM_PM = A_P;
 On=true;
}
```

The final public method is **Increment**. This method will modify the private time attribute **Seconds** by adding one to it, then if the **Seconds** is equal to 60, it will set the **Seconds** attribute to zero and add one to the **Minutes** attribute. If the **Minutes** attribute equals 60, then the **Minutes** attribute will be set to zero and the **Hours** attribute will be incremented. If the **Hours** attribute is incremented to 12, the **AM_PM** attribute will be toggled. If the **Hours** attribute is incremented to 13, it will be reset to 1.

```
void AlarmClock :: Increment()
{
 Seconds++;

 if (Seconds==60)
   {
    Seconds=0;
    Minutes++;
    if (Minutes==60)
      {
       Minutes=0;
       Hours++;
       if (Hours==12)
          if (AM_PM=='A')
            AM_PM='P';
          else
            AM_PM='A';
          else if (Hours==13)
            Hours=1;
       }
   }
 CheckAlarm();
}
```

Most of the information stored in the private section of the class is self-explanatory. All the attributes that we have in the class are stored in the private section because we do not wish other programmers to be allowed to modify them in any way other than that we have indicated with the public methods.

However, there is one **private** method that requires explaining. The method **CheckAlarm** will not be used by anyone outside the class. It is a helper method that we will write to simplify the **Increment** method. Since only methods defined inside the class will call it, we will place the declaration of it in the **private** section.

```cpp
void AlarmClock :: CheckAlarm()
{
 if (On && (Ahours==Hours) && (Aminutes==Minutes)
     && (Aseconds == Seconds) &&
      (A_AM_PM == AM_PM))
   cout<<"WAKE UP, ITS TIME TO GO TO SCHOOL!\n";
}
```

Now that we have the class **AlarmClock** defined as well as all of its methods, let's write a program using it:

```cpp
#include <stdlib.h>
#include <iostream.h>

//Class definition for AlarmClock goes here

void main()
{
 AlarmClock JeffClock;
 AlarmClock SchoolClock(8,10,0,'A');

 JeffClock.Display();
 SchoolClock.Display();

 SchoolClock.SetAlarm(8,20,0,'A');

 for(int i=0; i<5000; i++)
    SchoolClock.Increment();

 SchoolClock.Display();
}
```

10.5 Case Study (continued)

The program begins with declaring two objects of the class **AlarmClock**. The first, **JeffClock**, is declared using the default constructor since no parameters are given. Therefore, it is initialized with a time of 12:00:00 AM. The second, **SchoolClock**, is passed all the necessary parameters so the second constructor is called and it is initialized with a time of 8:10:00 AM.

Then the method **Display** is called for each object. Even though they were created with different constructors, all the other methods can be used as if the objects were created with the same constructor.

The **SetAlarm** method is then called for **SchoolClock**. This sets the private variables for us so that if we increment up to the alarm time of 8:20:00 AM, it will go off.

We then loop 5000 times incrementing **SchoolClock** by one second each time. When the time equals 8:20:00 AM, the alarm goes off.

The program finishes the loop, outputs the time, and then terminates.

END-OF-CHAPTER

♦ Key Terms

Attributes	Individual variables stored inside an object.
Classes	A template for creating objects that provide a blueprint for the types of data to be allocated and the operations that can be performed on it.
Constructor	A special method that is called automatically when an object is instantiated.
Encapsulation	The concept of hiding the inner workings of an object from the user.
Method	A special function that operates on an object of the class for which the method is created.
Object	The instantiation of a class.
Polymorphism	The concept that multiple objects can have operations with the same name.
Structure	A construct used to combine multiple values into a single structure.

◆ C++ Keywords Introduced

class	Defines a class in C++.
private	In a class, indicates all the methods and attributes defined here will be used only by methods defined within the class.
protected	In a class, indicates all the methods and attributes defined here will be used only by methods defined within the class and classes derived from it.
public	In a class, indicates all the methods and attributes defined here can be used by anyone.
struct	Creates a structure in C++.

◆ Answers to Drills

Drill 10-1

The structure definition for the drill is as follows:

```
struct DrillStructure1
{
    int Integer1;
    int Integer2;
    float Float1;
    float Float2;
};
```

Drill 10-2

The structure definition for the drill is as follows:

```
struct DrillStructure2
{
    int Integers[10];
    float Floats[10];
    char char[10];
};
```

Drill 10-3

The code required to create a variable called **StructureVariable** is as follows:

```
DrillStructure1 StructureVariable;
```

Drill 10-4

The code required to set the attribute **Integer1** to 100 is as follows:

```
StructureVariable.Integer1 = 100;
```

Drill 10-5

The code required to create a variable called **StructureVariable** is as follows:

```
DrillStructure2 StructureVariable;
```

Drill 10-6

The code required to initialize the first five integers for this drill is as follows:

```
StructureVariable.Integers[0]=1;
StructureVariable.Integers[1]=2;
StructureVariable.Integers[2]=3;
StructureVariable.Integers[3]=4;
StructureVariable.Integers[4]=5;
```

Drill 10-7

To declare an array of the five **DrillStructure1**'s we defined in Drill 10-1, we need the following code:

```
DrillStructure1 ArrayOfStructures[5];
```

Drill 10-8

To initialize the first array element of the array declared in Drill 10-7 to 1, 2, 3.5, and 4.5, respectively, we need the following code:

```
ArrayOfStructures[0].Integer1=1;
ArrayOfStructures[0].Integer2=2;
ArrayOfStructures[0].Float1=3.5;
ArrayOfStructures[0].Float2=4.5;
```

Drill 10-9

To declare an array of the five **DrillStructure1**'s we defined in Drill 10-2, we need the following code:

```
DrillStructure2 ArrayOfStructures[5];
```

Drill 10-10

To initialize the first five integers of the first array elements of the array declared in Drill 10-9 to 1, 2, 3, 4, and 5, respectively, we need the following code:

```
ArrayOfStructures[0].Integers[0]=1;
ArrayOfStructures[0].Integers[1]=2;
ArrayOfStructures[0].Integers[2]=3;
ArrayOfStructures[0].Integers[3]=4;
ArrayOfStructures[0].Integers[4]=5;
```

Drill 10-11

A class for **Radio** would be defined as follows:

```
class Radio
{
 public:
    Radio();
    void TurnOn();
    void TurnOff();
    void IncreaseVolume();
    void DecreaseVolume();
    void SetStation(float NewStation);
    void SwitchBand();
 private:
    int Volume:
    float Station:
    char Band;
    bool Power;
};
```

Notice that we have included one constructor. This would be necessary to turn the power off and select an initial station and volume setting. Also, although not indicated by the problem description, we have chosen to implement **SwitchBand** as a method that does not require a parameter. When we implement it, we will simply switch the AM band to FM and visa versa toggling back and forth. We have also chosen to store the AM/FM band as a single character. This choice can be left up to the programmer.

A more robust solution would be to have values to indicate the maximum and minimum range for a station and the volume. However, for simplicity we have left them out. An example of this type of implementation can be seen in our **CableBox** class defined in the next chapter.

Drill 10-12

The definitions for the methods defined in Drill 10-11 are as follows:

To define the constuctor we need to make sure we shut the power off and initialize the volume, band, and station. It makes sense to set the volume to 0. However, since there is no logical choice for the station and band, we'll set it to my favorite station, 610 on the AM dial. Could you guess it's a sports station? The code is as follows:

```
Radio :: Radio()
{
    Volume = 0;
    Band = 'A';
    Station = 610;
    Power = false;
}
```

The next two methods, **TurnOn** and **TurnOff**, simply toggle the **Power** attribute. The code follows:

```
void Radio :: TurnOn()
{
    Power = true;
}

void Radio :: TurnOff()
{
    Power = false;
}
```

The next two methods, **IncreaseVolume** and **DecreaseVolume**, increment and decrement the **Volume** attribute. Although not specified in the problem definition, our implementation will not allow a volume to be set less than zero or greater than 10. The code follows:

```
void Radio :: IncreaseVolume()
{
    if (Volume < 10)
        Volume++;
    else
        cout<<"The Volume is already maxed!";
}

void Radio :: DecreaseVolume()
{
    if (Volume > 0)
        Volume--;
    else
        cout<<"The Volume is already set to the lowest value!";
}
```

The method **SetStation** simply assigns the parameter to the **Station** attribute. The code follows:

```
void Radio :: SetStation(float NewStation)
{
    Station = NewStation;
}
```

The final method, **SwitchBand**, needs to toggle the **Band** attribute from 'A' to 'F' or from 'F' to 'A'. The code follows:

```
void Radio:: SwitchBand()
{
    if (Band == 'A')
        Band = 'F';
    else
        Band = 'A';
}
```

◆ Programming Exercises

1. Write a program that uses a structure to simulate the time in hours, minutes, and seconds. Write a function to set the time, another function to increment the time by a number of seconds, and a function to display the time.

2. Write a program to simulate an automated-teller machine. Create a structure that has four fields: user name, account number, pin number, and balance. In the main function, create an array of this structure and initialize it from a file storing valid account information. The program should contain a function for withdrawing money, one for depositing money, another for transferring money, and a fourth that displays the balance of an account specified. Money can be transferred only to and from accounts that are owned by the same person. The program should start by asking for the user name and then a pin number. If the pin number and name match, then the person is given a menu to choose whether to withdraw money or transfer money to another account. When the program completes, it should save the updated account information back to the account file.

3. Improve the previous program so that the array is stored using a pointer. Allocate the memory dynamically so that there is no need to limit the number of accounts that can be processed. To accomplish this, you will be required to read the file twice: once to determine the maximum number of accounts and once to actually read the data for each account.

4. Write a program to play checkers. Create a class called checkers. The constructor should initialize all the attributes within the class when it is called. There should be a method called play that runs the entire program. Other methods should be display and check for jump. Each user takes a turn. The board should be in a two-dimensional array. At each turn a user enters valid coordinates for where the piece is and another set of coordinates to move the piece. Regular rules of checkers are in effect. This game will force jumps. If a jump exists then the only valid move is a jump.

5. Write a program for a bank that calculates the percentage that an account should receive. The percentage rate is entered as a yearly rate but the user can choose to add the interest daily, monthly, or hourly. The program can also add an additional feature that will pay out a certain amount of money for a loan that the user may have at his or her bank. You may also set up direct deposit where the user will enter an amount that would be added to the account on a biweekly basis. A method needs to exist that will ask for how much time has been allotted. This method should then calculate the current balance in the account, taking into account all the information that has been entered.

◆ Additional Exercises

1. True or False: A structure can include members of different types.

2. Write the code required to define a structure for the following types of data:

   a. Time (hours, minutes, seconds)
   b. Date (name of the month, day, year)
   c. Bank account (includes balance, account number, name, type, etc.)

3. Declare an array of 10 structures for each of the data types you just declared:

   a. Time (hours, minutes, seconds)
   b. Date (name of the month, day, year)
   c. Bank account (includes balance, account number, name, type, etc.)

4. True or False: Structures cannot be passed as parameters to a function because they are too large to be passed by value.

5. In the following class, tell whether the members are attributes or methods, and whether they are private or public:

```
class MyClass {
public:
  void Display();
  int flag;
  int temp();

private:
  int first;
  int second();
  float third();
  void calculate();
};
```

6. Write two constructors for the class in exercise one. The first constructor should be the default, and should set all the attributes to an initial value and have no parameters. The second constructor should be passed two values, which are used to set two of the attributes. The other attributes should be set to an initial value.

7. Can a method inside of a class call another method inside of that same class? Can the method call another method in a different class if the name of the method does not exist in its own class?

8. Can a class can be written with no constructor? If so, explain when you would.

CHAPTER

11

More on Classes

Chapter Objectives

♦ Explain how to use dynamic memory and classes

♦ Introduce the destructor method

♦ Introduce predefined classes of `vector` and `string`

♦ Introduce the reuse of code via inheritance

▌▌ 11.1 OTHER BENEFITS OF CLASSES

One of the not so obvious benefits of classes is the ability to allow methods of different classes to have the same name. Think for a moment what you would do if you had multiple classes that all required a **Display** method. Imagine if you had our **AlarmClock** class as well as a new class called **Calendar**. With functions, you would be required to create a different function with a different parameter list and a different name for each function. Therefore, you would have a **DisplayAlarmClock** and **DisplayCalendar**. Although this may not seem too burdensome, imagine if you were to write a program that created all the different types of windows in your graphical user interface. You have windows with scroll bars, windows with buttons, windows that just present information, etc. You wouldn't want to have to come up with a different name for each display function —it would be far easier to simply call all the methods **Display**.

C++ allows us to do this easily. By attaching the method call to the object, the computer knows which **Display** method to call. Upon seeing a method call, the computer checks the class the object belongs to and calls the appropriate method. Additional methods from other classes are not even seen.

The following two programs initialize and display an alarm clock variable and a calendar variable. The first program uses structures and functions; the second program uses classes. It should be clear that the main routine in the second program is more readable and easier to write than the main routine in the first program.

```cpp
//Program 1, shows structures and functions

#include <stdlib.h>
#include <iostream.h>

//Structures
struct Calender
{
    int day;
    int month;
    int year;
};

struct AlarmClock
{
    //Time attributes
    int hours;
    int minutes;
    int seconds;
    char AM_PM;

    //Alarm attributes
    int Ahours;
    int Amintues;
    int Aseconds;
    char A_AM_PM;
    bool On;
};

//Prototypes
void DisplayAlarmClock(AlarmClock Time);
void InitializeAlarmClock(AlarmClock & Time, int h, int m, int s,
                          char P_AM_PM);
void DisplayCalander(Calender date);
void InitializaeDate(Calender & date, int m, int d, int y);

//Functions
void DisplayAlarmClock(AlarmClock Time)
{
    cout<<time.hours<<':'<<time.minutes<<':'<<time.seconds<<endl;
}

void InitializeAlarmClock(AlarmClock & Time, int h, int m, int s,
                          char P_AM_PM)
{
    Time.hours = h;
    Time.minutes = m;
    Time.seconds = s;
    Time.AM_PM = P_AM_PM;
}

void DisplayCalender(Calender date)
{
    cout<<date.month<<"//"<<date.day<<"//"<<date.year<<endl;
}
```

```
void InitializaeDate(Calender & date, int m, int d, int y)
{
   date.day = d;
   date.month = m;
   date.year = y;
}

void main()
{
   Calander Today;
   AlarmClock Now;

   InitializeCalender(Today, 9,15,2000);
   InitializeAlarmClock(Now, 12, 0, 0, 'A');

   DisplayCalender(Today);
   DisplayAlarmClock(Today);
}
```

```
//Program 2, showing classes

#include <stdlib.h>
#include <iostream.h>

//Include previous AlarmClock code here.

class Calender
{
   public:
     Calender(int m, int d, int y);
     void Display();
   private:
     int day;
     int month;
     int year;
};

Calender :: Calender (int m, int d, int y)
{
   day = d;
   month = m;
   year = y;
}

void Calender :: Display()
{
   cout<<month<<"//"<<day<<"//"<<year<<endl;
}
```

```
//Class definition for AlarmClock goes here.

void main()
{
    AlarmClock Now(12,0,0,'A');
    Calender Today(9,15,2000);

    Now.Display();
    Today.Display();
}
```

The difference between the two programs should be obvious. The second program with classes is much simpler. We can initialize the object at the time of declaration. If we do not wish to initialize it to specified values, we can set up default values and pass it nothing. To display the objects, we simply call the **Display** method. As more and more classes are defined, not having to remember different names for displaying the contents of an object will make our life simpler.

DRILLS

Assume for this drill that the following code was written after a program's structure and class definitions were coded. Where you can figure it out, indicate which lines of code have function calls and which have method calls. Also, indicate where, if any, constructors may be called. Note you must try to figure out from the code given whether the variable is created from a class or a structure.

Drill 11-1

```
//Drill 11-1

// Assume definitions before this point.

XXX FirstVariable;
YYY SecondVariable;

FirstVariable.Display();
DisplayYYY(SecondVariable);
```

11.2 DYNAMIC MEMORY AND CLASSES

Here is another example of a class, **Person**. **Person** is slightly more complicated than our **AlarmClock** example, because as you will see the **Person** class will dynamically allocate memory upon constructing the object.

Our **Person** class should contain a pointer to character for the name and an integer for the age of the person. Additionally, we should have a default constructor, a constructor with parameters, and a display method.

See the following definition of the **Person** class:

```
class Person
{
    public:
       Person();   //Default constructor
       Person(char * N, int A); //Constructor
       Display();
    private:
       char * Name; //dynamic array!
       int Age; //Integer age as always
};

Person :: Person ()
{
    Name = NULL;
    Age = 0;
}

Person :: Person (char * N, int A)
{
    int Len;
    Len = strlen(N);
    Name = new char[Len+1];
    strcpy(Name, N);
    Age = A;
}

Person :: Display()
{
    cout<<Name<<' '<<" is "<<Age<<" years old\n";
}
```

The class is self-explanatory except maybe for the constructor with parameters. Although we have seen this method used to allocate space for a string before, a new question is raised. What happens to the memory the constructor allocates when the variable goes out of scope or the program quits?

Let's look at the following program:

```
#include <stdlib.h>
#include <iostream.h>

//Assume Person class definition

void DummyFunction()
{
    Person("Jeff Salvage", 29);
    Person.Display();
}

void main()
{
    DummyFunction();
}
```

Memory is allocated in the **DummyFunction** to store the name Jeff Salvage, but when was it deallocated? It was not. If this function were called in a loop, eventually the heap would run out of memory and the system would crash.

PROGRAMMER'S NOTEBOOK

Any time memory is allocated dynamically, it must be returned manually to the system using a delete command. With classes, it is often useful to do this in the destructor method.

The problem is that there is no specific time to issue a delete command in the program where we might write code to issue a delete command. What we want is for the removal of any dynamic memory to occur automatically when the object goes out of scope. This can be done with a special method called a **destructor**. A destructor method is called as an object goes out of scope. This is the opposite of a constructor, which allocates and initializes the information required when the object is created.

The syntax is similar to the constructor, except a tilde operator is added before the destructor name:

```
Classname :: ~Classname()
```

Then all that is required is to write the code to delete any memory that we allocated either in the constructor of the class or any of its methods in the destructor method.

```
Person :: ~Person()
{
    delete [ ] Name;
}
```

 **DRILLS**

 Drill **11-2**

Modify the definition of the **Person** class so that it can take a first name and a last name for a person.

Drill **11-3**

Modify the constructor of the **Person** class so that it can take a first name and a last name for a person.

Drill **11-4**

Modify the destructor of the **Person** class so that it can handle a first name and a last name for a person.

 11.3 VECTOR CLASS

Modern C++ compilers include many classes that enhance the versatility of the C++ programming language. By using these classes, we gain the advantage of developers' efforts, without having to understand the intricacies of the implementation of these classes' implementations.

One such class is the **vector** class, which is very similar to the use of arrays, but as we will see vectors have many advantages. Unlike arrays, they can be allocated at run time. In addition, when required, vectors can be resized to accommodate additional space requirements. Another issue with arrays was that they were always passed by reference. There may come a time when we wish to pass an array by value—this can be accomplished with vectors.

Vectors also package a number of additional methods that give additional functionality, which are not provided with the simple array implementation provided in C++.

To use a vector, we must reference the include file that defines a **vector**. Therefore, add the following line to the beginning of your code in the include section:

```
#include <vector.h>
```

PROGRAMMER'S NOTEBOOK

Depending upon your compiler, you may have to add an additional line of code. For instance, with the Microsoft Visual C++ compiler Ver 6.0, the following line must be added:

```
using namespace std;
```

To declare a **vector** you have many options. First you must decide of what type variable your **vector** will be composed. Then you must decide whether or not you are going to hard-code the initial size of the **vector** or determine its size at run time. Finally, if you initialize the size of the **vector**, you can initialize all the values of the **vector** to a specific value. This can be seen in the following code:

```
vector <VariableType> VectorName(VectorSize, InitialValue);
```

If we wanted to declare a **vector** of integers without specifying the initial size, we would do so with the following code:

```
vector <int> Vector1;
```

If we wanted to declare a **vector** of 10 integers, we would do so with the following code:

```
vector <int> Vector2 (10);
```

Finally, if we wanted to declare a **vector** of 10 integers whose initial value would be 1, we would do so with the following code:

```
vector <int> Vector2 (10, 1);
```

Once we have a **vector** defined, we can access its elements in the same manner we used with arrays. Therefore, if we wanted to set element 0 to 10, element 1 to 15, and element 2 to 20, we could do so using the following code:

```
Vector2[0]=10;
Vector2[1]=15;
Vector2[2]=20;
```

One convenient feature of a **vector** is that we can programmatically determine its size even after it has been allocated. We can do this by using the **size** method. Observe the following example that reads values from a user until the **vector** is full.

```cpp
#include <stdlib.h>
#include <iostream.h>
#include <vector>

void main()
{
   vector <int> UserValues (10);

   int LoopCounter=0;

   while (LoopCounter<UserValues.size())
   {
      cout<<"Please enter a value to store in the vector"<<endl;
      cin>>UserValues[LoopCounter++];
   }
}
```

If we determine that the **vector** is full, we can ask the user how many values by which we would like to increase the size, and then by calling a method of the **vector** class called resize, we can add the additional space.

PROGRAMMER'S NOTEBOOK

Make sure that the value you pass resize is the new size of the vector, not the amount of additional values you wish to add to the vector.

This is shown in the following code snippet that could appear directly after the previous code:

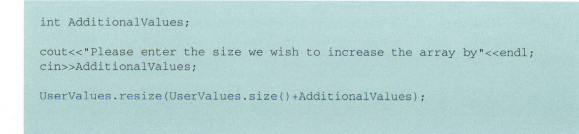

```cpp
int AdditionalValues;

cout<<"Please enter the size we wish to increase the array by"<<endl;
cin>>AdditionalValues;

UserValues.resize(UserValues.size()+AdditionalValues);
```

◼◼◼ 11.4 STRING CLASS

Another built-in class is the **string** class. By including it, we have access to a class that implements strings in a far more robust manner than we did with arrays. The **string** class allows us to manipulate strings without the hazards of the strings we implemented using arrays.

With the class **string**, we no longer have to worry about allocating the proper amount of space. These strings allocate the proper amount of space as we use it. By implementing a **string** class, the details of the implementation are hidden from the programmer.

In addition to not having to deal with the issues of memory allocation, the **string** class gives us a series of methods that provide additional functionality. We will demonstrate some of them, but for a complete list, consult your C++ compiler manual.

To get access to all these values, you must add an additional include file to your list of includes at the beginning of your program. Just add **<string.h>** to the top of your program and you will be set.

PROGRAMMER'S NOTEBOOK

Depending upon your compiler, you may have to add an additional line of code. For instance, with the Microsoft Visual C++ compiler Ver 6.0, the following line must be added:

```
using namespace std;
```

Much like other objects, when a string is declared it has a constructor to allow the creation of an empty string or a string that is initialized to a value. See the following code where the first string is not initialized and the second string is initialized to the expression "Go Sixers!":

```
string String1;
string String2("Go Sixers!");
```

These strings can be output using the **cout** command, with which we are already familiar. If we wanted to output the **String2** object we just created, we would output as we would any other object.

```
cout<<String2;
```

Some of the methods implemented allow us to determine the size of the string, find the starting location of a string within the string, obtain a substring from a string, determine what character is at a specific location of the string, determine the maximum size of a string, and more.

Here is an example of a program that demonstrates many of these methods:

```cpp
#include <string>
#include <stdlib>
#include <iostream>
using namespace std;

void main()
{
    string BasketBallTeam1("Philadelphia 76ers");
    string BasketBallTeam2("Indiana Pacers");

    string Champions;
    string Message;

    cout<<"BasketBallTeam1 contains "<<BasketBallTeam1<<endl;
    cout<<"BasketBallTeam2 contains "<<BasketBallTeam2<<endl;

    cout<<"The Max Size of a string is "
        <<BasketBallTeam1.max_size()<<endl;

    cout<<"The length of BasketBallTeam1 is "
        <<BasketBallTeam1.length()<<endl;

    cout<<"The 10th character of BasketBallTeam1 is "
        <<BasketBallTeam1.at(10)<<endl;

    cout<<"The string 76 is located at position "
        <<BasketBallTeam1.find("76")<<endl;

    cout<<BasketBallTeam1.substr(13,5)<<endl;

    Champions = BasketBallTeam1;

    cout<<"The championship team is the "<<Champions<<endl;

    Message = BasketBallTeam1+" will beat the "+BasketBallTeam2 +
            " next year!";

    cout<<Message<<endl;
}
```

The output of the program is as follows:

```
BasketBallTeam1 contains Philadelphia 76ers
BasketBallTeam2 contains Indiana Pacers
The Max Size of a string is 4294967293
The length of BasketBallTeam1 is 18
The 10th character of BasketBallTeam1 is i
The string 76 is located at position 13
76ers
The championship team is the Philadelphia 76ers
Philadelphia 76ers will beat the Indiana Pacers next year!
```

In addition to the methods mentioned, an additional feature of strings was utilized. The two operators that we are used to using for assignment and addition can be used with strings. They operate the way we would intuitively believe them to. The = operator will assign a string on the left whatever the value of the string on the right contains. The + operator will concatenate two strings similarly to the **StrCat** function we implemented earlier.

DRILLS

What is the output of the following code:

Drill **11-5**

```
#include <string>
#include <stdlib.h>
#include <iostream>
using namespace std;

void main()
{
    string Message("The Sixers will win the next championship!");

    cout<<Message.length()<<endl;
    cout<<Message.at(5)<<endl;
    cout<<Message.find("Sixers")<<endl;
    cout<<Message.substr(10,5)<<endl;
}
```

11.5 CODE REUSE VIA COMPOSITION AND INHERITANCE

When we develop a class, we often realize that after developing it, we may need another class that is very similar. Beginner programmers will copy the original class, make any changes necessary, and rename the old class. Although this works in the short term, it is problematic in the long term.

Imagine that you have created many classes using this technique. After using the new classes in various programs, you discover that there was a bug in the original code. Now you must go back and modify the code in all the classes into which you copied the bug.

The other problem, although not quite as severe, is that you waste a lot of unnecessary disk space by having multiple copies of the source code each time you copy it.

The solution to these issues is to use C++'s inheritance behavior of classes. Inheritance has many features and many flavors; however, we will focus on the basics and leave the complex examples to other texts.

Imagine if we had two classes: a simple **Clock** class and a simple **Date** class, as follows:

```cpp
#include <stdlib.h>
#include <iostream.h>

class Clock
{
   public:
     Clock();
     Clock(int h, int m, int s, char P_AM_PM);
     void SetTime(int h, int m, int s, char P_AM_PM);
     void Display();
   private:
     int hour;
     int minute;
     int second;
     char AM_PM;
};

class Date
{
   public:
     Date();
     Date(int m, int d, int y);
     void SetDate(int m, int d, int y);
     void Display();
   private:
     int month;
     int day;
     int year;
};

Clock :: Clock()
{
   hour=12;
   minute = 0;
   second = 0;
   AM_PM = 'A';
}

Clock :: Clock(int h, int m, int s, char P_AM_PM)
{
   hour=h;
   minute = m;
   second = s;
   AM_PM = P_AM_PM;
}

void Clock :: SetTime(int h, int m, int s, char P_AM_PM)
{
   hour=h;
   minute = m;
   second = s;
   AM_PM = P_AM_PM;
}
```

```
void Clock :: Display()
{
    cout<<hour<<":"<<minute<<":"<<second<<" ";
    if (AM_PM == 'A')
        cout<<"AM"<<endl;
    else
        cout<<"PM"<<endl;
}


Date :: Date()
{
    month = 1;
    day = 1;
    year = 2000;
}


Date :: Date(int m, int d, int y)
{
    month = m;
    day = d;
    year = y;
}


void Date :: SetDate(int m, int d, int y)
{
    month = m;
    day = d;
    year = y;
}


void Date :: Display()
{
    cout<<month<<"//"<<day<<"//"<<year<<endl;
}
```

These two classes can be used and independent objects can be created. However, we can expand their original design without having to know the inner workings of the classes themselves.

Has-A Relationships

Image if we wanted to create an appointment class that stored a time and date of an appointment. Do we need to start over from scratch? The answer is no.

If we wanted, it would be easy to design a class called appointment, where in essence, we rewrote all the code contained in the **Clock** and **Date** classes. However, that would be a waste of time. This is especially true if these classes were more complex than the simple classes that we have demonstrated.

Instead, we will design our **Appointment** class by including objects of the **Clock** and **Date** class within the **Appointment** class. This is commonly referred to as composition. See the following code for the **Appointment** class:

```
#include <stdlib.h>
#include <iostream.h>

class Appointment
{
   public:
     Appointment();
     Appointment(int ch, int cm, int cs, char P_AM_PM,
                 int dm, int dd, int dy);
     void SetAppointment(int ch, int cm, int cs, char P_AM_PM,
                         int dm, int dd, int dy);
     void Display();
   private:
      Clock Time;
      Date Day;
};

Appointment :: Appointment()
{
   Time.SetClock(12,0,0,'A');
   Day.SetDate(1,1,2000);
}

Appointment :: Appointment(int ch, int cm, int cs, char cP_AM_PM,
                           int dm, int dd, int dy);

{
   Time.SetClock(ch,cm,cs,cP_AM_PM);
   Day.SetDate(dm,dd,dy);
}

void Appointment :: SetAppointment(int ch, int cm, int cs,
                                   char cP_AM_PM, int dm, int dd, int dy);

{
   Time.SetClock(ch,cm,cs,cP_AM_PM);
   Day.SetDate(dm,dd,dy);
}

void Appointment :: Display()
{
   Time.Display();
   Day.Display();
}
```

The **Appointment** class demonstrates the **has-a relationship** of classes. An **Appointment** has-a **Time** and has-a **Day**. By using the predefined classes **Clock** and **Date**, we see that the complexity of the **Appointment** class is passed to the two previously defined classes. This reduces the time it takes to write, test, and debug the **Appointment** class.

There is one drawback to using this method. A program written with this method will operate slightly slower than one written as a single class. This is because there is an additional overhead that associated with the **Appointment** class calling the methods of the **Clock** and **Date** classes. However, unless performance is the most important concern or many levels of has-a relationships are introduced, the overhead is insignificant compared to the savings in complexity.

Is-A Relationships

The other type of relationship is an **is-a relationship.** Is-a relationships are used when we want to create an object that is a variation of another object. This is the classic model for **inheritance.** Imagine if we had previously defined a **Clock** class. Now instead of creating an **AlarmClock** class as we did earlier, we decide to create an **AlarmClock** class that is-a **Clock** with additional alarm features.

With almost no modifications to the original class, we can build upon it.

```
#include <stdlib.h>
#include <iostream.h>
#include <iomanip.h>

//Prototypes
void OutputTwoDigits(int Value);

//Functions
void OutputTwoDigits(int Value)
{
   cout<<setfill('0')<<setw(2)<<Value;
}

//Classes
class Clock
{
   public:
     Clock();
     Clock(int h, int m, int s, char P_AM_PM);
     void SetTime(int h, int m, int s, char P_AM_PM);
     void Display();
   protected:
     int hour;
     int minute;
     int second;
     char AM_PM;
};

class AlarmClock : Clock
{
   public:
     AlarmClock();
     AlarmClock(int h, int m ,int s, char P_AM_PM);
     SetAlarm(int h, int m, int s, char P_AM_PM);
     void Display();
   private:
     int Ahour;
     int Aminute;
     int Asecond;
     char A_AM_PM;
     bool On;
};
```

```
AlarmClock :: AlarmClock()
{
   On = false;
}


AlarmClock :: AlarmClock(int h, int m ,int s, char P_AM_PM)
{
   SetTime(h,m,s,P_AM_PM);
   On = false;
}


AlarmClock :: SetAlarm(int h, int m ,int s, char P_AM_PM)
{
   Ahour = h;
   Aminute = m;
   Asecond = s;
   A_AM_PM=P_AM_PM;
   On = true;
}

void AlarmClock :: Display()
{
   if (On)
   {
     Clock::Display();
     cout<<"The Alarm is Set to ";
     OutputTwoDigits(Ahour);
     cout<<":";
     OutputTwoDigits(Aminute);
     cout<<":";
     OutputTwoDigits(Asecond);
     cout<<" ";
     if (A_AM_PM == 'A')
   cout<<"AM"<<endl;
     else
   cout<<"PM"<<endl;
   }
}


Clock :: Clock()
{
   hour=12;
   minute = 0;
   second = 0;
   AM_PM = 'A';
}

Clock :: Clock(int h, int m, int s, char P_AM_PM)
{
   hour=h;
   minute = m;
   second = s;
   AM_PM = P_AM_PM;
}
```

```
void Clock :: SetTime(int h, int m, int s, char P_AM_PM)
{
    hour=h;
    minute = m;
    second = s;
    AM_PM = P_AM_PM;
}

void Clock :: Display()
{
    OutputTwoDigits(hour);
    cout<<":";
    OutputTwoDigits(minute);
    cout<<":";
    OutputTwoDigits(second);
    cout<<" ";
    if (AM_PM == 'A')
        cout<<"AM"<<endl;
    else
        cout<<"PM"<<endl;
}

void main()
{
    AlarmClock Now;
    Now.SetAlarm(5,5,5,'A');
    Now.Display();
}
```

By defining **AlarmClock** from the class **Clock**, we are only responsible for defining the new properties of the alarm. It will save us a great deal of time.

Let's start by looking at the constructor. We need the **AlarmClock** class to initialize the clock as before. Because we defined **AlarmClock** from **Clock**, we do not have to add any code to initialize the time. This is the power of inheritance. However, we must initialize one of the new attributes, **On**. We must set **On** to **false**. Therefore, we add this line to the constructor for **AlarmClock** and allow the time to be set automatically from the **Clock** constructor.

The method **SetAlarm** is new and has no counterpart in the base class **Clock**. Therefore, we code **SetAlarm** as we would any other method.

Finally, the **Display** method introduces a new concept. We require the method of the base class to be called as well as additional code to handle the derived classes' additional information, unlike with the constructor, in which C++ automatically called the base classes' constructor method. Methods that are of the same name in derived classes are called, but their base class counterparts are not called unless explicitly told to do so. Since in this case we want the base classes' information to be displayed as well as the additional derived class information, we call the base classes' method and then write the additional code required for the derived class.

To call a base class method from a derived class, use the following format:

```
BaseClass :: MethodName();
```

There are many more issues as we create complex inheritance models; however, used in moderation, it can be a very useful tool for the programmer. Although we could go through many more generic examples of classes, we will use classes through the rest of this book to implement the various data structures. This will further enhance your knowledge of classes.

11.6 Case Study

Problem Description

Let's write a program that simulates a cable box. Our box has the following characteristics and operations:

- `Power Button.` It allows the box to be turned on or off. No other buttons function when the power is off.
- `Volume Setting.` The volume can be set, but it has a minimum and maximum setting.
- `Channel Setting.` The channel can be set, but it has a minimum and maximum setting.
- `Company Identification.` The name of a cable company can be assigned to the box when it is created.
- `Display.` The box can output the name of the company it belongs to, as well as the current volume and channel settings.

Problem Discussion

Because our cable box will work with multiple cable systems, we will set it up with two constructor methods. The first will be the default constructor that is used if no options are given. This will set the company to "No Company Specified" and the min/max's for volume and channel to the default values 0, 10, 1, and 30, respectively.

However, if the user wishes to specify new values for these fields, we will create a second constructor that accepts these values as parameters to the constructor.

In both cases we have to allocate space for the name of the cable company and copy the string we want assigned to the newly allocated space.

The only issue we need to address in the destructor is to return the allocated memory for the company name to the system. This can be done with a single delete statement.

As for the `PowerButton` method, we need to write a method that flips the power setting from off to on or from on to off each time `PowerButton` is called. We could choose to write an if statement that determines whether the `Power` attribute is `true` and then assign it `false`, or if it is `false` assign it `true`. However, if we assign Power the logical negation of what it currently is assigned to, we will accomplish the same thing more efficiently.

11.6 Case Study (continued)

The methods **VolumeUp** and **VolumeDown** are similar. The only difference is that one will set the **Volume** attribute one setting higher and one will set it one setting lower. For the **VolumeUp** method, we must check to make sure the Power is on and if so, also check to see that the volume is not set to the maximum value. If these conditions are true, then we can simply increment the **Volume** attribute by one. For the **VolumeDown** method, we must check to make sure the power is on and if so, also check to see that the volume is not set to the minimum value. If these conditions are true, then we can simply decrement the **Volume** attribute by one.

The methods **UpChannel** and **DownChannel** are very similar to **VolumeUp** and **VolumeDown**, but instead of incrementing the **Volume** attribute, we increment/decrement the **Channel** attribute. However, because we want to remember the last channel selected, we must also set the current channel to the attribute **PreviousChannel**.

The method **SetChannel** accepts a parameter from the user. As long as the **Power** attribute is true and the channel we wish to set it to is valid, we first assign the **PreviousChannel** attribute to the current channel and then set the **Channel** attribute to the parameter.

The **ReturnToPrevious** method assigns the current channel the previous channel value and vice versa. We do not have to check if any values are valid, because only valid values could have been assigned initially. We must, however, make sure the **Power** attribute is set to **true**.

The final method, **Display**, outputs the cable company's name, volume, and channel settings, as long as the power is on.

Solution

```cpp
#include <stdlib.h>
#include <iostream.h>
#include <string.h>

#define DefaultMinVolume 0
#define DefaultMaxVolume 10
#define DefaultMinChannel 1
#define DefaultMaxChannel 30

class CableBox
{
   public:
     CableBox();
     CableBox(char * pCableCompany, int pMinChannel, int pMaxChannel,
              int pMinVolume, int pMaxVolume);
     ~CableBox();
     void PowerButton();
     void UpVolume();
     void DownVolume();
     void UpChannel();
     void DownChannel();
     void SetChannel(int pChannel);
     void ReturnToPrevious();
```

```cpp
      void Display();
   private:
      char * CableCompany;
      bool Power;
      int Channel;
      int MaxChannel;
      int MinChannel;
      int Volume;
      int MaxVolume;
      int MinVolume;
      int PreviousChannel;
};

CableBox :: CableBox()
{
   Power = false;
   CableCompany = new char[strlen("No Company Specified")+1];
   strcpy(CableCompany, "No Company Specified");
   MinVolume = DefaultMinVolume;
   MaxVolume = DefaultMaxVolume;
   MinChannel = DefaultMinChannel;
   MaxChannel = DefaultMaxChannel;
   Volume = DefaultMinVolume;
   Channel = DefaultMinChannel;
   PreviousChannel = Channel;
}

CableBox :: CableBox(char * pCableCompany, int pMinChannel,
                     int pMaxChannel, int pMinVolume,
                     int pMaxVolume)
{
   Power = false;
   CableCompany = new char[strlen(pCableCompany)+1];
   strcpy(CableCompany, pCableCompany);
   MinVolume = pMinVolume;
   MaxVolume = pMaxVolume;
   MinChannel = pMinChannel;
   MaxChannel = pMaxChannel;
   Volume = pMinVolume;
   Channel = pMaxVolume;
   PreviousChannel = Channel;
}

CableBox :: ~CableBox()
{
   delete [] CableCompany;
}

void CableBox :: PowerButton()
{
   Power = !Power;
}
```

```cpp
void CableBox :: UpVolume()
{
   if ((Power) && (Volume < MaxVolume))
     Volume++;
}

void CableBox :: DownVolume()
{
   if ((Power) && (Volume > MinVolume))
     Volume--;
}

void CableBox :: UpChannel()
{
   if ((Power) && (Channel < MaxChannel))
     PreviousChannel = Channel++;
}

void CableBox :: DownChannel()
{
   if ((Power) && (Channel > MinChannel))
     PreviousChannel = Channel--;
}

void CableBox :: SetChannel(int pChannel)
{
   if (Power)
   {
      if (pChannel >= MinChannel && pChannel <= MaxChannel)
      {
         PreviousChannel = Channel;
         Channel = pChannel;
      }
   }
}

void CableBox :: ReturnToPrevious()
{
   int TempChannel;

   if (Power)
   {
     TempChannel = PreviousChannel;
     PreviousChannel = Channel;
     Channel = TempChannel;
   }
}

void CableBox :: Display()
{
   if (Power)
     cout<<"Your "<<CableCompany<<" cablebox is set to channel "
     <<Channel<<" and its volume is set to "<<Volume<<endl;
}
```

11.6 Case Study (continued)

```cpp
//Sample program illustrating the use of the CableBox
void main()
{
    CableBox DefaultCompany;
    CableBox NewCompany("Ettinger's Cable Company", 2, 69, 0, 100);

    NewCompany.PowerButton();
    NewCompany.SetChannel(30);
    NewCompany.Display();

    DefaultCompany.PowerButton();
    DefaultCompany.Display();
}
```

PROGRAMMER'S NOTEBOOK

Do not assume that functions that we defined are automatically usable. In this case, we have included C++'s string.h file, which contains all the string functions defined earlier. We could use a more advanced string library that treats strings as an object, but we have stayed with the implementation with which you are most familiar.

END-OF-CHAPTER

◆ Key Terms

Composition	The creation of one class by including objects of previously defined classes.
Destructor	A special method that is called automatically when an object goes out of scope.
Has-a relationship	Resuing code by building a new class that contains objects of another class or classes.
Inheritence	Reusing code by building on previously defined classes.
Is-a relationship	A relationship between two classes where one is the base class and the other is a derived class that inherits the properties of the base case.

◆ Answers to Drills

Drill 11-1

The code in the drill allocates two variables: **FirstVariable** and **SecondVariable**. From the declaration you cannot assume whether the variables are created from a class or a structure. However, the line **FirstVariable.Display()** is clearly a method call. The **Display** method is called from the variable with no parameters. Since we know this to be a class and we do not have the class definition in front of us, it is impossible to say whether a constructor is called or not. If one is called, it would be called upon the declaration of the object.

The second variable, **SecondVariable**, is passed to the function **DisplayYYY**. From the code given, it is impossible to tell if the second variable was created from a class and thus passed as an object or was a structure and passed. However, because of the format of the call, we can say is that the line is a function call.

Drill 11-2

The definition of the class needs minor changes to accommodate the additional attribute. First we must add the attribute for the last name and first name. We should also remove the current attribute, since it would add confusion due to its vague naming choice. Then we must modify the constructor to take the additional parameters. You might think you need to change the destructor and you would be correct, but not the declaration of the destructor in the **Person** class. The code follows:

```
class Person
{
   public:
     Person();  //Default constructor
     Person(char * FN, char * LN, int A); //Constructor
     ~Person();
     Display();
   private:
     char * FirstName;
     char * LastName;
     int Age; //Integer age as always
};
```

Drill 11-3

There are two constructors whose bodies require modification. The first one is the one that takes no parameters. There we must assign both pointers to **NULL**. For the other constructor, we must mimic the actions currently coded for both **FirstName** and **LastName**. The code follows:

```
Person :: Person ()
{
   LastName = NULL;
   FirstName = NULL;
   Age = 0;
}
```

```
Person :: Person (char * FN, char * LN, int A)
{
    int Len;

    Len = strlen(FN);
    FirstName = new char[Len+1];
    strcpy(FirstName, FN);

    Len = strlen(LN);
    LastName = new char[Len+1];
    strcpy(LastName, LN);
    Age = A;
}
```

Drill 11-4

The destructor needs to be modified so that the two arrays allocated are deallocated, thus returning the memory used to the operating system. This can be seen as follows:

```
Person :: ~Person()
{
    delete [ ] FirstName;
    delete [ ] LastName;
}
```

Drill 11-5

The output of the program would be as follows:

The first line is the length of the string. Remember that the length does not include the string termination character, so the output is **42**.

The next line is the character at position 5. Remember that position 5 is actually the sixth character in the array. Therefore the output is **i**.

The next line is to return the output to the location of the string "Sixers". The string starts at the location at position 4. Therefore, the output is **4**.

The characters from position 10 to 14 are the final output, which therefore is **will**.

◆Programming Assignments

1. Write a program that asks for a student's age, name, birthday, and address. Store this information in a class. Include a method that will search through the list looking for information that matches. An example is to look for all students with a certain birthday, born in a certain month or a certain year. Create this class so that you can search for a student based on any of the attributes.

2. Modify the **Person** class used in this chapter to include two more methods. One method should be placed in the **public** section and should be named **Wages()**. The other method should be placed in the **private** section and should be called **Income()**. When the method **Wages()** is called, it should ask for the amount of money that the person makes per hour. Then **Wages()** should call the method **Income()**, which will calculate the weekly and yearly salary of that person. The **Display()** method should also be modified to show the yearly and weekly salaries. All necessary attributes should be added to the private section of the class.

3. Modify the **CableBox** class so that it allows up to five favorites to be specified and stored within the object. Provide a method **SetFavorites** that will ask users to enter their favorite five channels. Make sure that the channels entered are valid. Provide a method **SelectFavorite** that accepts an integer parameter to select a channel from the list of favorites.

4. Write a class called **Player**. This class should contain attributes for the player's name, average, and team. Write methods to display each attribute and methods to change them. Make sure that a constructor exists that asks for input to initialize all the attributes.

♦ Additional Exercises

1. Does the following code allocate the proper amount of memory and copy the string passed to the constructor to the attribute properly? Explain why or why not.

```
class classname :: classname(char * N)
{
 Name = new char [] strlen(N);
 strcpy(Name, N);
}
```

2. The destructors we showed in this chapter have dealt with dynamic memory. Is there a time that you can think of that you could use a destructor when not dealing with dynamic memory? Is so, describe it.

3. What are the valid indices for the following vector?

```
vector <int> vector(5);
```

4. Can a vector's size be reset at run time? If so, what happens to the current contents of the vector?

5. Name the advantages to using the built-in string class.

6. Are there any disadvantages to using the built-in string class?

7. Does writing code using inheritance cause extra overhead as opposed to simply recoding everything as traditional classes?

8. What kind of relationship do the following items have (IS-A, HAS-A)?

    a. Dog, mammal
    b. Clock radio, radio
    c. Car, engine
    d. Pentium III computer, IBM-compatible computer
    e. House, door

9. Can a class have more than one destructor? If you think it can, show an example.

In this part, we shift gears a bit. In the first two parts, we focused on learning the syntax of various C++ constructs. With our arsenal of programming tools developed and practiced through the many drills, we now learn practical uses for these tools. Although the number of drills is reduced per chapter, we have added numerous diagrams to assist you with the comprehension of the data structures we introduce.

We now focus on the creation of simple data structures to show you various ways information can be represented and accessed. So far we have shown you how to use computers to store, process, and retrieve information. However, how fast and efficiently they perform these operations is critical to the usability of the computer application.

If we asked users how fast or efficient an application needs to be, they might request a system that

- Is as fast as possible
- Requires the least amount of space possible
- Is capable of retrieving any value at any time

The problem with these requests is that in order to implement one of the requests, another request may be affected in a trade-off. For instance, it may be possible to increase the speed of a search, but the algorithm to increase the speed would require more space than the slower algorithm. Similarly, if we wish to be able to access any value at any time, we may have to sacrifice some speed over a system that allowed us to access only the last value entered or the earliest value entered.

Effective information systems professionals are ones that select the proper data structure for a specific problem. By understanding the types of access and speed versus space constraints, an information systems professional can select a data structure that operates quickly and uses the least amount of space required to access the data as specified by the end users.

Imagine two possible problems:

1. You wish to create a phone book containing people's names and their phone numbers. The people may not be entered in the proper order; however, you will want to be able to enter a person's name and retrieve his or her phone number quickly. This structure will take up more space as we wish the speed to improve. We will see why shortly.

2. You wish to write a program that will simulate people entering a bank and waiting in line to be serviced by a teller. You would need a data structure to store the people as they wait in line. Assuming that people don't cut the line, they would be serviced in the order they entered the line. Therefore, we would want a structure that quickly allowed removal from one end while it allowed insertion from the other. By not requiring access to the middle elements of the line and not requiring the items to be sorted in any way other than the order they entered, we can create a data structure that is extremely fast and requires minimal space.

We will discuss various data structures that can be used for these purposes. It is important to use the right data structure for the right problem.

CHAPTER
12

Stacks

Chapter Objectives

♦ Introduce the simplest data structure called a stack

♦ Master the operations of a stack

♦ Demonstrate algorithms that utilize a stack efficiently

♦ Implement a C++ class for a stack

▮▮▮ 12.1 WHY DO WE NEED STACKS?

One of the simplest data structures is called the stack. Whether or not a stack should be included in a text written for information systems professionals is debatable. Computer science majors use stacks more commonly than do information systems majors, but there are reasons to include stacks. Although stacks are not overly useful, as other more general data structures are, they are a good place to start. They introduce the concept that we can access information in a structure only by predefined operations. These operations provide a discipline over the structure so that unintended operations cannot be performed. By providing only certain operations, the structure of the stack and its operations are optimized. The major benefits of stacks are their ease of implementation and their speed of operation. However, as with all data structures, these benefits come at a price.

We want a data structure that can be accessed in any fashion with almost instantaneous performance. Stacks achieve this speed goal by allowing only the insertion and deletion of items from one place.

Values are inserted or removed from the top (only) of the stack. This creates problems when we wish to access values that are not on the top of the stack. If we need to access values in that fashion then we should use a different type of data structure.

The most common use of a stack is how our operating system handles function calls in C++. We saw in the recursive function chapter that we had to handle the ability to call a function over and over again. Each time the function called itself, we needed to remember the parameters, local variables, and the place to return on each call. When we returned from a function call it was important to return to the function that had previously called it. In essence, the last function called was the first function on the stack. This precedence is often referred to as Last In First Out (**LIFO**).

Remember, in Chapter 5, when we created the banner program? From the **main** routine, we called the **PrinterLetterF** function. From **PrintLetterF**, we called the **Stars** function, which in turn called the **Star** function. How did the computer know to return to the **Stars** function after the call to **Star** was complete? It remembered the entire function call sequence because each function call was stored in a stack. You can see that the order of the calls is preserved in a LIFO format.

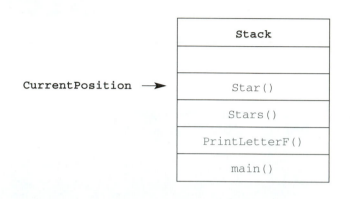

12.2 HOW DOES A STACK OPERATE?

LIFO precedence is exactly how a stack operates. The last value put on a stack is the first value removed from a stack. Observe the following graphical representation of a stack that has the four values 1, 2, 3, and 4 contained within it.

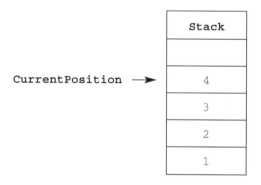

How can we create a **Stack** and use it? When a **Stack** is created, it is done so with no values on the **Stack**. To add values to a **Stack** we use the **Push** operation.

Push will accept a single value and insert it to the top of the **Stack**. The top of the stack is signified in our diagrams as the **CurrentPosition**. Observe the following sequence of operations on the **Stack** as we **Push** the values 1, 2, 3, and 4 onto the **Stack**, respectively.

After we push 1 onto the stack:

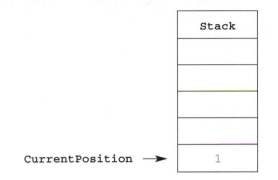

After we push 2 onto the stack:

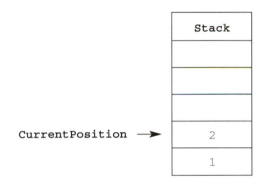

After we push 3 onto the stack:

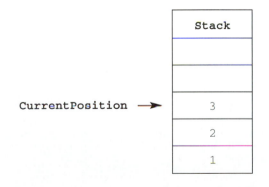

After we **Push** 4 onto the **Stack**:

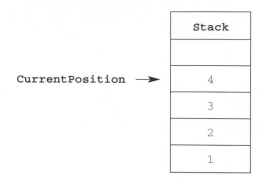

With each **Push** of a value onto the **Stack**, we see that the **CurrentPosition** is moved to point to the new value. All the preceded values are stored in the **Stack** in the sequence they were inserted.

We remove values from the **Stack** with a **Pop** operation. Although you might think it is useful to allow the removal from values in the order they were inserted, or better yet from any arbitrary position, we cannot. **Pop** will only allow you to remove the value pointed to from the **CurrentPosition**. This is done for speed and ease of implementation. If your application requires this type of operation, a **Stack** can be very useful.

So what happens when we execute the **Pop** command from the previous view of a **Stack**? The value 4 is returned and the **Stack** now looks as follows:

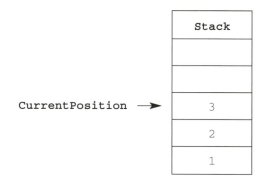

If we issue the **Pop** command again, the value 3 is returned and the **Stack** looks as follows:

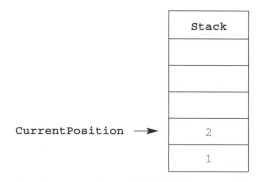

We can issue **Pop** again and the value 2 is returned with the **Stack** looking as follows:

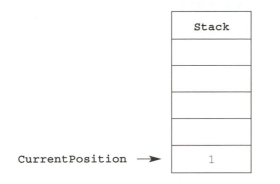

Finally, if we issue **Pop** again, we return the value 1 and the **Stack** is returned to its empty state.

Basically we have seen that if we issue a series of **Push** commands and then a series of **Pop** commands we will, in essence, reverse the order of the value on a **Stack**.

The other two operations that we might wish to implement are **Top**, which simply returns the value of the **Stack** pointed to by **CurrentPosition** without removing it from the **Stack**, and **Clear**, which resets a **Stack** to its original state.

We do have two additional concerns. What happens when we attempt to **Push** a value onto a **Stack** when there is no more room on the **Stack** to accept such a value? This is known as a **stack overflow**. You may have experienced this when you were learning recursive functions. If you wrote a function that called itself too many times, the operating system's **Stack** would have reached a point where there was no more room and would issue an error message. This is a fairly common occurrence and requires us to make sure our **Stack** guards against it.

A less common, but equally dangerous issue when dealing with **Stacks** is the concept of popping a value off the **Stack** when no values remain on the **Stack**. This is known as a **stack underflow**. It does not happen as often, but we must also guard against it.

DRILLS

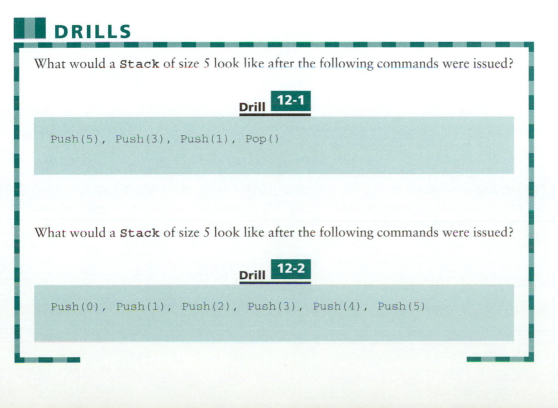

What would a **Stack** of size 5 look like after the following commands were issued?

Drill 12-1

```
Push(5), Push(3), Push(1), Pop()
```

What would a **Stack** of size 5 look like after the following commands were issued?

Drill 12-2

```
Push(0), Push(1), Push(2), Push(3), Push(4), Push(5)
```

12.3 STACK CLASS IMPLEMENTATION

There are many ways we can implement a **Stack**. The most common is to allocate an array statically to a fixed size. Because an array is declared to a fixed size, it is not as flexible as allocating the array dynamically, the method we have chosen. We allow the programmer to select the size of the array programatically, which maximizes flexibility and performance. Other methods exist, including using a linked list representation. We explain linked lists later and do not use them here, because a stack should be simple and quick. Linked lists add complexity that is not required.

Our **Stack** data structure will be implemented as a class. Although it can be implemented as a traditional structure and set of functions, we have decided to implement it as a class to provide further examples of how classes are implemented. The class definition is as follows:

```
//Program demonstrating the stack data structure

#include <stdlib.h>
#include <iostream.h>

#define DefaultSize 20

class Stack
{
    public:
        Stack();
        Stack(int StackSize);
        ~Stack();
        int Top();
        int Pop();
        void Push(int Value);
        void Clear();
        bool IsEmpty();

    private:
        int * Array;
        int CurrentPosition;
        int MaxCapacity;
};
```

Our **Stack** class has two constructors. A constructor for the stack must allocate the proper amount of memory and initialize the top of the **Stack**. If an object of type **Stack** is created with no parameters, then the **Stack**'s internal array is initialized to 20 indicated by the **DefaultSize** define statement. However, we also provide a second constructor that allows for the programmer to set the size. Notice that the second constructor checks to ensure that the size of the array is at least one; otherwise, it sets the size to the default size. This ensures that an empty or negative size stack cannot be specified.

```
Stack :: Stack()
{
    Array = new int[DefaultSize];
    MaxCapacity = DefaultSize;
    CurrentPosition = -1;
}

Stack :: Stack(int StackSize)
{
    if (StackSize > 0)
    {
        Array = new int[StackSize];
        MaxCapacity = StackSize;
    }
    else
    {
        Array = new int[DefaultSize];
        MaxCapacity = DefaultSize;
    }
    CurrentPosition = -1;
}
```

The destructor for a stack simply frees any memory allocated by the **Stack** constructors.

```
Stack :: ~Stack()
{
    delete [] Array;
}
```

You may think that in order to implement the **Top** method, we simply return the value at the top of the **Stack**. However, we need to make sure that the **Stack** is not empty. Therefore, before we return a value, we check to make sure that **CurrentPosition** is not negative. If it is, then we output a warning that the stack has been accessed illegally.

```
int Stack :: Top()
{
    if (CurrentPosition>=0)
        return Array[CurrentPosition];
    else
        cout<<"Stack Underflow"<<endl;
    return 0;
}
```

The **Pop** method operates similar to the **Top** method. We need to ensure that a value exists on the **Stack** before we remove it. If it does exist, we remove the value on the top of the **Stack** by decrementing the stack counter and returning the value from the method. As with the **Top** method, if the **CurrentPosition** is negative an error message is displayed.

```
int Stack :: Pop()
{
    if (CurrentPosition>=0)
      return Array[CurrentPosition--];
    else
      cout<<"Stack Underflow"<<endl;
    return 0;
}
```

The **Push** method operates in reverse of the **Pop** method. We need to ensure that there is room remaining in the **Stack** for the value. If there is, the value is placed on the **Stack**. Otherwise, an error message is generated. It is possible to implement the **Push** method so that if the **Stack** is full it allocates a new array with more space, copies over the previous contents of the **Stack**, and then frees the memory of the previous array. This will be left as an exercise.

```
void Stack :: Push(int Value)
{
    if (CurrentPosition<MaxCapacity-1)
      Array[++CurrentPosition]=Value;
    else
      cout<<"Stack Overflow"<<endl;
}
```

The **IsEmpty** method simply returns true if the **Stack** is empty. This is important, because it allows the user to determine if there is a value to remove before issuing the **Pop** method.

```
bool Stack ::IsEmpty()
{
    return (CurrentPosition == -1);
}
```

The final method is **Clear**. It simply empties the stack by resetting the **CurrentPosition** variable to its initial value. Although the values that previously existed on the **Stack** are still there, they are ignored the same way the constructor would initialize the **Stack** without blanking the memory that it allocated before it was used.

```
void Stack :: Clear()
{
   CurrentPosition = -1;
}
```

12.4   Case Study

What if we wanted to write a program to ask the user for a series of digits and then output the reverse of those digits? Unlike the example in the functions chapter where we read in an integer and output the reverse, in this case we can read in as many values as the stack can hold. Additionally, we would like to be able to write the algorithm without using recursion. The program will stop reading digits when a nondigit is read and then output the digits entered in the reverse order.

This program can be written using a stack and a variable to store a single character entered from the user. Without understanding the inner workings of a stack or even an array for that matter, we can write the program very succinctly. Simply create a stack and push each value read from the user onto the stack. When we encounter a nondigit, terminate the input loop and output all the values on the stack until the stack is empty.

The implementation follows:

```
void main()
{
   Stack ReverseDigits;

   //So that it can enter the while loop
   char InputChar='0';

   cout<<"Enter the Digits to Reverse"<<endl;
   while (isDigit(InputChar))
   {
      cin>>InputChar;
      if (isDigit(InputChar))
       ReverseDigits.Push(InputChar);
   }

   while (!ReverseDigits.IsEmpty())
   {
      InputChar = ReverseDigits.Pop();
      cout<< InputChar;
   }
   cout<<endl;
}
```

Be careful not to add the nondigit character entered by the user to the stack.

12.5 Case Study

Problem Description

Imagine if we wanted to write an application that checked to see if the input from the user has correct parentheses matching. By correct parentheses matching, we mean that an open parenthesis, '(' should be paired with a close parenthesis, ')', and a close parenthesis should not come before an open parenthesis. Our program should ignore any nonparentheses characters.

The following are considered valid parentheses expressions:
```
( 5 + 4 ) + ( 3 / 4 ) + ( ( 3 + 4) / 2)
( ( ( 3 ) + (3 + 4) + (1 + 1) ) / 3)
( )
```

The following are not considered valid parentheses expressions:
```
) (
( 4 + 5) + ) 4 + 3)
( ( ) ) )
```

Problem Discussion

To implement a simple solution, we can read characters from the user into an array. Then we can parse through the array and when we encounter an open parenthesis, we push it on the stack. When we encounter a close parenthesis, we pop an open parenthesis from the stack. If no open parenthesis exists, then we have encountered an error. If, when we reach the end of the input string we have any values of the stack left, then we also have an error in the input string.

Solution

```cpp
void main()
{
    Stack MatchParens;
    int i=0;
    char InputCharacters[100];
    bool ErrorFound = false;

    cout<<"Enter the Expression"<<endl;
    cin.getline(InputCharacters, 100);
```

```
        while (InputCharacters[i]!='\0')
        {
            if (InputCharacters[i] == '(')
              MatchParens.Push('(');
            else if (InputCharacters[i] == ')')
            if (!MatchParens.IsEmpty())
              MatchParens.Pop();
            else
              ErrorFound = true;
            i++;
        }
        if (ErrorFound)
          cout<<"An error was found!"<<endl;
        else
          cout<<"The input is fine!"<<endl;
    }
```

12.6 Case Study

Our final example is to improve the parentheses matcher we just created. Instead of simply matching parentheses as before, let's check to see if parentheses, brackets, and curly braces match. We will also make sure that these characters are ordered in the proper sequence.

Therefore, the following strings are valid:
```
( 5 )  { 5 }  [ 10 ]
( 5 * 4 [ 4 + 2] * { e f } )
{ [ ( ( [ ] ) ) ( ) ] { } }
```

but the following strings are not:
```
( 4 ]
( [ { ] } )
(((]]]
((()))))
```

Our solution does not vary much in structure from the previous example. We read the input string into an array of characters. We then loop through the array pushing values onto the stack when we encounter either a '(', '[', or '{'. If we encounter a ')', ']', or '}', we attempt to pop the corresponding character from the stack. If the stack is empty or if the incorrect character is popped, we set the error flag; otherwise we continue processing. Our implementation will take advantage of a **switch** statement to help better organize our program:

```
void main()
{
   Stack MatchParens;
   int i=0;
   char InputCharacters[100];
   bool ErrorFound = false;

   cout<<"Enter the Expression"<<endl;
   cin.getline(InputCharacters, 100);

   while (InputCharacters[i]!='\0')
   {
      switch (InputCharacters[i])
      {
         case '(':
         case '{':
         case '[':
           MatchParens.Push(InputCharacters[i]);
           break;
         case ')':
           if (MatchParens.IsEmpty() || (MatchParens.Pop() != '('))
             ErrorFound = true;
           break;
         case '}':
           if (MatchParens.IsEmpty() || (MatchParens.Pop() != '{'))
             ErrorFound = true;
           break;
         case ']':
           if (MatchParens.IsEmpty() || (MatchParens.Pop() != '['))
             ErrorFound = true;
           break;
      }
      i++;
   }
   if (ErrorFound)
     cout<<"An error was found!"<<endl;
   else
     cout<<"The input is fine!"<<endl;
}
```

◆ Key Terms

LIFO	An acronym for Last In First Out. It describes the order values are inserted and removed into a data structure.
Overflow	Occurs when a value is attempted to be inserted into a stack, but there is no room for it.
Pop	An operation on a stack that inserts a value to the top of the stack.
Push	An operation on a stack that removes the top value from the stack.
Stack	A simple data structure that allows insertions and deletions only from the top.
Underflow	Ocuurs when a value is attempted to be removed from a stack, but no values exist on the stack.

◆ Answers to Drills

Drill 12-1

After Push (5)   After Push(3)

After Push (1)   After Pop()

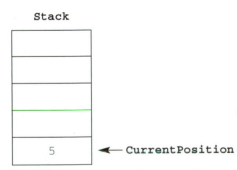

Drill 12-2

After Push (0)

After Push(1)

Stack

```
┌─────────────┐
│             │
├─────────────┤
│             │
├─────────────┤
│             │
├─────────────┤
│             │
├─────────────┤
│      0      │  ◄── CurrentPosition
└─────────────┘
```

Stack

```
┌─────────────┐
│             │
├─────────────┤
│             │
├─────────────┤
│             │
├─────────────┤
│      1      │  ◄── CurrentPosition
├─────────────┤
│      0      │
└─────────────┘
```

After Push (2)

After Push(3)

Stack

```
┌─────────────┐
│             │
├─────────────┤
│             │
├─────────────┤
│      2      │  ◄── CurrentPosition
├─────────────┤
│      1      │
├─────────────┤
│      0      │
└─────────────┘
```

Stack

```
┌─────────────┐
│             │
├─────────────┤
│      3      │  ◄── CurrentPosition
├─────────────┤
│      2      │
├─────────────┤
│      1      │
├─────────────┤
│      0      │
└─────────────┘
```

After Push (4)

After Push(5)

Stack

```
┌─────────────┐
│      4      │  ◄── CurrentPosition
├─────────────┤
│      3      │
├─────────────┤
│      2      │
├─────────────┤
│      1      │
├─────────────┤
│      0      │
└─────────────┘
```

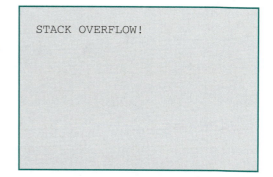

STACK OVERFLOW!

◆ Programming Exercises

1. Rewrite the Stack class so that it can accept characters instead of integers.

2. Rewrite the Stack class so that it can accept strings instead of integers.

3. Rewrite the Stack class so that it can accept a structure instead of integers.

4. Rewrite the Stack class that is implemented so that when an overflow occurs an array is allocated to double the current size of the Stack, so that all the values of the current Stack are moved to the new array, so that the old array is deallocated, and so that the newly allocated array is pointed to internally as the stack.

5. Write a program that would read characters from a file and check to see that the parentheses, brackets, and braces match as they do in section 12.6. You should use a Stack in the same manner as that case study as well.

◆ Additional Exercises

1. Given the following statements, will the stack overflow or underflow?

   a. ```
      Stack Test(3);
      Test.Pop();
      ```

   b. ```
      Stack Test(3);
      Test.Push(4);
      ```

   c. ```
      Stack Test(1);
      Test.Push(4);
      ```

   d. ```
      Stack Test(3);
      Test.Push(1);
      Test.Push(1);
      Test.Pop();
      Test.Push(1);
      Test.Push(1);
      ```

2. Draw what the Stack will look like after each of the following operations:

   a. ```
      Stack Test(10);
      Test.Push(1);
      Test.Push(2);
      Test.Push(3);
      Test.Pop();
      Test.Pop();
      Test.Push(4);
      ```

   b. ```
      Stack Test(10);
      Test.Push(4);
      Test.Push(3);
      Test.Push(2);
      Test.Pop();
      Test.Push(1);
      Test.Pop();
      ```

c.
```
Stack Test(1);
Test.Push(4);
Test.Pop();
Test.Push(3);
Test.Pop();
Test.Push(2);
Test.Pop();
Test.Push(1);
Test.Pop();
```

3. What does LIFO mean?

4. Does a Stack allow duplicate values to be inserted?

5. Does the term FILO (First In Last Out) properly describe the behavior of a Stack? Is it the same thing as LIFO?

6. Would a Stack be a fair way to store requests for a computer resource that is currently busy processing another request? Indicate why or why not.

13

Queues

Chapter Objectives

♦ **Introduce the simple data structure called a Queue**

♦ **Master the operations of a Queue**

♦ **Demonstrate algorithms that utilize a Queue**

♦ **Implement a C++ class for a Queue**

13.1 WHY DO WE NEED QUEUES?

Although `Stacks` may be easy to implement, their access restrictions make it difficult for them to be particularly useful to the information systems professional. A `Queue`, on the other hand, is another simple data structure that is fairly easy to implement. A `Queue` has the potential to be very useful for the information systems professional.

`Queues` have many uses; among the most popular is to use a `Queue` as a priority list. Unlike the Last In First Out nature of a `Stack`, `Queues` operate by allowing the First In to be the First Out (**FIFO**). This allows us to use a `Queue` to simulate, among other things, a line in a store or any other ordered list.

With a FIFO behavior, `Queues` operate the way we see many fair systems operate in the real world. If you went into a bank and got in line, would you want the system used to provide service to be LIFO or FIFO? A sarcastic answer would be LIFO, if you were the last person to enter the bank. However, if you agreed that the order people were serviced in the bank was to be the order in which they entered the bank, the only answer could be that you require a line that follows a FIFO precedence.

Because many simulations follow a FIFO precedence, `Queues` are a very popular data structure. In the real world, simulations are often run to see the effect of adding, removing, or reconfiguring physical setups—for example, a bank where a `Queue` is used to store the people who are waiting in line. Simulations can be run to see if it is more effective to have multiple lines, and thus multiple `Queues`, or a single line feeding multiple tellers. Similar examples can be seen if we wish to simulate the utilization of service bays in an auto repair facility.

Although we agreed that FIFO is the type of structure we want, we will see that it is not as simple to implement as a `Stack`. First we will demonstrate what happens with a simple implementation scheme. The FIFO structure will appear to work, but as we further study it, we will see that we require a slightly more complicated algorithm to accomplish our task.

13.2 HOW DOES A QUEUE OPERATE?

Let's use a simple array to store the `Queue`. Unlike `Stacks`, we require more than one index for a `Queue`. We require one index to point to the front of the `Queue`, where we remove values, and another index to point to the rear of the `Queue`, where we insert values. We will also need an integer variable to store the number of items in the `Queue`.

Observe a `Queue` that has had 1, 2, and 3 inserted into it, respectively.

The first value inserted was the value 1 and therefore the **Front** index points to it. Since the value 2 was inserted next, it follows in the `Queue` behind 1. Since 3 is the last value entered, it follows behind value 2 and has the **Rear** index pointing to it.

If we were to insert another value, 4, then it would be inserted into the `Queue` as follows:

So what would happen if we were to remove the first value from the `Queue`? Simple: We would pass the value 1 back, and move the **Front** index to point to 2. So what's the problem? Well, so far there is none. The following figure demonstrates how the `Queue` would look after we removed the first value:

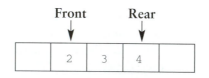

To see the problem with our **Queue** implementation, we simply need to insert two more values into the **Queue**. Let's insert 5, show you the figure, and then insert 6.

After 5 is inserted, the **Queue** is represented as follows:

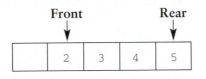

We have room for one more value in the **Queue**, but if we follow a simple incrementing scheme, when we try to add the next value, it would be inserted past the end of the array. Therefore, we must come up with a scheme to handle this situation.

There are many possibilities that do not require allocating extra memory in the array. One of the slickest is the concept of thinking of the array as circular instead of linear. When we think of an array this way, we need to think of the process of moving to the next cell as almost linear. The only difference is that when we wish to increment the index past the end of the array, we set the index to 0.

Therefore, if we used a circular implementation for a **Queue** and we were trying to insert the value 6 into the previous example, then the **Queue** would look as follows:

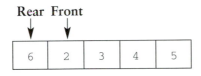

Another issue arises from this implementation. How do we tell if the **Queue** is full? The simplest solution is to store the current number of values in the **Queue** in a variable.

■ DRILLS

Drill 13-1

What would a **Queue** of size 5 look like after the following commands were issued?
```
Insert(5), Insert(112), Remove(), Insert(33), Remove(),
Insert(100)
```

Drill 13-2

What would a **Queue** of size 5 look like after the following commands were issued?
```
Insert(100), Insert(99), Insert(98), Insert(97), Remove(),
Remove()
```

■■ 13.3 QUEUE CLASS IMPLEMENTATION

As with the **Stack**, there are many ways we can implement a **Queue**. Again, the most common is to allocate an array statically to a fixed size. However, for the same reasons, we choose to allocate the array dynamically.

A **Queue** has the following operations: **Insert**, **Remove**, **First**, **IsEmpty**, and **Clear**. **Insert** allows the insertion of an item at the back of the **Queue**. **Remove** deletes the item from the front of the **Queue**. **First** returns the value at the front of the **Queue**, but it does not remove it from the **Queue**. **IsEmpty** simply checks to see if the **Queue** is empty. Finally, **Clear** reinitializes the **Queue** to its original empty status. Its definition follows:

```
#define DefaultSize 5

class Queue
{
    public:
        Queue();
        Queue(int QueueSize);
        ~Queue();
        int First();
        int Remove();
        void Insert(int Value);
        void Clear();
        bool IsEmpty();

    private:
        int * Array;
        int Front;
        int Rear;
        int ArraySize;
        int CurrentSize;
};
```

Constructor

The constructor for the **Queue** must set up an empty **Queue**. Our class defines two constructors. The first constructor assumes that the size of the **Queue** is set to the default size, and the second constructor takes a parameter that allows the user to specify the default size of the **Queue**. Beyond that, the two constructors operate the same.

We must allocate enough space for the **Queue**. We do this with a dynamic memory allocation to either the default size of the **Queue** or the size passed as a parameter.

Then we must set the current number of items in the **Queue** to zero. In addition, we must set the **Front** and **Rear** pointers to the proper indexes. **Front** should point to the first element of the array, and **Rear** should point to the last element. You may wonder why **Rear** is pointed to the last element. It's because when we insert items into the array we increment the **Rear** pointer before we insert the item. Therefore, we set **Rear** to the last element of the array so that when we are ready to insert a value, it will point to the first element of the array. Since these three assignments are repeated, we have added a **Clear** method that can be called from the constructor or a programmer who wants to reset the **Queue**.

A graphical representation of the **Queue** follows:

```
Queue :: Queue()
{
    Clear();
    Array = new int[DefaultSize];
    ArraySize = DefaultSize;
}


Queue :: Queue(int QueueSize)
{
    Clear();
    ArraySize = QueueSize;
    Array = new int[QueueSize];
}
```

Destructor

The destructor of a **Queue** is the same as in a **Stack**. We merely need to return any dynamically allocated memory to the computer. We do this by issuing a **delete** command.

```
Queue :: ~Queue()
{
    delete [] Array;
}
```

Insert

To insert a value into the **Queue**, there must be room for it. So first we make sure that the current size of the **Queue** is less than the maximum size. If so, we increment the **Rear** pointer so that it points to the next available cell of the array. If the **Rear** pointer is set to the last cell of the array, then we must set the **Rear** pointer to zero, thus implementing a circular array. Once the **Rear** pointer is set to the next available cell, we copy the insertion value to the cell and increment the current number of items by one.

```
void Queue :: Insert(int Value)
{
   if (CurrentSize > ArraySize)
   {
      cout<<"Queue is Full"<<endl;
      return;
   }

   if (Rear == ArraySize - 1)
     Rear = 0;
   else
     Rear++;
   Array[Rear] = Value;
   CurrentSize++;
}
```

Remove

To remove a value from the **Queue**, there must be a value on the **Queue**. Therefore, we first check to make sure that a value exists by comparing the current number of items to zero.

As long as a value exists, we return the value pointed to by the **Front** index and then increment the **Front** index. If the **Front** index is already at the last element of the array, we set it to zero.

```
int Queue :: Remove()
{
   int Temp;

   if (IsEmpty())
   {
      cout<<"Queue Underflow"<<endl;
      return 0;
   }

   Temp=Array[Front];

   if (Front == ArraySize - 1)
     Front = 0;
   else
     Front++;

   CurrentSize--;
   return Temp;
}
```

IsEmpty

Used by programmers or by the **Remove** method, **IsEmpty** returns **true** if the number of items in the **Queue** is greater than zero; otherwise it returns **false**.

```
bool Queue :: IsEmpty()
{
    return (CurrentSize == 0);
}
```

First

This method operates similarly to the **Remove** method, except that when it returns the first value of the **Queue** it does not remove it from the **Queue**.

```
int Queue :: First()
{
    if (!IsEmpty())
      return Array[Front];
    else
        cout<<"Queue Underflow"<<endl;
    return 0;
}
```

Clear

Used by programmers to reset the **Queue**, **Clear** will reset the indexes and counters of the class so that the **Queue** appears empty. The actual contents of the **Queue** will remain, but will be ignored.

```
void Queue :: Clear()
{
    Front = 0;
    Rear = ArraySize -1;
    CurrentSize=0;
}
```

13.4 Case Study

Problem Description

Let's write a simple simulation that models what happens when people enter a line and wait to be serviced. Each person who enters the line will be represented by a single integer that represents the number of requests that person will have when he or she reaches the front of the line.

Only one person in our simulation can be processed at a time. This will be the person at the front of the line. Because this person will be the one who entered the line before everyone else in the line, we will use a `Queue` called `Line` to store the people in the line.

The user of the simulation will have three options:

- If the user enters A, the user can add a person to the line and indicate the number of requests the person being added will require when he or she reaches the front of the line.
- If the user enters N, the user can do nothing and just allow the line to continue to be processed.
- If the user enters Q, the user can quit the simulation.

The program should output each time all of a person's requests are completed. When a user quits the simulation, it should output the total time of the simulation and how many people remained in the line.

Problem Discussion

The program will need a variable to track the system time, the time entered by the user that represents each person's requests, the current number of requests processed for the first person in the line, and a variable to store the number of people remaining in the line when the simulation ends.

We can set up a `do/while` loop that will prompt the user with a menu of options and then will process the menu option entered. If the Add option is selected, the user must be prompted to enter the number of requests the person being added will require. Then the program should ask for the number of requests and loop until it gets a valid input.

Once valid input has been entered, the person should be entered to the rear of the line.

Regardless of the input, we should process one request each time unit. Therefore, if a person is in line, the front person should have one request processed.

Once the user quits the program, the total system time is output and the number of people remaining in the line is calculated by looping until the `Queue` is empty. With each iteration of the loop, we will remove one person from the line. This information is output and the program terminates.

Solution

```cpp
void main()
{
    Queue Line;
    int PersonTime;
    int SystemTime=0;
    int CurrentProcessingTime=0;
    int PeopleRemaining=0;
    char Answer;

    do
    {

        cout<<endl<< "Enter the appropriate character"
            <<endl;
        cout<<"A]dd person to the line"<<endl;
        cout<<"N]obody enters the line"<<endl;
        cout<<"Q]uit the simulation"<<endl;
        cin>>Answer;

        if (Answer == 'A')
        {
            do
            {
                cout<<"Enter the amount of time the person wants to be serviced"
                    <<endl;
                cin>>PersonTime;
                if (PersonTime <= 0)
                    cout<<"You must enter a positive time"<<endl;
            } while (PersonTime <= 0 );

            Line.Insert(PersonTime);
        }

        if (!Line.IsEmpty())
          if (Line.First() == ++CurrentProcessingTime)
          {
              cout<<endl<<"A person has been serviced!"<<endl;
              Line.Remove();
              CurrentProcessingTime=0;
          }
        SystemTime++;
    }
    while (Answer != 'Q' && Answer != 'q');

    cout<<"The simulation ran for "<<SystemTime<<" time units"<<endl;

    while (!Line.IsEmpty())
    {
        PeopleRemaining++;
        Line.Remove();
    }
    cout<<PeopleRemaining
        <<" people remained in the queue at the end of the simulation"<<endl;
}
```

> ### PROGRAMMER'S NOTEBOOK
>
> Realize that the simulation does not really track "time." Instead, we track a simulated time that really represents the number of requests processed. This is done to simplify the implementation. Although we could track system time, this adds complexity to the application, which would distract us from our goal of learning the use of Queues.

> ### PROGRAMMER'S NOTEBOOK
>
> It is not enough simply to output a message that invalid input has occurred. It is often better to loop until valid input has been entered. In a more robust program, you may also give users an option to quit if they can't provide valid input.

END-OF-CHAPTER

◆ Key Terms

FIFO	An acronym for First In First Out. It describes the order values are inserted and removed into a data structure.
Front of queue	The pointer to where items are removed when dealing a with a queue.
Queue	A simple data structure that allows insertions and deletions following a FIFO behavior.
Rear of a queue	The pointer to where items are added when dealing with a queue.

◆ Answers to Drills

Drill 13-1

The following diagrams show the progression of the `Queue` as values are inserted and removed:

After Insert(5):

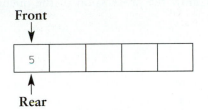

After Insert(112):

After Remove():

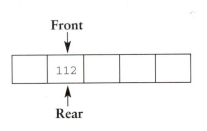

After Insert(33):

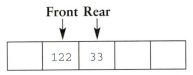

After Remove():

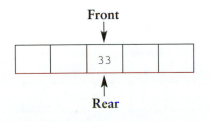

After Insert(100):

Drill 13-2

The following diagrams show the progression of the queue as values are inserted and removed:

After Insert(100):

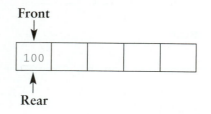

After Insert(99):

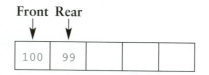

After Insert(98):

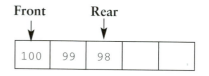

After Insert(97):

After Remove():

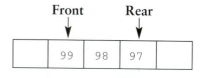

After Remove():

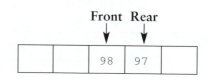

♦ Programming Exercises

1. Modify the `Queue` class so that it can store strings instead of integers.

2. Modify our case study so that it simulates people waiting in a line. But instead of just indicating when a person exits the line, indicate how long each person waits in the line. The time is not calculated from the computer system's time, but from a simulated time. Also, instead of asking the user for input, each person entering the line is assigned a random amount of time that his or her activity will take. This can be calculated using the **rand** function and the modulus operator. Each task should take from 1 to 3 units of time. As each person is serviced, the system time is incremented by the number of units of time that person has been assigned. Assume that there is only one line and anyone entering the bank gets on the end of it. You can calculate the wait time of a person as the time the person entered the `Queue` minus the time he or she begins to be serviced at the front of the line.

3. Create a more complicated simulation than the previous one. Instead of having only a single person served at a time, create a bank simulation where, although there is only one line, there are three tellers who can service the next person in the line. See how this improves performance.

4. Create a final simulation in which, instead of a single waiting line, three lines exist, one for each teller. When a person enters the bank, place him or her in the line with the least number of people. Otherwise, the simulation should operate in the same way as that in Assignment 3.

♦ Additional Exercises

1. Show what a `Queue` of size 5 would look like after the following actions are performed: Insert(1), Insert(2), Insert(3), Delete(), Insert(4), Delete(), Insert(5), Insert(6), Delete().

2. Show what a `Queue` of size 5 would look like after the following actions are performed: Insert(10), Insert(9), Insert(8), Delete(), Insert(7), Delete(), Insert(6), Insert(5), Delete().

3. Can a `Queue` have more inserts performed than deletes?

4. When we first discussed a `Queue`'s implementation, we demonstrated that a `Queue` had to be implemented in a circular fashion so that after items are removed we do not waste the space previously taken by values in the `Queue`. Describe another method of solving the deletion problem in `Queue`.

5. Assume that four items are in a `Queue` but you do not know what the values of the `Queue` are. Assume that the first value removed is the value 1. List the operations that must occur in order for you to return the `Queue` to contain the same values in the same order as it was just before it had the value 1 removed from it. You may use a single temporary variable to store the values as you remove them from the queue.

CHAPTER

14

Linked Lists

Chapter Objectives

♦ Introduce the first general-purpose data structure

♦ Master the operations of a linked list

♦ Demonstrate two methods for implementing a C++ class for linked lists

■■ 14.1 WHAT IS A LINKED LIST?

The problem with the data structures that we have learned so far is that they are only useful if we do not wish to access information in an arbitrary fashion. However, many real-world problems cannot be implemented efficiently if we use either the **Stack** or **Queue** data structures. Often, real-world problems involve storing lists of information, either sorted or unsorted. Although unsorted lists are quick to assemble and easy to maintain, modifying an unsorted list's implementation to insert the items in order is relatively easy and will improve the performance of searching the list.

Although a list of information can be implemented using an array, it is far more versatile to implement a list of information in a data structure we call a **linked list**. Chained nodes of information create a linked list, with each node providing a link to the next node. It is much like the game of telephone we played as kids. One friend tells another friend something. Then that person relays the information to the next person. If one person stops the chain, the rest of the people at the end of the chain are lost.

A huge advantage of using a linked list is that we do not need to indicate the number of values in our structure at one time. We can simply allocate and deallocate the nodes as required.

Figure 14.1 depicts a linked list of three nodes. Although this happens to be a sorted linked list, it is not a requirement. By keeping track of the head of the list, we can reference any value on the list by traversing down it.

Head

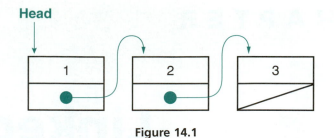

Figure 14.1

The basis for our list is a structure that contains two values: the value to store at each node and a pointer to the next node.

In our example, the value is an integer; however, it could just as easily be a character, floating point number, another structure, etc. It could also be a combination of any of those types of variables. C++ even provides a mechanism to create a template so that it can be mapped to any type of value you wish; however, we will leave that level of C++ explanation to other texts.

To define a node for our linked list, we declare a structure to hold the values that we require. Our node consists of two values: an integer that requires four bytes of memory and a pointer that requires four bytes of memory. Therefore, the entire structure requires eight bytes of memory. The structure is defined as follows:

```
struct ListNode
{
    int Value;
    ListNode * Next;
};
```

Once the structure is defined, we should also declare a variable that is a pointer to the structure we just created. It can be defined as follows:

```
typedef ListNode * ListNodePointer;
```

When creating dynamic structures it is very important to remember to create them using the dynamic memory routines in C++. If you simply declare variables of type **ListNode**, when you leave the function the variables you declared will go out of scope and disappear.

Therefore, when we declare a linked list we start by creating a pointer to a **ListNode** structure as follows:

```
ListNodePointer Head;
```

If you are not familiar with pointers, review the pointers chapter. Linked lists make heavy use of them.

If we wish to have a list with just one node containing an integer value of 5, then the memory allocation could look like Figure 14.2.

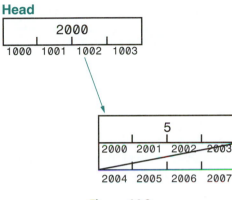

Figure 14.2

To create a list like the one depicted previously, we would execute the following statements:

```
ListNodePointer Head;

Head = new ListNode;

(*Head).Value = 5;
(*Head).Next=NULL;
```

First, a pointer, **Head**, is declared. The pointer will act as the start of our list. Then we need to allocate enough space for one node. By assigning **Head** to the newly allocated node, we are saying that **Head** points to the first node in the list. This can be seen in our example where the variable **Head** stores the address(2000) of the newly allocated node.

Since the **Head** pointer is the only way we can access the items within the newly allocated node, we must use the dereference ***** operator to access the structure. Since we are attempting to access individual parts of the structure at the memory address stored in **Head**, we must also use the **.** operator to specify which field in the structure we will access.

By referencing **(*Head).Value**, we are instructing the computer to go to memory address 2000, add the offset for **Value** (0), and then store the value 5 at that memory address.

By referencing **(*Head).Next**, we are instructing the computer to go to memory address 2000, add the offset for **Next** (4), and then store the **NULL** value at that memory address(2004).

Although using this scheme will allow us access to both values in the structure, C++ provides a shorthand notation that is more readable when dealing with pointers and structures. The line:

```
(*Head).Value = 5;
```

can be replaced with the following:

```
Head->Value=5;
```

The arrow takes the place of the ***** . notation and produces code that is more intuitive.

What if we wanted to create a linked list with three nodes, each containing 1, 2, and 3? Here are two methods of creating this list.

The first is to use individual pointers for each node of the linked list, allocate a node to each pointer, and then link the allocated nodes together. We can see the beginning of this process where we have declared the three pointers and allocated the nodes below:

```
ListNodePointer Head;
ListNodePointer Second;
ListNodePointer Third;

Head = new ListNode;
Second = new ListNode;
Third = new ListNode;
```

Notice from Figure 14.3 that all of the nodes have yet to be initialized.

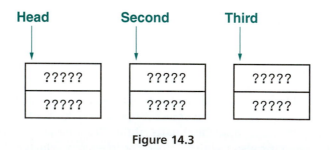

Figure 14.3

By adding the following code, we can link the individual nodes of our linked list.

```
Head->Next  = Second;
Second->Next = Third;
Third->Next = NULL;
```

Although depicted graphically, Figure 14.4 shows the individual nodes now linked. If we actually looked at the computer memory instead of the graphical arrows, the actual memory addresses of each node would be stored in the **Next** pointer field of each structure.

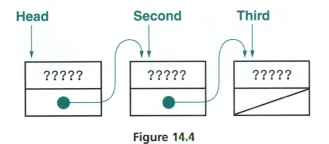

Figure 14.4

To complete our linked list, we execute the following statements to insert the values into the nodes:

```
Head->Value = 1;
Second->Value = 2;
Third->Value = 3;
```

The final linked list is now depicted in Figure 14.5

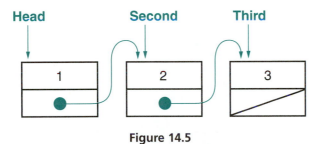

Figure 14.5

Although this method works fine, let's look at another method that would not require as many temporary pointers. Although we are not stating that this method is more efficient, the more ways that you are familiar with linked lists, the easier it will be to write general functions pertaining to linked lists later.

Here is the complete code to create the same linked list that we just implemented.

```
ListNodePointer Head = new ListNode;
Head->Value = 1;
Head->Next = new ListNode;
Head->Next->Value = 2;
Head->Next->Next = new ListNode;
Head->Next->Next->Value = 3;
Head->Next->Next->Next = NULL;
```

So that we fully understand the process, let's look at the code a statement or two at a time. First we declare the **Head** pointer, which will be our handle to the entire linked list. We allocate a node and set **Head** to point to that node. Then we initialize the value of the first node. This is depicted as follows:

```
ListNodePointer Head = new ListNode;
Head->Value = 1;
```

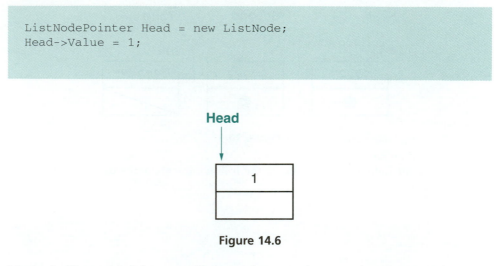

Figure 14.6

Notice in Figure 14.6 that we still do not have a value stored in the **Next** field. We will set the **Next** field to a newly allocated node with the following statement:

```
Head->Next = new ListNode;
```

Now the linked list looks like Figure 14.7.

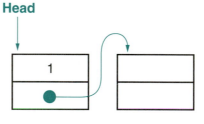

Figure 14.7

Initializing the value in the second node is no longer as simple as it was in our first implementation. To access the second node we need to access its memory address from the **Next** field of the first node. Therefore, we need to follow from the **Head** pointer through the **Next** field through to the **Value** field. This is done in the following line:

```
Head->Next->Value = 2;
```

Clearly there is a correlation between the arrows in the code and the arrows in the diagram; see Figure 14.8.

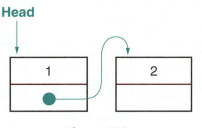

Figure 14.8

The next step is to allocate the third node in the list. We need to assign the memory address of the allocated node to the **Next** pointer in the second node of our list. This can be done with the following statement:

```
Head->Next->Next = new ListNode;
```

The final node now appears in Figure 14.9.

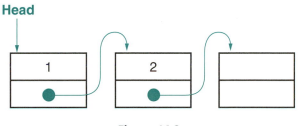

Figure 14.9

The last step is to initialize the values in the last node. To access them, we need to start at the **Head** pointer and work our way down the list until we reach the newly allocated node. Then it is a simple matter of assigning the value and **NULL** pointer as follows:

```
Head->Next->Next->Value = 3;
Head->Next->Next->Next = NULL;
```

The final linked list is depicted in Figure 14.10.

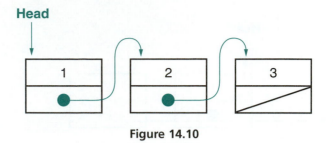

Figure 14.10

As we see, both methods work reasonably well, but what would happen if we needed to create a linked list with many nodes? Both of our current methods would be quite cumbersome. What we need to create is a methodology that allows us to repeat the operation of appending nodes to the linked list one at a time. Eventually we will want to write a function that will perform the insert for us; however, to aid in our understanding let's go through the following example of using a temporary pointer.

We start as we did when we created a **Head** pointer that will be the handle for the beginning of our list. We allocate the first node and assign the first value (1).

```
ListNodePointer Head = new ListNode;
Head->Value = 1;
```

Now we allocate the next node and create a temporary pointer, **Current**, that will point to the new node.

```
Head->Next = new ListNode;
ListNodePointer Current = Head->next;
```

Figure 14.11 depicts the current status of our linked list.

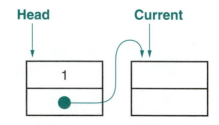

Figure 14.11

Now we can begin a repeating process of adding nodes to the linked list by using the **Current** pointer. See the following code to add the next node:

```
Current->Value = 2;
Current->Next = new ListNode;
Current = Current->Next;
```

This is depicted in Figure 14.12.

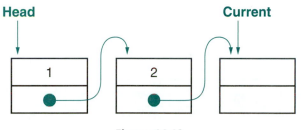

Figure 14.12

The process is repeated for each node we want to add to the list. Notice that the only code that changes is the value to be stored in the list.

```
Current->Value = 3;
Current->Next = new ListNode;
Current = Current->Next;
```

Imagine if we continued the process and added 100 items. The only code that would need to change is the code to add the last node to the list. This is because the last node must have a **NULL** pointer in the next field to signify the end of the list. This is shown in the following code:

```
Current->Value = 100;
Current->Next = NULL;
```

▌DRILLS

Drill 14-1

Write the code required to create the following linked list (you may use extra pointers if you require them):

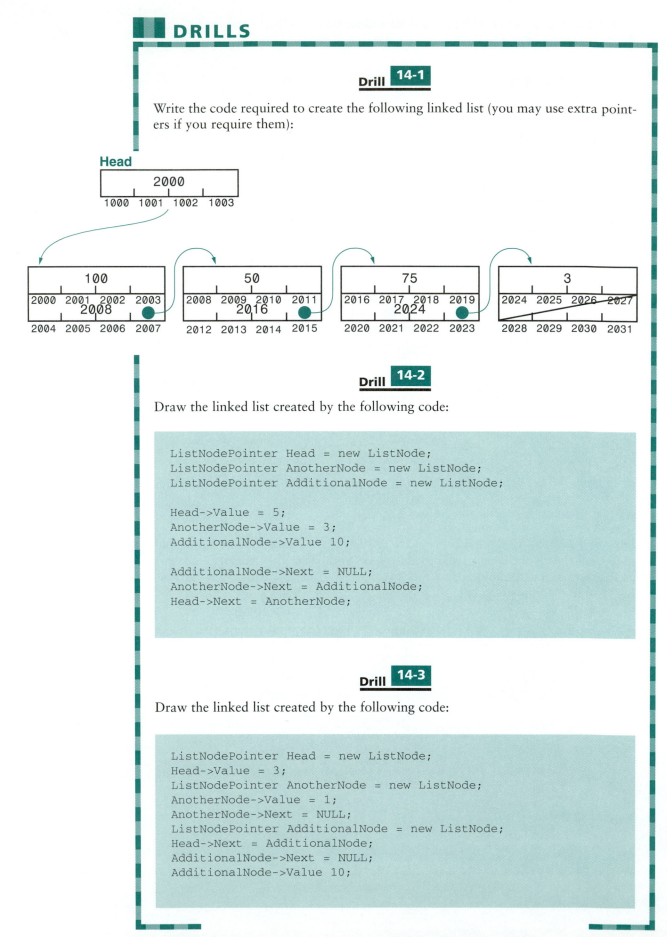

Drill 14-2

Draw the linked list created by the following code:

```
ListNodePointer Head = new ListNode;
ListNodePointer AnotherNode = new ListNode;
ListNodePointer AdditionalNode = new ListNode;

Head->Value = 5;
AnotherNode->Value = 3;
AdditionalNode->Value 10;

AdditionalNode->Next = NULL;
AnotherNode->Next = AdditionalNode;
Head->Next = AnotherNode;
```

Drill 14-3

Draw the linked list created by the following code:

```
ListNodePointer Head = new ListNode;
Head->Value = 3;
ListNodePointer AnotherNode = new ListNode;
AnotherNode->Value = 1;
AnotherNode->Next = NULL;
ListNodePointer AdditionalNode = new ListNode;
Head->Next = AdditionalNode;
AdditionalNode->Next = NULL;
AdditionalNode->Value = 10;
```

14.2 LINKED LIST CLASS IMPLEMENTATION

What we have just seen is the first step in writing a function to insert elements into a linked list. However, in a practical use of linked lists, we need to arbitrarily search, insert, and delete from a list. So instead of thinking about just writing a bunch of functions, let's use the proper C++ methodology and create a linked list class. By defining the interface from the beginning, we will have a clear understanding of the goals of our **List** class.

```
class List
{
    public:
        List();
        ~List();
        void Display();
        bool Search(int Val);
        void Insert(int Val);
        void InsertInOrder(int Val);
        void Remove(int Val);
    private:
        ListNodePointer Head;
};
```

The **List** class appears simple, but we will find that implementing it will not be quite so straightforward.

Constructor

The **List** class has a relatively simple constructor; all we need to do is initialize the **Head** pointer to **NULL**. This is implemented in the following code:

```
//List Class Constructor Code
List :: List()
{
    Head = NULL;
}
```

Destructor

However, implementing a properly written destructor for the **List** class will require returning all the dynamically allocated memory to the computer. This means that we must loop through the list, deleting each node along the way. See the following code:

```
List :: ~List()
{
    ListNodePointer Temp;

    while (Head)
    {
        Temp=Head->Next;
        delete Head;
        Head=Temp;
    }
}
```

PROGRAMMER'S NOTEBOOK

If you do not return all the memory used by a linked list, the programmer may not notice a problem initially, but as the program runs for a long time, memory will be lost and system problems will occur.

We create pointer called **Temp** for a very important reason. You might be tempted to delete the node pointed to by the **Head** pointer and then reassign the **Head** pointer to **Head->Next** until you get to the end of the list. However, if you are on a system that has more than one program running at once, then another program might allocate the memory you just returned to the system with the **delete** command. The system may change the value of the **Head** pointer before you can access **Head->Next**. This would lead to deleting memory not contained within your linked list and may crash your program, other programs, or the operating system.

Though we could rewrite the **while** condition as follows:

```
while(Head!=NULL)
```

This would be unnecessary. A **NULL** pointer will evaluate to **false**. Assuming **Head** is pointing to a node, the value at that node will then be removed; otherwise, the loop terminates.

Let's follow a step-by-step explanation of the deletion of the entire linked list containing the values 1, 2, and 3.

Initially, the list is intact and **Head** contains a non-**NULL** value. This is shown in Figure 14.13.

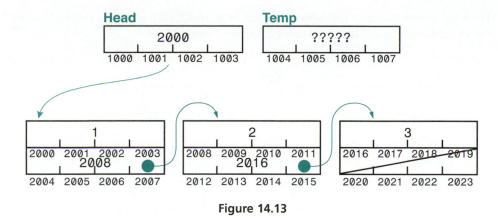

Figure 14.13

Since **Head** is not **NULL**, we enter the body of the **while** loop. The **Temp** pointer is assigned the address(2008) of the second node, shown in Figure 14.14.

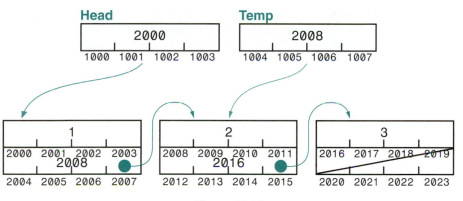

Figure 14.14

At this point, **Temp** is maintaining the link to the rest of the list. Therefore, we can delete the **Head** node. After deleting the **Head** node the value of **Head** is momentarily irrelevant (see Figure 14.15).

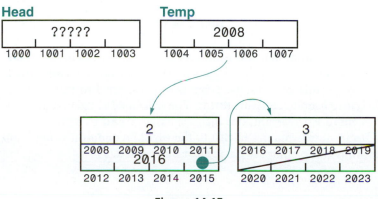

Figure 14.15

Then we assign **Head** to the address stored in **Temp**(2008), which is the address of the second node in the list. This can be seen in Figure 14.16.

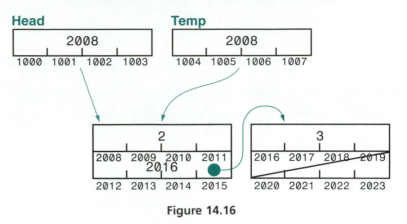

Figure 14.16

The **while** loop conditional test evaluates to **true** again, because **Head** is a non-**NULL** value. We enter the body of the **while** loop and the same process occurs. **Temp** is assigned the address(2016) of the third node. After deleting the **Head** node the value of **Head** is momentarily irrelevant, but then we assign **Head** to the address stored in **Temp**(2016), which is the address of the third node in the list. This can be seen in Figure 14.17.

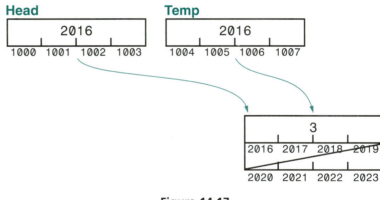

Figure 14.17

The **while** loop conditional test evaluates to true again, because **Head** is a non-**NULL** value. We enter the body of the **while** loop and the same **while** process occurs, but we get different results. **Temp** is now assigned to **NULL**, since the **Next** field of the current node contains **NULL**. The last node is deleted and momentarily the value of **Head** is irrelevant, but then we assign **Head** to **NULL** as well.

Since **Head** now evaluates to **NULL**, the **while** condition is false and the loop terminates, thus completing the **destructor** method.

Display

Display is a simple method that requires the traversal of a list similarly to the **destructor** method. However, instead of deleting each of the nodes as we visit them, we will display the contents of their **Value** fields. See the following code:

```
void List::Display()
{
    ListNodePointer Temp=Head;

    while(Temp)
    {
        cout<<Temp->Value<<endl;
        Temp=Temp->Next;
    }
}
```

If we wish to display a list, we must assign a temporary pointer to point to the first node. Otherwise, if we moved the **Head** pointer down the list after we displayed the list we would no longer have a handle to the beginning of the list. We will loop until the temporary pointer has the value **NULL**.

Assuming **Temp** is pointing to a node, the value at that node will be displayed. To move to the next node, we need to assign **Temp** the address stored in its **Next** field. This is accomplished with the following statement.

```
Temp = Temp->Next;
```

Figure 14.18 contains an example of the **Display** method being executed on a list containing the values 1, 2, and 3. Initially, the **Temp** pointer is assigned the value stored in the **Head** pointer. Therefore, the **Temp** pointer is pointing to the front of the list.

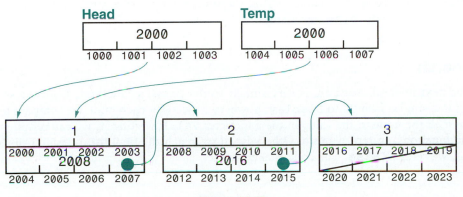

Figure 14.18

The value at the address stored in the **Temp** pointer (1) is displayed. **Temp** is then assigned the value in **Temp->Next** (2008). Now, **Temp** is pointing to the next node in the list as depicted in Figure 14.19.

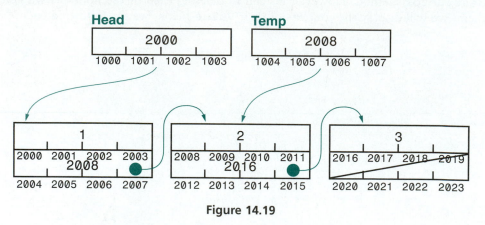

Figure 14.19

The value at the second node (2) is displayed and **Temp** is then assigned the value in **Temp->Next** (2016). Now, **Temp** is pointing to the final node in the list as depicted in Figure 14.20.

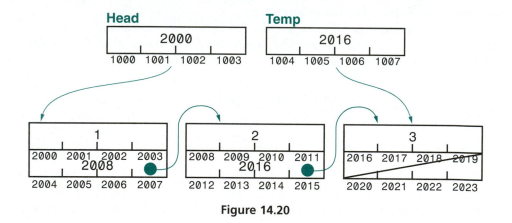

Figure 14.20

The value at the third node (3) is displayed and **Temp** is assigned the value in **Temp->Next**. Since **Temp** now equals **NULL**, the **while** loop terminates and we are finished executing the **Display** method.

Search

The next method, **Search**, is very similar to the **Display** method. We traverse a list in a similar fashion to **Display**; however, as we visit each node we compare the value at the node to the value in the parameter **Val**. If we find it, we can terminate the function and return **true**. Otherwise, if we reach the final **NULL** pointer in the list, we return **false**. The code is as follows:

```
bool List:: Search(int Val)
{
    ListNodePointer Temp=Head;

    while(Temp && Temp->Value != Val)
        Temp=Temp->Next;

    if (Temp)
        return true;
    else
        return false;
}
```

Let's trace through two examples of the **Search** method. First let's see what happens when we check if the value of parameter **Val** equals 2 and the list has the values 1, 2, and 3, respectively.

The method starts by assigning the **Temp** pointer to the address of the first node of the list, as seen in Figure 14.21.

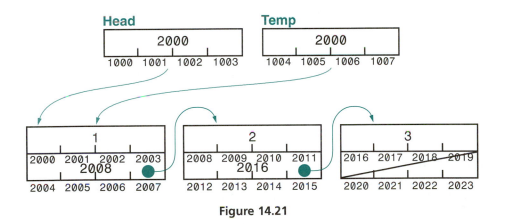

Figure 14.21

Now the condition in the **while** loop is evaluated, and since **Temp** is not **NULL**, the first half of the expression is **true**. **Temp->Value** evaluates to 1. Since this is not equal to the parameter **Val**, the second half of the expression is also **true**. Since both parts of the expression are **true**, the whole expression is **true**. Therefore, the body of the loop executes and the **Temp** pointer is reassigned to the next node. This can be seen in Figure 14.22.

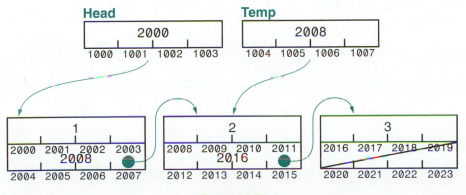

Figure 14.22

The condition of the **while** loop is evaluated again. **Temp** is still not **NULL**, so the first half of the expression is still **true**. However, now the second half of the expression evaluates to **false**. This is because the value of **Temp->Value** is now 2, which equals the value in the parameter **Val**.

Since the condition is **false**, the loop terminates and the final **if** statement is evaluated. Because we dropped out of the **while** loop before we reached the end of the list, the **Temp** pointer will contain an address other than **NULL**. Therefore, when we evaluate the **if** statement, **true** is returned from the function.

Now let's try an example of searching for a number that does not exist. If we attempt to search for the number 5 in a list containing 1, 2, and 3, respectively, we will proceed with the search the same way we did when searching for 2.

The method starts by assigning the **Temp** pointer to the address of the first node of the list, as shown in Figure 14.23.

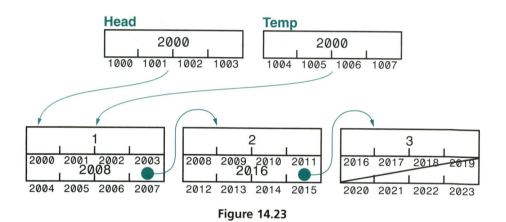

Figure 14.23

Then we proceed to check each node as we traverse down the list. As before, since **Temp->Value** evaluates to 1 and 1 is not the value we are searching for, we reassign the **Temp** pointer to the next node, shown in Figure 14.24.

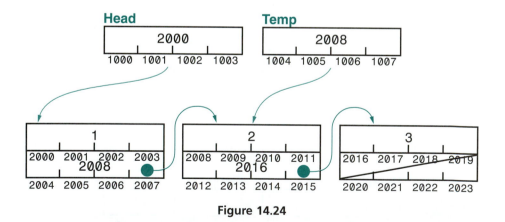

Figure 14.24

However, now when we enter the `while` loop, we do not terminate it as we did before. This time, although `Temp` does not evaluate to `NULL`, `Temp->Value` evaluates to 2, which is not the value we are looking for. Therefore, we execute the body of the loop again. This reassigns the `Temp` pointer to the value in the `Next` field of the node pointed to by `Temp`. This is shown in Figure 14.25.

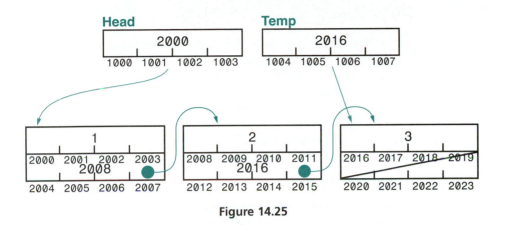

Figure 14.25

Once again we check to see if `Temp` evaluates to `NULL`, which it does not. Again we check to see if `Temp->Value` evaluates to the value we are searching for. Again, it does not. Therefore, we reassign the `Temp` pointer to the value in the `Next` field of the node pointed to by `Temp`. This is shown in Figure 14.26.

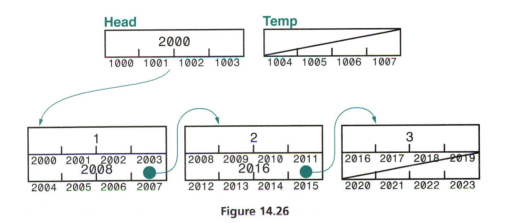

Figure 14.26

Notice that this time, the `Temp` pointer was assigned `NULL`. This is because there are no more nodes in the list. Therefore, when we evaluate `Temp` in the looping condition, the loop terminates.

Since the `Temp` pointer contains `NULL`, the final `if` expression evaluates to `false` and the method returns `false`.

PROGRAMMER'S NOTEBOOK

If a programmer has a pointer defined to point to a node, but the pointer equals NULL, the programmer cannot reference a value from that pointer using the -> operator.

Although the search code appears straightforward, there is one important subtlety that we have overlooked. Observe the following rewritten **while** statement:

```
while(Temp->Value != Val  && Temp)
```

The only change we have made is in the order of the evaluation of the terms of the **while** condition. Now we check in the **while** condition whether the value we are searching for is at the current node before we evaluate whether the **Temp** pointer is not **NULL**. However, this would be a big mistake. If the **Temp** pointer evaluates to **false**, thus containing the **NULL** pointer, then no node exists to check the first part of the condition. Although you might not think this is a problem, if **Temp** evaluates to false the entire expression will be false no matter what the first half of the condition evaluates to, so you would be setting your program up for a possible run-time error.

Imagine if **Temp** evaluated to 0, or **NULL**. When you ask to access **Temp->Value** you are asking to look at memory location 0. It is very possible that you will not have access to this location on your machine and will cause your application and maybe the operating system to crash.

The reason we write the expression in the original order is that C++'s short circuit evaluation prevents the second part of the conditional expression from being evaluated. In this case, if **Temp** evaluates to false, then there is no way for the expression to evaluate to be true, so the remainder of the condition is not evaluated. Short circuit analysis is discussed in detail in the conditional chapter.

Insertion

Inserting a value into the list can be done two ways. The easier process is to allocate and place a node at the beginning of the list, as we will see with the **Insert** method. The slightly more complicated process is to allocate the new node and place the value in its proper place (so that all the items in the list are in ascending order) as we will see with the **InsertInOrder** method.

Simple Insert

The simple **Insert** method doesn't specify that an order to the linked list needs to be maintained, therefore we insert the values at the front of the list. To accomplish this we:

- Store the new node with a temporary pointer
- Store the value to be added in the newly allocated node
- Point the **Next** pointer of the new node to **Head**
- Set **Head** to the temporary pointer

The code is as follows:

```
void List :: Insert(int Val)
{
    ListNodePointer Temp = new ListNode;
    Temp->Value = Val;
    Temp->Next = Head;
    Head = Temp;
}
```

In understanding the code, we need to examine two cases, even though they execute the same code.

First let's look at the case when nothing is contained in the list and the **Head** pointer equals **NULL**. The **Temp** pointer has been declared, but no memory address has been assigned to it yet (see Figure 14.27).

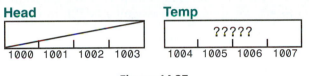

Figure 14.27

The first step is to allocate a new node and assign its address to the **Temp** pointer. In our example, the node allocated starts at memory address 2000, so 2000 is stored in the **Temp** pointer (see Figure 14.28).

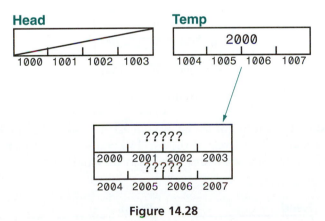

Figure 14.28

The next step is to initialize the new node's value to the value we wish to insert (see Figure 14.29).

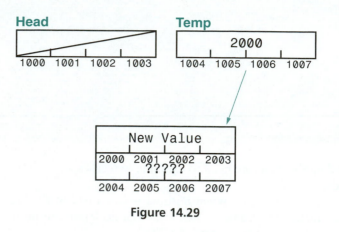

Figure 14.29

Now we need to assign the **Next** pointer of the node pointed to by **Temp** to the remainder of the list. However, in this case, there is no remainder, so when we assign **Temp->Next** to **Head**, we are actually assigning NULL to the **Next** pointer (see Figure 14.30).

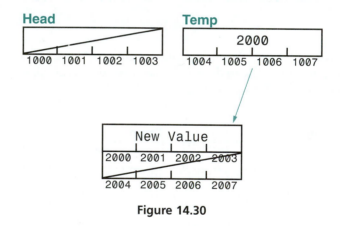

Figure 14.30

Finally, we assign **Head** to point to the same place as **Temp**, thus making the node pointed to by **Temp** the first node of the list. In Figure 14.31 you can see the completed insert of a value into what was previously an empty list.

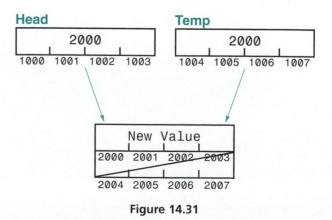

Figure 14.31

The second case is similar. In this case, we have a list that already contains nodes as seen in Figure 14.32.

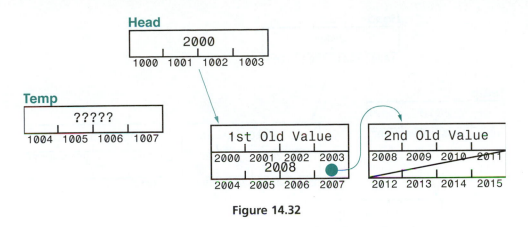

Figure 14.32

We start as we did in the previous example by assigning the **Temp** pointer to a newly allocated node. The new node in our example is located at memory address 2016 (see Figure 14.33).

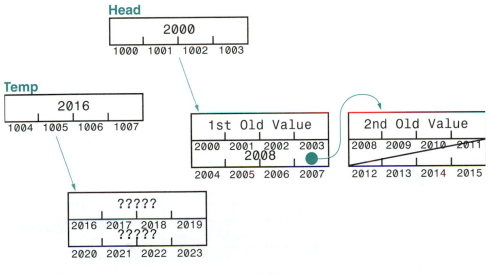

Figure 14.33

Similarly to the first example, we initialize the new node's value to the value we wish to insert (see Figure 14.34).

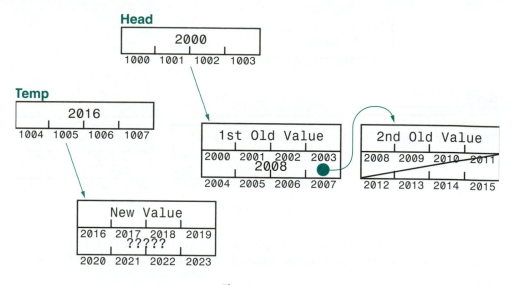

Figure 14.34

However, now when we assign the next pointer of the node pointed to by the **Temp** pointer to the **Head** pointer, the **Head** pointer contains the address of the first node in the remainder of the list (see Figure 14.35).

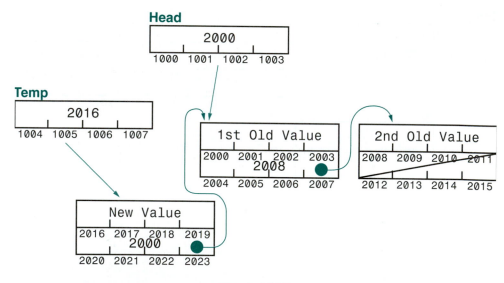

Figure 14.35

Finally, we assign `Head` to point to the same node as the node pointed to by the `Temp` pointer, thus making the node pointed to by `Temp` the first node of the list (see Figure 14.36).

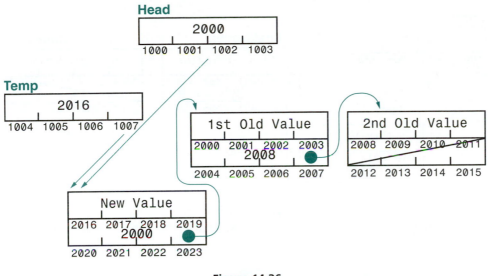

Figure 14.36

Be aware, when dealing with linked lists, the order of our statements is extremely important. If we wrote our insert method in the following order, what do you think would happen?

- Store the new node with a temporary pointer
- Store the value to be added in the newly allocated node
- Set `Head` to the `Temp` pointer
- Point the `Next` pointer of the new node to `Head`

Everything appears fine until the last step is executed. When we attempt to set the `Next` pointer of the new node to what should be the remainder of the list, we find that `Head` already contains the pointer to the new node. This means the remainder of the list is lost. The process is shown in Figures 14.37 and 14.38.

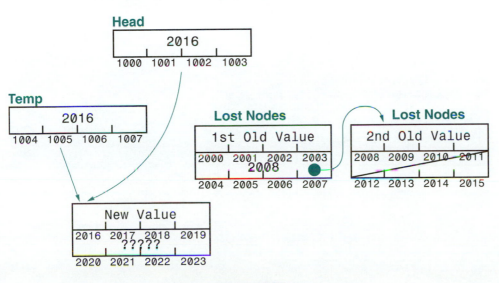

Figure 14.37
Everything is fine after first two steps.

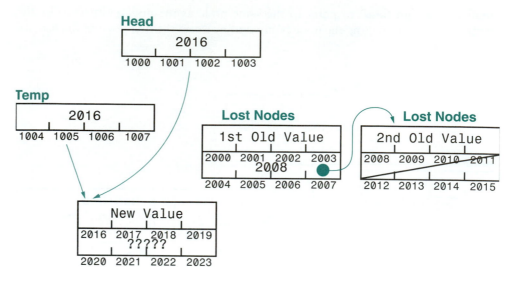

Figure 14.38
Old values in list are no longer pointed to after third step is executed!

> **PROGRAMMER'S NOTEBOOK**
>
> At no point while processing linked lists should you ever break the chain from the beginning of the list to the end, unless you previously have stored the broken link in a temporary pointer.

Insert in Order

Although the earlier **Insert** method is simple to implement, it is not very useful if we wish to display the items of the list in order. By changing the implementation to insert the values in order we slow the execution of the **Insert** method, but improve the speed of searching with only minor modifications to the **Search** method. Furthermore, we are not required to make any changes to the **Display** method, even though now it will print the values in order. The code is as follows:

```cpp
void List::InsertInOrder(int Val)
{
    ListNodePointer Curr = Head;
    ListNodePointer Prev = NULL;

    ListNodePointer Temp = new ListNode;
    Temp->Value = Val;
```

```
    // Loop through the list until the end or item is found
    while((Curr) && (Curr->Value < Val))
    {
        Prev =  Curr;
        Curr = Curr->Next;
    }

    //Perform the actual insert.
    Temp->Next = Curr;
    if (Prev)  //Inserting in the middle of the list
       Prev->Next = Temp;
    else  //Inserting into the front of the list
       Head = Temp;
}
```

To understand the code we must analyze four cases:

- Inserting into an empty list
- Inserting into the beginning of a list already containing nodes
- Inserting into the middle of a list already containing nodes
- Inserting at the end of a list already containing nodes

Inserting into an Empty List

To insert into a empty list, we are stating that the **Head** pointer is equal to **NULL**. Therefore, the **Curr** and **Prev** pointers get initialized to **NULL** at the beginning of the method. In all cases, we will allocate a new node and set the **Temp** pointer to the address of the new node. We initialize the value field of the newly allocated node to the **Val** parameter.

We evaluate the conditional expression of the **while** statement, but since **Curr** is equal to **NULL**, it evaluates to false and the body of the loop never executes. We now compare the pointer **Prev** in the conditional expression of the **if** statement and it evaluates to false. Therefore, we assign the **Head** pointer to the address of the new node. Finally, we set the **Next** field of the new node to equal the address stored in the **Curr** pointer. Since **Curr** equals **NULL**, the **Next** field is assigned **NULL**. We are left with a list containing one node, the newly inserted one.

Inserting into the Beginning of a List Containing Nodes

Next, we need to step through the case where we insert a new value into an existing list, inserting it before all the nodes previously contained in the list. Observe the following example as we insert the value 10 into a list that previously contained the values 20 and 30.

Initially, the list is composed of two nodes containing the values 20 and 30. The **Curr** pointer is set to the first node and the **Prev** pointer is set to **NULL**. We allocate a new node and set the pointer **Temp** to its address. We also set the value field of the newly allocated node to 10. This can be seen in Figure 14.39.

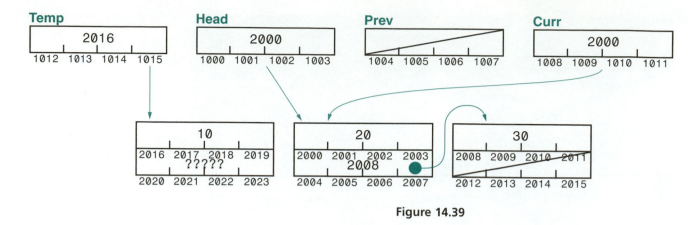

Figure 14.39

The next step is to evaluate the **while** loop expression. Since **Curr** points to the first node, it contains the value 2000 and is not **NULL**. Therefore, the first half of the expression evaluates to true. However, the second half of the expression compares the value in the first node of the list to the value we wish to insert. Since 20 is not less than 10, the second half of the **while** condition evaluates to false. Therefore the entire **while** loop expression evaluates to false and we do not execute the body of the **while** loop.

We continue executing the method by assigning the **Next** field in the newly allocated node to the address of the node pointed to by **Curr**(2000). This can be seen in Figure 14.40.

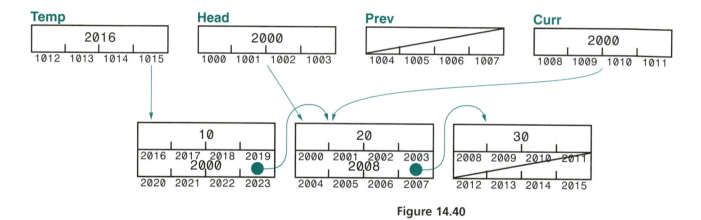

Figure 14.40

Finally, the **if** statement expression is evaluated. Since we have not moved down the list at all, the **Prev** pointer still contains the value **NULL**, and therefore the expression evaluates to **False**. Assigning the **Head** pointer to the address of the newly allocated node thus completes the **Insert**. This can be seen in Figure 14.41.

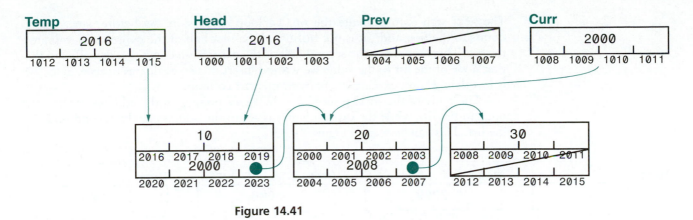

Figure 14.41

Inserting into the Middle of a List Containing Nodes

The next case we need to step through is when we wish to insert a new value into an existing list, inserting it in between nodes previously contained in the list. Observe the following example as we insert the value 25 into a list that contains the values 20 and 30.

Initially, the list is composed of two nodes containing the values 20 and 30, respectively. As in the previous example, the **Curr** pointer is set to the first node and the **Prev** pointer is set to **NULL**. We allocate a new node and set the pointer **Temp** to its address. We also set the value field of the newly allocated node to 25. This can be seen in Figure 14.42.

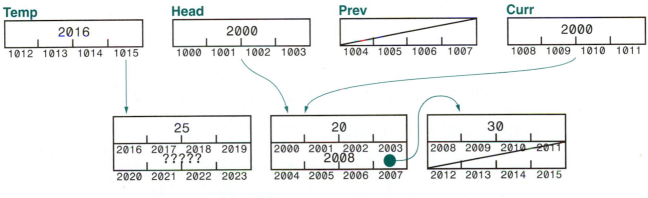

Figure 14.42

The next step is to evaluate the **while** loop expression. As before, since **Curr** points to the first node, it is not **NULL** and the first half of the expression evaluates to true. This time when the second half of the expression compares the value in the first node of the list to the value we wish to insert, it also evaluates to true. Since 20 is less than 25, we execute the body of the **while** loop.

The body of the **while** loop sets the **Prev** pointer to the address of the first node in the list, while the **Curr** pointer is set to the address of the second node in the list. This can be seen in Figure 14.43.

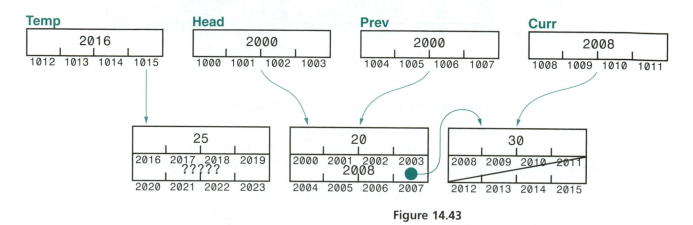

Figure 14.43

The **while** loop expression is evaluated again. The **Curr** pointer is still non-**NULL** because it points to the second node in the list. However, the value at that node is no longer less than the value we wish to insert, therefore the **while** loop terminates.

Next we assign the **Next** field in the newly allocated node to the address of the node pointed to by **Curr**. Temporarily, the node containing 30 is pointed to by two nodes. This will be fixed momentarily. This can be seen in Figure 14.44.

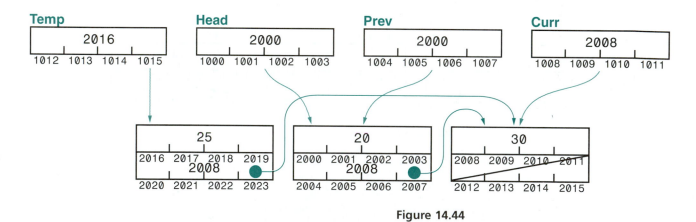

Figure 14.44

Finally, the `if` statement expression is evaluated. Since we have moved down the list, the `Prev` pointer is set to the node directly before where we are going to insert the new node. We must assign the `Next` field of that node to the newly allocated node thus completing the `Insert`. This corrects the problem of two nodes pointing to the node containing 30. This can be seen in Figure 14.45.

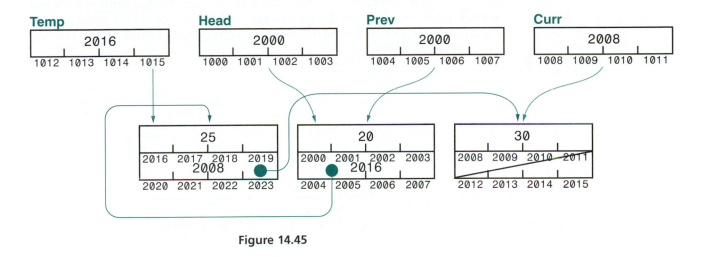

Figure 14.45

Our job is now complete; however, let's reorganize the diagram so that it is easier to read, as shown in Figure 14.46.

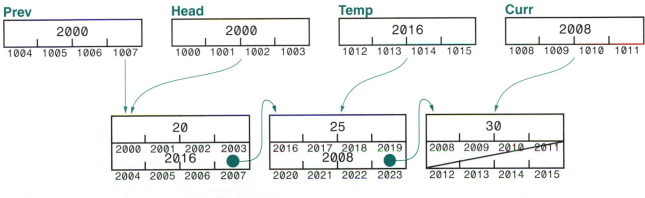

Figure 14.46

Inserting at the End of a List Containing Nodes

The final case we step through is to insert a value at the end of a list that already contains nodes. The following example inserts 40 into a list that previously contained 20 and 30.

Initially, the list is composed of two nodes containing the values 20 and 30, respectively. As in the previous example, the **Curr** pointer is set to the first node and the **Prev** pointer is set to **NULL**. We allocate a new node and set the pointer **Temp** to its address. We also set the value field of the newly allocated node to 40. This can be seen in Figure 14.47.

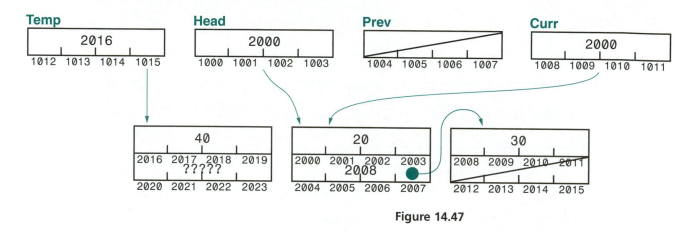

Figure 14.47

The next step is to evaluate the **while** loop expression. As before, since **Curr** points to the first node, it is not **NULL** and the first half of the expression evaluates to **true**. The second half of the expression compares the value in the first node of the list to the value we wish to insert; it also evaluates to **true**. Since 20 is less than 40, we execute the body of the **while** loop.

The body of the **while** loop sets the **Prev** pointer to the address of the first node in the list, and the **Curr** pointer is set to the address of the second node in the list. This can be seen in Figure 14.48.

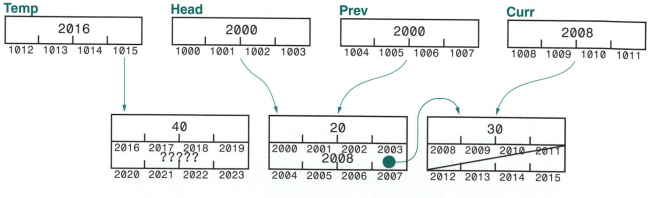

Figure 14.48

The `while` loop expression is evaluated again. The `Curr` pointer is still non-`NULL` because it points to the second node in the list. The second half of the expression still evaluates to `true` since the value pointed to by `Curr` is 30 and the value we are inserting is 40. Therefore we execute the body of the `while` loop one more time. This time, `Prev` is set to point to the last node in the list, and `Curr` is set to `NULL`. This is because the `Next` field of the node containing 30 contains `NULL`, as shown in Figure 14.49.

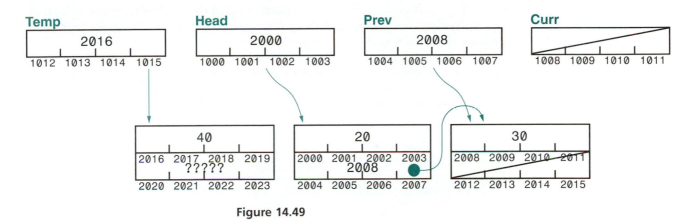

Figure 14.49

Now when we evaluate the `while` loop condition, it evaluates to `false` and drops out of the loop. The `Next` field of the node pointed to by `Temp` is set to the value in `Curr(NULL)`. The final step is to set the `Next` field of the node pointed to by `Prev` to the address stored in the `Temp` pointer(2016). This connects the end of the list to the new node. This is shown in Figure 14.50.

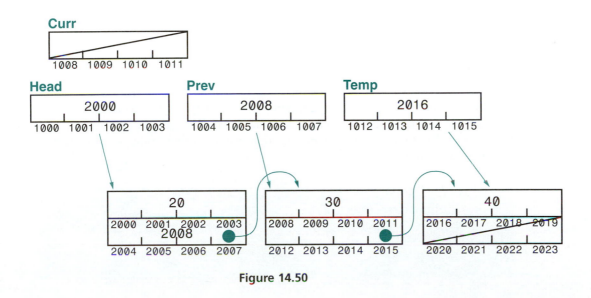

Figure 14.50

Improved Search

Now that we have added the method **InsertInOrder**, we can assume that the items in the list are already in ascending order. We can make the assumption that if the current value in the list is greater than the value we are searching for, that the value we are searching for is not contained in the list.

All that is required is to modify the **while** condition, so we add the clause to check if the current value is less than the parameter **Val**. If so, that indicates that we want to continue searching. It is important to list the conditions in the order that they are presented. Otherwise, if the pointer **Temp** evaluates to **NULL** we may get a run-time error upon evaluating **Temp->Value**.

The other change we must make is to add a condition to the **if** expression to check if we dropped out of the **while** loop because we found the value we were searching for. Again the order of the expressions is important for the same reasons as before. The new code follows:

```
bool List:: Search(int Val)
{
   ListNodePointer Temp = Head;

   while(Temp && Temp->Value < Val)
     Temp=Temp->Next;

   if ((Temp) && (Temp->Value == Val))
     return true;
   else
     return false;
}
```

Remove

Finally, we implement the **Remove** method. To remove a value from a list, we are required to find the node that contains it. Similarly to the **InsertInOrder** method, we are required to keep a trailing pointer to the node we just visited. Then when we realize that we need the pointer that points to that node, we already have it. Observe the following code.

```
void List::Remove(int Val)
{
   ListNodePointer Curr = Head;
   ListNodePointer Prev = NULL;
```

```
    while(Curr)
    {
        if (Curr->Value == Val)
        {
            if (Prev == NULL) //Removing first node
                Head = Curr->Next;
            else //Removing a normal node
                Prev->Next = Curr->Next;
            delete Curr; //In either case
            return;
        }
        else //Move to the next item in the list
        {
            Prev = Curr;
            Curr = Curr->Next;
        }
    }
}
```

To understand the code we must analyze three cases:

- Removing from the beginning of a list containing nodes
- Removing from the middle of a list containing nodes
- Removing from the end of a list containing nodes

Removing from the Beginning of a List Containing Nodes

To understand the removal of a node at the beginning of the list, observe the following example as we wish to remove the value 10 from a list that contains the values 10, 20, and 30.

Initially, the **Curr** pointer is set to the first node of the list and the **Prev** pointer is set to **NULL**, as shown in Figure 14.51.

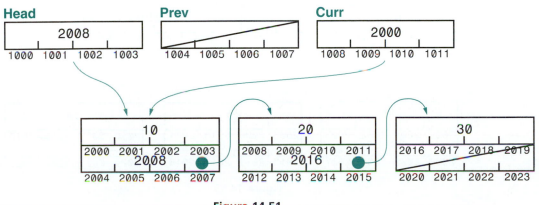

Figure 14.51

We evaluate the looping condition, and because **Curr** contains the address of the first node, it is not **NULL** and therefore **true**.

Next, we evaluate the first **if** statement expression and find that the **Value** field of the current node is equal to the value we wish to remove. We then check to see if we are removing the first node, which we are. Therefore, we set the new beginning of the list to the node indicated in the **Next** field of the **Curr** pointer. This can be seen in Figure 14.52.

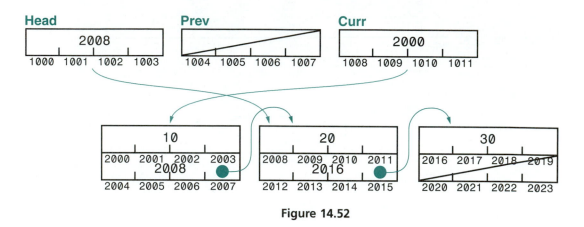

Figure 14.52

The final step is then to issue a **delete** command so that the memory of the node we are removing is returned to the operation system.

Removing from the Middle of a List Containing Nodes

To understand the removal of a node at the middle of the list, observe the following example as we wish to remove the value 20 from a list that contains the values 10, 20, and 30.

As in the previous example, initially the **Curr** pointer is set to the first node of the list and the **Prev** pointer is set to **NULL**, as shown in Figure 14.53.

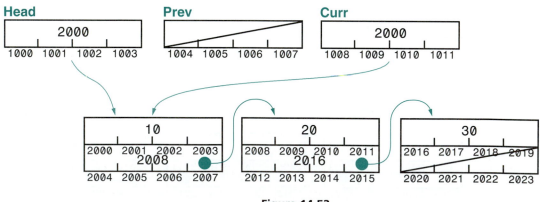

Figure 14.53

We evaluate the looping condition, and because **Curr** contains the address of the first node, it is not **NULL** and is therefore **true**.

Next, we evaluate the first **if** statement expression and find that the value field of the current node is not equal to the value we wish to remove. Therefore, we execute the **else** statement and move the **Curr** pointer to the second node and set the **Prev** pointer to the first node, as shown in Figure 14.54.

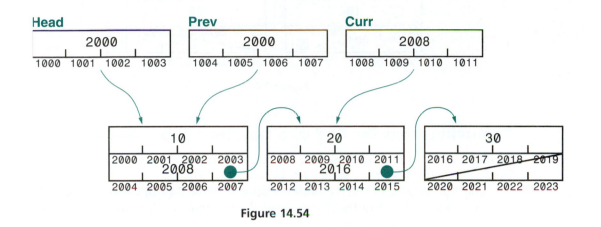

Figure 14.54

Once again we evaluate the looping condition and find that **Curr** contains the address of the second node. It is not **NULL** and is therefore **true**.

Next, we evaluate the first **if** statement expression and find that the **Value** field of the current node is now equal to the value we wish to remove.

We then check to see if we are removing the first node, which we are not. Therefore, we set the **Next** field of the node pointed to by **Prev** to the **Next** field of the node we are going to remove. This can be seen Figure 14.55.

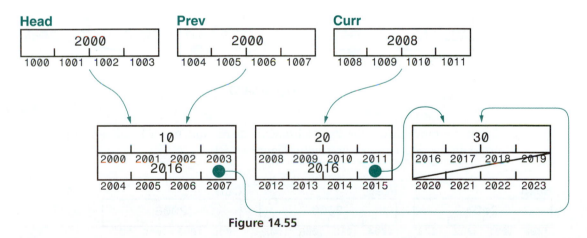

Figure 14.55

The final step is then to issue a **delete** command so that the memory of the node we are removing is returned to the operation system, as shown in Figure 14.56.

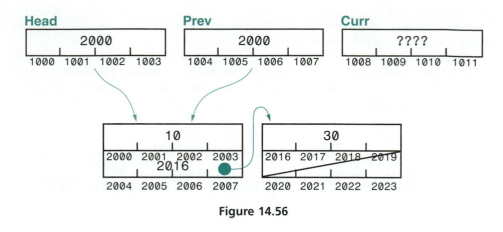

Figure 14.56

Removing from the End of a List Containing Nodes

To understand the removal of a node at the end of a list, let's remove the value 30 from a list that contains the values 10, 20, and 30.

The beginning execution is exactly the same as in the previous example. Initially the **Curr** pointer is set to the first node of the list and the **Prev** pointer is set to NULL, as shown in Figure 14.57.

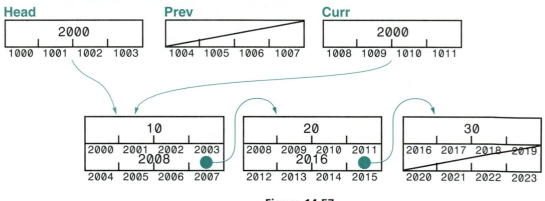

Figure 14.57

Again we move down the linked list with **Curr** and **Prev** being set to the next nodes in the list. This can be seen in Figure 14.58.

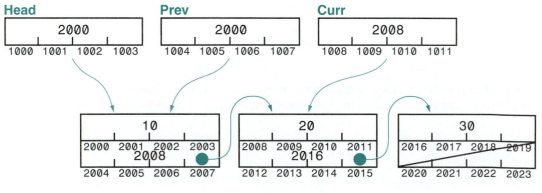

Figure 14.58

However, since we are attempting to remove the node containing 30 from the list, we no longer break out of the **while** loop as in the previous example.

Since the **Curr** pointer is not equal to **NULL**, we enter the **while** loop. Since the value stored at the node is not equal to 30, we execute the **else** statement. This increments the **Prev** and **Curr** pointers to the next nodes in the list. This can be seen in Figure 14.59.

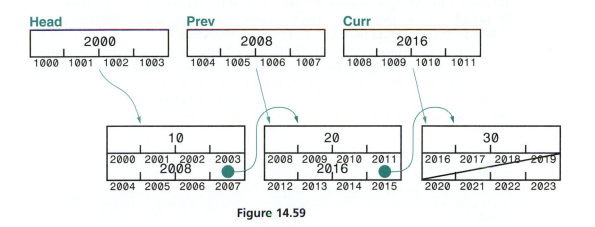

Figure 14.59

Once again the **while** loop condition evaluates to true and we enter the **while** loop. This time however, the **if** statement evaluates to **true**. Since **Prev** is not equal to **NULL**, the **else** statement is executed. Therefore the **Next** field of the node pointed to by **Prev** is set to the **Next** field of the node pointed to by **Curr**. Since the **Next** field of the node pointed to by **Curr** is equal to **NULL**, then the **Next** field of the node pointed to by **Prev** is set to **NULL**. Additionally, the **Curr** node is deleted. This can be seen Figure 14.60.

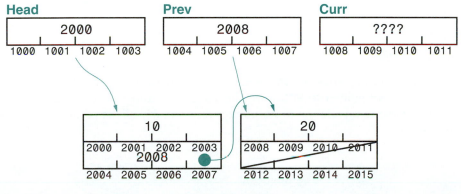

Figure 14.60

14.3 HEADER NODE LINKED LIST IMPLEMENTATION

Although the linked list code we wrote executes correctly, you may have noticed the code we implemented has special cases because we have to worry about whether the list is empty or if the first node is the one we wish to delete. Our class can be simplified by adding only a single node to the front of the list in the constructor method. By adding a blank node to the front of the list, we no longer have the special case of **Head** equaling **NULL**; thus we alleviate these problems.

Observe the cleaner, newly written class for **List**. Notice that the class definition itself doesn't change, which is extremely important when considering code maintenance. It means that any code written using the **List** class will not have to be modified when we switch implementations of the **List** class. If possible, modifications to a class for efficiency purposes should remain internal to the class.

```
class List
{
    public:
       List();
       ~List();
       void Display();
       void Insert(int Val);
       void InsertInOrder(int Val);
       bool Search(int Val);
       void Remove(int Val);
    private:
       ListNodePointer Head;
};
```

Constructor

The first method that must be changed is the constructor method. Instead of initializing the **Head** pointer to **NULL**, we allocate a node and set the **Head** pointer to it. We also must terminate the **Next** pointer of the newly allocated node. The new code follows:

```
List::List()
{
    Head = new ListNode;
    Head->Next= NULL;
}
```

Therefore, every list upon creation will look like Figure 14.61.

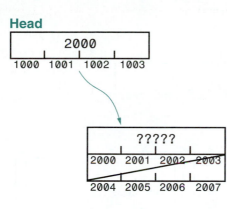

Figure 14.61

Although we could place a value in the **Value** field of the header node, there is no advantage to this. We will be ignoring this value in all of our methods.

Destructor

The next method, the destructor, does not change at all from the previous implementation. We must start at the **Head** pointer and traverse the list deleting all the nodes along the way.

Display

We are, however, required to modify the **Display** method. No longer do we wish to display the value of the first node in the list. Remember, the first node's **Value** field is never assigned. Therefore, we simply start the **Temp** pointer at the **Head->Next** node instead of the one pointed to by **Head**. The modified code follows:

```
void List::Display()
{
    ListNodePointer Temp = Head->Next;
    while(Temp)
    {
        cout<<Temp->Value<<endl;
        Temp = Temp->Next;
    }
}
```

In Figure 14.62 we can see the starting location of the **Temp** pointer. Once the **Temp** pointer is in this position, the remainder of the **Display** method functions as it did in the previous implementation.

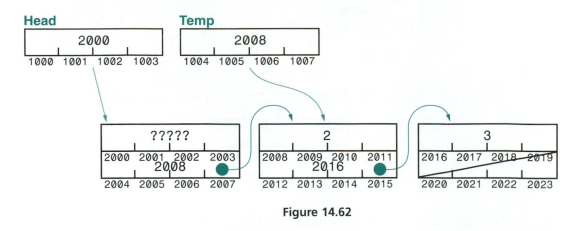

Figure 14.62

Search

The modified **Search** method parallels the **Display** method. The only difference between the new and old implementation is that the **Temp** pointer is initialized to **Head->Next** instead of **Head**. As with the **Display** method, this simply skips the header node before we begin to search the list. The code follows:

```
bool List:: Search(int Val)
{
    ListNodePointer Temp=Head->Next;

    while(Temp && Temp->Value < Val)
        Temp=Temp->Next;

    if ((Temp) && (Temp->Value == Val))
        return true;
    else
        return false;
}
```

Insert

Although this method will not really be necessary once we rewrite the **InsertInOrder** method, for consistency purposes we will add it.

The simple **Insert** method requires only minor modification from the previous implementation. All we need to change is the reference to **Head** in the previous code. It will be set to **Head->Next** in the modified code.

The modified code is as follows:

```
void List :: Insert(int Val)
{
    ListNodePointer Temp = new ListNode;
    Temp->Value = Val;
    Temp->Next = Head->Next;
    Head->Next = Temp;
}
```

The first two statements in the method are identical to the previous version of **Insert**. Assuming that values existed in the list before the **Insert** method is called, the memory allocation would look like Figure 14.63.

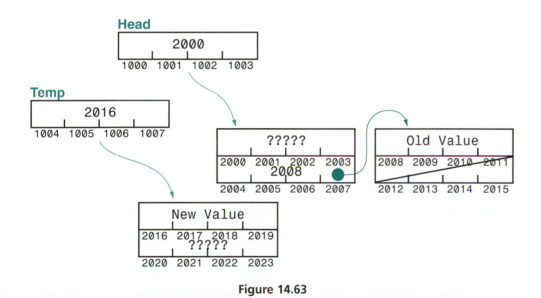

Figure 14.63

The next statement links the new node into the list after the header node, but before the remainder of the nodes. First it must assign the **Next** field of the newly allocated node to point to the same place as the **Next** field of the header node. This can been seen in Figure 14.64.

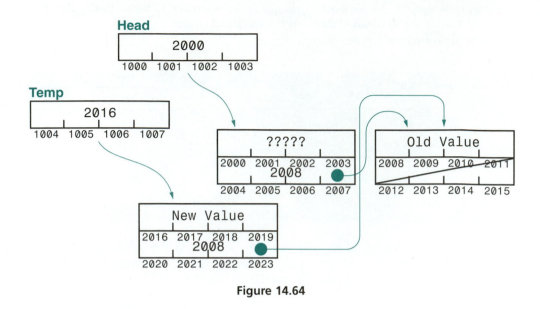

Figure 14.64

Finally, we need to set the **Next** pointer of the header node to the address of the newly allocated node. Upon completing this step, the list is intact with the newly allocated node in the proper place (see Figure 14.65).

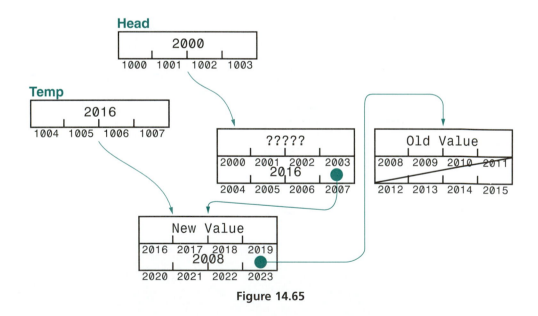

Figure 14.65

Figure 14.66 is a cleaner representation of Figure 14.65.

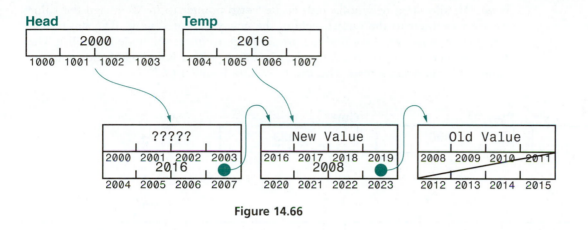

Figure 14.66

Insert in Order

To maintain a list in ascending order, upon each insertion we need to search for the proper place to insert the item. We wish to insert it so that the node before it contains a value that is less than the value we are inserting, and the node after the new node contains a value greater than the value we are inserting.

While searching for the place to insert we must keep track not only of the current node, but of the previous node as well. As in the non-header node code, we require a pointer to the node that is less than the value we wish to insert, as well as a pointer to the node that is greater than the value we wish to insert. This way we can easily link the new node into the list. The main difference between the non-header node implementation and this implementation is that we no longer need a special case of checking to see if we are inserting at the beginning of the list. See the following code:

```
void List::InsertInOrder(int Val)
{
    ListNodePointer Curr = Head->Next;
    ListNodePointer Prev = Head;

    ListNodePointer Temp = new ListNode;
    Temp->Value = Val;

    while((Curr) && (Curr->Value <= Val))
    {
        Prev=Curr;
        Curr=Curr->Next;
    }
    Prev->Next = Temp;
    Temp->Next = Curr;
}
```

This code could be rewritten so that we only maintained one temporary pointer, **Prev**; however, the code would be slightly more complicated so we have avoided it.

In the following example, we insert 25 into a list that contains 10, 20, and 30.

Initially, we have a list with three values 10, 20, and 30, and a blank header node. We allocate a new node and set the **Temp** pointer to it. We assign the value we wish to insert to the **Value** field of the newly allocated node. The **Next** field remains unknown until we find the proper place to insert the node in the list. The **Prev** pointer is set to the header node. The **Curr** pointer is set to the node with the value 10 in the **Value** field. This can be seen in Figure 14.67.

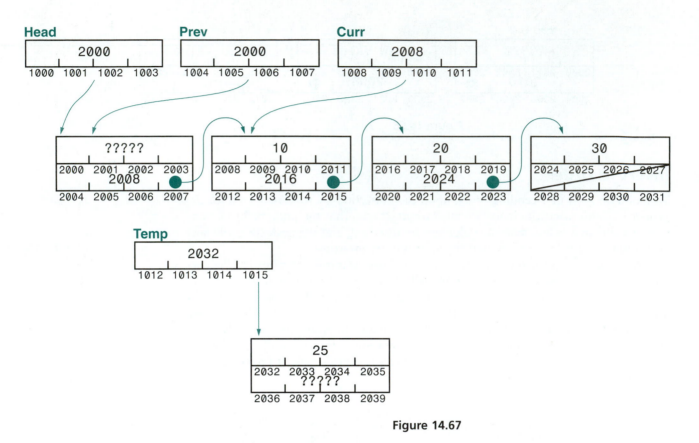

Figure 14.67

We execute the **while** loop until the value at the node pointed to by **Curr** is less than or equal to 25. Since 10 is less than 25, we reset the **Prev** and **Curr** pointers so they each point to the next node in the list. This can be seen in Figure 14.68.

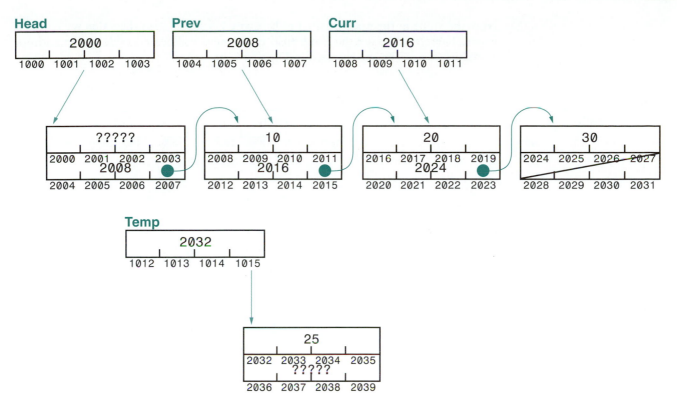

Figure 14.68

Again the value in the node pointed to by **Curr** is less than 25, so we reset the **Prev** and **Curr** pointers again. This can be seen in Figure 14.69.

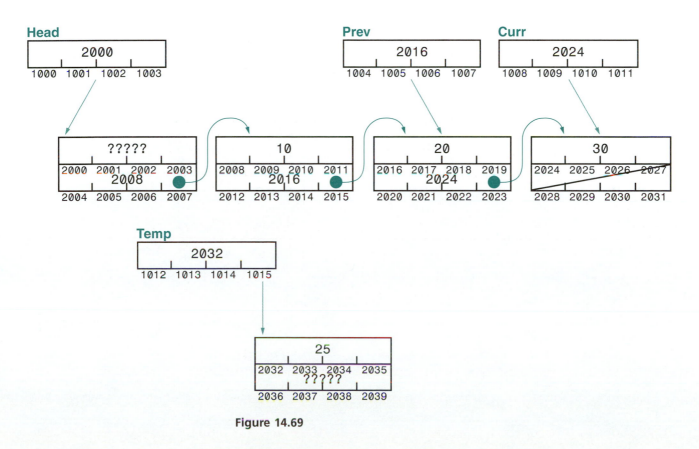

Figure 14.69

Now the value in the node pointed to by **Curr** is greater than the value we want to insert. Therefore, we set the **Next** field of the newly allocated node to the address stored in **Curr**. This can be seen in Figure 14.70.

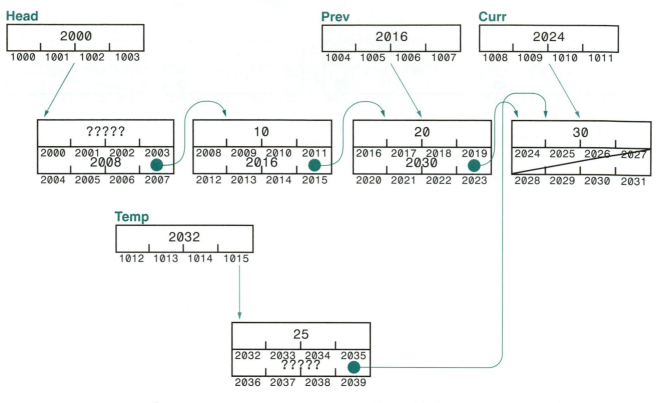

Figure 14.70

The last step is to assign the **Next** field of the node pointed to by **Prev** to the address of the newly allocated node, as shown in Figure 14.71.

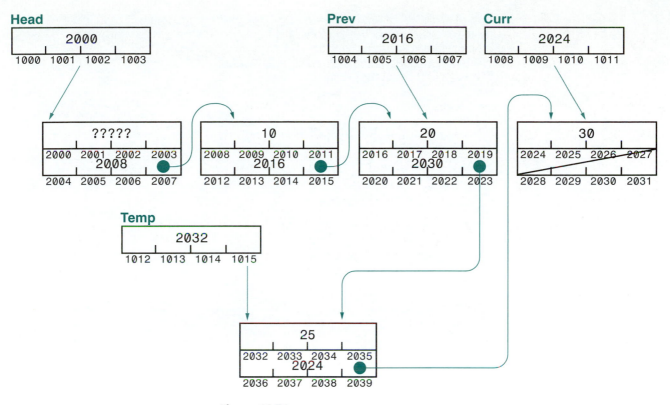

Figure 14.71

Remove

To remove a node in a header list we need to search for the item to remove. While searching for the node we must keep track not only of the current node, but the previous node as well. As in the nonheader node code, we require a pointer to the node that is prior to the one we wish to delete so that we can maintain the link from the previous node's **Next** field to the node after the one we wish to delete.

Because of the header node at the beginning of the list, we no longer require a special case to initialize our method. We set the **Prev** pointer to the header node's address and set the **Curr** pointer to the address contained in the header node's next field.

We search through the list, moving both the **Curr** and **Prev** pointers down the list, until we find the value we are looking for. Once found, we set the **Next** field of the **Prev** pointer to the address stored in the **Next** field of the **Curr** node. Then we delete the node pointed to by **Curr** and the task is complete. See the following code:

```
void List::Remove(int Val)
{
    ListNodePointer Curr = Head->Next;
    ListNodePointer Prev = Head;

    while(Curr)
    {
      if (Curr->Value == Val)
      {
          Prev->Next = Curr->Next;
          delete Curr;
          return;
      }
      else //move to the next item in the list
      {
          Prev = Curr;
          Curr = Curr->Next;
      }
    }
}
```

Observe the code in action with an example of removing the node with a value of 2 from a list containing 1, 2, and 3.

Initially, we have a list with three values 1, 2, and 3, and a blank header node. The **Prev** pointer is set to the header node. The **Curr** pointer is set to the node with the value 1 in the **Value** field (see Figure 14.72).

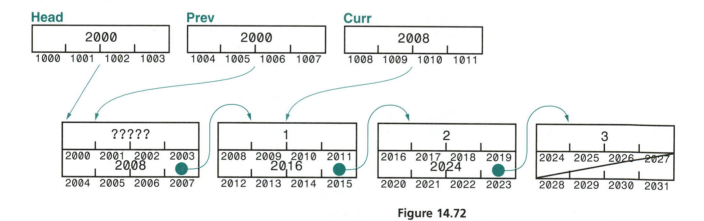

Figure 14.72

Since the value of the current node is 1 and does not equal the value we are searching for, we set **Prev** to the address stored in **Curr** and then set **Curr** to the address stored in the **Next** field of the **Curr** pointer (see Figure 14.73).

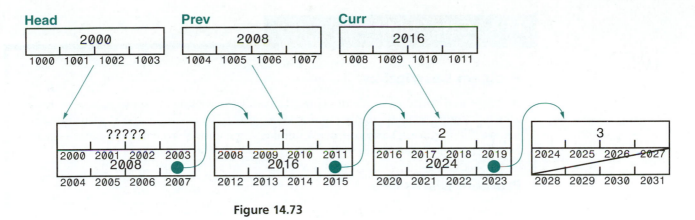

Figure 14.73

Now that **Curr** is pointing to the node with 2 contained within it. We enter the body of the **if** statement. The **Next** field of **Prev** pointer is set to the address stored in the **Next** field of the **Curr** node as shown in Figure 14.74.

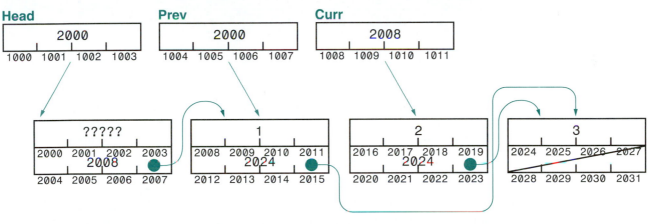

Figure 14.74

Once the link had been established it is OK to delete the node pointed to by the **Curr** pointer, as shown in Figure 14.75.

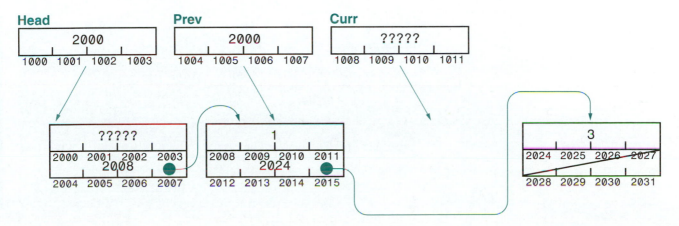

Figure 14.75

14.4 Case Study

Problem Description

A simple real-world example of using a linked list is writing an application to track a student's social security number and average grade. To track the social security number we will require a **long** to track a number large enough to handle a social security number and a **float** to store the average grade for the student.

Problem Discussion

To make a linked list class work with this data we will have to make some modifications. We can start by changing the structure to the linked list node as follows:

```
struct ListNode
{
    long SSN;
    float Average;
    ListNode * Next;
};
```

In addition, we need to make a few modifications to the **List** class. It should be obvious that we need to modify the **Insert** and **InsertInOrder** methods to accept a social security number as well as an average grade. In addition, the **Remove** method must be changed so that it accepts a social security number as well. Finally, the **Search** method must be modified so that it accepts a social security number to search for as well as an average grade that will be returned. However, because we need to return whether or not the social security number is found as well as the actual average associated to the social security number, we need to pass the average grade by reference.

Solution

```
class List
{
    public:
        List();
        ~List();
        void Display();
        bool Search(long SSN, float & Average);
        void Insert(long SSN, float  Average);
        void InsertInOrder(long SSN, float Average);
        void Remove(long SSN);
    private:
        ListNodePointer Head;
};
```

The actual method implementation requires minor changes and is left as an exercise to the reader.

To use our new **List** class, see the following example. In it we read 100 sets of social security numbers and grades. Then the program asks the user to enter social security numbers to search the list for. The program ends when a negative number is entered for a social security number.

```cpp
#include <stdlib.h>
#include <iostream.h>


//Tree definitions included here

void main()
{
    List StudentsAverages;
    int StudentCounter;
    long StudentNumber;
    float StudentAverage;

    //Read in 100 grades and insert them into the Tree.
    for(StudentCounter=0; StudentCounter < 100; StudentCounter++)
    {
        cout<<"Enter the Student's Social Security Number"<<endl;
        cin>>StudentNumber;
        cout<<"Enter the Student's average"<<endl;
        cin>>StudentAverage;
        StudentAverages.Insert(StudentNumber, StudentAverage);
    }


    do
    {
        cin>>StudentNumber;
        if (StudentNumber >= 0)
        {
            StudentAverages.Search(StudentNumber, StudentAverage)
            cout<<"The student's average is "
                <<StudentAverage<<endl;
    } while (StudentNumber >=0)
}
```

♦ Key Terms

Empty list	A linked list that contains no nodes. It is simply a NULL pointer.
Header node	A blank node in a special type of linked list. It is the first node and its existence makes writing the methods for a linked list simpler.
Linked list	A general-purpose dynamic data structure that allows its size to grow without having to decide its exact size at its time of instantiation.
Next pointer	A pointer in a node of a linked list that connects the current node to the next node in the list.
Node	A structure that contains the information for an item in the list as well as a pointer to the next node in the list.
Ordered list	A linked list than maintains the items in the list in order.
Unordered list	A linked list that does not maintain an order to the items contained in the list.

♦ Answers to Drills

Drill 14-1

The code required to create the linked list in the drill is as follows. It is easiest to allocate each node with a separate pointer, so we have done so.

```
ListNodePointer Head;
ListNodePointer Node2;
ListNodePointer Node3;
ListNodePointer Node4;

Head = new ListNode;
Node2 = new ListNode;
Node3 = new ListNode;
Node4 = new ListNode;

Head->Next = Node2;
Node2->Next = Node3;
Node3->Next = Node4;
Node4->Next = NULL;

Head->Value = 100;
Node2->Value = 50;
Node3->Value = 75;
Node4->Value = 3;
```

Drill 14-2

We will show the creation of the linked list in sections. After the following lines of code are executed, a graphical representation of the linked list would look like Figure 14.76.

```
ListNodePointer Head = new ListNode;
ListNodePointer AnotherNode = new ListNode;
ListNodePointer AdditionalNode = new ListNode;
```

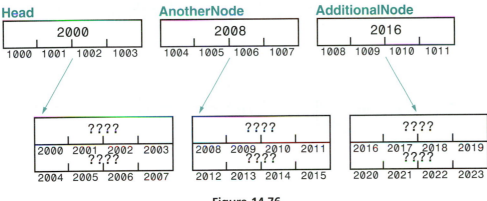

Figure 14.76

After the next three lines of code are executed, the graphical representation of our linked list looks like Figure 14.77.

```
Head->Value = 5;
AnotherNode->Value = 3;
AdditionalNode->Value 10;
```

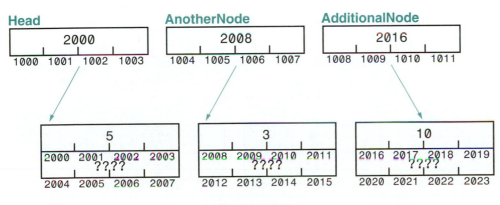

Figure 14.77

After the final three lines of code are executed, the graphical representation of our linked list looks like Figure 14.78.

```
AdditionalNode->Next = NULL;
AnotherNode->Next = AdditionalNode;
Head->Next = AnotherNode;
```

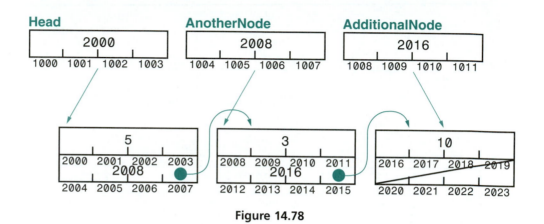

Figure 14.78

Drill 14-3

We will show the creation of the linked list in sections. After the following lines of code are executed, a graphical representation of the linked list would look like Figure 14.79.

```
ListNodePointer Head = new ListNode;
Head->Value = 3;
ListNodePointer AnotherNode = new ListNode;
```

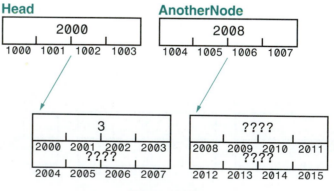

Figure 14.79

After the next three lines of code are executed, the graphical representation of our linked list looks like Figure 14.80

```
AnotherNode->Value = 1;
AnotherNode->Next = NULL;
ListNodePointer AdditionalNode = new ListNode;
```

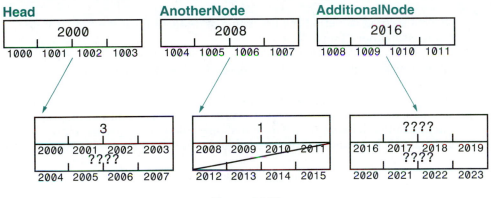

Figure 14.80

After the final three lines of code are executed, the graphical representation of our linked list looks like Figure 14.81.

```
Head->Next = AdditionalNode;
AdditionalNode->Next = NULL;
AdditionalNode->Value 10;
```

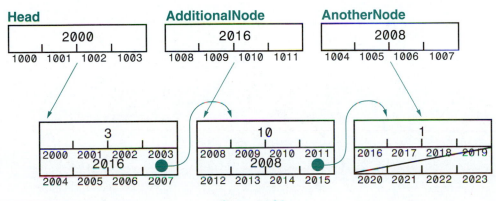

Figure 14.81

♦ Programming Exercises

1. Modify the linked list code in the chapter so that it can handle characters instead of integers.

2. Modify the linked list code in the chapter so that it can handle strings instead of integers.

3. Write a method to return the sum of all integers stored in a linked list.

4. Write a method to return the last integer stored in a linked list.

5. Write a method to output the first value of a linked list if it exists. If it does not exist, output "Empty."

6. Write a method that returns the number of items in a linked list.

7. Write a program that has a linked list class that processes bank accounts. It should store a name (as an array of characters), an account number (as an integer), and a balance (as a float). It should allow deposits, withdrawals, and balance inquiries as well as the ability to add and remove accounts.

8. Complete the implementation of the case study discussed in this chapter.

♦ Additional Exercises

1. What is a dynamic structure?

2. Why shouldn't linked lists be created statically at the beginning of a program? What are the advantages of creating them dynamically?

3. What happens if we do not issue a delete command on a pointer to a node that we are removing from a linked list? Will the user of a program written this way know immediately that there is a problem? Indicate why or why not.

Trees

▌▌ 15.1 WHAT IS A BINARY SEARCH TREE?

Although our implementation of linked lists left us with a data structure that is versatile and solves many of our list processing needs, is it efficient? If your problem involves just a few items, it should be more than fast enough. However, what happens as we increase the number of items contained in the list? Just as we saw with the implementation of a linear search, a linked list representation will become inefficient as the number of items in the list increases. Our solution to the searching problem was to create a binary search algorithm that divided the problem in half each time until we found the item we were looking for. Though this allowed for fast lookups, the problem with the array implementation of the structure was that inserting new items into it was cumbersome and inefficient.

A solution to this problem is to create a structure we call a tree. A tree combines the versatility of a linked list's memory allocation with the efficiency of the binary search's divide and conquer approach.

There are many different types of trees; we will implement what we call a **binary search tree.**

A binary search tree is composed of nodes. A tree that contains no nodes is called an **empty tree.** If a tree is considered a binary search tree, then it must follow these rules:

- The first node of the tree is called the **root node.** There can be only one root node per tree.

- Each node in the tree may be linked with up to two nodes. These nodes are considered the **children** of the current node and the current node is considered the **parent** of its children. There may be a left child that represents all of the values less than the current node as well as a right child that represents all of the values greater than the current node. A node that contains no children is called a **leaf node.**

- Each node in the tree may have only one parent node.

Figure 15.1 shows examples of binary search trees.

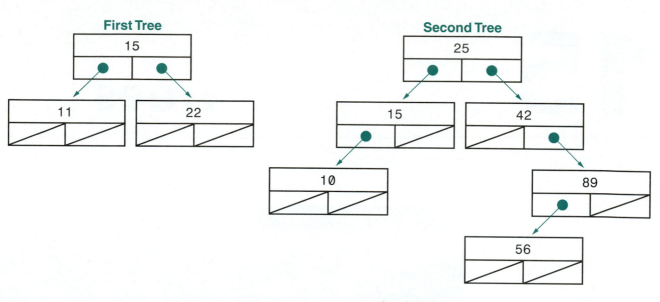

Figure 15.1

Let's examine the first tree more closely and label each of the nodes in the tree. The tree contains three nodes. The root node contains the value 15 and has two children associated with it. Since it is the root node, it has no parent. The left child to the root node contains the value 11. It has no children and its parent is the root node. The root node's other child contains the value 22. As with the left child, it has no children associated with it.

The first tree is a valid binary search tree because

- It has one root node, the node containing 15
- It has at most two children from any node
- The values in the nodes that are left children are less than the parent
- The values in the nodes that are right children are greater than the parent

See Figure 15.2.

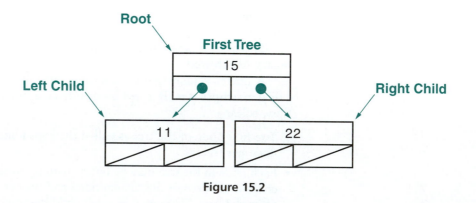

Figure 15.2

One more note about the first tree. Both children are also considered leaf nodes, because neither child has any children associated with it.

Second Tree

The second tree starts with the root node that contains the value 25. It has two child nodes associated with it. The left child contains the value 15 and has one child associated with it. It has no right child, and its left child contains the value 10. The node with the value 10 does not have any children and is considered a leaf node.

The right child of the root node contains the value 42. This child has no left child, but it does contain a right child that contains the value 89. This node contains no right child, but it does contain a left child node with the value 56. The node containing 56 has no children, so it is a leaf node.

See Figure 15.3.

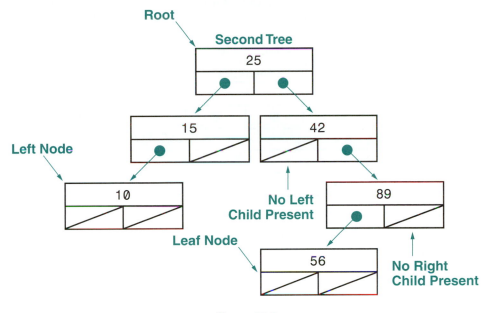

Figure 15.3

Invalid Binary Search Trees

Figure 15.4 contains examples of trees that are not considered valid binary search trees.

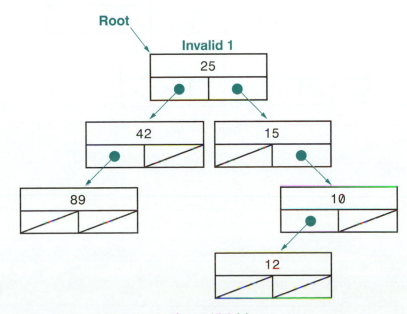

Figure 15.4 (a)

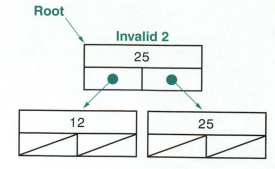

Figure 15.4 (b)

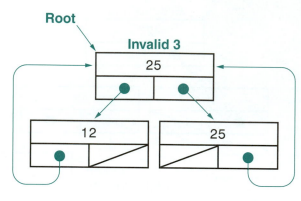

Figure 15.4 (c)

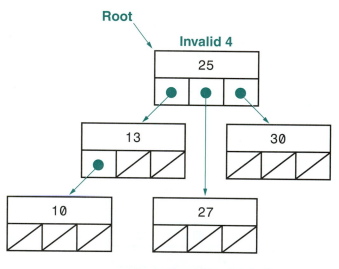

Figure 15.4 (d)

Invalid 1 is not a valid binary search tree, but it is technically a binary tree. It contains one root node, but the left children do not contain values less than their parent nodes. Additionally, the right children do not contain values greater than their parent nodes.

Invalid 2 is not a binary search tree because it contains duplicate nodes. The value 25 is stored in the root node and the right child of the root node. Although duplicates are not expressly mentioned as illegal, it is implied by the rule stating a left child node must be less than the parent and a right child node must by greater than the parent.

Invalid 3 is not a binary search tree because the root node containing the value 25 has two nodes pointing to it. This violates the rule that a node may not have more than one parent.

Invalid 4 is not a binary search tree because a node has three children. A binary search tree may contain only two children.

DRILLS

Which of the trees in Figure 15.5 are valid binary search trees?

Drill **15-1**

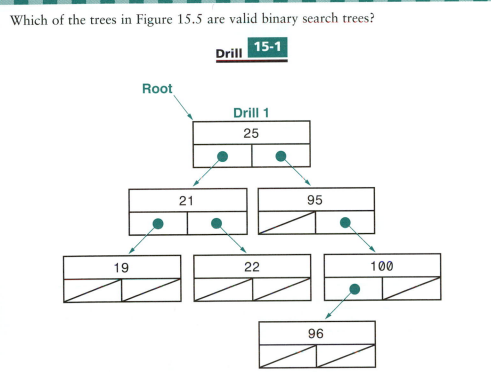

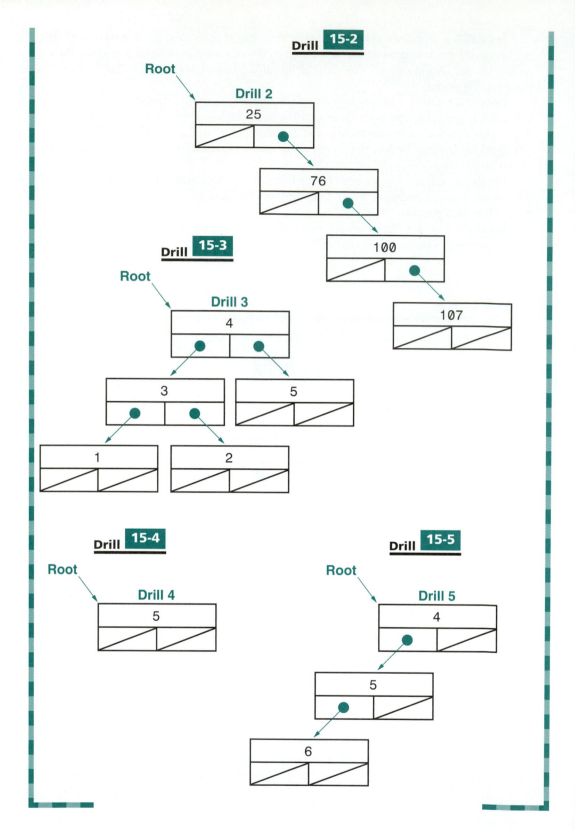

A binary search tree is of a different class of structure than the previous stuctures we have discussed. Previously all of the structures were linear in nature. Each item on the structure was listed in a linear progression from the previous item. However, with the introduction of trees we introduce the concept of a hierarchical structure.

15.2 BINARY TREE CLASS IMPLEMENTATION

To implement a tree data structure, we will need to define a template for how it will be allocated, and define the operations that can be performed on it.

Let's start the implementation of our tree by defining a structure that will be used as a node for our tree. Our node consists of three fields: an integer that requires 4 bytes of memory and two pointers, one to point to the children on the left and one to point to the children on the right that each require 4 bytes of memory. Therefore the entire structure requires 12 bytes of memory. The code to define our node structure follows:

```
struct TreeNode
{
    int Value;
    TreeNodePointer Left;
    TreeNodePointer Right;
};
```

As with our linked list example, we are going to create a class called **Tree** so that we can encapsulate all the methods and variables in one interface. Our class will contain the customary constructor and destructor as well as a method to display the tree, insert an item into the tree, and search the tree. Noticeably absent is the method to delete an item from a tree. This requires a more tricky implementation than we wish to cover right now. The following code defines our **Tree** class.

```
class Tree
{
    public:
        Tree();
        ~Tree();
        void Display();
        void Insert(int Val);
        bool Search(int Val);
        bool Delete();

    private:
        TreeNodePointer root;
        void InsertTree(TreeNodePointer & Root, int Val);
        void DisplayTree(TreeNodePointer Root);
        bool SearchTree(TreeNodePointer Root, int Val);
        void DeleteCompleteTree();
        boolDeleteValueTree();
};
```

You may be wondering why we have two methods for each operation, one private and one public; we will explain this shortly.

Constructor

The **Tree** class has as simple a constructor as the **List** class we implemented earlier. All that is required is that we set the **Root** to NULL. When the **Root** is equal to **NULL**, it indicates that the tree is empty. The code follows:

```
Tree :: Tree()
{
    Root = NULL;
}
```

This can be seen in Figure 15.6.

Root

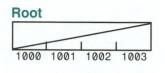

```
1000  1001  1002  1003
```

Figure 15.6

PROGRAMMER'S NOTEBOOK

The next few methods can be implemented easily only if you have a good understanding of recursion. If you do not, please review that section of the functions chapter.

Insertion

Remember that recursion is used when we wish to break a problem into smaller and smaller problems, until we reach a problem that is small enough to solve easily. With trees, recursion is pervasive, because it is natural to break the problem into two possible parts: the left and the right. By making the decision to solve the problem to the left or right of the current node, we are (on average) reducing the problem in half.

To implement the **Insert** method we need to find the location to insert the new node. Recursion fits nicely into the solution because starting from the root, we can decide if the insertion value belongs to the left, to the right, or at the current node. When we decide that the node belongs either to the left or right, we are in essence starting the problem over from the left or right node. This continues until we find the proper place to insert the node.

We cannot implement the method yet, because we are left with another complication. When we call the **Insert** method from an object, we do not wish to specify the root pointer in the call. In fact, the user of the **Tree** class should not even know that the root node exists. This would be a violation of accessing private data outside the class definition. However, when dealing with recursive methods/functions, we need to standardize the parameters being passed. If on all subsequent calls we are going to pass a pointer, how can we avoid it on the initial call to **Insert**?

The solution is to create a method that is called by the user and then one method called internally. The method called by the user will accept only one parameter, the value we wish to insert. The only purpose of this method will be to call a private method that takes a pointer to the current node as well as the value we wish to insert. Since the **Insert** method is part of the class **Tree** we can access the private attribute **Root** and pass it to the private method **InsertTree**. The code for **Insert** and **InsertTree** follows.

```
void Tree :: Insert(int Val)
{
   InsertTree(Root, Val);
}
```

```
void Tree :: InsertTree(TreeNodePointer & Root, int Val)
{
   if (Root==NULL)
   {
    Root= new TreeNode;
    Root->Left=NULL;
    Root->Right=NULL;
    Root->Value = Val;
    return;
   }

   // Handle duplicate
   if (Val == Root->Value)
     return;

   //Search left
   if (Val < Root->Value)
     InsertTree(Root->Left, Val);

   //Search right
   else
     InsertTree(Root->Right,Val);
}
```

When executing the **InsertTree** method we have four options:

- Insert at the current location
- Return because a duplicate value was requested to be inserted
- Look to insert the value to the left of the node
- Look to insert the value to the right of the node

Insert at the Current Location The first case occurs either when we have traversed down the entire tree and reached a leaf node, or if the tree is empty. Since there are no more nodes to traverse, we insert the node here. We must allocate a new node, set the left and right pointers to **NULL**, and initialize the value field to the value we wish to insert. At this point we are done and we issue a return statement. This is one of the stopping cases of the recursion.

Let's observe the steps taken when we insert into an empty tree. First, we allocate the node and set the root pointer to its address (see Figure 15.7).

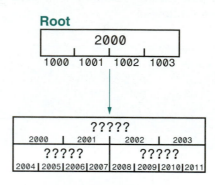

Figure 15.7

Next both pointer fields (**Left** and **Right**) are set to **NULL** (see Figure 15.8).

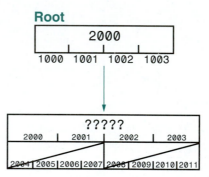

Figure 15.8

Finally, the value field is set (see Figure 15.9).

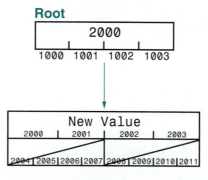

Figure 15.9

Return Because of Duplication This routine actually has two stopping cases. Since we do not wish for duplication of values in our tree, upon finding a value already contained in the tree that we are trying to insert, we simply return having done nothing.

Look to Insert the Value to the Left If the value we are attempting to insert is less than the node pointed to by the current node, then we want to search for the proper insertion point to the left. This is one of the two recursive steps of this routine.

Observe the following example of inserting the value 1 into the tree in Figure 15.10.

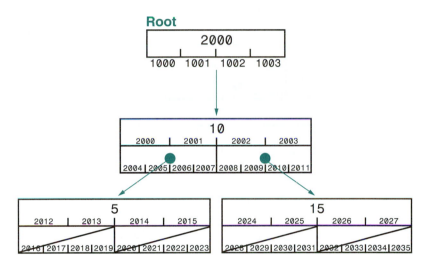

Figure 15.10

The call to insert would look as follows:

```
ExampleTree.Insert(1);
```

The public **Insert** method calls the private method called **InsertTree** with the address of the root node (2000). This can be seen with the following code:

```
InsertTree(Root, 1);
```

On each call to **Insert**, information about the calls will be stored in a system stack.

Call	Root	Called from
1	2000	Initial

The first step is to locate the proper place to insert the value 1. So, since **Root** is not **NULL**, we compare the value at **Root->Value** to 1. Since 1 is less than 10, we need to search to the left. This is accomplished by a recursive call with the value of **Root->Left** replacing the current value of **Root** (see Figure 15.11).

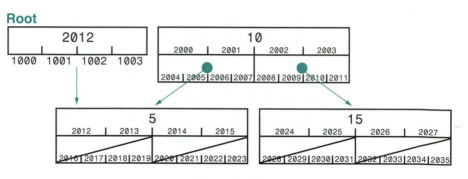

Figure 15.11

Call	Root	Called from
2	2012	Left
1	2000	Initial

Again we compare the value at **Root->Value** to 1. Since 1 is less than 5, we need to search to the right. However, this time when we make the recursive call to the right, **Root** is set to the **NULL** pointer of the current node (see Figure 15.12).

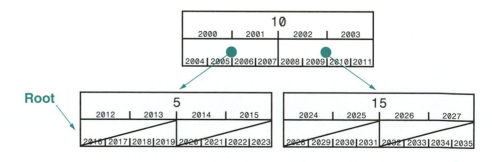

Figure 15.12

Call	Root	Called from
3	NULL	Left
2	2012	Left
1	2000	Initial

Now when we enter the call to **InsertTree**, we are ready to insert the new node. This occurs exactly as it did in the example when the tree was empty. The pointer containing the value **NULL** is changed to point to a newly allocated node (see Figure 15.13).

PROGRAMMER'S NOTEBOOK

What's That & Doing There?

Although unmentioned, notice that there is an & operator in the parameter list. Without it, the method will not work at all. If you run the code through a debugger, it will appear to work; however, once you leave the method, the node of the tree that you created will disappear.

This is because of a subtlety of C++. Normally when we have passed a pointer to a function or method, we were changing that value at that pointer. However, in this case, we wish to change the pointer itself. Since C++ defaults to pass by value, even for pointers, we must specifically indicate that the pointer variable Root should retain its new value.

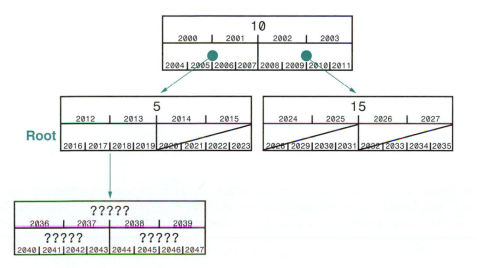

Figure 15.13

Then the pointers of the newly allocated node are set to **NULL**, as shown in Figure 15.14.

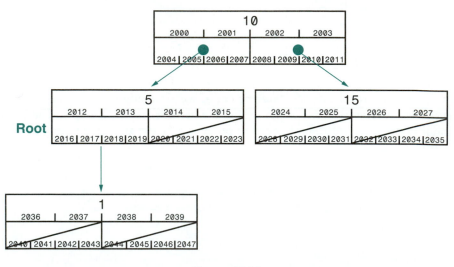

Figure 15.14

Finally, the value field of the newly allocated node is set to 1 (see Figure 15.15).

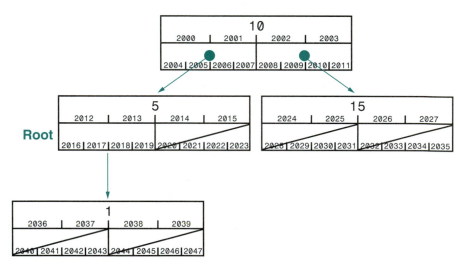

Figure 15.15

When we reach a root value containing **NULL**, the code does not call **Insert** again as it has been. The termination case of the recursion is reached. Therefore, the method returns to where it was called. In this case, it is the **InsertTree** method. In each case of returning from **InsertTree**, there remains nothing left to do, so it returns all the way back to the original call to **Insert**, where the method calls end.

Look to Insert the Value to the Right If the value we are attempting to insert is greater than the node pointed to by the current node, then we want to search for the proper insertion point to the right. This would follow the exact same methodology as inserting to the left.

Observe the following example of inserting the value 25 into the tree shown in Figure 15.16.

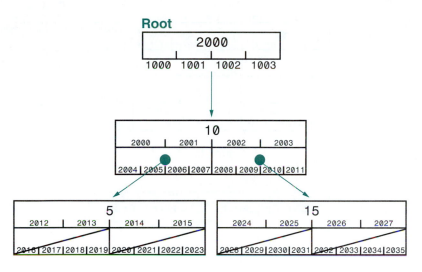

Figure 15.16

The call to **Insert** would look as follows:

```
ExampleTree.Insert(25);
```

The public **Insert** method calls the private method called **InsertTree** with the address of the root node (2000). This can be seen with the following code:

```
InsertTree(Root, 25);
```

On each call to **Insert**, information about the calls will be stored in a system stack.

Call	Root	Called from
1	2000	Initial

The first step is to locate the proper place to insert the value 25. So, since **Root** is not **NULL**, we compare the value at **Root->Value** to 25. Since 25 is more than 10, we need to search to the right. This is accomplished by a recursive call with the value of **Root ->Right** replacing the current value of **Root** (see Figure 15.17).

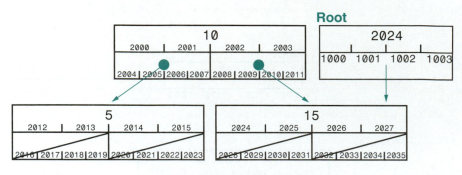

Figure 15.17

Call	Root	Called from
2	2024	Right
1	2000	Initial

Again we compare the value at **Root->Value** to 25. Since 25 is greater than 15, we need to search to the right. However, this time when we make the recursive call to the right, **Root** is set to the **NULL** pointer of the current node (see Figure 15.18).

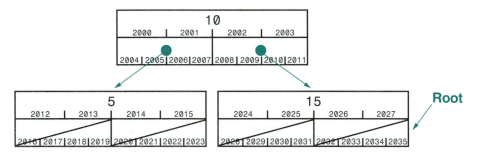

Figure 15.18

Call	Root	Called from
3	NULL	Left
2	2024	Left
1	2000	Initial

Now when we enter the call to **InsertTree**, we are ready to insert the new node. This occurs exactly as it did in the example when the tree was empty. The pointer containing the value **NULL** is changed to point to a newly allocated node, as shown in Figure 15.19.

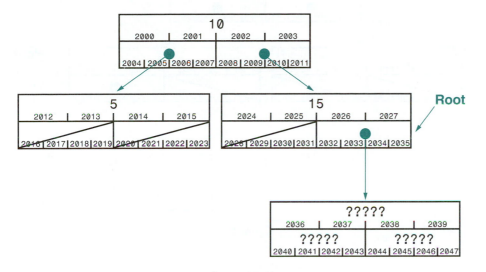

Figure 15.19

Then the pointers of the newly allocated node are set to **NULL** (see Figure 15.20).

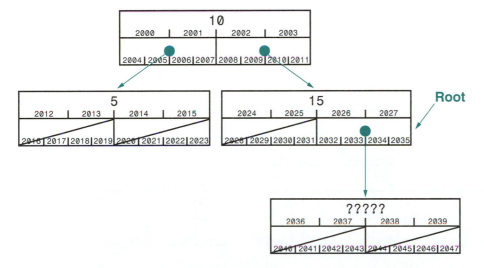

Figure 15.20

Finally, the value field of the newly allocated node is set to 25 (see Figure 15.21).

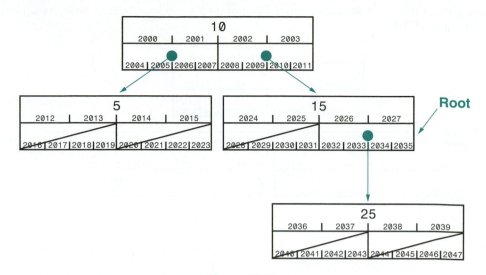

Figure 15.21

As before, once the node is inserted, we return through the calls to `InsertTree` and finally `Insert` and terminate the method calls.

General Case Insert Also realize that one might have to go to the left and then the right and vice versa during the course of finding the proper location to perform the `Insert`.

Figure 15.22 contains an example of inserting 12 to a binary search tree.

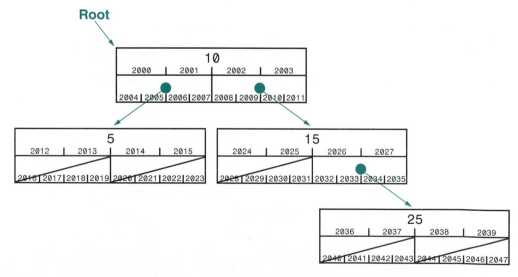

Figure 15.22

The call to insert would look as follows:

```
ExampleTree.Insert(12);
```

The public **Insert** method calls the private method called **InsertTree** with the address of the root node (2000). This can be seen with the following code:

```
InsertTree(Root, 12);
```

On each call to **Insert**, information about the calls will be stored in a system stack.

Call	Root	Called from
1	2000	Initial

The first step is to locate the proper place to insert the value 12. So, since **Root** is not NULL, we compare the value at **Root->Value** to 12. Since 12 is more than 10, we need to search to the right. This is accomplished by a recursive call with the value of **Root ->Right** replacing the current value of **Root** (see Figure 15.23).

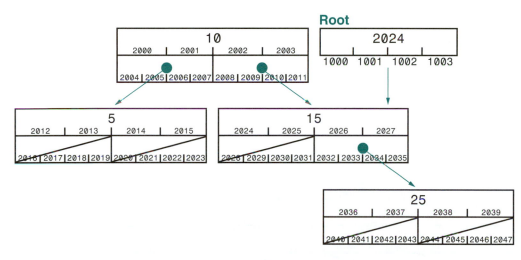

Figure 15.23

Call	Root	Called from
2	2024	Right
1	2000	Initial

Again we compare the value at **Root->Value** to 12. Since 12 is less than 15, we need to search to the left. However, this time when we make the recursive call to the left, **Root** is set to the **NULL** pointer of the current node (see Figure 15.24).

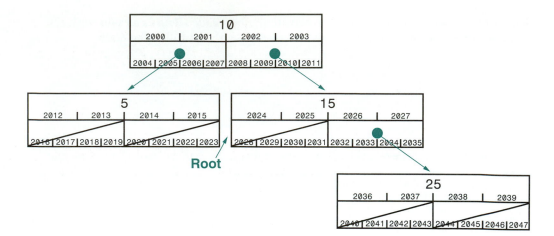

Figure 15.24

Call	Root	Called from
3	NULL	Left
2	2024	Left
1	2000	Initial

Now when we enter the call to **InsertTree,** we are ready to insert the new node. This occurs exactly as it did in the example when the tree was empty. The pointer containing the value **NULL** is changed to point to a newly allocated node (see Figure 15.25).

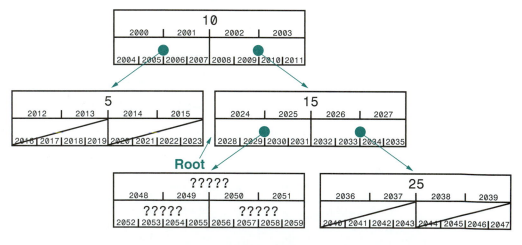

Figure 15.25

Then the pointers of the newly allocated node are set to **NULL** (see Figure 15.26).

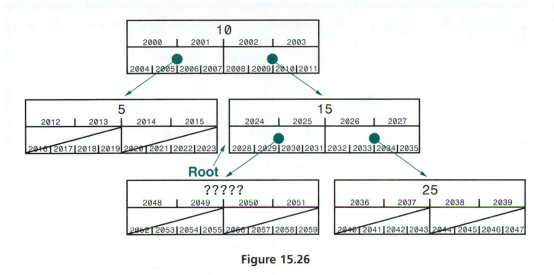

Figure 15.26

Finally, the value field of the newly allocated node is set to 12 (see Figure 15.27).

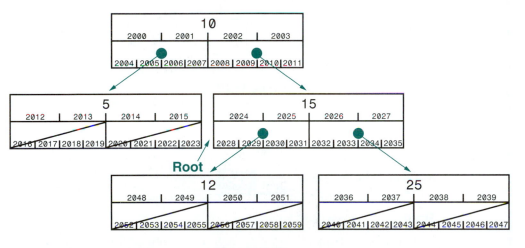

Figure 15.27

As before, once the node is inserted, we return through the calls to **InsertTree** and finally **Insert** and terminate the method calls.

▌DRILLS

Given the tree in Figure 15.28, show what happens when we attempt to insert the value 110.

Drill 15-6

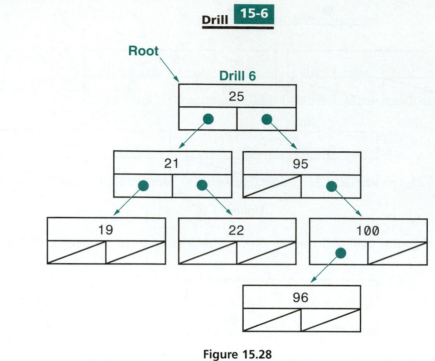

Figure 15.28

Given the tree in Figure 15.29, show what happens when we attempt to insert the value 77.

Drill 15-7

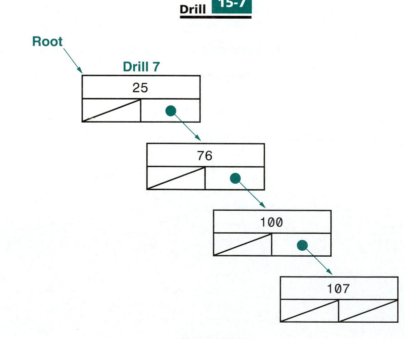

Figure 15.29

Given the tree in Figure 15.30, show what happens when we attempt to insert the value 0.

Drill 15-8

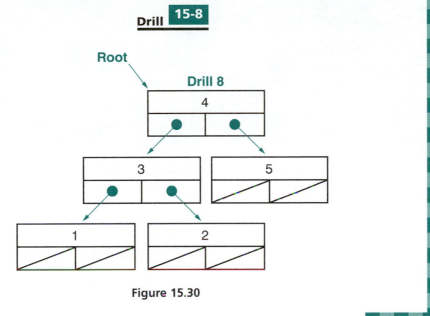

Figure 15.30

Display

There are many ways to write a **Display** method for a tree. We are going to implement one that outputs the elements at the nodes of the tree in ascending order. As with the **Insert** method, the **Display** method will be called by the user, while in turn **Display** will call a private method, **DisplayTree**, that passes the extra parameter needed for the recursion.

The method **Display** requires no parameters and is coded as follows:

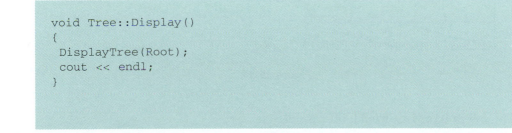

```
void Tree::Display()
{
  DisplayTree(Root);
  cout << endl;
}
```

To implement the private method **DisplayTree** we must first understand how to traverse a tree to output the values in ascending order. If we start at the **Root**, all nodes to the left of the root are less than the **Root**. Therefore, it would make sense that they must be output before the **Root**. The same can be said about any node in the tree. All the elements in a node to the left of a node are less than that node. Therefore, we must output all values of the nodes to the left before we output the nodes to the right.

Once we have output all the nodes to the left, we return to the parent node of the leftmost node. Since that node, by definition, is less than all the nodes to its right, we output that node before we traverse the nodes to the right of it.

By defining this routine recursively, we can traverse to the left, output the current value, and then traverse to the right with minimal code. No loops are required at all. See the following code:

```
void Tree :: DisplayTree(TreeNodePointer Root)
{
 if (Root != NULL)
   {
    DisplayTree(Root->Left);
    cout<<Root->Value<<' ';
    DisplayTree(Root->Right);
   }
}
```

Figure 15.31 shows as an example of displaying a tree.

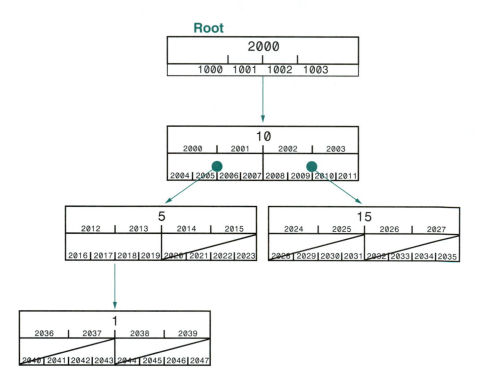

Figure 15.31

The call to **Display** would look as follows:

```
ExampleTree.Display();
```

The public **Display** method calls the private method called **DisplayTree** with the address of the root node (2000). This can be seen with the following code:

```
DisplayTree(Root);
```

On each call to **Display**, information about the calls will be stored in a system stack.

Call	Root	Called from
1	2000	Initial

Upon entering **DisplayTree**, since **Root** is not equal to **NULL**, we begin to recurse to the left. This sets the value of **Root** to the address of the node containing 5. When we return from this call, the value 10 will be output, but currently nothing is displayed.

When we recurse, we must place the information about the recursive call on the stack. The new root is now 2012 and we must remember that we came from the left. This can be seen in Figure 15.32.

Call	Root	Called from
2	2012	Left
1	2000	Initial

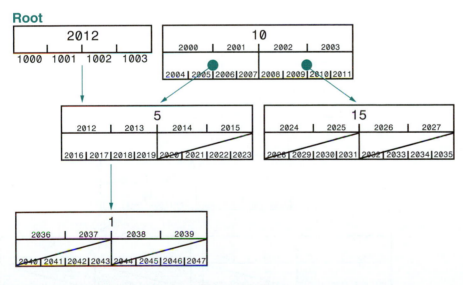

Figure 15.32

Since **Root** is still not equal to **NULL**, we once again traverse to the left via a recursive call. Now **Root** is equal to the address of the node containing 1 (see Figure 15.33).

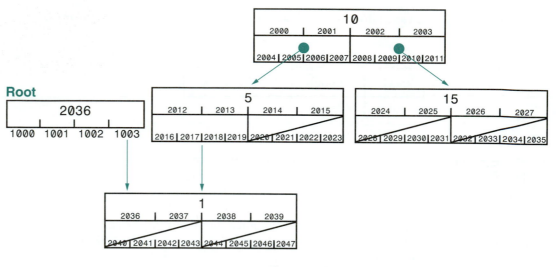

Figure 15.33

Again, the **Root** is still not equal to **NULL**. However, this time when we recurse to the left, the **Root** is set to **NULL**. Again when we recurse, we must place the information about the recursive call on the stack. The new root is now 2036 and we must remember that we came from the left. This can be seen in Figure 15.34.

Call	Root	Called from
3	2036	Left
2	2012	Left
1	2000	Initial

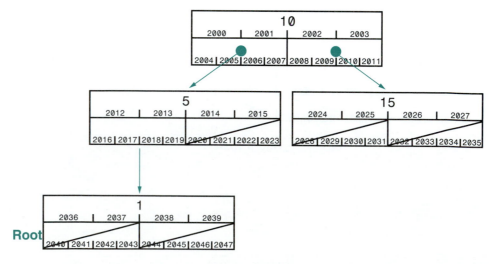

Figure 15.34

We call `Display` again with the root node equaling **NULL**. The stack now looks as follows:

Call	Root	Called from
4	NULL	Left
3	2036	Left
2	2012	Left
1	2000	Initial

Since the **Root** is equal to **NULL**, we return to the previous function call. However, when we return from the previous call we return to the middle of the execution of the previous call to **DisplayTree**. The next instruction to execute is the **cout** statement. Since the **Root** pointer is pointing to the node containing the value **1**, the value **1** is output. Then the function traverses to the right.

Since traversing to the right follows a **NULL** pointer, we again have entered the method simply to return. This is shown in the following representation of the stack and tree (see Figure 15.35).

Call	Root	Called from
4	NULL	Left
3	2036	Left
2	2012	Left
1	2000	Initial

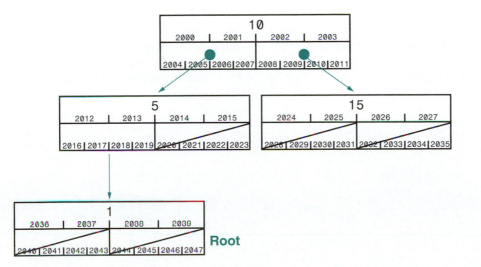

Figure 15.35

As before when the **NULL** pointer is passed to **DisplayTree**, we simply return. However this time, when we return to the call of **DisplayTree**, we have finished executing all of the code for the node where **Root** points to the node containing the value 1. Therefore, we return to the call of **DisplayTree**, which called it. This would be the call from the node containing the value 5 (see Figure 15.36).

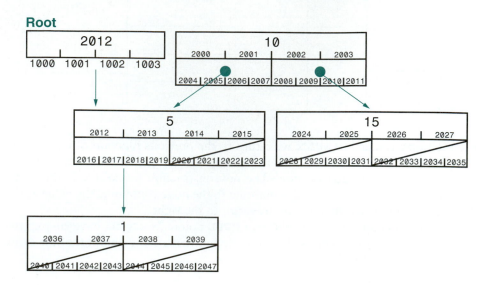

Figure 15.36

Call	Root	Called from
2	2012	Left
1	2000	Initial

Now, the value at the node is output, **5**. Then we traverse to the right, but as before when the pointer is **NULL**, we return without outputting any other values. Since there is no more code to execute from the current node, we return to the call of **DisplayTree** that called it. See Figure 15.37 and the updated stack representation.

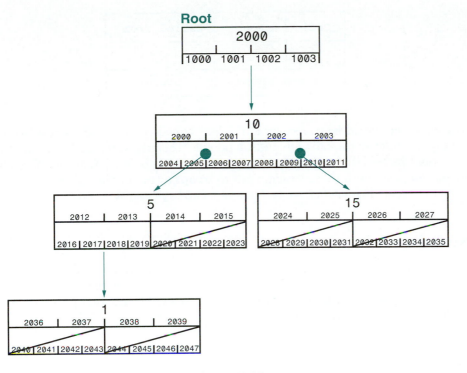

Figure 15.37

Call	Root	Called from
1	2000	Initial

Now, the value of **10** is output. Unlike the other nodes, the current node has a non-**NULL** right pointer. Therefore, we recurse down the **Right** pointer as shown in Figure 15.38.

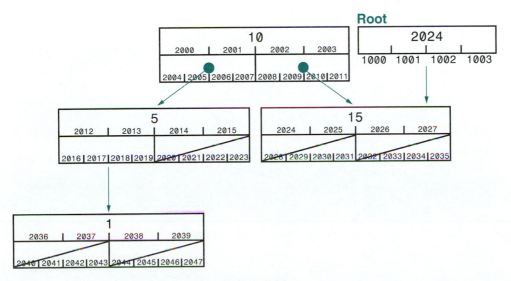

Figure 15.38

Call	Root	Called from
2	2024	Left
1	2000	Initial

The next step would be to recurse to the left. However as we now know, we will simply return from the call with a **NULL** pointer. Then the value **15** is output. Next we would recurse to the right, but again, it is a **NULL** pointer. With no more code to execute, we return to the original call to **DisplayTree**. Since there is no more code to execute there either, we return and **DisplayTree** is complete.

Search

Implementing the **Search** method parallels the **Display** method's implementation. As with the **Display** method, the **Search** method will be called by the user, and in turn, **Search** will call a private method, **SearchTree**, that passes the extra parameter needed for the recursion.

```
bool Tree:: Search(int Val)
{
    return SearchTree(Root, Val);
}
```

SearchTree traverses the tree in the same manner as **DisplayTree**, except instead of outputting each value as it visits a node, it checks to see if the value at the current node is equal to the value we are searching for.

The method either returns **true** when it finds the value it is looking for, or it returns **false** when it reaches a **NULL** pointer in the leaf. The implementation of **SearchTree** follows:

```
bool Tree:: SearchTree(TreeNodePointer Root, int Val)
{
    if (Root == NULL)
      return false;
    if (Root->Value == Val)
      return true;
    if (Val < Root->Value)
      return SearchTree(Root->Left, Val);
    return SearchTree(Root->Right, Val);
}
```

The following is an example of a main routine declaring, inserting, displaying, and searching for values in a **Tree**.

```
void main()
{
    Tree Root;

    Root.Insert(5);
    Root.Insert(20);
    Root.Insert(1);
    Root.Insert(100);
    Root.Display();

    if (Root.Search(100))
      cout<<"FOUND\n";
    if (!Root.Search(50))
      cout<<"NOT FOUND\n";
    cout<<'\n';
}
```

PROGRAMMER'S NOTEBOOK

Although binary search trees can more efficient than linked lists, this is true only if values are inserted into the tree in a fairly random order. If items are entered in order, the binary tree becomes a linked list with all the values being linked on the right pointer.

Destructor

The **DeleteCompleteTree** method traverses the tree to left and to the right upon returning from the transversal it frees the memory allocated for the node. See the following code. As with the **Insert** method, the Destructor method will be called by the user, and in turn, Destructor will call a private method, **DeleteCompleteTree**, that passes the extra parameter needed for the recursion.

```
void Tree::Tree()
{
 DeleteCompleteTree(Root);
}
```

```
void Tree :: DeleteCompleteTree(TreeNodePointer Root)
{
 if (Root != NULL)
   {
     DeleteCompleteTree(Root->Left);
     DisplayCompleteTree(Root->Right);
     delete Root;
   }
}
```

Figure 15.39 is an example of a destructor being called for an existing tree.

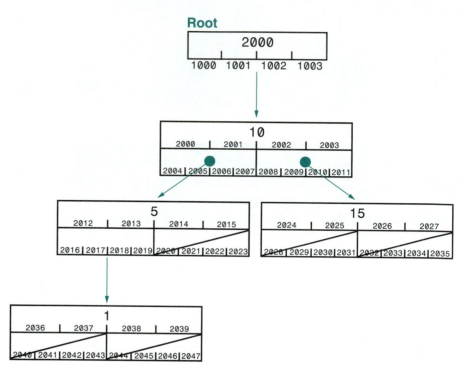

Figure 15.39

Unlike the previous method calls, there is no direct call to the destructor; instead, the destructor is called automatically when the tree goes out of scope. However, once the destructor is called, we need a method of recursing like the other methods we have created.

The public **Destructor** method calls the private method called **DeleteCompleteTree** with the address of the root node (2000). This can be seen with the following code:

```
DeleteCompleteTree(Root);
```

On each call to **DeleteCompleteTree**, information about the calls will be stored in a system stack.

Call	Root	Called from
1	2000	Initial

Upon entering **DeleteCompleteTree**, since **Root** is not equal to **NULL**, we begin to recurse to the left. This sets the value of **Root** to the address of the node containing 5. When we return from this call, we will traverse to the right, and then when we return to the node the second time we will delete the node and return its memory to the operating system.

When we recurse to the left, the new root is now 2012 and we must remember that we came from the left. This can be seen in Figure 15.40.

Call	Root	Called from
2	2012	Left
1	2000	Initial

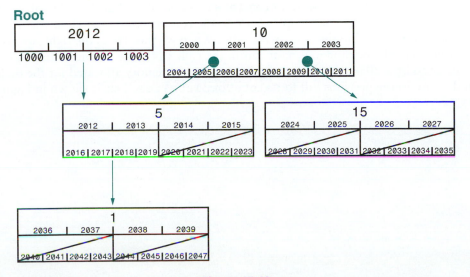

Figure 15.40

Since **Root** is still not equal to **NULL**, we once again traverse to the left via a recursive call. Now **Root** is equal to the address of the node containing 1 (see Figure 15.41).

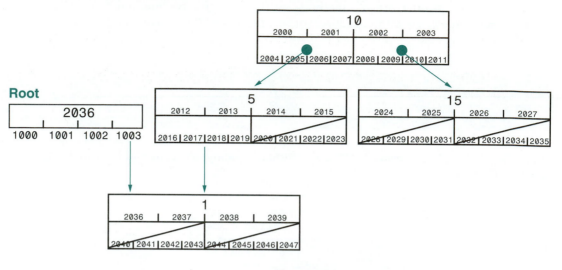

Figure 15.41

Again, the **Root** is still not equal to **NULL**. Again when we recurse, we must place the information about the recursive call on the stack. The new root is now 2036 and we must remember that we came from the left. This can be seen in the following diagram:

Call	Root	Called from
3	2036	Left
2	2012	Left
1	2000	Initial

The next time we recurse **DeleteCompleteTree** is called, but the value of **root** equals **NULL**. Therefore, we simple return to the third call of the method where we continue to recurse, but this time to the right. When we traverse to the right, we also pass **NULL** to the method and return from the call. Upon the second return to the node at address 2036, we call **Delete** to return the memory allocated for the node and return to the previous call to **DeleteCompleteTree**. This is shown in Figure 15.42.

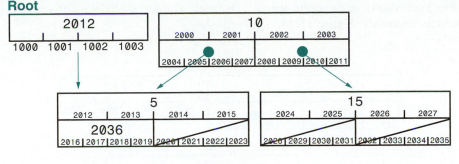

Figure 15.42

Notice that although the node at address 2036 is now removed, the pointer to it in the node at the address 2012 still contains the address 2036. This is not a problem, because after we recurse to the right we will return to this method call and remove the node at address 2012 without accessing the left pointer again. Therefore we do not have to set it to **NULL**. Doing so will just waste processing time.

We continue our traversal by following the right link from the node at address 2012. However, since the link is **NULL** we simply return. However, now it is time to delete the node at address 2012 from memory.

This can be seen in Figure 15.43.

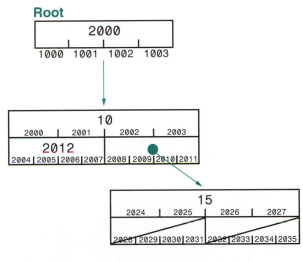

Figure 15.43

Currently, we have returned to the original node and must traverse to the right. The left pointer of the current node is set to 2012, but we will not be traversing to the left any more, so we don't have to worry about resetting it.

Call	Root	Called from
1	2000	Right

When we traverse to the right, we visit the node at address 2024 for the first time. This can be seen in Figure 15.44.

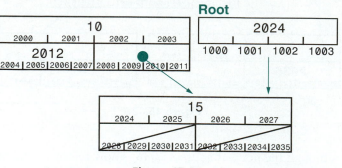

Figure 15.44

Call	Root	Called from
2	2024	Initial
1	2000	Right

When we traverse from the node at memory address 2024, we will traverse to the left and to the right only to reach **NULL** pointers. Therefore, we return to this state ready to delete the node.

After deleting the node and returning to the original call to the **DeleteCompleteTree** method, we have Figure 15.45.

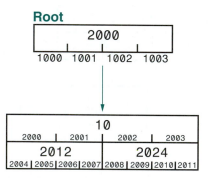

Figure 15.45

Upon returning to the node at address 2000 for the second time, we have no more traversals left and simply remove the node from memory and return to the call from the destructor, and we have completed the destructor call.

Problem Description

In this chapter, we will solve the same problem that we did in the last chapter. However, because we realize that a linked list can be slow, we will implement the student grade application with a tree.

When the number of students to search is small, there is not a large difference between the number of nodes we check between a linked list implementation and a tree implementation. However, as the number of nodes increases, trees become much more efficient.

To compute the amount of nodes for the search in the average case for a linked list, we simply calculate half the total number of nodes in the linked list. To calculate the number of nodes for the search in a binary search tree, the calculation is slightly more complicated. In a balanced tree, each time we check a node to see if it is the one that we are searching for, we cut the number of nodes we are searching in half. This continues until we either find the node or traverse to a leaf node. Fortunately, we can calculate this by taking the logorithm base 2 of the number of nodes in the tree. The following chart is provided so you don't have to calculate it.

Number of Nodes	Linked List	Tree	Number of Nodes	Linked List	Tree
1	1	1	1,024	512	10
2	1	1	2,048	1,024	11
4	2	2	4,096	2,048	12
8	4	3	8,192	4,096	13
16	8	4	16,384	8,192	14
32	16	5	32,768	16,384	15
64	32	6	65,536	32,768	16
128	64	7	131,072	65,536	17
256	128	8	262,144	131,072	18

We can easily see that once we have over 1000 nodes a tree structure is significantly faster. So with that said, what changes do we need to make to the tree class in order to handle tracking a student's social security number and average grade?

Problem Discussion

We can use the existing code of a tree class to track the student's social security number, assuming we change the value to a long instead of an integer. However, we need to add another field to track grades associated with each student.

First, we need to change the structure for the tree node as follows:

```
struct TreeNode
{
    long SSN;
    float Average;
    TreeNodePointer Left;
    TreeNodePointer Right;
};
```

Additionally, the **Tree** class must be modified so that the **Insert** and **InsertTree** methods accept a social security number and a grade. We should also change the method **Search** to accept a social security number instead of the integer **Value**, and because we need to return the student's average grade if the student is found, we need to pass a varible by reference so that its value may be returned to the calling function.

Solution

```
class Tree
{
    public:
        Tree();
        ~Tree();
        void Display();
        void Insert(long SSN, float Average);
        bool Search(long SSN, float & Average);
        bool Delete();

    private:
        TreeNodePointer root;
        void InsertTree(TreeNodePointer & Root, long SSN, float Average);
        void DisplayTree(TreeNodePointer Root);
        bool SearchTree(TreeNodePointer Root, long SSN, float & Average);
        void DeleteCompleteTree();
        boolDeleteValueTree();
};
```

The actual method implementation requires minor changes and is left as an exercise to the reader.

To use our new **Tree** class, see the following example. In it we read 100 sets of social security numbers and grades. Then the program asks the user to enter social security numbers to search the tree for. The program ends when a negative number is entered for a social security number.

```cpp
#include <stdlib.h>
#include <iostream.h>

//Tree definitions included here

void main()
{
    Tree StudentsAverages;
    int StudentCounter;
    long StudentNumber;
    float StudentAverage;

    //Read in 100 grades and insert them into the tree.
    for(StudentCounter=0; StudentCounter < 100;StudentCounter++)
    {
        cout<<"Enter the Student's Social SecurityNumber"<<endl;
        cin>>StudentNumber;
        cout<<"Enter the Student's average"<<endl;
        cin>>StudentAverage;
        StudentAverages.Insert(StudentNumber, StudentAverage);
    }


    do
    {
        cin>>StudentNumber;
        if (StudentNumber >= 0)
        {
            StudentAverages.Search(StudentNumber, StudentAverage)
            cout<<"The student's average is "
                <<StudentAverage<<endl;
    } while (StudentNumber >=0)
}
```

END-OF-CHAPTER

◆ Key Terms

Binary search tree	A special kind of tree that contains only two children. All children to the left of a node contain values that are less than the parent node. All children to the right of a node contain values that are greater than the parent node.
Child node	A node that is pointed to by another node in a tree.
Empty tree	A tree that contains no nodes. It is essentially a pointer set to NULL.
Leaf node	A child node that contains no children.
Parent node	A node that has at least one of its pointers not equal to NULL.
Root node	The very first node of a tree. No other nodes point to it.
Tree node	A building block of a tree. It contains at least one value and pointers to other nodes.

◆ Answers to Drills

Drill 15-1

The first tree is a valid binary search tree. We can start the analysis by noting that there is only one root node, the node containing the value 25. All of the other nodes are descendants of this node. Furthermore, no nodes have more than two children and each child has only one parent. Since this is true, to verify that the tree is valid, all we need is to show that each node's right children are either nonexistent or contain a value greater than the parent node's value. Additionally, the value of each node's left children are either nonexistent or contain a value less than the parent node's value. In all cases this is true, so the tree is a valid binary search tree.

Drill 15-2

The second tree is also a valid binary search tree. In fact everything that we checked for the example in Drill 15-1 holds true for this example. The only difference is that this tree contains only right children. There is nothing in the rules of binary search trees that states a tree must have a left child. Therefore, this tree is valid.

Drill 15-3

The third tree is not valid. To prove a tree invalid is easier than proving it valid. All that is required is showing a single instance where the rules of binary search trees are violated. In this case, look at the node containing the value 3. Its left child contains the value 1. This is legal, because we want the left children of a node to contain values less than the parent. However, the right child node contains the value 2. This is not allowed. The right child node's value should be greater than the value contained in the parent.

Drill 15-4

The fourth tree is valid. Although it is a tree that contains only one node, there is nothing wrong with this. A binary search tree may contain one node and therefore it is valid.

Drill 15-5

The fifth tree looks like a mirror image of the structure of the second tree. However, this tree is not valid. Although it is acceptable to have trees with only left children, each child must have a value less than the value of the parent node. In each case the child node has a value greater than the parent node, so this tree is obviously invalid.

Drill 15-6

Inserting the value 110 into the following tree is accomplished as follows:

We start by comparing the value at the root, 25, to the value that we are inserting, 110. Since 110 is greater than 25, we traverse the tree to the right.

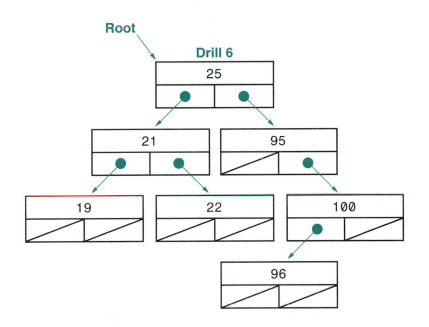

We continue by comparing the value at the current root, 95, to the value that we are inserting, 110. Since 110 is greater than 95, we traverse the tree to the right.

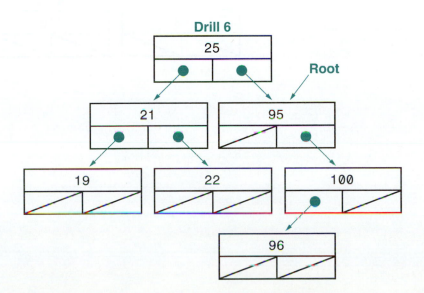

We continue by comparing the value at the current root, 100, to the value that we are inserting, 110. Since 110 is greater than 100, we traverse the tree to the right.

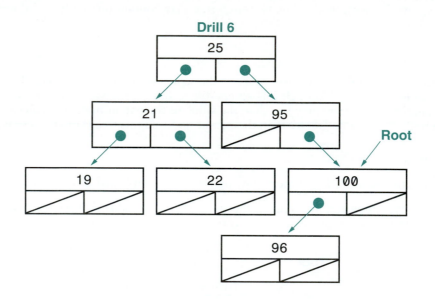

Now, we reach the NULL pointer. Therefore, we allocate space for the new node and link it from the node containing 100. Finally, we set the newly allocated node to the value 110.

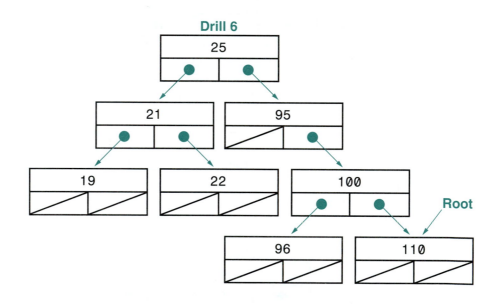

Drill 15-7

Inserting the value 77 into the following tree is accomplished as follows:

We start by comparing the value at the root, 25, to the value that we are inserting, 77. Since 77 is greater than 25, we traverse the tree to the right.

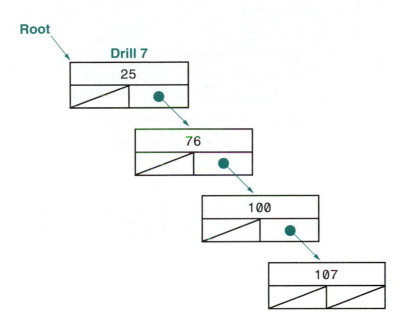

We continue by comparing the value at the current root, 76, to the value that we are inserting, 77. Since 77 is greater than 76, we traverse the tree to the right.

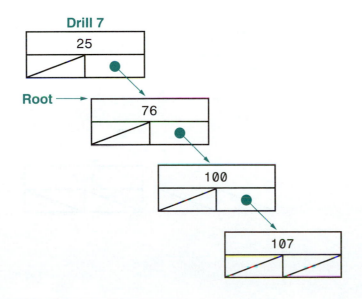

We continue by comparing the value at the current root, 100, to the value that we are inserting, 77. Since 77 is less than 100, we traverse the tree to the left.

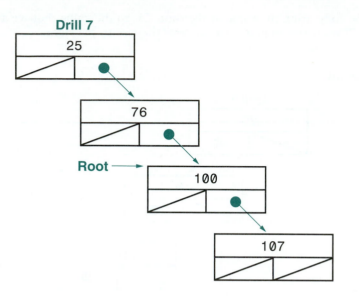

Now, we reach the NULL pointer. Therefore, we allocate space for the new node and link it from the node containing 100. Finally, we set the newly allocated node to the value 77.

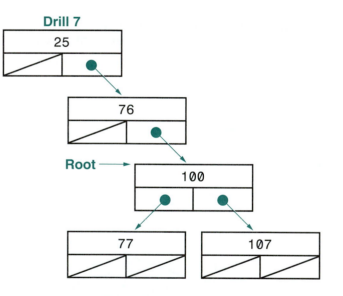

Drill 15-8

We start by comparing the value at the root, 4, to the value that we are inserting, 0.
Since 0 is less than 4, we traverse the tree to the left.

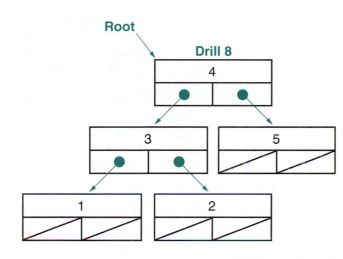

We continue by comparing the value at the current root, 3, to the value that we are
inserting, 0. Since 0 is less than 3 we traverse the tree to the left.

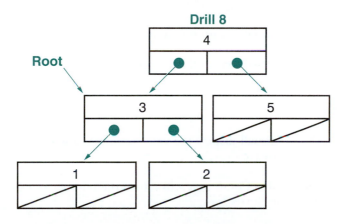

We continue by comparing the value at the current root, 1, to the value that we are
inserting, 0. Since 0 is less than 1, we traverse the tree to the left.

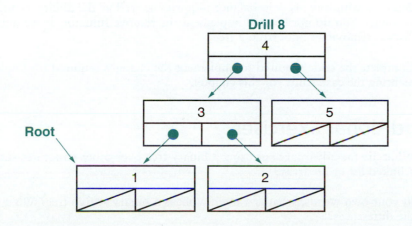

Now, we reach the NULL pointer. Therefore, we allocate space for the new node and link it from the node containing 1. Finally we set the newly allocated node to the value 0.

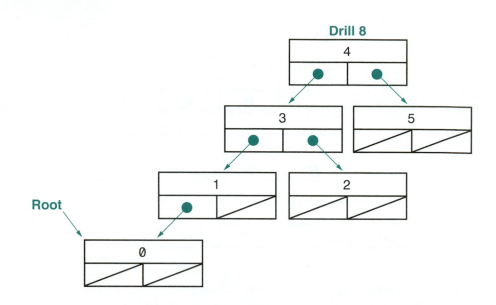

Drill 8

Root

♦Programming Exercises

1. Write a method that will return the minimum value of a binary search tree.

2. Write a method that will return the maximum value of a binary search tree.

3. Write a method that will return the sum of all values contained in a binary search tree.

4. Write a method that will display the values contained within a binary search tree in descending order.

5. Write a method called Count that will return the number of nodes contained within a binary search tree.

6. Rewrite your program from the linked list exercise to process bank accounts. However, instead of using a linked list object, now you need to implement it using a binary search tree. It should store a name (as an array of characters), an account number (as an integer), and a balance (as a float). It should allow deposits, withdrawals, and balance inquiries as well as the ability to add accounts. You do not have to implement the remove function as we did not discuss removing nodes from a tree.

7. Complete the code required to implement the changes required for implementing the case study for this chapter.

♦Additional Exercises

1. What are the advantages of using a binary tree over other structures such as a linked list or an array?

2. In your own words, what is a tree? What is a binary search tree? What are the differences?

3. Can a child node also be a parent node?

4. How does a leaf node differ from a child node?

5. What is the maximum number of children that a node can have in a binary tree?

6. Does the addition of a new node always mean that it will be a leaf node?

7. What is the minimum number of nodes that a tree can have? What is the maximum?

8. Draw the binary search tree formed by inserting the following values: 100, 56, 11, 111, 77, 120, 101, 99.

9. Draw the binary search tree formed by inserting the following values: 50, 60, 70, 40, 30, 20, 35, 45, 55, 65.

10. Draw the binary search tree formed by inserting the following values: 10, 90, 500, 1000, 1300.

11. Draw the binary search tree formed by inserting the following values: 1300, 1000, 500, 90, 10.

12. Does the order values are entered into a tree affect the speed in which a value is found when it is searched for?

13. What would be an easy method to allow deletion from a tree that would not require any pointer manipulations?

16

Hash Tables

Chapter Objectives

♦ Introduce a simple efficient data structure optimized for searching

♦ Master algorithms required for hash table implementation

♦ Develop a C++ class for implementation of a hash table

16.1 WHAT IS A HASH TABLE?

So far we have seen data structures that allow adding, removing, searching, and displaying values, but how efficient were they? We can easily see how a binary tree, in most cases, performs its operations faster than a linked list. However, how fast is fast enough? As they said in *Top Gun,* "I feel the need, the need for speed." Although speed is good, how much speed required depends upon your application and the amount of data that application deals with. Imagine if you were to write a program similar to software used to run a search engine like Yahoo!. You would be indexing millions, potentially billions, of Web pages and key words. Clearly a linked list would be too slow to handle the multitudes of requests made every second. Even a binary tree would be too slow.

Since the majority of actions performed on such a structure would be searches, it would make sense to optimize your structure for searches. Have you ever noticed that although you can look pages up on a search engine very quickly, if you want to add your page to a search engine, it takes up to a couple of days or even weeks to have your page added. You will soon see why.

Although the search engines may not use the structure we are about to introduce, the concepts of a **hash table** are used in many database applications and provide an excellent way for us to improve search time. However, this speed does not come without a cost. Inserts in some conditions can be time consuming and the space required for hash tables can be considerable. Let's ignore these issues initially and dive into an example.

Imagine if you had to track whether or not you had a particular baseball card. Baseball cards typically have a number on the back. With a linked list or tree structure you could insert each number into a list and then search for the number of a particular card. Although this process will work, it would be time consuming if the number of cards were large.

Instead, imagine if we set up an array. The array would have as many elements as potential cards. By initializing the entire array to false, we could then set the array element that corresponded to the card number to true. Now how long would it take to discover whether or not we owned a particular card? The amount of time it would take to look up one array element. You can't get much faster than that!

The problem is that in the real world, our problems do not map so easily to the simple array model. Imagine if you had to track something other than baseball cards. Imagine if instead you choose to track whether a particular person attended your school. How do you map such a person to an array? You might think about using a person's social security number. Will that work? Sure, if you have an array with over one billion cells. This would seem like quite a waste if your school only wished to track 10,000 students.

That's where a hash table comes in. We need to develop a methodology that allows us to have the efficiency of the array implementation discussed with a mechanism for handling the issue of space. This will require a compromise to be made. The compromise is the traditional one: space versus time. As we decrease the size of our array, the efficiency of our data structure will decrease.

However, a bigger issue ensues. As we decrease the size of our array, we need a way to decide the location in the array in which to store the information we are tracking. In addition, as we reduce the size of the array, different values will map to the same location. We will need to develop ways to handle this as well. How we handle these issues will determine the type of hash table we have.

16.2 HOW DOES A HASH TABLE OPERATE?

If we want to solve the problem of mapping people's social security numbers to an array, many approaches exist. A simple one is to use a portion of a person's social security number as the index to the array. What if we choose the last three digits of a social security number as the index? Then we could map anyone to any location within the array. However, although this may seem like an answer to our problems, a new problem arises. What do we do if two people have the same last three digits? We can still use our basic idea if we develop an efficient methodology for dealing with duplicates, and if we ensure that duplicates do not occur frequently.

When two values map to the same location in the hash table, we call it a **collision**. A good rule of thumb to ensure a low incidence of **collisions** is to create an array that is at least double the size of the number of elements we wish to track. The simplest method for handling duplicates is called **chaining**. As duplicates occur, we can add them to the array by placing them onto a linked list that is pointed to by the array element.

Figure 16.1 shows the insertion of six social security numbers (065-11-1234, 992-12-0923, 123-45-6789, 435-33-5234, 549-01-9923, 190-42-0004) into a hash table of size 10. For purposes of simplicity, we will use the last digit of the social security number as a map into the array.

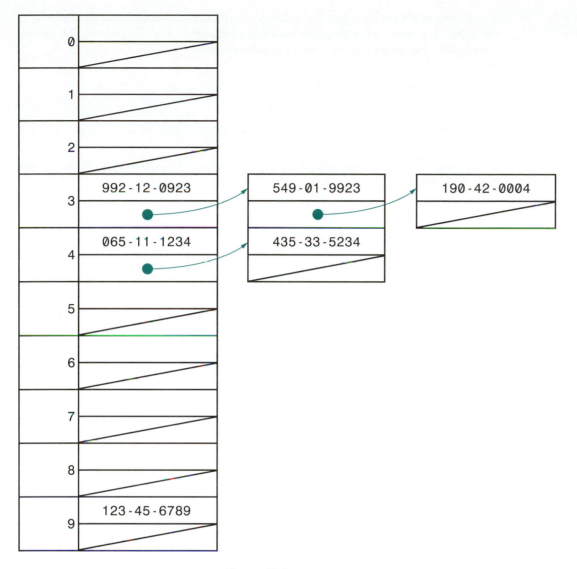

Figure 16.1

You can see that when the last digit is the same, the duplicate social security numbers appear as nodes on a linked list.

An easier solution is to place the duplicate somewhere else within the hash table. There are two methods of placing duplicates that we will explore, **linear probing** and **quadratic probing**.

Linear probing attempts to place the duplicate value in the next available cell. This requires that we modify our search routine so that if we search for an item and it is not contained within the cell that we are looking for, we continue to search until we find it or find an unoccupied cell.

Since we can potentially store different values in the same array cell, we must use something more than a Boolean flag indicating that a value exists. Now we must store both whether or not the cell contains a valid value as well as the value itself.

The following example stores three-digit numbers in a hash table of size 10. To determine the cell in which we place the three-digit value, we divide by the size of the table (10) and use the remainder as the index to the hash table. In our example, it is easy to determine the index, because it is the last digit of the value. This will not always be the case.

A simple way to calculate the index is to calculate the modulus of the value with the table size. Remember that the modulus operator is the % operator. Therefore, to calculate the index we could use the following:

```
CellIndex = Value % TableSize;
```

If we wanted to insert the numbers 404, 203, 109, 33, and 105, our table would look as follows:

Index	Stat First	After	Stat Second	After	Stat Third	After	Stat Fourth	After	Stat Fifth	After
0	U		U		U		U		U	
1	U		U		U		U		U	
2	U		U		U		U		U	
3	U		O	203	O	203	O	203	O	203
4	O	404	O	404	O	404	O	404	O	404
5	U		U		U		O	33	O	33
6	U		U		U		U		O	105
7	U		U		U		U		U	
8	U		U		U		U		U	
9	U		U		O	109	O	109	O	109

U = Unoccupied   O = Occupied

First we insert 404. To insert 404, we must determine the proper index within the hash table. The index, 4, is determined by the calculation 404 % 10. Since nothing is stored in the fourth slot, we can store 404 there.

Similarly, when we wish to insert 203, we calculate the cell index, 3, by the calculation 203 % 10. Since cell 3 is available we can store our number there.

109 is also inserted into the table in a similar manner. We calculate the cell index, 9, by the calculation 109 % 10.

However, when we attempt to insert 33, we encounter our first collision. The cell index, 3, is calculated by 33 % 10. But cell 3 of the hash table is already occupied by the value 203. Therefore, we search for the next available spot, 4, and see if it is available. Unfortunately, it also is already occupied by the value 404. We continue to the fifth spot and find it is available, so the value 33 is placed in the fifth spot.

When we attempt to insert 105, another collision occurs. Despite the fact that no previous entry ended in a 5, this collision occurs because the previous entries had collisions. To insert the 105 value properly, we simply move to the next available spot, 6, and insert it there.

In order for a hash table to be effective, it is important to keep the number of collisions to a minimum. One easy way to do this it to mandate that when a table becomes half full, that we double the table size and rehash all the values into the new table.

In the following example, the following seven items are inserted into a hash table: 89, 100, 9, 45, 33, 13, and 65. We will follow all of the previous rules; however, now we will increase the table size when the table is half full.

Index	Stat	After First	Stat	After Second	Stat	After Third	Stat	After Fourth	Stat	After Fifth
0	U		O	100	O	100	O	100	O	100
1	U		U		O	9	O	9	O	9
2	U		U		U		U		U	
3	U		U		U		U		O	33
4	U		U		U		U		U	
5	U		U		U		O	45	O	45
6	U		U		U		U		U	
7	U		U		U		U		U	
8	U		U		U		U		U	
9	O	89	O	89	O	89	O	89	O	89

After the fifth insertion, we need to double the size of our array. Now our array contains 20 elements. The hash function can no longer use the shortcut of looking at the last digit of the number; instead, it needs to be the remainder of the value when divided by the table size.

To get the optimum efficiency of our newly created table we need to remap all the previously inserted values using our new hash function. Since we do not store the order of insert in our hash table, the process of doubling our hash table continues by looping from the first index to the last and reinserting any occupied cells into the new table.

Observe the reinserted hash table as it is created:

Index	Stat	After First	Stat	After Second	Stat	After Third	Stat	After Fourth	Stat	After Fifth
0	O	100	O	100	O	100	O	100	O	100
1	U		U		U		U		U	
2	U		U		U		U		U	
3	U		U		U		U		U	
4	U		U		U		U		U	
5	U		U		U		O	45	O	45
6	U		U		U		U		U	
7	U		U		U		U		U	
8	U		U		U		U		U	
9	U		O	9	O	9	O	9	O	9
10	U		U		U		U		O	89
11	U		U		U		U		U	
12	U		U		U		U		U	
13	U		U		O	33	O	33	O	33
14	U		U		U		U		U	
15	U		U		U		U		U	
16	U		U		U		U		U	
17	U		U		U		U		U	
18	U		U		U		U		U	
19	U		U		U		U		U	

If, instead, we insert the values in their original order, the table would be created as follows:

Index	Stat	After First	Stat	After Second	Stat	After Third	Stat	After Fourth	Stat	After Fifth
0	U		O	100	O	100	O	100	O	100
1	U		U		U		U		U	
2	U		U		U		U		U	
3	U		U		U		U		U	
4	U		U		U		U		U	
5	U		U		U		O	45	O	45
6	U		U		U		U		U	
7	U		U		U		U		U	
8	U		U		U		U		U	
9	O	89	O	89	O	89	O	89	O	89
10	U		U		O	9	O	9	O	9
11	U		U		U		U		U	
12	U		U		U		U		U	
13	U		U		U		U		O	33
14	U		U		U		U		U	
15	U		U		U		U		U	
16	U		U		U		U		U	
17	U		U		U		U		U	
18	U		U		U		U		U	
19	U		U		U		U		U	

Think for a moment about the two methods of growing the hash table. Although it is easy for a human to look back at the order we entered items into the hash table, it is not always so easy for a computer to remember the original order. If we wanted a hash table to remember the order of the inserted items, it would take longer to process inserts and it would waste a lot of space. Therefore, the computer must rehash using the order they were stored in the array. So we must use the first table of the previous two to continue with the insertion of our final values, as shown here.

The final two items can now be added:

Index	Stat	After Sixth	Stat	After Seventh
0	O	100	O	100
1	U		U	
2	U		U	
3	U		U	
4	U		U	
5	O	45	O	45
6	U		O	65
7	U		U	
8	U		U	
9	O	9	O	9
10	O	89	O	89
11	U		U	
12	U		U	
13	O	33	O	33
14	O	13	O	13
15	U		U	
16	U		U	
17	U		U	
18	U		U	
19	U		U	

Often when collisions occur, the values may tend to group together. To combat this, we use another method called **quadratic probing**. It functions similarly to linear probing; however, when multiple collisions occur, instead of stepping to the next cell we use the following formula:

Linear Probing
```
Hash(x) % TableSize
(Hash(x)+1) % TableSize
(Hash(x)+2) % TableSize
(Hash(x)+3) % TableSize
Etc....
```

Quadratic Probing
```
(Hash(x)+0² )% TableSize
(Hash(x)+1² )% TableSize
(Hash(x)+2² )% TableSize
(Hash(x)+3² )% TableSize
Etc.....
```

The following example inserts the following seven items into a hash table using quadratic probing instead of linear probing: 89, 100, 9, 45, 33, 120, and 0. We will follow all of the previous rules, except when collisions occur.

Index	Stat	After First	Stat	After Second	Stat	After Third	Stat	After Fourth	Stat	After Fifth
0	U		O	100	O	100	O	100	O	100
1	U		U		U		U		U	
2	U		U		U		U		U	
3	U		U		O	9	O	9	O	9
4	U		U		U		U		O	33
5	U		U		U		O	45	O	45
6	U		U		U		U		U	
7	U		U		U		U		U	
8	U		U		U		U		U	
9	O	89	O	89	O	89	O	89	O	89

We wish to insert 89, so we calculate the cell index, 9, by the calculation 89 % 10. Since cell 9 is available we can store 89 in cell 9.

Next we insert 100 by calculating the cell index, 0, with the calculation 100 % 10. Since cell 0 is available, we can store 100 in cell 0.

So far both insertions would be placed in the same cell location whether we used linear probing or quadratic probing.

However, when we attempt to insert the value 9, we calculate the cell index, 9, with the calculation 9 % 10. Since cell 9 is not available and since we are using quadratic probing, we calculate the next possible cell with the calculation $(Hash(x)+1^2)$ % TableSize. Since Hash(x) equals 9 and 1^2 equals 1, a simplified form of the cell index calculation is (9 + 1) % 10. Therefore, the next cell to try is cell 0.

Unfortunately cell 0 is also occupied. Therefore we must calculate the next possible cell with the calculation $(Hash(x)+2^2)$% TableSize. Since Hash(x) still equals 9 and 2^2 equals 4, a simplified form of the index calculation is (9 + 4) % 10. Therefore, the next cell to try is 3. Since cell 3 is available, we can store 9 in cell 3.

Next we insert 45 by calculating the cell index, 5, with the calculation 45 % 10. Since cell 5 is available, we can store 45 there.

However, when we attempt to insert 33, the first cell index calculated, 3, is occupied. 3 is calculated by 33 % 10. To calculate the next possible cell to insert 33, we use the formula $(Hash(x)+1^2)$ % TableSize, or (3+1) % 10. Therefore, we attempt to insert the value into cell 4. Since cell 4 is unoccupied, we can insert 33 there.

After the fifth insertion, we need to double the size of our array. Now our array contains 20 elements. As with linear probing, the hash function that we use can no longer be the last digit; it needs to be the remainder of the value when divided by the table size.

As with linear probing, to obtain the optimum efficiency of our newly created table we need to remap all the previously inserted values using our new hash function. Since we do not store the order the items we were inserting in our hash table, the process of doubling our hash table continues by looping from the first index to the last and reinserting any occupied cells into the new table. This may give us a different hash table than if we insert the items in the same order that they were initially.

Observe the reinserted hash table as it is created:

Index	Stat	After First	Stat	After Second	Stat	After Third	Stat	After Fourth	Stat	After Fifth
0	O	100	O	100	O	100	O	100	O	100
1	U		U		U		U		U	
2	U		U		U		U		U	
3	U		U		U		U		U	
4	U		U		U		U		U	
5	U		U		U		U		U	
6	U		U		U		U		U	
7	U		U		U		U		U	
8	U		U		U		U		U	
9	U		O	9	O	9	O	9	O	9
10	U		U		U		U		O	89
11	U		U		U		U		U	
12	U		U		U		U		U	
13	U		U		O	33	O	33	O	33
14	U		U		U		U		U	
15	U		U		U		O	45	O	45
16	U		U		U		U		U	
17	U		U		U		U		U	
18	U		U		U		U		U	
19	U		U		U		U		U	

The final two items can now be added:

Index	Stat	After Sixth	Stat	After Seventh
0	O	100	O	100
1	O	120	O	120
2	U		U	
3	U		O	0
4	U		O	0
5	U		U	
6	U		U	
7	U		U	
8	U		U	
9	O	9	O	9
10	O	89	O	89
11	U		U	
12	U		U	
13	O	33	O	33
14	U		U	
15	O	45	O	45
16	U		U	
17	U		U	
18	U		U	
19	U		U	

When we attempt to insert 120, the first cell index calculated, 0, is occupied. 0 is calculated by 120 % 10. To calculate the next possible cell to insert 120, we use the formula $(Hash(x)+1^2)$ % TableSize, or $(0+1)\%10$. Therefore, we attempt to insert the value into cell 1. Since cell 1 is unoccupied, we can insert 120 there.

The final insertion, 0, also has collision issues. The first cell index calculated, 0, is occupied. 0 is calculated by 0 % 10. To calculate the next possible cell to insert 0, we use the formula $(Hash(x)+1^2)$ % TableSize, or $(0+1)$ % 10. Since cell 1 is also occupied, we calculate the next possible insertion position by using the formula $(Hash(x)+2^2)$ % TableSize, or $(0+4)$ % 10. Since cell 4 is not occupied, the value 0 can be stored there.

Deletion of a Value

So far we have shown you how to add values to a hash table, but not how to remove them. Observe what would happen if we executed the following code:

```
#include <stdlib.h>
#include <iostream.h>

//Hash table definitions included here

void main()
{
   HashTable Values;

   Values.Insert(107);
   Values.Insert(106);
   Values.Insert(206);
   Values.Delete(106);
   if (Values.Search(206))
     cout<<"Found"<<endl;
   else
     cout<<"Not Found"<<endl;
}
```

The hash table would look as follows:

Index	Stat	After First	Stat	After Second	Stat	After Third	Stat	After Delete
0	U		U		U		U	
1	U		U		U		U	
2	U		U		U		U	
3	U		U		U		U	
4	U		U		U		U	
5	U		U		U		U	
6	U		O	106	O	106	U	
7	O	107	O	107	O	107	O	107
8	U		U		O	206	O	206
9	U		U		U		U	

After the first three inserts, the hash table looks as we would expect. The problem comes when we delete a value, for example, 106. If we now search for a value like 206, we first search for 206 at the hash function value (6), and we find the cell unoccupied. Therefore we would return false when 206 really is contained in the hash table.

The correction to this problem is simple. We must mark a cell when it has been deleted. Then we write our search algorithm to look for the desired value until an unoccupied cell is discovered instead of an occupied cell.

By modifying the hash table we now see the corrected hash table that will allow for correct searches after a delete has occurred.

Index	Stat	After First	Stat	After Second	Stat	After Third	Stat	After Delete
0	U		U		U		U	
1	U		U		U		U	
2	U		U		U		U	
3	U		U		U		U	
4	U		U		U		U	
5	U		U		U		U	
6	U		O	106	O	106	D	
7	O	107	O	107	O	107	O	107
8	U		U		O	206	O	206
9	U		U		U		U	

U = Unoccupied　　　O = Occupied　　　D = Deleted

Inserting Strings

While the examples we looked at work great for numbers, what do you do when the item you are trying to add to the hash table does not have a number assigned to it? Some might suggest assigning a student number to a person, but methods such as these usually do not work well with individuals forgetting their numbers. An easier way is to develop a hash function that creates a numeric key from a word or name.

The simplest, but not very effective, of these would be to count the number of letters in a first and last name and use that as a key. However, with just a few names, this method would become flooded with duplicates.

A better method might be to add the ASCII values of the letters in a person's first and last name and take the modulus of the table size. Although duplicates will still occur, they will occur with much less frequency than just counting letters. C++ allows us to do this very easily, because a character is really implemented as an integer. You can simply create a sum variable. Initialize it to zero and then add all the characters to it.

This can be seen in the following function:

```
int HashFunction(char * Name, int TableSize)
{
    int Sum=0;
    while (*Name !='\0')
        Sum+=*Name;
    return Sum%TableSize;
}
```

For hash tables to be effective, duplicates must be minimized and the hash function itself must execute quickly. More complicated hash functions usually lead to less duplicate keys, but increased search time. A balance must be met that works for the application for which the hash table is being developed.

DRILLS

Show what the hash table would look like after each action of the hash table is called first using linear probing, then using quadratic probing. Assume that the hash tables are empty, initially. Observe the rules for doubling the array size as described in this chapter.

Drill 16-1

```
HashTable Values;
Values.Insert(1);
Values.Insert(11);
Values.Insert(111);
Values.Insert(0);
```

Drill 16-2

```
HashTable Values;
Values.Insert(199);
Values.Insert(87);
Values.Insert(55);
Values.Delete(87);
Values.Insert(77);
Values.Delete(199);
Values.Insert(65);
Values.Insert(66);
```

16.3 HASH TABLE CLASS IMPLEMENTATION

Our implementation of hash tables is implemented with a class to abstract the details of the implementation from the user. Externally, the user of the hash table sees three methods to allow for insertion, deletion, and searching of the hash table.

Internally, we compose the hash table as an array of structures. The structure defines space for the value we wish to store and a status. In our implementation, the values being stored are integers, but with a minor modification the hash table can store any data type. The three values for the status field can be **Occupied**, **Unoccupied**, or **Deleted**. These values are specified using a **define** statement so that throughout the code we can refer to them by name instead of their integer equivalent.

```cpp
#include <stdlib.h>
#include <iostream.h>

//Used to indicate the status of a hash table cell
#define Occupied 0
#define Unoccupied 1
#define Deleted 2

//Used to indicate a search failed
#define NotFound -1

//Initial size of the hash table
#define DefaultSize 13

//Structure for a hash table cell
struct HashElement
{
    int Value;
    int Status;
};

//Hash table class
class HashTable
{
    public:
        bool Insert (int Value);
        bool Delete(int Value);
        int Search(int Value);
        HashTable();
        ~HashTable();
    private:
        void Clear();
        int HashFunction(int HashValue);
        int TableSize;
        int CurrentSize;
        HashElement * Array;
};
```

A constructor is defined that allocates the necessary memory and calls a `Clear` method to initialize the status of each cell in the hash table.

```
//Constructor
HashTable :: HashTable()
{
    TableSize=DefaultSize;
    Array = new HashElement[TableSize];
    Clear();
}
```

```
//Initialize a hash table to unoccupied
void HashTable :: Clear()
{
    int TempIndex = TableSize - 1;

    //Loop through the table setting each value to unoccupied
    while(TempIndex)
      Array[TempIndex--].Status = Unoccupied;

    CurrentSize = 0;
}
```

A destructor is defined that deallocates any memory that has been allocated for the storage of the hash table.

```
//Destructor simply deallocates memory for the table
HashTable :: ~HashTable()
{
    delete [] Array;
}
```

A method called `HashFunction` provides the conversion from an item we wish to place in the hash table and the index of the initial possible location.

```
//Map a value to the hash table
int HashTable :: HashFunction(int HashValue)
{
    return HashValue % TableSize;
}
```

The user and the **Delete** method use a method called **Search** to determine if a value is currently stored in the hash table. By calling the **HashFunction** method, the **Search** method determines the first possible location of the value passed as a parameter and stores it in **CurrentPosition**. **Search** then loops as long as the status of the cell pointed to by **CurrentPosition** is not unoccupied and is not the value we are searching for. If we reach the end of the array, we reset the **CurrentPosition** index to 0. You may worry that this could cause an infinite loop, but remember that we stated no hash table will ever be more than half full. Therefore, it is impossible to reach the first location that we check for.

```
//Find the value and if it exists mark the cell deleted.
bool HashTable :: Delete(int Value)
{
    int CurrentPosition;

    CurrentPosition = Search(Value);

    if (CurrentPosition == NotFound)
        return false;

    Array[CurrentPosition].Status = Deleted;
        return true;
}
```

The **Delete** method calls the **Search** method to get the location of the value to be removed from the hash table. If **Search** returns that the value is not found, the **Delete** method will return **false**, indicating that no value was removed. However, if **Search** returns a valid index, the status of the cell at the index is set to **Deleted**. When a valid deletion occurs, the method returns **true**.

```
//Perform search for cell
int HashTable :: Search(int Value)
{
    int i=0;
    int CurrentPosition;

    //Perform initial mapping
    CurrentPosition = HashFunction(Value);

    //Perform linear probing
    while (Array[CurrentPosition].Status != Unoccupied &&
            Array[CurrentPosition].Value != Value)
        if (++CurrentPosition >=TableSize)
            CurrentPosition = 0;

        if (Array[CurrentPosition].Status==Unoccupied ||
            Array[CurrentPosition].Status==Deleted)
            return NotFound;
        else
            return CurrentPosition;
}
```

The final method, **Insert**, is the most complicated. We start by finding the initial place the value might be inserted into the hash table. Then we perform a linear search as we did in the **Search** method, to find the first available location to insert the value.

Once the proper location has been found, if the insertion value already exists there, then the method returns false, since duplicates are not allowed in a hash table. If the value does not exist, then the insertion value is placed at the index pointed to by **CurrentPosition**, and the number of items contained in the hash table is increased. Another check must now be performed to determine whether or not the hash table is too full. If the number of items is greater than or equal to half the total capacity of the hash table, then we must double the size of the array storing the hash table.

To double the size of the array we must allocate an array twice the size of the current array. However, instead of allocating the memory and assigning it to a new pointer, we create a temporary pointer to the old array so that we do not lose the existing values in the hash table. We then allocate the new array to the existing hash table pointer. Then we step through the old array and insert each value found in an occupied cell of the old hash table. When all the values in the old array are transferred, we return the memory used by the array by issuing a **delete** command.

```
bool HashTable :: Insert (int Value)
{
   //Search table for value
   int CurrentPosition;

   CurrentPosition = HashFunction(Value);

   while (Array[CurrentPosition].Status != Unoccupied &&
          Array[CurrentPosition].Value != Value)
   {
      CurrentPosition++;

      //Check to see if we have stepped past the end of the array
      if (CurrentPosition >=TableSize)
        CurrentPosition = 0;
   }

   //If the value exists, return without it being inserted
   if (Array[CurrentPosition].Status == Occupied)
     return false;

   //Add the info to the cell.
   Array[CurrentPosition].Status = Occupied;
   Array[CurrentPosition].Value = Value;
   CurrentSize++;

   //Check to see if the size is not > than half.
   if (CurrentSize*2 < TableSize)
     return true;

   //If the table is more than half full, double the
   //size of the array and rehash the values.

   HashElement * OldTable = Array;  //Points to the old array

   CurrentSize = 0;
```

```
    //Allocate the new array.
    Array = new HashElement[TableSize*2];

    //Insert all occupied values into new table.
    for (int i=0; i<TableSize; i++)
      if (OldTable[i].Status == Occupied)
        Insert(OldTable[i].Value);

    TableSize *=2;   //Double the size

    //Delete the old table.
    delete [] OldTable;
    return true;
}
```

16.4 Case Study

Problem Description

Our case study for this chapter will continue with the same example as the previous two chapters. When the number of items tracked starts to grow, sometimes a tree is not fast enough. By using a hash table we increase the performance considerably.

Problem Discussion

As before, the code provided in this text is not sufficient to handle a real-world problem. In the real world we will usually require a hash table to store more than just a single value. Imagine if we wanted to track a student's average grade for a class. We would need to track both the grade of the student and a unique identifier for the student. We can use the existing code of a hash table to track the student's social security number, assuming we change the value to a long instead of an integer. However, we need to add another field to track grades associated with each student.

To accommodate this, we need to modify the **HashElement** structure to hold both the social security number and a grade. This is shown in the following code:

```
//Structure for a hash table cell
struct HashElement
{
   long SSN;
   gloat Average;
   int Status;
};
```

Additionally, the **HashTable** class must be modified so that the **Insert** method accepts a social security number and a grade. We should also change the methods **Delete**, **Search**, and **HashFunction** to accept a social security number instead of the integer **Value**.

Solution

```
//Hash table class
class HashTable
{
   public:
      bool Insert (long SSN, float Average);
      bool Delete(long SSN);
      float Search(long SSN);
      HashTable();
      ~HashTable();
   private:
      void Clear();
      int HashFunction(long HashValue);
      int TableSize;
      int CurrentSize;
      HashElement * Array;
};
```

The actual method implementation requires minor changes and is left as an exercise to the reader.

To use our new **HashTable** class, see the following example where we read 100 sets of social security numbers and grades. Then the program asks the user to enter social security numbers to search for in the hash table. The program ends when a negative number is entered for a social security number.

```
#include <stdlib.h>
#include <iostream.h>

//Hash table definitions are included here.

void main()
{
   HashTable StudentsAverages;
   int StudentCounter;
   long StudentNumber;
   float StudentAverage;

   //Read in 100 grades and insert them into the hash table.
   for(StudentCounter=0; StudentCounter < 100; StudentCounter++)
   {
      cout<<"Enter the Student's Social Security Number"<<endl;
      cin>>StudentNumber;
      cout<<"Enter the Student's average"<<endl;
      cin>>StudentAverage;
      StudentAverages.Insert(StudentNumber, StudentAverage);
   }
```

```
   do
   {
    cin>>StudentNumber;
    if (StudentNumber >= 0)
      cout<<"The student's average is "
           <<StudentAverages.Search(StudentNumber)<<endl;
   } while (StudentNumber >=0)
   }
```

◆ Key Terms

Chaining	A method used to handle collisions that requires a linked list to be used to store the additional values mapped to the same index.
Collision	A term used to describe when two values map to the same index of a hash table.
Hash table	A data structure used to allow speedy searches of values, which requires a great deal of space.
Linear probing	A method used to handle collisions that requires searching for the proper index by continually moving to the next cell until the value is found (search/delete) or until a blank space is found (insert).
Modulus operator	An operator used to determine the remainder of a division. This is used to ensure that the calculated index of a hash table is not beyond the upper bound of the hash table.
Quadratic probing	A method used to handle collisions that requires searching for the proper index by using a quadratic formula until the value is found (search/delete) or until a blank space is found (insert).

◆Answers to Drills

Drill 16-1

Linear Probing

Index	Stat	After First	Stat	After Second	Stat	After Third	Stat	After Fourth
0	U		U		U		O	0
1	O	1	O	1	O	1	O	1
2	U		O	11	O	11	O	11
3	U		U		O	111	O	111
4	U		U		U		U	
5	U		U		U		U	
6	U		U		U		U	
7	U		U		U		U	
8	U		U		U		U	
9	U		U		U		U	

We wish to insert 1, so we calculate the cell index, 1, by the calculation 1 % 10. Since cell 1 is available we can store 1 in cell 1.

Next we insert 11 by calculating the cell index, 1, with the calculation 11 % 10. Since cell 1 is not available and we are using linear probing, we check the next cell, 2. Since cell 2 is available, we can store 11 in cell 2.

Next we insert 111 by calculating the cell index, 1, with the calculation 111 % 10. Since cell 1 is not available and we are using linear probing, we check the next cell, 2. However, cell 2 is also unavailable. Therefore, we check the next cell, 3. Since cell 3 is available, we can store 111 in cell 3.

Finally, we insert 0 by calculating the cell index, 0, with the calculation 0 % 10. Since cell 0 is available we can store 0 there.

Quadratic Probing

Index	Stat	After First	Stat	After Second	Stat	After Third	Stat	After Fourth
0	U		U		U		O	0
1	O	1	O	1	O	1	O	1
2	U		O	11	O	11	O	11
3	U		U		U		U	
4	U		U		U		U	
5	U		U		O	111	O	111
6	U		U		U		U	
7	U		U		U		U	
8	U		U		U		U	
9	U		U		U		U	

The insertion of 1 and 11 occur the same way, whether we are using linear probing or quadratic probing; but when we go to insert value 111 we see that a different location is calculated.

First we calculate the cell index, 1, with the calculation 111 % 10. Since cell 1 is not available and we are using quadratic probing we must check for the next possible location using the calculation $(Hash(x)+1^2)$ % TableSize. A simplified form of the cell index calculation is $(1 + 1)$ % 10. Therefore, the next cell to try is cell 2.

Unfortunately cell 2 is also occupied. Therefore we must calculate the next possible cell with the calculation $(Hash(x)+2^2)$% TableSize. Since Hash(x) still equals 1 and 2^2 equals 4, a simplified form of the index calculation is $(1 + 4)$ % 10. Therefore, the next cell to try is 5. Since cell 5 is available, we can store 111 there.

Finally, we insert 0 by calculating the cell index, 0, with the calculation 0 % 10. Since cell 0 is available we can store 0 in cell 0 as we did with linear probing.

Drill 16-2

Linear Probing

Index	Stat	After First	Stat	After Second	Stat	After Third	Stat	After Delete	Stat	After Fourth
0	U		U		U		U	U		
1	U		U		U		U	U		
2	U		U		U		U	U		
3	U		U		U		U	U		
4	U		U		U		U	U		
5	U		U		O	55	O	55	O	55
6	U		U		U		U		U	
7	U		O	87	O	87	D	87	O	77
8	U		U		U		U		U	
9	O	199	O	199	O	199	O	199	O	199

Index	Stat	After Delete	Stat	After Fifth	Stat	After Sixth
0	U		U		U	
1	U		U		U	
2	U		U		U	
3	U		U		U	
4	U		U		U	
5	O	55	O	55	O	55
6	U		O	65	O	65
7	O	77	O	87	O	87
8	U		U		O	66
9	D	199	D	199	D	199

The first three inserts are straightforward and have no collisions. Therefore, 199 maps to cell 9, 87 maps to cell 7, and 55 maps to cell 5, using the calculations 199 % 10, 87 % 10, and 55 % 10, respectively. Then a `delete` command is issued for value 87. The 87 is not removed, but the status of its cell is marked as Deleted. Then when the value 77 is inserted, it can be written over the 87 and the status of cell 7 is set to Occupied.

When 199 is deleted, its cell is marked Deleted as well. We then insert the value 65 using the calculation 65 % 10. Since cell 5 is occupied, the next available cell, 6, is used to insert the value 65.

Finally when the value 66 is inserted, we have a collision at cell 6, so we try cell 7, but that value is occupied as well, so we insert 66 in cell 8.

PROGRAMMER'S NOTEBOOK

Although there were six insertions in this example, because the array was never half full, we never had to double the size of the array.

The initial five inserts and two deletions operate the same way as with linear probing, so we will pick up our answer with the insertion of the value 66.

Quadratic Probing

Index	Stat	After Sixth
0	O	66
1	U	
2	U	
3	U	
4	U	
5	O	55
6	O	65
7	O	87
8	U	
9	D	199

First we calculate the cell index, 6, with the calculation 66 % 10. Since cell 6 is not available and we are using quadratic probing we must check for the next possible location using the calculation $(Hash(x)+1^2)$ % TableSize. A simplified form of the cell index calculation is $(6 + 1)$ % 10. Therefore, the next cell to try is cell 7.

Unfortunately cell 7 is also occupied. Therefore we must calculate the next possible cell with the calculation $(Hash(x)+2^2)$% TableSize. Since Hash(x) still equals 1 and 2^2 equals 4, a simplified form of the index calculation is $(6 + 4)$ % 10. Therefore, the next cell to try is 0. Since cell 0 is available, we can store 66 there.

◆Programming Exercises

1. Rewrite the hash table class so that it handles strings instead of integers as values.

2. Rewrite the hash table class so that it handles quadratic probing instead of linear probing.

3. Rewrite the hash table class so that it handles chaining instead of linear probing.

4. Complete the code required to implement the changes required by implementing the case study for this chapter.

◆Additional Exercises

1. Given a hash table with an initial size of 10 that uses linear probing, show what the hash table would look like after each insert when the following values are inserted: 13, 4, 23, 99, 100, 25, 33. *Make sure that you remember to increase the size of the hash table at the proper time and rehash the values properly.*

2. Given a hash table with an initial size of 10 that uses linear probing, show what the hash table would look like after each insert when the following values are inserted: 22, 12, 11, 188, 100, 101, 81. *Make sure that you remember to increase the size of the hash table at the proper time and rehash the values properly.*

3. Given a hash table with an initial size of 10 that uses quadratic probing, show what the hash table would look like after each insert when the following values are inserted: 13, 4, 23, 99, 100, 25, 33. *Make sure that you remember to increase the size of the hash table at the proper time and rehash the values properly.*

4. Given a hash table with an initial size of 10 that uses quadratic probing, show what the hash table would look like after each insert when the following values are inserted: 22, 12, 11, 188, 100, 101, 81. *Make sure that you remember to increase the size of the hash table at the proper time and rehash the values properly.*

5. Do hash tables allow duplicate values?

6. Does the order that values are inserted into a hash table make a difference in how quickly a specific individual value is found when it is searched for?

◆ A Final Word About Program Order

When we first started programming, we dictated to you an order in which components of your code should be placed in your program. Now that you have a firm grasp on these components, let's review their order of placement in your program. The reasons we dictated the order we did will become clear.

Program Purpose

We started by telling you to place the program's name and purpose at the beginning of each file. This is done to ensure that you can quickly identify the program and the reason it was written. You would not want to place it anywhere other than the beginning, because if you had to search through your code to find it, it would take too long.

Include Files

The next section was to list all of the include files that you will be using. The reason for listing this before any code that you might write is that you might reference items from the include files in your code. If you reference something before it has been defined for the C++ compiler, it will return an error. Since the system include files will not be attempting to reference your code, there is no need for the system include files to be placed anywhere but the beginning of your program.

Constants and Defines

After include files are declared, the next section is to list any constant definitions and `define` statements. Both of these types of statements may be used by the rest of the program, but would not reference any other constructs that you will define later.

Structures

Structures are the next section of code to be defined. They will define new types of variables for your program; therefore, they need to be defined before you use them in global variable, function, prototype, or class definitions. They must be defined after the constant and define statements, because a definition such as the size of an array may use a constant of define value.

Classes

Classes are defined next. They cannot be defined before structures, because a structure may be referenced from within the class. They must be defined before the global variables, functions, and prototypes, because the classes defined will be used with a function.

Globals

At this point in the program, we have defined any new types of variables that can be created. Therefore, now we can list any global variables that the program will use. These global variables can be used in functions. They will not be listed in prototypes, so technically they could be listed after the function prototypes. However, we feel it is better style to place them after the constructs from which they may be defined are declared.

Function Prototypes

Before any function is defined, we must list its prototypes. Though these can be listed before the global definitions, we feel it is better style to list them afterward.

Functions

There are two styles for placing your function definitions. You can place the **main** function first and then all the other function definitions after it or you can place all the function definitions first and list the **main** function definition last. Function definitions should not be too long. Therefore, with the **main** function definition last, it is easy to find.

Multiple File Programs

The preceding has been a template for program layout that will work wonderfully if followed. However, as programs get very large, it is sometimes convenient to store a program in multiple files. This would change the order of program layout somewhat. Since this is meant as an introductory text and there are many ways of laying out multiple file programs, we will leave that issue to other texts.

Quality Programming

What makes a good program? Beginning students often argue that since their programs function properly, they should receive an A. A program that meets the specifications dictated to the programmer meets only the first criterion of a quality program. A quality program should have all of the following characteristics.

Readability

In the real world, specifications for a program constantly change. After a programmer meets the initial requirements, users often see the value of their new application and want additional features. This maintenance phase of a computer project actually can be more expensive than the original development process. Therefore, it is imperative that the program is understandable not only to the original programmer, but to other programmers as well.

To improve readability, a key method a programmer can employ is to add comments to the program. Comments are statements in a program that explain the program's purpose and any unclear pieces of code along the way. These comments should be written into the code when the code is written, not after the entire program is completed. Sometimes comments within the code are not enough; it is often necessary to produce external documentation to round out the explanation of a project.

Beginning programmers, as well as some seasoned professionals, will jokingly argue that they do not comment their code to ensure job security. In reality, a programmer who develops readable, reliable code is far more valuable to a company than one who hoards knowledge in cryptic code. Additionally, a programmer who becomes the sole person to understand the code often ends up maintaining that code instead of moving on to more exciting and lucrative projects.

Additionally, having a programming standards document is extremely important. In the corporate programming environment, many programmers work together as a team to develop a single program. It is imperative that everyone follows the same conventions. These can include indenting code in a consistent manner, capitalizing the first letter of each word in a variable name, and using the same abbreviations each time a long word is abbreviated.

Modularity

To reduce the cost of maintenance, code must be modularized. This requires that programs be written in an orderly fashion, with problems divided into smaller subproblems and then assembled in a logical order. Each piece of code should accomplish one task and be capable of standing on its own.

Efficiency

The next issue is the tradeoff between writing compact, super-efficient code versus writing clear, readable code that may run a little more slowly and take up slightly more room. Which is more desirable? Well, that depends on the situation. If the code is being written for an air-to-air combat system, then speed of execution and size are the most important issues. However, most applications spend a majority of time dealing with the input of data. Speeding up seldom-used areas of code for such applications will not produce significantly improved performance. Therefore, you are adding complexity without a true increase in overall performance. In most cases, a marginal increase in the size of application is not a critical design factor. Rapidly declining prices of computer memory and storage have decreased the importance of reducing the size of most applications.

It is important to realize that the amount of characters you write in your program does not necessarily relate to program size. Sometimes small amounts of code require far more space than the remainder of the program.

If you add cryptic lines of code for the purposes of speed or size, then you should do two things: one, explain the intricacies of the code in full detail, and two, if a simpler way exists to implement the code, indicate so in the comments. This will assist future programmers in modifying your code, even if they do not understand your shortcut.

Robustness

If a program is written to do a particular task, how does it handle cases when the input to the program is not as expected? Does it crash? Does it go into an infinite loop? Or does it display a message indicating the information entered is incorrect and gracefully allow the user to exit or continue?

Usability

The last issue is probably the most difficult to master. A program must be correct to be useful. Whether the project is an assignment in class or a task given by your boss at work, if the project does not meet the needs of the end user, regardless of the elegance of your solution, it may never be used.

These are all issues that should be considered while programming. Following them will lead to a successful program and will produce much less stress in getting there.

APPENDIX

B

ASCII
Character Set

0 null '\0'	22 syn	44 comma	66 B	88 X	110 n
1 soh	23 etb	45 minus	67 C	89 Y	111 o
2 stx	24 can	46 period	68 D	90 Z	112 p
3 etx	25 em	47 /	69 E	91 [	113 q
4 end transmission	26 sub	48 0	70 F	92 \	114 r
5 enquire	27 escape	49 1	71 G	93]	115 s
6 acknowledge	28 fs	50 2	72 H	94 ^	116 t
7 ring a bell '\a'	29 gs	51 3	73 I	95 underscore	117 u
8 backspace '\b'	30 rs	52 4	74 J	96 back quote	118 v
9 tab '\t'	31 us	53 5	75 K	97 a	119 w
10 new line '\n'	32 blank	54 6	76 L	98 b	120 x
11 vertical tab '\v'	33 !	55 7	77 M	99 c	121 y
12 form feed '\f'	34 "	56 8	78 N	100 d	122 z
13 carriage return '\r'	35 #	57 9	79 O	101 e	123 {
14 so	36 $	58 :	80 P	102 f	124	
15 si	37 %	59 ;	81 Q	103 g	125 }
16 dle	38 &	60 <	82 R	104 h	126 ~
17 dc1	39 single quote	61 =	83 S	105 i	127 delete
18 dc2	40 (	62 >	84 T	106 j	
19 dc3	41)	63 ?	85 U	107 k	
20 dc4	42 *	64 @	86 V	108 l	
21 nak	43 +	65 A	87 W	109 m	

APPENDIX

C

COMMONLY USED C++ INPUT/OUTPUT TECHNIQUES

Manipulation of a program's input and output (I/O) is an unglamorous but very necessary task that a programmer must perform. Fortunately that task is made easier for the C++ programmer by the extremely rich I/O environment of streams, flags, and manipulators. This environment is so extensive that complete coverage would require more space than we can allocate here, so this appendix covers only the most commonly used features of the C++ I/O environment.

BASIC IOSTREAMS

The C++ IOStream library contains three stream objects that are linked to the computer's I/O channels.

`cin`-Used to receive input and connected to the computer's keyboard.

`cout`-Used to display output and connected to the computer's video display unit.

`cerr`-Used to display error messages and also connected to the computer's video display unit.

From the user's perspective there is no difference in viewing a message produced by a `cout` or `cerr` stream, since they both appear on the screen. For a programmer, these streams offer a convenient way to document the difference between an error message and normal output as shown in the following example.

```
#include <iostream.h>

int main()
{
   int n,d;
   cout << "Enter a number to be divided -> ";
   cin >> n;
   cout << "Enter the divisor -> ";
   cin >> d;
   if(d == 0) cerr << "Division by zero not allowed";
   else
   cout << "Quotient = " << n/d;
   return 0;
}
```

```
Enter a number to be divided -> 8
Enter the divisor -> 0
Division by zero not allowed

Enter a number to be divided -> 8
Enter the divisor -> 2
Quotient = 4
```

The double left-facing arrow (<<) is referred to as the insertion or output operator because the messages are inserted into the output or error streams. The double right-facing arrow (>>) is referred to as the extraction or input operator, because the numbers are extracted from the input stream. The rule-of-thumb for remembering which operator to use is: *Data flow is in the direction of the arrows*.

I/O FORMATTING FLAGS

There are many flags or switches that can be utilized to alter the formatting of the IOStreams discussed earlier. These flags use a binary pattern to convey their state to the stream. A one bit means that the switch is on; that is, the flag representing that particular formatting feature is set.

Flag Name	Flag Value	Flag Function
skipws	0x0001	Skips whitespace on input
left	0x0002	Left justification of output
right	0x0004	Right justification of output
internal	0x0008	Place spaces after sign or base indicator when a field width is specified
dec	0x0010	Show integers in decimal format
oct	0x0020	Show integers in octal format
hex	0x0040	Show integers in hexadecimal format

showbase	0x0080	Show the numbers base for octal and hexadecimal numbers
showpoint	0x0100	Show decimal point for all declared decimal numbers, even those without a fractional component
uppercase	0x0200	Display the hex base indicator and characters in uppercase for hexadecimal and scientific notation
showpos	0x0400	Show plus sign, + , for positive numbers
scientific	0x0800	Show exponential notation for all decimal numbers
fixed	0x1000	Show decimal notation for all decimal numbers regardless of size
unitbuf	0x2000	Flushes output buffers after each stream insertion
stdio	0x4000	Flushes **cout** and **cerr** buffers after each insertion

Table C.1

The flag values are shown in hexadecimal. These flags may be set by invoking functions in IOStream or IOManip libraries that must be included in any program that attempts to change them. The following example will show how we can determine the flag settings for the compiler being used, change them, and reset them to their original settings by using functions in the IOStream library.

```
#include <iostream.h>

int main()
{
  int initial, middle, last;
  initial = cout.flags(); // Gets the compiler's initial output flag setting
  cout.setf(ios :: hex); // Sets the hex flag so hex digits are displayed
  middle = cout.flags(); // Gets the flag settings after the hex flag is set
  cout << endl << initial << "   " << middle;
  cout.setf(ios :: showbase); //Sets the showbase flag
  cout << endl << initial << "   " << middle;
  cout.unsetf(ios :: hex | ios :: showbase ); //  Clears previously set flags
  last = cout.flags(); // Gets flag settings after the clear
  cout.setf(ios :: hex); // Sets the hex flag so hex digits are displayed
  cout << endl << initial << "   " << last;
  return 0;
}
```

```
2001  2041
0x2001  0x2041
2001  2001
```

This example and its output require a detailed explanation. The variable `initial` receives the default output flag setting of the compiler. Then the `hex` flag is set so the flag settings may be viewed in hexadecimal. `Middle` then receives the flag settings at that point in the program. Then the values of `initial` and `middle` are displayed as `2001` and `2041`, respectively. However, a person viewing these numbers would have no indication that they are hexadecimal. To provide that indication, the `showbase` flag is set. Now the values of `initial` and `middle` are displayed as `0x2001` and `0x2041`, respectively, with the `0x` indicating they are in hexadecimal.

Each hexadecimal digit can be represented with four binary digits. The four binary digit position values reading from left to right are 8421. A '1' indicates a bit has a value.

```
Group value    2    0    0    1
0x2001  =  0010 0000 0000 0001 Each group can indicate up to 4 flag settings
              ↑                      ↑   skipws flag value
              └──── unitbuf flag value
```

```
Group value    2    0    4    1
0x2041  =  0010 0000 0400 0001
              ↑         ↑        ↑   skipws flag value
              └── unitbuf flag value
                        └── hex flag value
```

The function call `cout.unsetf(ios :: hex | ios :: showbase )` unsets the `hex` and `showbase` flags, which restore the compiler to the default flag settings. These settings are placed in `last`. The third output line shows the `initial` and `last` flag settings are identical.

The general form for the arguments passed to the IOStream `setf` or `unsetf` functions is `ios :: flag name`. The C++ bitwise OR operator, `'|'`, can be used with any of the flag-changing functions to change multiple flags in a single call.

I/O FORMAT MANIPULATORS

In addition to the flags just discussed, C++ has other manipulators that can be used to control formatting. The manipulators shown in Table C.2 are in the IOManip library.

Manipulator	Manipulator Purpose
`setbase(val)`	Sets number base of display to the number specified by `val`
`setfill('val')`	Sets the fill character to the char specified by `val`
`setw(val)`	Sets field width to the size specified by `val`
`setprecision(val)`	Sets number of places for decimal numbers to that specified by `val`
`setiosflags(ios :: name)`	Sets the flag specified by name
`resetiosflags(ios :: name)`	Resets the flag specified by name

Table C.2

The next example uses calls to IOManip functions to demonstrate additional flag setting effects. The C++ bitwise OR operator, '|', used in the previous example can also be used in calls to the IOManip functions of **setiosflags** and **resetiosflags** as shown next.

```
#include <iostream.h>
#include <iomanip.h>

int main()
{
    float x = 140, y = -140;
    int fvalue;
    cout << endl << x << "   " << y << " Default flag output";
    // Sets showpos and showpoint flags
    cout << setiosflags(ios :: showpos | ios :: showpoint);
    cout << endl << x << "   " << y << " showpos & showpoint flag output";
    cout << setiosflags(ios :: scientific); // Sets scientific flag
    cout << endl << x << "   " << y << " showpos, showpoint, & scientific flag output";
    // Flag for uppercase hex and exponential display
    cout << setiosflags(ios :: uppercase);
    cout << setbase(16); // Sets display to base 16, hexadecimal
    fvalue = cout.flags(); // Gets flag settings
    cout << endl << fvalue << " Hex flag settings ";
    cout << resetiosflags(ios :: showpoint); //Resets showpoint flag
    cout << endl << x << "   " << y << " showpos , scientific & uppercase flag output";
    cout.flags(0); // Restores flag settings to default values
    cout << endl << x << "   " << y << " Restored default flag output";
    return 0;
}
```

140 -140	Default flag output
+140.000000 -140.000000	showpos & showpoint flag output
+1.400000e+02 -1.400000e+02	showpos, showpoint, & scientific flag output
2F41	Hex flag settings
+1.4E+02 -1.4E+02	showpos, scientific & uppercase flag output
140 -140	Restored default flag output

In the preceding example, **x** and **y** are declared as floating point variables and given values that do not contain any decimal values. The first line of output shows the values of the floating point variables as whole numbers, with only the negative number showing the sign. The next line shows the output after the **showpos** and **showpoint** flags are set. Number signs are now shown for both the positive and negative numbers. Six decimal places are displayed reflecting the default compiler precision setting. Precision is discussed later. The next line shows the number in exponential notation; the result of setting the **scientific** flag. Next the **uppercase** and **hex** flags are set; then the flag settings are captured and displayed. Note that hexadecimal value 15 is displayed as an uppercase F.

Group value   2   F   4   1
0x2041 = 0010 1111 0400 0001 Each group can indicate up to 4 flag settings

↑ skipws flag value

unitbuf flag value

scientific flag value

hex flag value

showpos flag value

showpoint flag value

uppercase flag value

The next line shows the result of resetting the **showpoint** flag. Note that the exponential indicator is now displayed as an uppercase E now that the **uppercase** flag is set. The function call **cout.flags(0)** is used to reset *all* the flags that were set in the program and restore the flag settings to their default values. This is demonstrated by a comparison of the first and last lines of output. Multiple bitwise OR's could have been used in the arguments of a call to the **resetiosflags** function to accomplish the same thing as **cout.flags(0)**, as could multiple calls to **resetiosflags**.

The next example illustrates most of the remaining flags and the **setw** and **setprecision** manipulators.

```cpp
#include <iostream.h>
#include <iomanip.h>
int main()
{
  float x = -3.1234567;
  float decimal[] = {1.111, 22.225, 333.336, 4444.40};


   //Sets field width to 20 sets internal flag
  cout << endl << setw(20) << x << setiosflags(ios :: internal)
       << setw(20) << x;
   //Sets field width to 20 sets left flag
  cout << endl << setw(20) << x << setiosflags(ios :: left)
       << setw(20) << x;
  cout.flags(0); // Resets flags to default
  cout << endl << "group 1";
  for(int i = 0; i < 4; i++)
    cout << endl << decimal[i];
  cout << endl << setprecision(2) << endl << "group 2";// sets precision to 2
  for(i = 0; i < 4; i++)
    cout << endl << decimal[i];
  cout << endl << setiosflags(ios :: fixed) << endl << "group 3"; // sets fixed flag
  for(i = 0; i < 4; i++)
    cout << endl << setw(7) << decimal[i];
  cout << setiosflags(ios :: showpoint); //Sets showpoint flag
  cout << endl << endl << "group 4";
  for(i = 0; i < 4; i++)
    cout << endl << setw(7) << decimal[i];
  return 0;
}
```

```
          -3.123457-         3.123457
-          3.123457-3.123457
group 1
1.111
22.225
333.335999
4444.399902

group 2
1.11
22.23
```

```
333.34
4.44e+03


group 3
   1.11
  22.23
 333.34
4444.4


group 4
   1.11
  22.23
 333.34
4444.40
```

In the first line of the output, the first number is right-justified in a field with width set to 20. This is the normal positioning for numbers. The next number shows the result of turning the **internal** flag on. This causes the field positions between the sign and the number to be padded with blanks. The first number on the second line shows the same conditions. The second number shows the result of setting the **left** flag on. This causes the number to be left-justified within the field. The two flags **internal** and **left** create an ambiguous condition. For the compiler this example used, the **left** flag had a higher precedence than **internal** flag. This may not hold true for all compilers. The safe course of action for the programmer is to reset the **internal** flag before setting the **left** flag. All flags are reset after the second line of output.

The next four output groups show how decimal numbers may be formatted. The numbers in the decimal array 1.111, 22.225, 333.336, 4444.40 have been chosen to provide them with specific characteristics. The first has a single integer digit and the third decimal place is less than 5. The second has two integer digits and the third decimal place is 5. The third has three integer digits and the third decimal place is more than 5. The last number has four integer digits, is greater than 999.99, and has a zero as a trailing decimal place.

The output of group 1 shows how the numbers will be displayed without any flags set or manipulators used. The differences in the values displayed and the number's original value is caused by the fact that numbers stored in a computer are not stored in decimal form.

Group 2 output is after the **setprecision** manipulator is used to set the precision of the display to two. The first number has the same two decimal places as its original value. The next two numbers have had the second decimal place increased by one. This is the result of the third decimal place in these numbers being 5 or larger. The third number is displayed in scientific notation, even though that flag was not set. *Any decimal number with a value greater than 999.99 will automatically be displayed in exponential form.*

Group 3 output is the result of using **setw** to set a field width of seven and setting the **fixed** flag on. The numbers are displayed right-justified in the field as they should be. With the exception of the last number, the decimal points are aligned and the numbers show two decimal places. This is because **setprecision** acts like a flag. It is only necessary to set it once in a program. The manipulator **setw**, however, must be used in front of any value for which you wish to specify a width. The reason that the last number has only one decimal place is that C++ *will not show trailing zeros unless the showpoint flag is set.*

Group 4 shows the output after the **showpoint** flag is set. All numbers show two decimal places and the decimal points are aligned. The field width of seven is the minimum width necessary to hold the largest number 4444.40, which has exactly seven positions including the decimal point.

The last example for this section illustrates the **setfill** manipulator and some additional decimal number characteristics.

```cpp
#include <iostream.h>
#include <iomanip.h>

int main()
{
  float x = 140.00;
  float decimal[] = {1.111, 22.225, 333.336, 4444.40};
  cout << x << endl;
  cout << setiosflags(ios :: showpoint); //Sets showpoint flag
  cout << x << endl;
  cout << setprecision(2) << x << endl; //Sets precision to 2
  cout << setiosflags(ios :: fixed); //Sets fixed flag
  cout << endl << "group output";
  for(int i = 0; i < 4; i++)
                                //Sets fill character to *
    cout << endl  << "$" << setfill('*') << setw(14) << decimal[i];
  return 0;
}
```

```
140
140.000000
140.00

group output
$**********1.11
$*********22.23
$********333.34
$*******4444.40
```

In the first example, x was initialized to 140. Here, it is initialized to 140.00. Comparing the first line of each program's output shows that the addition of the trailing zeros makes no difference; C++ ignores them. In the second line of output, setting the **showpoint** flag not only shows the decimal point, but any decimal places up to the default setting of the complier. The third line is the result of setting the precision to 2. The group output shows the result of setting the **setfill** manipulator to set the fill character to asterisk. Any unoccupied field position now shows an asterisk instead of a blank. The fill character in C++ is set to a space. If the fill character is changed by using the **setfill** manipulator, it remains set at the new character until it is changed back to a space.

ESCAPE SEQUENCES

An escape sequence is so named because the first character of a two-character sequence alters the way the computer interprets the second character. It causes an "escape" from the norm. The backslash, ' \ ', is the escape character used in C++. Table C.3 shows the C++ escape sequences.

Escape Sequence	Meaning	Purpose
\b	backspace	Moves back one position
\f	form feed	Moves to top of next page
\n	new line	Moves to next line
\r	return	Moves to beginning of line
\t	tab	Moves to next tab setting
\\	backslash	Inserts a backslash
\'	single quote	Inserts a single quote
\"	double quote	Inserts a double quote

Table C.3

Two of the characters in the second position of the escape sequence have meaning as part of the C++ syntax. The single quote symbol is used to delimit a single character; the double-quote character delimits a character string. Any attempt to display them would result in a syntax error, since the compiler would try to interpret them as part of a command. The backslash by itself would also cause an attempt at execution since it denotes the beginning of the escape sequence. An escape sequence may be embedded in a string or used as a character within single quotes. The following example demonstrates escape sequence usage.

```cpp
#include <iostream.h>
#include <iomanip.h>

int main()
{
    cout << "\nabcde\bZ";
    cout << "\n123456789012345678901234567890";
    cout << "\n\t*" << '\t' << '*';
    cout << "\n\rTo move to a tab position use \\t";
    cout << "\nThe politician was quoted in \'TIME\' as saying \"I\'m innocent\"";
    return 0;
}
```

```
abcdZ
123456789012345678901234567890
        *             *

To move to a tab position use \t
The politician was quoted in 'TIME' as saying "I'm innocent"
```

There is a one-to-one correspondence between the cout program lines and each line of output. The first line demonstrates the use of \b. The letters abcde were displayed, but they were followed by \bZ. This caused the display to backspace and show the letter Z in the position previously occupied by the letter e. The new line escape sequence '\n' is used to advance to the next line. This escape sequence may be surrounded by single quotes and used as a character, or embedded into a string. Either '\n' or "\n" requires four keystrokes; the same as **endl**. A good rule-of-thumb is: *If the output requires a string and a new line, place* \n *in the string; otherwise use* **endl**.

The second line of output simply numbers the positions of the display so the effect of the tab escape sequence \t may be observed. Line three shows that the effect of the tab is to cause the display to move a fixed number of positions each time it is encountered; eight places for the compiler used. The method shown in the example can be used to verify the tab setting for any compiler.

Line four embeds \r with the \n and uses \\ to insert a backslash into the string. The \r has no effect on the display. For the display, each time an \n is encountered, the display moves to the first position of the next line negating the need for the \r. Printing, discussed later, will demonstrate how \r is used.

Line five demonstrates how \' and \" are used to surround words with single quotes and double quotes, respectively. The \' is also used to insert an apostrophe. Any attempt to insert these characters in the string without using the appropriate escape sequence would result in a syntax error.

CHARACTER I/O

The first example showed that the **skipws** flag was set on as a default condition for the compiler used. This flag setting essentially causes characters being input to be delimited in the same manner as integers; either by a space or the Enter key. The following example demonstrates the effect of this flag and introduces a method of getting each character entered regardless of this flag setting.

```
#include <iostream.h>
#include <iomanip.h>
#define SIZE 13

void input1(char []),input2(char []), input3(char *);
void display(char []);
int main()
{
  char carray[SIZE];
  input1(carray);
  display(carray);
  input2(carray);
  display(carray);
  input3(carray);
  display(carray);
  return 0;
}
void input1(char array[])
{
  char c;
  const char END = '?';
  cout << "\nEnter UP TO " << SIZE-1 << " characters ";
  cout << "\nSeparate each letter with a space. Exit early with a ?";
  cout << "\nEnter your characters -> ";
  for(int i = 1; i < SIZE; i++)
  {
    cin >> c;
    if(c == END) break;
    array[i] = c;
  }
```

```
      array[0] = i;
      cin.get();
}

void input2(char array[])
{
    char c; int i = 1;
    const char END = '\n';
    cin >> resetiosflags( ios :: skipws);
    cout << "\n\nEnter UP TO " << SIZE-1 << " characters ";
    cout << "\nSeparate each letter with a space. Exit early by
                                        pressing enter";

    cout << "\nEnter your characters -> ";
    do
      {
        cin >> c;
        if(c == END) break;
        array[i++] = c;
      }
    while(i < SIZE && c != END);
    array[0] = i;
    cin >> setiosflags( ios :: skipws);
}

void input3(char *a)
{
    const char END = '\n';
    char *ptr = a,c;
    int i = 1;
    ptr++;
    cout << "\n\nEnter UP TO " << SIZE-1 << " characters ";
    cout << "\nSeparate each letter with a space. Exit early by
                                        pressing enter";

    cout << "\nEnter your characters -> ";
    while(((c = cin.get()) != END)  && i < SIZE)
    { *ptr++ = c; i++; }
    *a = i;
}



void display(char array[])
{
    for(int i = 1; i < array[0]; i++)
      cout << array[i];
}
```

```
Enter UP TO 12 characters
Separate each letter with a space. Exit early with a ?
Enter your characters -> q w


e r
t y ?
qwerty
```

This I/O was produced by the functions `input1` and `display`. It illustrates the effect of the `skipws` flag being on. This is the default condition explained in the explanation of the second. After the arrow, the two characters `q` and `w` were typed. Then the Enter key was pressed three times. Then the characters `e r` were entered and the `Enter` key pressed. Finally, the characters `t y ?` were entered and the Enter key pressed. The output line, `qwerty`, shows that the spaces between the characters and the Enter key character `\n` were ignored; however, the `last \n` was left in the input buffer. The significance of this condition and the use of `cin.get()` will be explained later.

> Enter UP TO 12 characters
> Separate each letter with a space. Exit early by pressing enter
> Enter your characters -> q w e r t y
> q w e r t y

The preceding I/O was produced by the functions `input2` and `display`. It illustrates the effect of the `skipws` flag being reset or turned off. In this example the characters `q w e r t y` were input on one line and the Enter key pressed. The END constant in this example was given the value of `\n` and used to terminate data entry in contrast to the `?` used in input1. The character `\n` is inserted into the input stream each time the Enter key is pressed. The output line, `q w e r t y`, shows that all characters input including the spaces were read into the character `c`. The `skipws` flag was set to its original value by the last statement of `input2`.

> Enter UP TO 12 characters
> Separate each letter with a space. Exit early by pressing enter
> Enter your characters -> q w e r t y
> q w e r t y

A major problem with resetting the `skipws` flag is that *it prevents numbers from being delimited in the normal manner*. The preceding I/O was produced by the functions `input3` and `display`. Input3 uses an alternate method of reading all of the characters from the keyboard. That method uses the `cin.get()` function. It is very advantageous to use this function instead of resetting the `skipws` flag since that flag affects numbers as well as characters. Without the `skipws` flag being set, the normal `cin >> c;` statement is not capable of reading the Enter key character `\n`. The purpose of the `cin.get();` statement, the last statement of `input1`, is to pull the `\n` out of the buffer. If this had not been done, `input2` would never have allowed any input, since it would have automatically read the `\n` from the input buffer and terminated the loop immediately. No output would have been produced. You may wish to verify this by running this example with the last statement of `input1` commented out. The I/O produced by the third group is identical to that of the second group without it being necessary to reset any flags. The function `cin.get()` has the capability to read any ASCII character entered from the keyboard. A good rule-of-thumb is: *Avoid resetting the* `skipws` *flag, particularly in a mixed character and number input environment; use* `cin.get()` *instead.*

STRING I/O

There is no string type in C++. What is commonly referred to as a string is an array of characters with a special terminating character, '\0', used to mark the end of the string. The lack of this character can create some unusual results. The following example illustrates this problem and demonstrates some techniques for string I/O.

```cpp
#include <iostream.h>
#include <iomanip.h>

int main()
{
  char longstr[] = "This is a verrrrrrrry longgggggggg string";
  char c, shortstr[15], *ptr;
  int i = 0;
  cout << "\n1) " << longstr;
  cout << "\n\nEnter a short string -> ";
  while(((c = cin.get()) != '\n'))
       shortstr[i++] = c;
  cout << "2) Did you enter this mess ? " <<  shortstr;
  shortstr[i] = '\0';
  cout << "\n3) You really entered this -> " << shortstr;
  i = 0;
  cout << "\n\nEnter another string -> ";
  while(((c = cin.get()) != '\n'))
       longstr[i++] = c;
  cout << "4) Did you enter this string ? " <<  longstr;
  longstr[i] = '\0';
  cout << "\n5) You really entered this -> " << longstr;
  ptr = longstr;
  while(*ptr != '\0') ptr++;  ptr++;
  cout << "\n6) The rest of the string is still here -> " << ptr;
  cout << "\n\nEnter a different string -> ";
  cin.get(longstr,80);
  cout << "7) Here is the string you entered -> " << longstr;
  cout << "\n\nEnter a new string -> ";
  cin.get(longstr,80);
  cout << "\n8) B" << longstr << "E";
  return(0);
}
```

1) This is a verrrrrrrry longgggggggg string

Enter a short string -> qwerty
2) Did you enter this mess ? qwerty^@*&
3) You really entered this -> qwerty

Enter another string -> Another String
4) Did you enter this string ? Another Stringrrrrrry longgggggggg string
5) You really entered this -> Another String
6) The rest of the string is still here -> rrrrry longgggggggg string

Enter a different string -> Different String
7) Here is the string you entered -> Different String

Enter a new string ->
8) BE

Line 1 of the output simply displays the contents of **longstr** so its contents can be compared to later output. The characters **qwerty** are then entered and input using **cin.get()**. This form of the overloaded **cin.get** function will read one character at a time from the keyboard, including the **\n** produced by pressing the Enter key. This character is used to terminate the loop that places the characters entered into array **shortstr**. The output of line 2 displays the contents of **shortstr**. The characters **^@*&** appended to the end of the string show what happens when an array not containing **\0** is displayed as a string. Without the **\0**, the **cout** statement continues through memory, displaying anything present until it finds a reason to stop. Under certain circumstances, it is quite possible a stopping point will not be found. When that happens, the computer usually locks and ceases to function. Line 3 shows the result of displaying **shortstr** after the **\0** has been added; the letters **qwerty** are displayed correctly.

This same technique is used to read the characters into the existing string **longstr**. Line 4 shows that the characters entered replace the first 14 characters in **longstr**. All characters in **longstr** are displayed by the **cout** statement until the terminating **\0** is encountered. Line 5 shows the result of inserting **\0** after the **g** in the word string; The **cout** statement now stops at the first **\0** it encounters. **Another String** is displayed just as it was input.

You may be wondering what happened to the other characters in **longstr**. The answer is that they are still there. A pointer is attached to **longstr** and moved one position past the inserted **\0**, and the string beginning at the memory address in the pointer is displayed. Line 6 is the result of displaying **longstr** from the pointer location until the original terminating **\0** is encountered.

Although **cin.get()** can be used to input strings as shown, it clearly has limitations. There is another form of this overloaded function, **cin.get(name, N)**, that is much easier to use, but still has limitations. The first argument, **name**, must be the name of a character array or a pointer to an array. The second argument, **N**, represents the number of characters the programmer desires to input. A safety feature of this function reduces the number of characters withdrawn from the input stream by one to allow space in the string for the terminating **\0**. The **\0** is appended to the end of the character string automatically. In other words, if the programmer wishes to input five characters, N must be 6. It is up to the programmer to ensure that the string is of sufficient size to hold the number of characters and the **\0**. Another feature of **cin.get(name, N)** is the ability to stop extracting characters from the input stream when the **\n**, the Enter key character, is encountered. When the **\n** character is encountered, input ceases and **\0** is appended to the characters already extracted. The **\n** remains in the input buffer. This can create problems later in the program. To take advantage of this feature, the programmer often enters **N** as a much larger number than that actually required by the string length. In the example **Different String** is entered in response to the prompt. There are 16 characters in this string. The minimum **N** that would be required to input all 16 characters and also allow for the **\0** would be 17. By specifying 80, character input stops when the **\n** is encountered and **\0** is appended. This is a very useful feature when dealing with string input such as names that have different lengths. Line 7 shows that this input was successful.

The next segment of the example shows the problem created by the **\n** remaining in the buffer. There is no opportunity to enter any characters in response to the prompt **Enter a new string ->**. Because the **\n** is still in the buffer, the **cin.get(longstr,80)** ceases extraction and places the **\0** into the first position of array **longstr**. The beginning and end markers of line 8 show that there are no reachable characters in the string. The markers **BE** are displayed next to each other. A **cin.get()** placed in the program anywhere after the first **cin.get(longstr,80)** would have removed the **\n** and allowed the second **cin.get(longstr,80)** to function as expected.

The next example introduces a third form of the overloaded `cin.get` and introduces a new string input function, `cin.getline`, which is also overloaded.

```cpp
#include <iostream.h>
#include <iomanip.h>
int main()
{
  const int SIZE = 5;
  char str1[SIZE],str2[SIZE];
  char str3[SIZE],str4[SIZE];
  cout << "Enter a 12 character string -> ";
  cin.get(str1,SIZE);
  cin.get(str2,SIZE);
  cin.getline(str3,80);
  cout << "1) " << str1 << " " << str2 << " " << str3;
  cout << "\n\nEnter a string with an \'e\' in it -> ";
  cin.get(str1,80,'e');
  cout << "2) " << str1;
  cin.getline(str2,80);
  cout << "\n3) " << str2;
  cout << "\n\nEnter a string with an \'e\' in it -> ";
  cin.getline(str3,80,'e');
  cout << "4) " << str3;
  cin.getline(str4,80);
  cout << "\n5) " << str4;
  return 0;
}
```

```
Enter a 12 character string -> abcdefghijkl
1) abcd efgh ijkl

Enter a string with an 'e' in it -> qwerty
2) qw
3) erty

Enter a string with an 'e' in it -> qwerty
4) qw
5) rty
```

Line 1 of the output shows that three four-character strings were extracted from the 12 characters that were input. The first two `cin.get` statements used the constant **SIZE** (5) as the second argument. Since an `\n` was not encountered, four characters were extracted from the input buffer, a `\0` appended, and the string placed in the array. Using a constant for both the number of characters argument and to dimension the array ensures that the array will always hold the desired number of characters. The new string input function `cin.getline` is used to extract the remaining characters from the input buffer. This function works similar to the `cin.get` statement, but has a major difference. Both will stop when they reach the `\n`, the Enter key character, and will append the `\0` to the characters extracted, but unlike the `cin.get` function, the `cin.getline` function *removes the* `\n` *from the buffer*. This eliminates the problems discussed in the previous example.

Both the `cin.get` and `cin.getline` functions have another form using a third parameter. By default, both of these functions stop at the `\n`. This default stopping point can be altered by the addition of a third parameter. In the next segment of the example, the statement `cin.get(str1,80,'e')` is used to stop extracting characters from the buffer when the letter `'e'` is found, instead of the default `\n`. Line 2 of the output, **qw**, shows that this was the case. Then `cin.get-line(st2,80)` was used to extract the rest of the characters. Line 3 of the output, **erty**, shows that the `'e'` remained in the buffer.

The next segment of the example repeats the previous sequence except that `cin.getline(str1,80,'e')` is used instead of `cin.get(str1,80,'e')`. A comparison of line 4 to line 2 of the output shows they are the same. A comparison of line 5 to line 3 of the output shows they are the different. The `cin.getline(str1,80,'e')` discarded the letter `'e'`. A good rule-of-thumb is: *Use* `cin.getline` *in any form when you want to remove the stopping character from the buffer and discard it; use* `cin.get` *when you want to keep the stopping character in the buffer.* In their two-parameter form, both functions stop at `\n`.

FILE I/O

A file is a collection of data residing on a nonvolatile storage device, usually a disk, that can be referenced under a common name. The physical name of the file is the name that may be seen if a directory command is used. Thus this name may have length limits imposed by the operating system or environment. If you are unsure of the allowable length limit to use, a maximum length of eight characters, not including any extension to the name, should be used. Within a C++ program an internal or logical name is used to reference the file data. As will be demonstrated in the following examples of file usage, a linkage between these internal and external names must be provided by the programmer. Within the C++ language, I/O is in the form of streams. The examples up to this point have used the **cin, cout,** and **cerr** streams. File I/O utilizes three stream objects contained in the **fstream** library to access file data.

ifstream-Used to receive program input from a file.

ofstream-Used to send program output to a file.

fstream-Used to receive program input from a file or to send program output to a file.

Before a file can be used it must be opened, that is, a linkage established between the physical file and the logical file name used in the program. Table C.4 shows the modes with which a sequential access text file may be opened.

File Mode	Mode Purpose
ios :: app	Opens the file for appending data; places file pointer after last datum
ios :: in	Opens file for input from it; default for **ifstream**
ios :: nocreate	Does not create a file if none exists; open fails
ios :: noreplace	Does not open a file if one exists; open fails
ios :: out	Opens a file for output to it; default for **ofstream**

Table C.4

Because they are streams, the preceding functions pertaining to **cin, cout** discussed previously may also be used with file streams. In addition to these there are several functions and constants that are useful in processing file data. These are shown in Table C.5.

Function	Function Purpose
close()	Closes the associated file
EOF	A true valued constant
eof()	Returns a true value if end-of-file is reached
fail()	Returns a true value if the file operation fails
flush()	Flushes the buffer associated with the file
ignore(val)	Ignores the number of characters specified by val, or 1 if val is omitted
NULL	A false valued constant
open()	Opens the associated file
peek()	Returns the value of the next character in the input buffer without extracting it
put(char)	Places one character in the output stream
putback(char)	Places a character into an **input** stream at the file pointer position

Table C.5

Let us assume we have created a text file called **numtest** and it is located on a disk in the same directory as our program. The file has five numbers in it. Each number is delimited by a space. The file will look like this: **11 22 33 44 55EOF**. The EOF value is added to the end of the data automatically when the file is created. While the EOF value is there, it is not visible. The following program establishes a link to this file and reads the numbers from the file until EOF is encountered and then calculates their average.

```
#include <iostream.h>
#include <fstream.h>
int main()
{
                          //innum is the logical name of the file
    ifstream innum;       //Declares innum to be of type ifstream

    int num, cnt = 0;   //Initializes counter to 0
    float sum = 0.0;
        // Establishes the link between logical
        // and physical names
    innum.open("numtest"); // Opens the file

    while(!innum.eof())         // Processes data until EOF is reached
    {
        innum >> num;           // Reads a number from the file
        sum += num;
            // Displays number and counter
        cout <<  endl << num << "   " << ++cnt;
    }
        innum.close();        //Closes file after use

        //Calculates and displays average
```

```
        cout << "\nAverage = " << sum/cnt;
        return 0;
}
```

```
11  1
22  2
33  3
44  4
55  5
55  6
Average = 36.666667
```

At first glance, it may seem the program functioned properly, but it did not. Even though there are only five numbers in the file, the counter indicates six numbers were read, the last number seeming to have been read twice. The reason for this is that *in a C++ stream environment, end-of-file is not encountered when the last data value is read.* Another read is necessary to get end-of-file. The end-of-file marker does not enter the variable, so **num** retains the last data value read, 55. The program has another weakness; no check was made for the existence of the file before attempting to read from it. An attempt to read from a nonexistent file is usually disastrous. The following example corrects these weaknesses.

```
#include <iostream.h>
#include <stdlib.h>
#include <fstream.h>

int main(){
            //innum is the logical name of the file
  ifstream innum;        //Declares innum to be of type ifstream

  int num, cnt = 0;   //Initializes counter to 0
  float sum = 0.0;
          //Establishes the link between logical and physical names
  innum.open("numtest"); // Opens the file
  if(innum.fail())          // Tests for unsuccessful opening
  {
    cerr << "\nCould not open file\n";
    exit(1);                    // Exits program
  }
  while(innum.peek() != EOF)  // Processes data until EOF is reached
  {
    innum >> num;            // Reads a number from the file
    sum += num;

      //Displays number and counter
          cout <<  endl << num << "   " << ++cnt;
  }
    innum.close();   //Closes file after use

    //Calculates and displays average
  cout << "\nAverage = " << sum/cnt;
  return 0;
}
```

```
11  1
22  2
33  3
44  4
55  5
Average = 3
```

The `innum.fail()` function was used to check for unsuccessful opening of the file. You should verify that if an incorrect physical file name or path is placed in the `open` string, the program will terminate via the `exit(1);` statement. On some compilers it might be necessary to use this form of `open` to set the fail bit: `innum.open("numtest", ios :: nocreate)`. The `innum.peek()` function was used in conjunction with the `EOF` constant to look into the buffer and detect end-of-file before it was actually encountered.

Suppose that someone created the file **numtest** by entering one number per line and pressing the Enter key. Remember, the Enter key inserts `\n` each time it is pressed.

The file would now look like:

```
11\n
22\n
33\n
44\n
55\n
EOF
```

Running the last example produces the same incorrect output as the first.

```
11  1
22  2
33  3
44  4
55  5
55  6
Average = 36.666667
```

The reason for this seeming anomaly is that `peek()` only looks ahead one character; so that the `while` loop finds the `\n` and not end-of-file. A correction can be made by inserting the statement `if(innum.eof())` break; after the `innum >> num;` statement. This will restore correct program function for the file as last shown. A good rule-of-thumb is: *Always check for end-of-file after the first read*. A check for end-of-file in this position can allow the programmer to dispense with the conditional check in the `while` loop, but it is not good form to do so. Many apparent program errors are actually caused by incorrect assumptions made about the contents of a file.

Suppose that we want to write a program that will allow the creation of an output file and guard against accidentally overwriting this file, but allow the addition of more data to this file.

```cpp
include  <iostream.h>
#include <iomanip.h>
#include <fstream.h>

void tryfile(void);
void getdata(ofstream &);

int main()
{
  tryfile();
  return 0;
}

void tryfile(void)
{
   int n;
   char fname[30];  //Allocates storage for the file name
   ofstream outfile; // Declares outfile as type ofstream
   cout << "\nEnter name & path of file -> ";
   cin.getline(fname,80);  // Reads file name from keyboard
   outfile.open(fname, ios :: noreplace);  //Opens file for output
   if(outfile == NULL)  //Checks for invalid file pointer
   {
     cerr << "File " << fname << " already exists";
     cerr << "\nOpening " << fname << " for append only";
     outfile.open(fname, ios :: app);  // Opens existing file for append
   }
   else
       cout << "File " << fname << " succesfully opened for output";
   getdata(outfile);  //Passes file pointer to function getdata
   outfile.close(); // Closes the file
}



void getdata(ofstream &ofile)
{
    float bal; int cnt = 0;
    // Sets output file flags
    ofile << setiosflags(ios :: fixed | ios :: showpoint);
    ofile << setprecision(2);
    cout << "\n\nExit with a negative number or ";
    do
      {
    cout << "\nEnter Person\'s balance -> ";
    cin >> bal;
    if(bal < 0) break;
    ofile << bal;  //Writes contents of bal to file as formatted
    cnt++;
    if(cnt > 5){  // Limits data items to 5 per line
        ofile.put('\n');  // Puts newline character into the file
        cnt = 0;
    }
    else        {
        ofile.put(' ');  // Puts a space into the file
        cnt++;
```

```
        }
     ofile.flush();   //Causes immediate flush of buffer to the physical
file
     }
  while(bal >= 0);
}
```

Enter name & path of file -> a:numtest
File a:numtest succesfully opened for output

Exit with a negative number or
Enter Person's balance -> 11.11
Enter Person's balance -> 22.22
Enter Person's balance -> 33.33
Enter Person's balance -> 44.44
Enter Person's balance -> 55.55
Enter Person's balance -> 66.66
Enter Person's balance -> -9

Contents of file a:numtest: 11.11 22.22 33.33 44.44 55.55
                            66.66EOF

When the text a:numtest was entered in response to the prompt, the specified path
was checked by the **outfile.open(fname, ios :: noreplace);** statement.
Since no file having the name **numtest** was found, the file was opened for output.
Then the statement **if(outfile == NULL)** used the constant **NULL** to determine
if the file was successfully created. It was, so the logical file name was passed to
function **getdata**. Note the use of the address operator **'&'** in both the prototype
and the function. Using the address operator is absolutely necessary to insure correct program function. Within function **getdata**, the statements **ofile <<
setiosflags(ios :: fixed | ios :: showpoint);** and **ofile << set-
precision(2);** were used to set the output flags and manipulators in the
ofstream ofile. Note that these flags and manipulators are the same ones that were
discussed in conjunction with the **cout** stream earlier. Flags and manipulators may
be applied to any appropriate stream. After a number is entered, it is placed in the
file by the **ofile << bal;** statement. The delimiters for numbers are either the
space or the newline character. Placing these character delimiters in the file is done
by using the **put(char)** function. After five numbers have been entered, the
ofile.put('\n'); statement inserts the **'\n'** character into **ofstream
ofile**. The statement **ofile.put(' ');** similarly inserts a space. C++ streams
are fully buffered. When the buffer is full or the file is closed, the contents of the
buffer are transferred to the physical file. If there is a power interruption, the data
in the buffer would never be transferred to the physical file. The statement
ofile.flush(); is used to write the contents of the buffer to the physical file.
The **flush()** function should be used only when necessary, since it defeats the
speed advantage of buffering.

The second time we run the program the results are different.

Enter name & path of file -> a:numtest
File a:numtest already exists
Opening a:numtest for append only

Exit with a negative number or
Enter Person's balance -> 77.77
Enter Person's balance -> 88.88
Enter Person's balance -> 99.99
Enter Person's balance -> -9

Contents of file a:numtest: 11.11 22.22 33.33 44.44 55.55
66.66 77.77 88.88 99.99EOF

As before when the text **a:numtest** was entered in response to the prompt, the specified path was checked by the **outfile.open(fname, ios :: noreplace);** statement. This time a file having the name **a:numtest** was found so it was not opened. The statement **if(outfile == NULL);** used the constant **NULL** to determine that the file was not successfully opened. The file was then opened for append by the statement **outfile.open(fname, ios :: app);** and appropriate messages displayed. The contents of the file show that the three new numbers entered were appended to the existing data and the end-of-file indicator moved accordingly.

The file examples up to this point have used only single data elements. Groups of data about entities are associated with each other to form records or data sets. Suppose we want to build a person's credit record having the attributes or fields called account number, balance, credit code, and name. A sample record would look like: **00004 347.92 C I. M. Broke**. The next example demonstrates the notion of associated data and uses **fstream** first to build the file and then to produce a report from the file data.

```cpp
#include <iostream.h>
#include <iomanip.h>
#include <fstream.h>
#include <string.h>
#include <ctype.h>
#include <stdlib.h>

void makefile(void),report(void), getname(char *);
void prtheader(), prtline(char *, char *, float);
void prtfooter(float),getdata(int&,float&, char&, char*);
void tryfile(fstream &, char *);
int main()
{
  makefile();
  report();
  return 0;
}

void makefile(void)
{
  char fname[30],acct[6],name[25], c;
  char *ptr,temp[6];
  float bal;int a, x;
  fstream file; //Declares an fstream variable
  getname(fname); //Gets filename from keyboard
  file.open(fname, ios :: out); //Opens file for output
  tryfile(file,fname); //Checks for successful opening
  file << setiosflags(ios :: fixed | ios :: showpoint);
```

```
    file << setprecision(2);//Sets file flags & manipulators
    do{
        getdata(a,bal,c,name); //Gets data to place in file
        if(a < 1)break; //Checks for terminating entry

        //Changes integer to 5 character string
        strcpy(acct,"00000");
        ptr = acct;
        itoa(a,temp,10);
        ptr += (strlen(acct) - strlen(temp));
        strcpy(ptr,temp);

        //Writes record to file
        file << acct << ' ' << bal << ' ' << c << ' '
           << name << '\n';
    }
    while(a >= 1);
    cin.get();//Removes last \n
    file.close(); //Closes file
}

void getdata(int &a, float &b, char &c, char*n)
{
    cout << "\nEnter negative number to exit or";
    cout << "\nEnter account number -> ";
    cin >> a;
    if(a < 0) return;
    cout << "\nEnter customer balance -> ";
    cin >> b;
    cout << "\nEnter credit code -> ";
    cin >> c;
    c = toupper(c);
    cin.get();
    cout << "\nEnter customer name -> ";
    cin.getline(n,80);
}

void getname(char *name)
{
    cout << "\nEnter the name of the file -> ";
    cin.getline(name, 80);
}

void tryfile(fstream &file, char *name)
{
    if(!file)
    {
        cerr << "\nFile " << name << " could not be opened";
        cerr << "\nEnding program";
        exit(1);
    }
    else
        cerr << "\nFile " << name << " opened successfully \n\n";
}

void report(void)
```

```cpp
{
  const char OLD = 'Z';
  char c,fname[30],acct[6],name[25];
  float bal,sum = 0.0;
  fstream infile; //Declares fstream variable
  getname(fname); //Gets filename from keyboard
  infile.open(fname, ios :: in); //Opens file for input
  tryfile(infile,fname); //Checks for successful opening
  prtheader(); //Displays output header
  while(!infile.eof())//Checks for end-of-file
  {
    infile.get(acct,6); //Reads account number
    if(strlen(acct) == 0) break; //Breaks on zero length
    infile >> bal; //Reads balance
    infile.ignore();//Ignores space after balance
    c = infile.get();//Reads credit code
    if(c == OLD) //Checks for invalid code
    {
      infile.putback(c);//Puts back invalid code
      infile.getline(name,80); //Reads remaining characters
      continue; //Skips rest of loop
    }
      else
         infile.ignore(); //Ignores space after credit code
    sum += bal;     //Accumulates balance
    infile.getline(name,80); //Reads name
    prtline(acct,name,bal);  //Displays line for valid record
  }
  prtfooter(sum); // Displays accumulated totals
  infile.close(); // Closes file
}

void prtheader(void)
{
  cout << "\n                CREDIT REPORT";
  cout << "\n   Account      Name                Balance\n";
  cout << setiosflags(ios :: fixed | ios :: showpoint);
  cout << setprecision(2);
}

void prtline(char *a, char *n, float b)
{
  cout << "\n     " << a << "  " << setw(17) << n
    << setw(10) << b;
}


void prtfooter(float s)
{
  cout << endl << setw(39) << "_____\n";
  cout << setw(38) << s;
}
```

The first prompt that appears on the screen asks that the name of the file be entered:

> Enter the name of the file -> record
> File record opened successfully

The statement `file.open(fname, ios :: out);` attempts to open the file for output. If the file could not be opened successfully, the message "File **record** could not be opened" is displayed and the program is immediately terminated. If the file was opened successfully, the message "File **record** opened successfully" is displayed and prompts for data entry to begin. Note that the check for file opening was accomplished via function **tryfile**. Placing the code for file checking allows this code to be used with any **fstream** file. The statement `if(!file);` is the third method that has been presented to check for the existence of a file. The function call `get-data(a,bal,c,name);` is used to display a series of the following prompts.

> Enter negative number to exit or
> Enter account number -> 1
> Enter customer balance -> 111.11
> Enter credit code -> d
> Enter customer name -> Joe Oneman

The process continues until a negative number is entered in response to the "Enter account number -> " prompt.

> Enter negative number to exit or
> Enter account number -> -9

The function **itoa** is used in conjunction with string operations to format the integer into a five character string so the record could be formatted as required. The **toupper** function is used to ensure that all credit codes entered are placed in the file as uppercase letters. The statement `file << acct << ' ' << bal << ' ' << c << ' ' << name << '\n';` writes the data to the file. It is the programmer's responsibility to delimit each field with a blank space as shown and to place the \n at the end of the output line to delimit one record from another. The records in the file look like this:

```
00001 111.11 D Joe Oneman
00002 222.22 Z Joe Twofaced
00003 3333.33 A Joe Threepenny
00004 347.92 C I.M. Broke
EOF
```

After the last record is entered, the file is closed and function **report** is called. The prompt that appears on the screen asks that the name of the file be entered:

> Enter the name of the file -> record
> File record opened successfully

The statement `file.open(fname, ios :: in);` attempts to open the file for input. If the file could not be opened successfully, the message "File **record** could not be opened" is displayed and the program is immediately terminated. If the file was opened successfully, the message "File **record** opened successfully" is displayed. Since we want the header to appear only once in the output, the function call `prtheader();` is placed above the loop. The `infile.get(acct,6);` is used to read the five-character account number from the file. Then the statement `if(strlen(acct) == 0) break;` is used to detect EOF. The statement `if(infile.eof());` could also be used to detect EOF. Remember, EOF is *not* read when the last piece of valid data is. If one of these statements is not included, the last balance amount would be displayed twice and the sum would be incorrect. You should comment out the statement `if(strlen(acct) == 0) break;` and view the resultant report. The statement `infile >> bal;` is used to read the balance from the file. It is not necessary to be concerned about the space after the account number since spaces are ignored when reading a number. This is not true for characters; consequently, the statement `infile.ignore();` is used to ignore the space after the balance and before the credit code. Then the statement `c = infile.get();` is used to read the credit code into the variable c. The credit code is compared to a constant Z representing an obsolete credit code. If the credit code matches the constant, the character c is placed back in the buffer by the statement `infile.putback(c);`. The rest of the record is taken out of the buffer by reading it into the name array by the statement `infile.getline(name,80);`. Then the `continue;` statement is used to skip the remaining statements in the loop. For records not containing a credit code of `Z`, the statement `infile.ignore();` is used to skip the space after the credit code and before the name. Finally the statement `infile.getline(name,80);` is used to read the customer's name. Function `prtline` displays one output line. When EOF is detected, function `prtfooter` displays the accumulated sum. The displayed report is shown here:

CREDIT REPORT

Account	Name	Balance
00001	Joe Oneman	111.11
00003	Joe Threepenny	3333.33
00004	I.M. Broke	347.92
		3792.36

At first glance the report seems correct, but a closer inspection shows that the names are right-justified instead of the left-justification expected of characters. This occurs because C++ stores characters as one-byte numbers corresponding to their ASCII code. To left-justify the characters the **cout** statement in function **prtline** must be changed to the following:

```
cout << "\n    " << a << "  " << setw(17) << setiosflags(ios :: left)
     << n << setw(10) << resetiosflags(ios :: left) << b;
```

First the left flag is set before the name is displayed. This causes the names to be left-justified in the field. Because this flag acts as a switch and stays on, it must be reset before the balances are displayed. Failure to do this would cause the numbers to be left-justified. The corrected report looks like this:

```
              CREDIT REPORT
  Account        Name              Balance

  00001        Joe Oneman          111.11
  00003        Joe Threepenny     3333.33
  00004         I.M. Broke         347.92
                                  _____
                                  3792.36
```

PRINTER OUTPUT

Because of the consistent way C++ I/O commands are structured, most of the techniques required to send output data to the printer have already been demonstrated. However, before a printer can be accessed, the system device name for the printer must be determined. For most DOS/Windows-based computers, the device name for the printer is **LPT1** or **PRN**; at least for those computers not connected to a network. If the following test program will not produce the correct output on your network, consult your network administrator.

```cpp
#include <iostream.h>
#include <fstream.h>

int main()
{
    fstream prtfile;
    int page = 1;
    prtfile.open("LPT1", ios :: out); //Or next line
    // prtfile.open("PRN", ios :: out);// Or previous line
    if(!prtfile)
    {
      cerr << "Could not access printer";
      return 1;
    }
    prtfile << "This is page " << page++;
    prtfile << "\fThis is page " << page;
    prtfile << "\f";
    prtfile.close();
    return 0;
}
```

The statement **prtfile.open("LPT1", ios :: out);** attempts to access the printer. The check for file opening is as previously discussed. The statement **prtfile << "This is page " << page++;** should print **This is page 1** on the first line positioned upper left on the first page according to the margin settings of the printer. The statement **prtfile << "\fThis is page " <<**

page; should print **This is page 2** on the first line of the second page. The \f is the form feed character as shown in Table C.3. Then the statement **prtfile <<
"\f";** is used to eject the page immediately. A comparison of the two printed lines shows they are both printed on the first line, but not in the same columns.

> This is page1
> This is page 2

The reason for this is that no line control characters were used. Most nonimpact printers require explicit control of lines and returns. The next example, which uses the same file created for the **fstream** example, demonstrates this.

```cpp
#include <iostream.h>
#include <iomanip.h>
#include <fstream.h>
#include <string.h>
#include <stdlib.h>

void report(void), getname(char *);
void prtheader(fstream &), prtline(fstream &,char *, char *, float);
void prtfooter(fstream &,float), tryfile(fstream &, char *);

int main()
{
  report();
  return 0;
}

void tryfile(fstream &file, char *name)
{
  if(!file)
  {
    cerr << "\nFile " << name << " could not be opened";
    cerr << "\nEnding program";
    exit(1);
  }
    else
      cerr << "\nFile " << name << " opened successfully \n\n";
}

void report(void)
{
  char c,fname[30],acct[6],name[25];
  float bal,sum = 0.0;
  fstream infile,prtfile; //declares fstream variable
  getname(fname); //Gets filename from keyboard
  infile.open(fname, ios :: in); //Opens file for input
  tryfile(infile,fname); //Checks for successful opening
  getname(fname);//Gets printer device name from keyboard
```

```
  prtfile.open(fname, ios :: out);//Opens printer
  tryfile(prtfile,fname); //Checks for successful opening
  prtheader(prtfile); //Prints output header
  while(!infile.eof())//Checks for end-of-file
    {
     infile.get(acct,6); //Reads account number
     if(infile.eof()) break; //Breaks on EOF
     infile >> bal; //Reads balance
     infile.ignore(3);//Ignores 3 spaces after balance
     sum += bal;    //Accumulates balance
     infile.getline(name,80); //Reads name
     prtline(prtfile,acct,name,bal);  //Prints line for valid record
  }
prtfooter(prtfile,sum); // Prints accumulated totals
infile.close();prtfile.close(); //Closes both files
}

void getname(char *name)
{
    cout << "\nEnter the name of the file -> ";
    cin.getline(name, 80);
}

void prtheader(fstream &file)
{
    file << "\n\r             CREDIT REPORT";
    file << "\n\r   Account    Name                  Balance\n\r";
    file << setiosflags(ios :: fixed | ios :: showpoint);
    file << setprecision(2);
}

void prtline(fstream &file,char *a, char *n, float b)
{
    file << "\n\r     " << a << "  " << setw(17) << setiosflags(ios :: left)
         <<  n << setw(10) << resetiosflags(ios :: left) << b;
}

void prtfooter(fstream &file,float s)
{
  file << "\n\r" << setw(39) << "_____\n\r";
  file << setw(38) << s;
  file << "\f";
}
```

As before, the first prompt that appears on the screen asks that the name of the file be entered; it is then followed by the prompt asking for the printer device name.

```
Enter the name of the file -> record
File record opened successfully

Enter the name of the file -> prn  (or lpt1)
File prn opened successfully
```

Notice that all of the functions that show any output—**prtheader**, **prtline**, and **prtfooter**—have been changed to accept the **fstream** variable as the first parameter. The **fstream** variable attached to the printer in function **report** is **prtline**. All the output functions now show **prtline** instead of **cout**. The **\r** has been added after each occurrence of **\n**. Most printers are now nonimpact printers using ink jet, laser, or bubble technology. These printers do not execute a return to column 1 when a new line command is received as did older dot matrix printers. The **\r** causes the print mechanism to return to column 1. A good rule of thumb is: *Always add **\r** every time you use **\n** when you are printing.* This does no harm if you happen to be using a printer that encapsulates the return with the new line character. If your printer requires the **\r** and you don't use it, you will find each line being placed on the paper further to the right until they are truncated at the right margin. The printed report is displayed here:

CREDIT REPORT

Account	Name	Balance
00001	Joe Oneman	111.11
00002	Joe Twofaced	222.22
00003	Joe Threepenny	3333.33
00004	I.M. Broke	347.92
		4014.58

If you cannot access the printer directly because of network limitations, simply substitute the name of a disk file for the printer device name. When the program is complete, print the file using a word processing program. Make sure you use a *non proportional font* in order to preserve the spacing made by the C++ program. To conserve time and paper, it is a good idea to try formatting your output on the screen using **cout** before sending it to a printer.

HELPFUL OUTPUT FUNCTIONS

The ANSI C++ standard does not include a function for clearing the screen. Most compiler vendors provide such a function, but the name may vary from vendor to vendor. It is easy to write one.

```
void clear(void)
{
   const int LINES = 30;
   int n = 0;
   while(n < LINES){
   cout << endl;
   n++;}
}
```

The constant LINES may be adjusted to suit your environment. A variation of this function may be used to provide vertical spacing. The call to **vspaces(5)** would cause five blank lines to be written.

```
void vspaces(int spaces)
{
  int n = 0;
  while(n < spaces){
  cout << endl;
  n++; }
}
```

Function **spaces** is designed to provide horizontal spacing in an output statement.

```
char *spaces(int n)
{
  const int SIZE = 40;
  static char s[SIZE] = "
  char *e = s;
  e += SIZE-1;
  for(int i = 0; i < n; i++)
   e--;
  return e;
}
```

Consider the effect of placing the following **cout** statements in a program containing function **spaces**. The number lines are used to verify how many spaces are inserted.

```
cout << "012345678901234567890"0\n";
cout << "B" << spaces(9) << "E" << spaces(5) << '*' << spaces(12) << '+';
cout << "\n012345678901234567890\n";
```

This is the output produced by these lines:

```
012345678901234567890
B        E   *            +
012345678901234567890
```

The C++ flags and manipulators may be used to show a number to two decimal places, but no dollar sign or commas are included. The C++ standard does not include a function for formatting a number as currency. The following function, while rather cumbersome, will perform that task.

```
char *currency(double n)
{
  const int DIV = 10;
  char whole[50],decimal[50];
  static char complete[50];
  char *ptr,*pr,*pi;
  long dec, integer = long(n);
```

```cpp
   double fraction = n - integer;
   int x,cnt = 0;
   if(fraction > 0.0) {
      pr = decimal;
      fraction =  fraction  +.00555555;
      dec = fraction * 100;
      for(int i = 0; i < 2; i++)  {
         x = dec % DIV;
         itoa(x,pr++,DIV);
         dec = dec / DIV;    }
      *pr = '\0';
   }
      else strcpy(decimal,"00");
   ptr = whole;
   if(integer == 0) *ptr++ = '0';else{
   if(fraction >= 1) integer ++;
   while(integer) {
      x = integer % DIV;
      itoa(x,ptr++,DIV);
      integer = integer / DIV;
   } }
   *ptr = '\0';
   pr = complete;pi = whole;
   cnt = 0; *pr++ = '.';
   while(*pi != '\0'){
      *pr++ = *pi++;
       cnt++;
      if(cnt == 3){*pr++ = ',';cnt = 0;}
   }
   if(*(pr-1) == ',') pr—; *pr = '$';pr++; *pr = '\0';
   strrev(complete);
   strrev(decimal);
   strncat(complete,decimal,2);
   ptr = complete;
   return complete;
}

char *currency(double);

int main()
{
  double num[6] = {0.0,.05,1.010, 12.975,999.994 , 123456789.995};
  for(int i = 0; i < 6; i++)
   cout << "\n The formatted string is " << currency(num[i]);
   return 0;
}
```

The output of the above program is shown here:

```
The formatted string is $0.00
The formatted string is $0.05
The formatted string is $1.01
The formatted string is $12.98
The formatted string is $999.99
The formatted string is $123,456,790.00
```

BIBLIOGRAPHY

Cohoon, James P. and Jack W. Davidson. *C++ Program Design, An Introduction to Programming and Object-Oriented Design*. McGraw Hill, 1999.

Dale, Nell and Chip Weems. *Programming and Problem Solving with C++*. Jones and Bartlett Publishing, 1997.

Dale, Nell and Chip Weems. *Programming in C++*. Jones and Bartlett Publishing, 1998.

Friedman, Frank L. *Problem Solving, Abstraction, and Design Using C++*. Addison Wesley, 1997.

Lippman, Stanley B. *C++ Primer*. Addison Wesley, 1995.

Main, Michael and Walter Savitch. *Data Structures and Other Objects Using C++*. Addison Wesley, 1998.

Perry, Jo Ellen and Harold D. Levin. *An Introduction to Object-Oriented Design in C++*. Addison Wesley, 1996.

Savitch, Walter. *Problem Solving with C++, The Object of Programming*. Addison Wesley, 1999.

Schildt, Herbert. *C/C++ Programmer's Reference*. Osborne McGraw Hill, 1997.

Weiss, Mark A. *Data Structures and Algorithm Analysis in C++*. Addison Wesley, 1999.

INDEX